PERSONAL EFFECTS

PERSONAL EFFECTS
The Social Character of Scholarly Writing

edited by

DEBORAH H. HOLDSTEIN
DAVID BLEICH

UTAH STATE
UNIVERSITY PRESS
Logan, Utah

Utah State University Press
Logan, Utah 84322-7800

Copyright © 2001 Utah State University Press
All rights reserved.

"The Anxiety and Nostalgia of Literacy," by Morris Young, is part of a longer work forthcoming from Southern Illinois University Press, copyright © (forthcoming) by the Board of Trustees, Southern Illinois University. Reprinted with permission.

"The Social Construction of Expressivist Pedagogy," by Karen Surman Paley, was originally published in *I-Writing*, copyright © 2001 by the Board of Trustees, Southern Illinois University. Reprinted with permission.

Manufactured in the United States of America.
Cover design by Mazyne, Inc.

Library of Congress Cataloging-in-Publication Data

Personal effects : the social character of scholarly writing / edited by Deborah Holdstein, David Bleich.
   p. cm.
Includes bibliographical references and index.
 ISBN 0-87421-429-7 (alk. paper)
 1. English language--Rhetoric--Study and teaching--Social aspects. 2. Academic writing--Study and teaching--Social aspects. 3. Academic writing--Social aspects. I. Holdstein, Deborah H., 1952- II. Bleich, David.
 PE1404 .P457 2001
 808'.042'0711--dc21
                 2001004766

CONTENTS

Introduction: Recognizing the Human in the Humanities   *1*
    David Bleich and Deborah H. Holdstein

I IDEALS AND CAUTIONS

1 Scholarly Memoir: An Un-"Professional" Practice   *27*
    Margaret Willard-Traub

2 In the Name of the Subject: Some Recent Versions of the Personal   *51*
    Jeffrey Gray

II SELF-INCLUSION IN LITERARY SCHOLARSHIP

3 Radical Introspection: The Personal in Scholarship and Teaching   *79*
    Brenda Daly

4 Loss, Memory, and the Work of Learning: Lessons From the Teaching Life of Anne Sexton   *93*
    Paula M. Salvio

III TEACHING AND SCHOLARSHIP FACE TO FACE

5 "Knowledge Has a Face": The Jewish, The Personal, and the Pedagogical   *121*
    Susan Handelman

6 Who Was that Masked Author? The Faces of Academic Editing   *145*
    Louise Z. Smith

IV TEACHING AND SCHOLARSHIP PUBLIC AND PRIVATE

7 Autobiography: The Mixed Genre of Public and Private   *165*
    Madeleine R. Grumet

8 The Social Construction of Expressivist Pedagogy   178
     Karen Surman Paley

9 The Scope of Personal Writing in Postsecondary
    English Pedagogy   199
     Diane P. Freedman

10 Personal Experience Paper   220
     Rachel Brownstein

11 "The World Never Ends": Professional Judgments
    at Home, Abroad   232
     Joycelyn K. Moody

V THE SOCIAL CHARACTER OF PERSONAL NARRATIVE

12 Learning to Take it Personally   253
     Kate Ronald and Hephzibah Roskelly

13 Cuentos de mi Historia: An Art of Memory   267
     Victor Villanueva

14 Personal Landmarks on Pedagogical Landscapes   277
     Katya Gibel Azoulay

15 The Anxiety and Nostalgia of Literacy: A Narrative about Race,
    Language, and a Teaching Life   296
     Morris Young

16 Where I'm Coming From: Memory, Location, and the (Un)making
    of National Subjectivity   317
     Christopher Castiglia

17 The Personal as History   335
     Richard Ohmann

References   357

Contributors   377

Index   381

INTRODUCTION
Recognizing the Human in the Humanities

David Bleich
Deborah H. Holdstein

In the 1996 issue of *PMLA* considering "the personal" in scholarship, Michael Bérubé suggests that scholarly use of personal narrative represents "some kind of generic violation of scholarship in the human sciences." But he concludes that "as long as the scholarship in question concerns humans and is written by humans, readers should at least entertain the possibility that nothing human should be alien to it." This conclusion, so self-evident, is only now becoming acceptable in the humanities—that is, to admit the full range of human experience into formal scholarly writing.

The study of language and literature without reference to its roles in scholars' lives and communities has been the most common academic practice; such study is also academic in the pejorative sense of its being "not practical" or moot or removed from real life. The adjective "academic" has meant, among other things, that scholarly writing about language and literature assumes that the subjectivity and social memberships of scholars are *not* factors in their humanistic knowledge in the same sense as physical scientists assume that their subjectivities are not factors in their knowledge of science. Because humanists have used the scientific sense of objectivity to conceptualize their own work, and because humanistic scholarship does not have as great an economic and physical consequence as science, humanities have come to seem less important as subject matters than science, law, or business.

This volume collects essays that, taken together, try to show how fundamental it is in humanistic scholarship to take account, in a variety of ways and as part of the subject matter, of the personal and collective experiences of scholars, researchers, critics, and teachers. The volume advances the view that humanistic inquiry can not develop successfully at this time without reference to the varieties of subjective, intersubjective, and collective experience of teachers and researchers. We of course do not think that such reference is a requirement or that it should appear in every study; rather, that regardless of the announced level of subjective involvement of the scholarly author, both authors and readers need to have on their hermeneutic agenda, as readers and as writers, the task of locating scholarly authors through personal and social criteria. This presupposition may then apply to different authors in different degrees, as it does in this volume: authors choose how to identify themselves. But in each case, we readers and interpreters have at least before us the *issue* of the subjective and intersubjective situation of the author(s) *as part of the subject matter*.[1]

To one degree or another, scholarly authors' lived experiences are already part of the different subject matters in the humanities. However, the conventions of writing urge writers away from the citation or use of these experiences. In secondary and postsecondary writing pedagogy, authorial detachment is part of the curriculum; self-inclusion, particularly the use of the "I," is strongly discouraged. Students are not taught that *sometimes* the first person is effective, or that one's own experience may well matter in one's way of announcing knowledge, but that it is actually *not acceptable* to use the I or to fold in personal experience in substantive ways in academic writing. In this way, matters of writing pedagogy are closely related to matters of writing conventions in the humanities. Humanists are often unconscious to a great extent of just how coercive these conventions are. While many may wish to use self-reference and self-reflection, combining the genres of scholarship with the genres of personal experience and observation is confined to texts that are prominently marked "memoir," "autobiography," or other life-writing genres. One may include reference to scholarly work in life-writing, but one cannot include life-writing in scholarly work. This is the conventional means of minimizing the human presence in the humanities.

The foregoing description represents what motivates our effort to bring out this volume. But we did not anticipate how, exactly, it would materialize. We had a call for papers, and we had a zone of interest which we know has been growing in the past two decades. We waited for the essays to arrive and to see what they said. We sorted the proposals and the essays until we thought that each essay contributed something distinctive. Our last step was to face the issue of how the essays added up to a comprehensive perspective, to a vision that could provide guidance to other teachers and scholars. We thought that unless contributors wrote about what they themselves thought were the important issues, we would not be able to "add up" anything that truly reflected our constituency, or that would speak to the many colleagues and disciplines beyond our own. We tried to withhold judgment about what we wanted to accomplish in collecting these essays, rather than decide beforehand and instruct potential contributors on what we envision. We understood the risks of this procedure, but we thought it was more in keeping with our sense of ourselves as students: learning from our contributors. After collecting the essays we were able to sample what our colleagues were thinking, and then to decide, on the basis of their work, how the issues that they raised connected to the ones with which we started.

These issues are reflected in the five divisions of the volume following the introduction. Each division characterizes what we think is the principal choice by the authors on how they could best contribute to our topic. By juxtaposing each individual essay with others, we give each an accent beyond what the authors may have foreseen or intended. The volume's title reflects our sense of how the essays, taken together, add up to a picture of part of our profession, to a view of how we are changing, and to a set of advocacies of how we might change further. In addition to what our title actually says, here are a few other general issues, touched on to one degree or another by all the essays, which have emerged in our reading and interpreting these essays and that we think are also marked by the title.

The inseparability of teaching and scholarship. Readers may notice how many contributors treat teaching and scholarship as aspects of a single process. Including personal experiences and narratives in the presentation of scholarship lends scholarship its pedagogical authority: it is not just plain "knowledge." It is knowledge derived by someone and told to someone. It is knowledge that *this* person found in *this* community or society and is sharing with *this* other group of people. Contributors to this volume take pains to account for how they are situated, and, therefore, how their claims may then by taken up and evaluated by us readers. Scholarship that is "from" and "to" someone is, yes, "personal," but its personal location is only a feature of something that can be taken up in collective contexts and in non-personalized senses. Teaching that takes place in particular locations is "local" teaching, but it is also teaching that tells us the character of knowing, especially the knowing of language and literature. If the scholarship is about Joyce Carol Oates or Anne Sexton because Brenda Daly and Paula Salvio chose these authors, it is also about other authors who are read by other students and researched by other scholars. The persons, the scholarship, and the teaching are combined.

The connections of personal experiences with the subject of language and literature. Peter Elbow has asked, "What is English?" Our answer has been that "English" is *both* "our" language *and* the subject of language and literature. These essays say, in part, that we must be aware that we are studying *our* language—the language of a specific society that is host to many cultures and many values, but that we are also studying something that all people have, language and literature. Contributors to this volume come from many (though not all) zones of American society represented in the academy. Yet each is committed to "English" the subject, each speaks "English" the language, and many speak other languages, know other subjects and cultures, and bring their special knowledge to bear on the study of language and literature, as do Susan Handelman, Katya Azoulay, Victor Villanueva, Morris Young, and Chris Castiglia. Yet many other contributors also bring special perspectives on English the language and English the subject—those of profession, gender, history, pedagogy, to name a few. Almost every essay raises this issue: how English is *both* our language and a subject matter that extends to all language and literature.

The connections of literature and composition studies. This has been a continuing problem in "English" for perhaps a century and a half in modern times.[2] Yet most contributors to this volume have not subscribed to this division of subject matter and academic interest. To them, writing, language, language use, and literature have been part of one picture that has made a point of recognizing the human in the use and study of language and literature. Richard Ohmann's several works, for example, have presupposed a unified subject. In his contribution, he adds his own responses to teaching and to university administration, and suggests thereby what may be new relations of language and society, of English and America. Victor Villanueva, a teacher and administrator of English and Spanglish, is someone whose story and whose memory may itself fall among literary genres. Essays like Rachel Brownstein's take over the "student" genre, while her students take over oral genres, and the classroom account she gives can count as an ethnographic genre. Most of the contributions to this volume are not easily identified generically because they cross genre boundaries and show by repeated example how the many genres of "writing" speak against a propadeutic subject of "composition" as being distinct from a scholarly and culturally privileged subject of "literature."

Taken together, the essays in this volume fall into the category of "scholarly writing." Yet, they also create new subcategories of scholarly writing as they change the received genres. The essays have a social character, yet they are all still personal, even those, such as Willard-Traub's and Gray's, which seem to use more traditional scholarly conventions of writing. Their subject matters as well as their styles change their genres and form the basis for new pedagogical initiatives—ones that permit the risks, the personal reflections, the experiments, the errors, the awkward moments characteristic of real teaching and real research. Narratives such as Joycelyn Moody's challenge the customary conventions of teacher-student interaction in her "diary," yet the total effect of such an essay is to invite other such diaries that tell of the real levels of relatedness between students and teachers. This is a "scholarly" diary that speaks with a personal, individual, human, voice to those of us who are listening.

This volume continues and extends the efforts of a group of scholars who have begun to introduce their own lives and experiences as social factors in the scholarship of language and literature. In particular, these authors view their personal and social circumstances as part of their subject matter—whether implicitly or explicitly. Robin Lakoff's *Language and Women's Place* (1975) includes a discussion about the "place" from which she begins her thinking about language use. Lakoff ultimately expands this sense of place to include psychotherapy, the law, the culture of beauty, and the academy. In each instance, however, Lakoff explicitly describes her vantage point in terms more personal than those of a great majority of other scholars. Similarly, Adrienne Rich's collection, *On Lies, Secrets, and Silence* (1979), and Diane Freedman, Olivia Frey, and Frances Zauhar's volume, *The Intimate Critique: Autobiographical Literary Criticism* (Duke UP, 1993), examine even more closely the embedded self within scholarly work. Patricia Williams' *The Alchemy of Race and Rights* (1990) is an especially persuasive instance of how important it is to refer to one's own experience in discussing something as broadly applicable as the law. Scholarly uses and examinations of personal experiences help to articulate relationships among a variety of disciplines, as well as interestingly unarticulated links between composition studies and literary studies.

We see this in the work of one particular scholar: Jane Tompkins's "Sentimental Power: *Uncle Tom's Cabin* and the Politics of Literary History" (1981) examines how her own otherness led to her critical assessment of the same in the work of Harriet Beecher Stowe. Tompkins's rhetorical strategy features aspects of her own life as the introductory portion to more traditional forms of academic argument. Most recently, in *A Life in School* (1996), Tompkins examines her own life as the context for her scholarly work. Nancy K. Miller's work is also noteworthy, particularly *Getting Personal: Feminist Occasions and Other Autobiographical Acts*; Janet Varner Gunn in *Autobiography* suggests a perspective having to do with "taking oneself up and bringing oneself to language"; Shari Benstock asks, in "Authorizing the Autobiographical," how writing mediates ". . . the space between 'self' and 'life' that the autobiography would traverse and transgress." Benstock suggests that ". . . the place to begin our investigation of autobiography might be at the crossroads of writing and selfhood."

Composition studies has continued to delineate these personal-scholarly contexts since its emergence as a formal discipline in the late 1960s and early 1970s, examining both writer and students of writing. Deborah Brandt details, for instance, the acquisition of literacy among workers and the social forces that contextualize multiple literacies. Victor Villanueva, Jr., in *Bootstraps: From an American Academic of Color* (NCTE, 1990), examines how his "position" in the world provided the pedagogical and philosophical contexts for his work in composition. NCTE has also published *Teaching in College English and English Education* (1998) a volume in which editors Richard Larson, Thomas McCracken, and Judith Entes feature work by scholars writing about how they came to be postsecondary teachers of literature and composition. These very few examples from literary and composition studies suggest that such substantive accounts of the "inner" academic life provide appropriate and rich contexts for further study and analysis—and for interaction between these two areas of inquiry.

Personal writing has become a collective interest as a necessary context for scholarship and pedagogy. The 1996 issue of *PMLA*, cited above, provides potentially productive links between the literary scholars featured in *PMLA* and the work of composition scholars. For instance, Donald Palumbo-Li notes that the "racialized personal in scholarship" inevitably contributes to the creation of the personal, along with the "consequences of institutional change." He notes, "If we value the humanistic enterprise precisely because it allows us to explore our humanity, the link our particular lives have with others, then the minority scholar has a particular set of negotiations foisted on him or her, for the appearance of race in the university is an unstable one."

Cathy Davidson furthers the debate to embrace issues of genre (not unlike the work of Diane Freedman in *An Alchemy of Genres: Cross-Genre Writing by American Feminist Poet-Critics* (1992). She points out that "the conventions of genre for personal writing are every bit as scripted as the conventions of scholarship . . ." She notes that she makes the same kinds of aesthetic judgments about personal writing ". . . as I do about novels, plays, short stories, essays, or articles in *PMLA*." Concludes Davidson, "Whether we put ourselves in or think we are leaving ourselves out, we are always in what we write." Davidson here teases out multiple layers of the personal—the actual use of the personal in literary criticism as well as the inescapable "I" that must be part of even the most allegedly "impersonal" scholarship. If, indeed, "The politics of multiculturalization involve a rethinking of every participant's personal place," as Palumbo-Li attests, then Sylvia Molloy's view, "that the use of the personal is a decidedly political act," seems a logical, concurrent step. Molloy believes that a use of the personal is ". . . the only way at times to draw attention to the necessary duplicity of all texts and discourses." While Molloy realizes "the enormous responsibility of the personal," she acknowledges that it can become "too easy, too close to commodification in a safe academic setting." As such, it needs "rethinking." Molloy acknowledges that personal "intrusions" can be "jarring or at least cause discomfort and because they effectively call attention to seams, gaps, differences that a general, impersonal discourse would ignore." In view of both the problems and new opportunities it offers, personal-scholarly writing represents a new direction for academic work. It is clear that "old" directions remain, with only new moves, new gestures, when added to what has been done, suggesting new directions.

Perhaps an appropriate place to start understanding these new directions, new gestures, in a detailed way is to pay attention to our own stories as editors. We are not confiding or confessing anything to you, our colleagues, but we provide a different level of justification for opening this path more energetically. We consider it essential to show that our own lives have led us to this point of commitment and self-inclusion, yet still with circumspection at each point in the process. We have lived as if included in all other areas, but as scholars and teachers, we have written (before now, and very often) as if we were not a part of the groups to which our thoughts are directed and about whom we want to know. We had attempted to remove ourselves from our scholarly writing as if to suggest, by the absence of the personal "I-voice," that we were members of that rhetorically conventional and established group. We aim now to participate in the work of those whose thoughts collected in this volume by assuming the first person and observing what emerges. We want to test what some of the writers in this volume suggest, either through demonstration or declaration, that including reference to personal experience or even acknowledging it causes discomfort for them and for others. But we also want to feel the authority that may come from an elaborated and developed style of personal candor, and we want to propose understanding that is more helpful because more clearly anchored in human experience.

DEBORAH H. HOLDSTEIN

For some of us, I think, using the personal in academic scholarship provokes a profound sense of unease. As I reread this first sentence, I am struck by my need to make a personal statement by saying "for some of us" instead of "for me." I suppose I could be personal—sort of, by not focusing entirely on myself but *meaning* myself. Perhaps I am all too in touch with my inner adolescent, the one who is told by adults, "It's not about *you*; it's not *you* who's important. It's the community."

I believe completely Cathy Davidson's assertion, noted above, that "Whether we put ourselves in or think we are leaving ourselves out, we are always in what we write." Perhaps, then, for me, it's a matter of degree. While we might very well "be" in what we write, the varieties of academic rhetoric, however only *allegedly* objective, still, to me stand apart from the truly *personal,* in which narratives involving one's life are revealed within or instead of more conventional academic forms. I cannot legitimately rail against androcentric, academic argument; I am not entitled to do so, as I have not yet dominated it. The conventions of academic argument, I fear, might exceed my grasp. David Bleich, like Richard Ohmann in this volume, has thoroughly mastered (deliberate word choice) the various rhetorics of academe; indeed, he has improved them, shaped them, reshaped them. He has *earned the right to be personal* and given his authority within the profession, he is undiminished by its use. His credibility as a scholar remains.

Perhaps, too, I'm convinced that if something comes readily to me—as it has often seemed when I've written about family stories—that it cannot demonstrate the same degree of discipline, of accomplishment, as that which comes at greater effort. If that is the case, then, I am obligated to attempt those things that come less easily. Don't we, shouldn't we, exhort our students to strive for that which seems difficult, challenging? The so-called conventional, scholarly essay represents a form of that personal exhortation for me. Aren't the scholarly excavations required towards acceptable scholarship, paradoxically, among the most personal of ventures towards collective acceptance?

As Susan Handelman asserts, "knowledge has a face," but "the individual, 'confessional voice' is not such a major component of classical Jewish discourse, in part because Judaism is not a 'confessional' faith. . . . but instead a covenental membership in a People with a collective history, fate, and destiny." While several of our contributors point out that the "community" or collective nature of academe doesn't really exist—that we prize the individual, privatized work of the "solitary scholar"—there are nonetheless sets of scholarly conventions within each discipline that suggest membership. Perhaps I find my voice as an academician tempered by what I perceive to be the various histories and expanded canons of my ongoing academic experience, a voice that finds comfort only if the confessional is balanced by near-universally agreed upon conventions of scholarly work. I think of a personal favorite, the Jane Tompkins essay on *Uncle Tom's Cabin* cited above, which, at the time of its publication in 1981 dared to break the rhetorical conventions of academic prose by beginning as follows:

> Once during a difficult period in my life, I lived in the basement of a house on Forest Street in Hartford, Connecticut, which belonged to Isabella Beecher Hooker—Harriet Beecher Stowe's half-sister. This woman at one time of her life had believed that the millennium was at hand and that she was destined to be the leader of a new matriarchy. When I lived in that basement, however, I knew nothing of Stowe, or of the Beechers, or of the utopian visions of nineteenth-century American women. I made a reverential visit to the Mark Twain house a few blocks away. (20)

Tompkins's essay uses the personal as a touchstone for what is ultimately a strongly argued, scrupulously researched, scholarly work about the value of "sentimental fiction" by women bringing note to an era more readily associated with Whitman and Twain. I often use the Tompkins essay as a model with students to discuss the rhetorical conventions of academic writing, praising her impeccable, useful contrast between personal narrative and intellectually strenuous argument. [I contrast her essay with an equally useful piece of conventional academic argument: Edward Hirsch's award-winning essay in *PMLA*, "The Imaginary Irish Peasant," notable as an example of excellent, traditional academic scholarship as well as for its clarity. (And the latter leads to an entirely different discussion which I will not take up here.)]

In each of these essays, I admire the hard work, the discipline, the reconfiguring of the self into an academic self that must take place for such difficult work to occur. As the daughter of immigrants, I was encouraged to listen to popular music and to watch television as ways to make certain, my parents believed, that I would be completely, fully "American." While there are limits to the possibilities for *any* objectivity in language, I still believe, more often than not, that being "too" personal is a luxury, the privilege of those who have somehow arrived. (Conversely, and in other hands, when the confessional appears in the guise of the academic, it might be seen as the mark of the naïve.) A number of our contributors discuss the various "selves" of scholarship and teaching; certainly there are ways to be multiple selves that are true to who we are: for instance, the George Will I would rather not read as a political columnist, is, alas, the same, wonderful George Will who writes about baseball. Similarly, I do not become any less the working-class, Jewish girl from New York if I successfully achieve the conventions of academic prose. I do not assimilate away (even if I want to) by achieving the difficult.

As context for what to me is a hard-won place in the community (or, as you wish, non-community) of academe, I often tell the story of one of my high school English teachers, Mrs. Ludwick. On the first day of honors English class during my Junior year in high school, she held up a cartoon from *The New Yorker*—a magazine that other people's parents read instead of *Life* and *Reader's Digest*—that featured three witches around a cauldron. The actual caption escapes me now, but I recall her saying, "If you have not read Shakespeare's *Macbeth*, you would not understand to what this cartoonist was alluding. You would not be a cultured person." (That she said "Shakespeah," "cahtooonist," and "allooding," did not escape my adolescent notice, providing an interesting contrast to her well-meaning notions of "cultcha.") She concluded, as if to set the major goal of the rest of the year, "It is my job to give your culture." ("Cultcha") And in her way, Mrs. Ludwick was right: the culture with which she hoped to inoculate us was the culture of T. S. Eliot, to me and to my other white ethnic and African-American counterparts, "the other"—to us, the unattainable, something to which we could aspire. In a curriculum that had also featured *The Autobiography of Malcolm X*, a book I might add, to which we could "relate," it was Eliot and company—and we thought of

Richard Wright as part of the same company—whose oeuvre we had to work to attain, to dominate, to prove ourselves additionally capable of interpreting simply because these writers were in every way, shape, and form, the "*not* us."

That I work mostly in composition and rhetoric—and often in technology—enhances my desire to dominate conventional academic prose. Many of us remember the typical essay in *College English* during the 1960s that always seemed to begin like this: "I walked into my Dean's office, put my feet up on his desk, and told him 'We need to do something about the ways our freshmen write.'" To this day our colleagues with credible scholarship in conventional terms struggle to achieve tenure in a profession that views with skepticism some research in composition studies, judging the work undisciplined and self-indulgent (despite a growing body of work to the contrary). Too often, despite the increasing prominence of composition and rhetoric, there are those who wait for the moments at which compositionists might recede into what is in the view of some the uncritical, unexamined storytelling—the (gasp) "personal"—that makes the field suspect to begin with.

But just as we tell our students that there are different occasions for writing, so too are there different occasions for us: the conventions of the scholarly review in *Genre*, say, are different from the scholarly review in *The New York Review of Books*. These, in turn, differ from scholarly essays in *College English*, *PMLA*, and *American Literature*, which, in turn, differ among themselves within certain unarticulated but defined parameters. Perhaps, then, that which we already know is a compromise mediating my discomfort: that like anything else, the place for the transparent personal within scholarship is a matter of degree, its prominence varying among and within academic genres. In all, however, I remain wary of those colleagues who encourage the wholly, transparently personal from their students to the neglect of conventional rhetorics—of the sort these colleagues themselves have mastered. In doing so, and in the guise of "empowering personal voices," they hypocritically deny students access to the same privilege, deny them the potential to change academic conventions from within.

DAVID BLEICH

I remember learning academic writing. It was in college, and I had to write my bachelor's thesis. I read all the criticism on T. S. Eliot's plays. I had read so much that, unconsciously, I had assimilated the cadences and styles of the commentators on Eliot and his work. I did not know this had happened, but when I sat down to write the last draft, the language came out in the form of "Eliot criticism." For me, this was a genre in itself. A year later, I had the chance to get a job at McGraw-Hill as an entry level editor. The test for this job was to write as if I were a reporter and "report" on the advance presentation of a new kind of railroad system. After studying the imaginary "announcement" by the company, I wrote a newspaper story about this new system. I had assimilated the language of the promotion and converted it into journalese: my story sounded exactly like a newspaper story, and I was offered the job.

It was not until having to write my dissertation and announce a professional identity—how I would say who I am to people who would hire me on a career basis—that I observed my own absence from the scene of writing. It was during this time that I had become interested in the subjectivity of reading. Yet, the subjectivity of writing seemed still to be a forbidden topic. Then, and now, many consider subjectivity a zone of insubstantiality. Although readers' responses are treated somewhat more respectfully, there are still few, if any, accepted languages for announcing the subjectivities that emerge in reading and for translating them into other genres and styles of language. But in writing, the problem is more acute, as, despite the increasing numbers of people wanting to write as if they were part of the field of observation, it is still a choice that rarely leads to the same respectful response as does the voice of the detached scholar.

In college, when I learned the voices of the critics by reading studies of Eliot, Chaucer, Shakespeare, and others, the professional status of my choice of dissertation led me to utopian literature, a field whose idealism I could at once criticize and admire. However: *I felt and knew that my deeper relation to this subject matter was out of bounds for a scholarly project.* This meant: the subject that I chose to launch my professional identity had to be presented without reference to my privately acknowledged sense of its importance to me. At that moment, in the mid-sixties, I suppressed my wish to face this problem of formal academic writing until perhaps fifteen years later, when I turned actively toward the profession of writing pedagogy and tried to work within its space to face the more general issues of how the use of language can help to bring us more together with each other in academic life.

In case any readers of this volume want to know, my dissertation is available in the libraries as *Utopia: The Psychology of a Cultural Fantasy*, published by the UMI Research Press sixteen years after it was written, thanks to the generosity of Professor Robert Scholes, who picked it out of oblivion and recommended its publication. Its idea is that utopian authors have not advanced past adolescence, and the lack of literary quality or power found in most utopian novels derives from the adolescent fantasy of dominion over society being given to them by benevolent parents, fathers, circumstances. I used this idea to relate Thomas More to Edward Bellamy and H. G. Wells; I claimed that their lives were incomplete and in major ways, juvenile. They were boys, good rather than evil, whose gang psychology was translated, if fatuously, into being the gang-leaders of a peaceful and benevolent society.

Perhaps I could not say then about this piece of scholarship and criticism what I can say now: it was my moment of trying to grow beyond adolescence by criticizing the adolescence of others. However, during the writing of this dissertation, I was enjoying an adolescence I had previously missed having gone to all-male schools—high school and college. Was it hypocritical to have experienced this counterpoint: above adolescence in my dissertation, adolescent in real life? Perhaps it was; perhaps many academic statements, claims, advocacies are subject to the same intrapsychic trope. Yet it is also true that each zone of my mind had an appropriate public context. The question is: how full a picture of adolescence (for example) is available to the scholar *not aware of his or her own implication* in the issue? Had I been examining the psychology of these authors with my own situation more clearly in view, might I not have written about them with more sympathy, perhaps even with more alertness to the gender issues they raise, and which I had to raise when preparing the piece for publication? Doesn't the author's awareness of self play a role in how the writing is done, what stances to take as a public figure, and particularly, what tone and attitude as a person among others to take? Might I not have noticed earlier in life the endemic arrogance of the academic posture, an arrogance that is generated by the *convention* of detachment, learned in postsecondary writing courses? Might I, like many in my position, also have learned to notice my male adolescence with more perspicacity and to understand its socially given expectations? Might I have related these expectations to the postures I felt myself taking as an academic writer? Might I have become aware sooner of how fully expectations of masculinity have guided many academics, including many women, to write dishonestly—that is—without regard to who they believe they are in society?

So for me it is no longer personal to be personal—it is fundamental. Once I include myself in the "audience" my contribution changes: my words lose their hortatory status, and take on instead the role of invitation, contribution, membership, and studenthood. I am no longer bound to argue, to make points and cases, or to think that whoever reads my work must be persuaded. I am, rather, more conscious of being among others with comparable, though not identical, interests. Writing and speaking among others is different from doing the same things as performances. It is not *just* personal or *just* performing; it is a wide variety of stances that become available, once at least some terms of personal commitment are included, some aspect of one individual history as a living being and a social constituent, is invited into scholarly discussion.

This is how I feel in the presence of the other contributors to this volume. I feel ready to take up their formulations seriously and perhaps to overtake them, to "steal" them and place them into my own vocabularies. I feel authorized to traverse the differences that there obviously are between me and them. My individual voice provides a basis for hearing other individual voices as having struggled with similar counterpoints, similar previously private misgivings. Each of our formulations justifies all the others, and, gradually, the collection of individuals in this book come somewhat closer to one another and seem, when viewed from a greater distance, to be the beginning of a new community.

Certainly, in my responding to Deborah's invitation to collaborate with her on this volume, a fledgling new community was formed. Our relation to one another began to change from what it was in the past. We worked in this "project" but the interaction brought other issues before us, issues of interpersonal style as we tried to guide our differences toward complementarity that will help us and other contributors. We have not worked through or defined in any formal way what our differences are, and we have not formulated how our strong common cultural ties as Jews with immigrant parents growing up in Queens played a role in putting together this volume. At this time, I can't say at length how these common values work, but one thing is clear, I think: we have recognized the inseparability of individual from collective experience as a value taken from our parents and our culture. We have recognized how our talk shifts peremptorily from the private and hidden to the personal and shared, to the individual and the published. We take these common moves routinely in our discussions of essays and values, and we communicate with one another because we have noted this sense of common style, attitude, and public purpose. We engage in this volume because, perhaps, we want to eradicate people's feeling of exclusion, especially on the basis that their personal history departs from what was previously understood as "normal." We re-direct our historic opposition to exclusion in this local context, and we are grateful for the chance to pursue this purpose in the form of a scholarly enterprise.

IDEALS AND CAUTIONS

Our individual reflections, above, have already presented both our ideals and our cautions. From Deborah we heard how if this new direction in language and literary studies proceeds, little is accomplished if it is merely a new venue for the already confident. From David we heard how if the ideals of scholarship as now received are presented to the next generation, little is accomplished. In the first section, there are two wide-ranging reviews of this balance of values.

Margaret Willard-Traub's essay is part of the theoretical consideration of new approaches to self that don't censor it as a living idea. She focuses specifically on how feminist theory in literature and writing has begun to affect the

14   PERSONAL EFFECTS

"scholarly self," the voices we hear in reading our colleagues work, in rethinking how we are going to interact, in classrooms and in conferences, without the traditional tropes of academic egolalia. This essay, both critical and reflective, engages the provocative work of such figures as Ruth Behar, Nancy Miller, and Jane Gallop, and she provides guidance about how personal accounts do, could, and should lead us to issues of collective concern, without, however, letting the special identities of the personal narratives disappear. In particular, her discussion of loss, like Salvio's, leads toward the view of how academic genres are changing toward more active self-inclusion, and that these new genres are the signs of new social relations less prone to posturing, to idle abstraction, and more oriented around the unity of teaching and scholarship. In this process, she and Salvio are trying to teach how not to avoid pain and frustration in our attempts to tell, teach, study, and share the truth.

Jeffrey Gray, in reviewing a range of work in postmodern and postcolonial literary theory, considers an issue posed and implied by many contributors and those doing related work: how is it that personal styles, tropes, awarenesses and identities continue in our discussions in spite of the critique of the unitary self in postmodern thought? In spite of the proliferation of anti- essentialism, anti-foundationalism, fragmentations-of-self ideas that people entertain, postmodern theory seems still to retain a dimension of liberal humanism. The language of self and individual consciousness, he suggests, is not going out of style. Rather, in its place in language retains, with other ideas, a pragmatic reality in our lives. Other essays in this volume have shown the dimensions of this reality.

Juxtaposed to one another, these essays portray the issue of scholarly self-inclusion in its resistance to being dogmatized. As humanistic scholars gradually acquire the courage to disclose their stakes in their new understandings of the subject matter, they also recognize how much more latitude the subject gives to write from a variety of sites in the profession and in society. In the next section two unusual sites are considered.

SELF-INCLUSION IN LITERARY SCHOLARSHIP

Brenda Daly's essay is, in part, an answer to the cautions of Deborah Holdstein and Jeffrey Gray. Daly's site is definitely one of the more dangerous ones in the academy and in society. We are first beginning to face the common occurrence of the incestuous derogation of women's and children's lives. Brenda Daly's lifetime scholarly achievement has helped to open this path for this part of social experience and she has showed how it may enter the curriculum while we stay alert to its risks. While "radical introspection" may have been a part of classical Greek society, it has, today, a new meaning, one that could be taken up by all people, not only the privileged.

Before feminism became a factor in academic life, the genre of autobiography existed and was treated with respect—provided it knew its place. As Deborah Holdstein has observed, only some have been permitted the luxury of "writing my autobiography": these were the writers, critics, and travelers who already reached a relatively advanced age, had many public accomplishments, and now in a leisurely sense, they could "look back," make assessments, tell their stories. Brenda Daly's essay tells us how this can no longer be the case. Daly's writing says that a person's life can never again be a mere curiosity—the things that happen to us, our struggles, our accession to the privileges of academic life, our pre-academic family life, these too are fundamental. She suggests how these events teach us how to read, how to choose what we read and what we announce in our curricula. Daly's story is one of family concealment that leads to personal concealment. The processes of suppression and repression of the dangerous truths about some families' lives have been especially damaging to the ability of women to have lives of candor in public and in private. It is as if, in childhood, and unbeknownst to many women, the gift of self-esteem has been taken away, and as they grow into adulthood, are left to comprehend how this happened. Daly's story is, luckily, one of recovery from this near-permanent removal of self-esteem. She suggests how scholarly reading and criticism meant recovery for her and a path toward contact with student who may also have had to conceal the fundamental experiences of their lives. Daly shows that the one window of hope for her and others like her was the chance to publish in self-disclosing genres, to bring to light, to announce to others that, yes, "It really did happen," much as Patricia Williams's sister urges her (in *The Alchemy of Race and Rights*) to say "it happened" just because there will be a mendacious chorus saying "it didn't happen."

Paula Salvio achieves a similarly compelling synthesis of perspectives and genres. Dealing with a situation of the loss of a beloved parent whose loss is also resented because it was unnecessary and paradoxical, Salvio folds her story into that of Anne Sexton. Salvio's story follows her sense of loss and resentment into her scholarship and her teaching, and in the process, urges us to anticipate our unconscious responses to the literature we teach. Many of us literature teachers teach what we love. But the terms of our love of particular works are usually seen as not requiring any formal examination or social reference. Salvio, however, shows that whatever our attachments to literature and to writers, the fact that there are such attachments means that their roots in our life histories are significant, and that looking for them, finding them, and disclosing them as part of both the pedagogical and scholarly processes enriches these efforts for students and teachers. Sure, there is pain and discomfort for both Daly and Salvio. Yet one "fundamental" feature of our professional commitment is examining the unexamined for what it will teach us and future generations. Daly's and Salvio's essays show emphatically the seriousness and necessity of personal courage to disclose issues that younger, less able, less experienced, less comprehending people don't yet know to pursue. Their work shows teaching and scholarship at its deepest and how personal inquiry is a necessary part of them both.

TEACHING AND SCHOLARSHIP FACE TO FACE

Daly and Salvio show that including themselves in literary teaching and scholarship involves "facing" the forgotten, repressed, and suppressed in their individual histories of experience: they look memories and moods in the face by recording, narrating the movement between self and text, self and author, self and co-reader. Susan Handelman shows how, through Jewish history, the relation of teacher to student has always had a similar "face-to-face" status, that student and teacher face each other in the same sense that each of us "face" experience and history. This is not the case for the history of our own society, but, most of us would agree, that, as Richard Ohmann and most other contributors acknowledge, the individual facing oneself cannot be taken out of any teaching. In fact, we might as well admit, we have given the one-to-one tutorial the status as an ideal teaching unit, and this ideal materializes in the dissertation phase of doctoral study. Handelman shows how serious an ideal this is: it is not just a tutorial—it is "eye contact," the necessary face-to-face that must be part of the process of teaching and learning. Handelman documents this necessity in the long tradition of Jewish scholarly commentary. At the base of historic Jewish inquiries into what laws shall hold society together is the experience of face-to-face learning.

One cannot help but notice the connection between Handelman's ideal and the very differently put discussion of Madeleine Grumet, who, earlier in her career, stressed the connection between the bonds of parent and child and the bonds of teacher and student. In both Handelman's and Grumet's ideals, personal experience is already collective, already made up of two people facing each other, learning from that juxtaposition. Some language philosophers such as Lev Vygotsky and George Herbert Mead have described how language begins through one's experience with two or more people; social processes then create individual language capability as a phase of the socialization process. This is the similar weight of Handelman's contribution: there is a certain primoridiality of the face-to-face, the foundation of the wider collective, the source of our sense of the individual.

A great deal of academic editing in the humanities renders this face-to-face category a problem. In the rapidly growing practice of anonymous review, the editor "faces" the author and the reviewer, but the latter two don't face each other. Louise Z. Smith considers how these editing practices affect the process of moving the individual voice to face the public. Different relationships between author and reader are implied by the different modes of personal address—the personal and impersonal "you" that may be discerned in many essays written in personal modes. Smith is particularly concerned that when the more familiar "*du*" mode is used criticism crosses over into exposé—a sudden devaluation of the very act meant to make abstractions feel more consistent with experience. While agreeing that personal address is inescapable, and that there are instances of personal criticism that are not self-indulgent, for an editor to face authors as persons is a challenge. Smith relates the needs of the editor of a large, high-circulation journal (*College English*) to the needs of the profession to begin to include reference to personal experience. In the context of editing, she observes, practices like double-blind review, while helpful to those getting started, still do not remove the editor from interacting with contributors in the traditional person-to-person mode. Her experience could be an instance of Jeffrey Gray's—and Cathy Davidson's (cited by Holdstein, above)—similar observation that the person—the single face, the single voice, the active subject—is going to be there *in some form*, regardless of political change or intellectual fashion. Smith's account alerts us to how, if we take into account the continuity of day-to-day experiences, we necessarily write our scholarship through the *combination* of personal and collective values, modes of interaction, ways of speaking, styles of writing.

TEACHING AND SCHOLARSHIP, PUBLIC AND PRIVATE

The scholarly tutorial (such as obtained in dissertations and "independent study" arrangements for students) and the double-blind review are extremes of pedagogical and scholarly interpersonal relations which occur in lesser degrees and in mixed forms in other social relations in the academy. These relations include the identified ones of journal reviews, academic conferences, department meetings that review curricula.

Madeleine Grumet's commentary on how the interest in autobiography has evolved and on how the genre has varied suggests its broad range of application in the teaching and scholarship. Coming from a basic sympathy with the practices of family, children, and rational subjectivity, Grumet reflects on her own growth, especially on her responses to postmodern critiques of individual life that challenge these sympathies. Remembering herself as "Miss Subjectivity of 1978," she now asks that autobiography not stop with the personal narrative but guide us also to generalizations about selves in society. She reminds us that if we think of ourselves as teachers, the process of sharing the private in public is never purely either public or private. It is only that our ways of thinking about one another change as we change our genres of writing, as we include reference to our own growth, our "aging," our consciousness of the passing of loved ones. She urges that we remember that our self-awareness, as teachers and as citizens, is finally oriented around contributions to society, to collective life.

Karen Paley follows this line of thought in her discussion of the need to remember the collective value of "expressive" writing. She notes how we have come into a mood in which "expressive" is equated with self-indulgence and narcissistic "emoting." In fact, she, like Grumet, has viewed expressive and personal writing as an element in a social project that aimed for full equality in society for all groups, all memberships. As individualism has become redirected into narrow, power-oriented values through the influence of corporate culture, those writing teachers who have insisted that people continue to tell their stories have felt the pressure of condescension. Writing teachers, always the lowest on the academic totem, are now feeling the effects of this new pretext for diminishing their work. Paley takes up the task of revoking this new criticism with evidence from classrooms and counter-arguments to critics. She shows what many have assumed: the announcement of experience has both a social and a personal weight, and their *combination*, not their separation, is the responsibility of those of us teaching writing and other subjects presented in writing.

Diane Freedman's essay, also answering Grumet's challenge to use all the forms of autobiography, surveys the pedagogical contexts in which writing "that matters" can be taught, where the writing refers equally to the literature and to the comments and analyses given by students. She shows how accounts of teaching experiences are becoming more self-consciously integrated with scholarly genres. Freedman has a broad range of reference to scholarly work that has increasingly used self-inclusion—anthropology, sociology, education, as well as literary criticism—but then returns to show and document the salutary effects on students' motivation when they are able to read, write, and discuss with full reference to experiences, including painful ones, of their lives. Like Brenda Daly, Freedman is interested in the transition of writers' senses of audience from individual to class to public. Freedman's essay shows genres in the process of change and her citations of students' work also help to show why they change. Today, she observes, that on the part of writers, teachers, and students, there is a willingness to loosen received generic boundaries, because people in all parts of society, many from communities entering postsecondary education for the first time, have narratives that help to end the rule of "master" narratives. She shows how school work is life work—a calling for some, work about people's lives for others, the movement through stages for still others. Each of these works entails a new view of language and literature, a new sense of how to overtake it and fold it into our minds.

Rarely in the professional literature do we find accounts of pedagogical experiences in graduate school. Rachel Brownstein overtakes the students' voices in her title, "Personal Experience Paper" and then considers the fact that pedagogical experiences are *necessarily* personal, another version, perhaps, of Handelman's subject. Writing in an informal and decidedly non-ethnographic style, Brownstein implies a degree of her discomfort, but also dramatizes her kinship with the students. She is responding to the traditional academic hesitations about taking personal responses to literature seriously by asking if she is wasting students' time seeking, listening to, and then integrating their responses and other allusions to their personal lives into her more traditional judgments of literature's meaning and value. She cites undergraduate as well as graduate responses. Yet the different kinds of students entering her classes are non-traditional, so that her account of their experiences of one another brings a fresh accent to the genre of classroom accounts. Her discussion puts the question of personal response to literature in a somewhat different light: if we are aiming to encourage a wide reading latitude by postsecondary and graduate students, how do we use the experience and expertise of the scholar who has devoted decades to the study of the same works? When listening to this account with the "third ear," one hears perhaps the thought of how protective traditional scholarship had been of the subjective and the private.

A decisive shift from Brownstein's voice is that of Joycelyn K. Moody, who moves forcefully into risky territories about which many teachers have expressed hesitations. In recounting a teaching situation in which she lived in close proximity to her students, she observes in revealing detail the feelings, moods, interpersonal psychology of trying to challenge students while relating to them in fully personal ways, including dancing with them. This engrossing account raises an issue that has been sensitive for centuries—from Abelard and Heloise through Jane Gallop (whose experience is mentioned by Ohmann and Holdstein)—the temptation toward erotic feelings between teachers and students. Moody's essay does not, of course, provide answers and solutions in the usual sense. Rather, she provides a *personal narrative* that permits us to conceptualize, and in part to judge for ourselves, the effects of what we usually think of as dangers. We may feel the teaching situation in which she worked, and perhaps because it takes place abroad, we may perceive a distance that encourages us to compare it to our own teaching.

THE SOCIAL CHARACTER OF PERSONAL NARRATIVE

One of the reasons for the exclusion of the first person in scholarly writing is the ideal that because scholarship is for everyone, narcissism is unwelcome. Yet, in scholarly writing, narcissism has taken indirect forms (such as the excessive citation of one's own work), and in professional life it is already rampant among academics. For too many, the measure of success is the length of one's vita; for many graduate students and not-yet-tenured scholars, there are many efforts undertaken "because it will look good on my vita." The process by which faculty members are judged and evaluated already says that you either succeed as an individual, or you risk failure. The censorship of the first person in scholarly writing is accompanied by a standard that discourages the identification of second and third persons as scholarly collaborators, thus encouraging narcissism indirectly.

In "Collaboration and Concepts of Authorship"[3] Lisa Ede and Andrea Lunsford, two scholars who have collaborated with one another for a long time, observe that in spite of attempts to find alternatives to the "adversarial academy" in recent decades, "the deep structure of the academy remains relatively untouched." (358) This statement refers, in part, to how the primacy of individual authorship as an ideal has continued to discourage the recognition of the value of collaborative work as a practice deserving of professional credit at least as much as individual authorship. The axiom of individual authorship, as backed by centuries of copyright law, is justified by the presumed "objectivity" of the individual author. The inclusion of subjective stances in the work of individual authors would, under this axiom, discredit the authority of the author. However, as Ede and Lunsford (as well as many other scholars collaborating with one another on an equitable basis) have repeatedly demonstrated, collaborative efforts provide more space for personal writing to enter the text: the two voices' subjectivities, as well as their intersubjectivities, help to remove the sense of narcissism that could accrue to the self-references and self-disclosures of single authors.

At the same time many styles of offering personal narratives about scholarly lives perform the same scholarly function of enhancing public understanding that other, less personally articulated writings have performed in the past. As Virginia Woolf writes in *A Room of One's Own*, the turn to biography and autobiography as a source of new information provided her the means to overcome ideological biases found in traditional (male oriented) scholarship.

The account of collaboration given by Kate Ronald and Hephzibah Roskelly points us in the directions outlined by Ede and Lunsford. Their account suggests how individuals' sense of membership in the academy and in society is cultivated through collaboration. In our (Holdstein's and Bleich's) collaboration, we chat a great deal about everything but our work. Sometimes, our concern for one another as total figures upstaged our responsibility to proceed with this volume in a timely manner. Nevertheless, here it is, done perhaps not as soon as we would have liked, but with the sense that it is our common project, with our extra attachment to it. This last observation is one of our gestures of connection with Kate Ronald and Hephzibah Roskelly, who have collaborated with each other as friends and colleagues for two decades. They met in graduate school, found a common language, obviously both personal and professional mixed in with one another, and then found that this language led to projects that need their collaborative attentions. Just how personal a story is this? Well, of course it is personal, but it is like the relations of many faculty members who, unlike Ronald and Roskelly or Ede and Lunsford, have not recognized the value and advantage of discussing their collaborations as part of their scholarly practice. Hundreds of us faculty members collaborate with one another in different ways. Sometimes it is just a matter of "many hands making light work." Other times it is common for a project to demand the perspective of two or more people. We may not be used to hearing the story, account, or explanation of the collaboration attached to the given work, but those genres insert our human experiences into our writings. Such genres seem to emerge only on dramatic occasions, such as the account of how the double helix may have been discovered. Ronald and Roskelly's essay shows how that acknowledging our dependency on our friends and colleagues emphasizes the social basis of personhood, while helping to move us away from the adversarial academy.

Victor Villanueva's essay, a combination of genres reminiscent of his own, Diane Freedman's, and Patricia Williams's books teaches us how mixed and multiple genres urge us to notice the mixed and multiple constituencies in our society. He reminds us of the contemporary meaning of "pathos." Our culture, he notes, is very familiar with logos and ethos, but as most contributors to this volume acknowledge, pathos is a problem for academic writers. Pathos, like the first person, has been relegated to autobiography. When it appears in scholarly writing, it is perceived as sentiment. With a dramatic combination of genres, including so-called "fictional" ones, Villanueva, like Freedman and Williams, is teaching how to create genres that include, but do not focus exclusively on, our emotional stakes in our histories and in our language uses. His purposeful inclusion of colloquialisms, poetry, partial memory narratives make his own present tense live in new ways. How many of us professors are willing to describe our own habits of mind in this way that demonstrates how fully a part of others we already are, even as individual authors?

Katya Gibel Azoulay, an anthropologist who has already written self and society into the academic record, tells another personal story that documents the Western refusal to acknowledge in public the ubiquity of ancestral mixtures. Of the many issues treated in her essay, perhaps the matter of scientific racism is the obstacle most decisively opposed by her forceful account of "what actually happened." She observes that racism backed by science—"is stronger than the disclaimers that race is a social construction." Science and local mythologies have combined to perpetuate false habits of perception; her experience, recorded in her recent book, counters the centuries-old axiom of assuming the primordiality of "the self in isolation." Her voice and her story revoke the ideal of the primacy of the isolated individual by telling her own experience as a *family* history. Because of this emphasis, "I accentuate the complicated histories of people, the emergence of diasporic communities, and the significance of interrogating political signifiers." This in turn leads to the effort to create "courses, syllabi selections, and research projects . . . shaped and crafted from the advantage of multiple perspectives."

Like Azoulay's accent on family, the essays by Morris Young and by Chris Castiglia take us back to the *childhood* experiences that contributed to their scholarly identities. Young's re-creation of the experiences in the office of the "speech therapist" dramatizes how collectively held attitudes and practices tried to guide the individual child into inappropriate categories. He goes through a series of incidents, showing how the uncertain responses of strangers gradually foster in him the sense of uncertainty: his appearance always gave a first impression of being "foreign," even though he was born in the United States—Hawaii.

Those of us who have not experienced this unsettling but conventional response may not understand its effects. One presents as native-born in every way. But appearance is used to turn the otherwise certain identity into an anomaly. Young demonstrates the cumulative effect of experiencing these responses over childhood and youth. By the time he arrives at the front of the room as a university faculty member, he anticipates them. He realizes the inertia of his position, how slowly it would change. Yet he also realizes that the moment of this writing is also a moment of change. "The use of story (and not simply to resist or invert dominant culture) creates the possibility of expressing a fuller experience." In this way, Young gives us the sense that "assimilation" is for *everyone*. The narratives of childhood recovery help us readers to create a more inclusive society, rather than just to resist a hegemony or to enhance an individual. Young's pedagogy and scholarship grow from this narrative.

Christopher Castiglia's is the story of an individual deriving collective values from home to overcome the isolation in academic life. Like Young, he is on a borderline: his appearance, however, works to conceal salient features of individuality rather than revoke salient features of membership. Again, a productive response to having been placed in this situation is to tell the story. Castiglia is the suburban youth who is really gay. His essay counteracts "the academic desire to segregate the personal." Placing this issue in the arena of sexual identity emphasizes its national, even global, dimensions. Segregating the personal in our own society quietly performs the collective bigotry of keeping people "in the closet." When Castiglia tells the story, his participation in national culture emerges, his kinship with familiar symbols and practices are rendered as lived experiences. The examination of his own life suggests that the success of his citizenship in family and society "has in many ways made me a poor academic—too hungry for community, too quick with tactless speech." But by telling the story, Castiglia moves the academy closer to society. The reader immersed in his appealing, articulate renditions of youth in Northern New Jersey, feels the connections Castiglia has had to feel only through pain. Yet he too is teaching us through the voice heard in this volume.

Richard Ohmann's narrative takes us to a time when "student centered" teaching was not widely known and argued about. His trepidations as a young teacher, while common enough among today's young teachers, make us smile as we know him as one of the leaders of our profession, one of those whose lifetime achievement has helped render the academy a place where more and more of us can find fulfillment. Ohmann's descriptions of his youthful experience makes us conscious of our own historicity as well as our social privileges.

Interestingly enough, the personal voice we find in this essay has been there, it now seems, all along! How similar it is to the voice of *English in America*, as well as to those of Ohmann's many other contributions. Yet his essay also shows that although we may admire a personal *voice*, it is not the same as to use that voice, or any other, to *write oneself into the subject matter*, and this is what his essay achieves on this occasion. His experiences at Harvard, at Wesleyan as Vice Provost, as editor of *College English*: these now are part of "English in America" the subject matter, the profession, the pedagogy, the academic community.

As a citizen of his university community, indeed, as one of its pedagogical, intellectual, professional, and administrative leaders, he may have to take positions that do not represent his political convictions. What is he to do? He places this issue in the context of his story, his long search for what is right for *both* himself and society. Is this a "personal" story. Some will say, "easily," but it is not so clear, unless we have already cordoned off the "personal" into some narrative form that has many "I's" in it. Here the writer's question remains unanswered; his memberships, while clear, dictate no clear rules for how to meet the contingencies of social circumstances. Yet, including the individual perspective dramatizes just how incomplete this perspective is if taken alone to be fundamental.

It is interesting to us as editors how stubborn this *combination* of personal, impersonal, and collective uses of language is. We believe that these essays show conclusively that one cannot separate "the personal" anything (well, maybe the toothbrush), from what belongs to or is associated with the "our," the some of us, and the all of us. In a sense this collection is a voice opposing strong boundaries while recognizing a wide variety of limited uses of boundaries. This collection has found and also advocates for the reduction of censorship, for the construction of different ways of communication, and for the informed interest in what others feel it essential to report.

We are aiming for new values for ourselves and our profession. We want to remove the implied coerciveness of the term "profession," a word that says in one way or another, "you can't say this, you can't say that." At the same time we seek in the combination of the personal and the professional ways to reduce idle combativeness that dates back to the age of classical Greek rhetoric and to 12th century university pedagogy through which students' Latin debates were tests of their readiness to become licensed teachers. *Of course* we hear voices preparing to say that opposing adversariality is adversarial. But we have an answer, which, we claim, is forceful but not adversarial: "A foolish consistency is the hobgoblin of little minds." We ourselves think that this is neither inconsistency, nor paradox, nor hypocrisy. We can dispute and oppose; we can combine, create, and transcend mistaken views; we can include ourselves among as many others as appropriate. And we can honor revisions of our selves, our memberships, and our societies, without declaring their demise.

NOTES

1. This same issue, as it applies in physical and social sciences as well as in the humanities, is taken up in the volume forthcoming from Duke University Press edited by Olivia Frey and Diane Freedman, *Personal Thoughts*. A still compelling volume making a similar point about science is *Discovering Reality: Feminist Perspectives on Epistemology, Metaphysics, Methodology, and Philosophy of Science*, eds. Sandra Harding and Merill B. Hintikka. Boston: Reidel, 1983.
2. Its problematic status can be traced back much further to the separation of the written from the oral uses of language that is, actually, thousands of years old, though not altogether universal in Western culture.
3. *PMLA*, March 2001, 354-369.

PART ONE
Ideals and Cautions

1 SCHOLARLY MEMOIR
An Un-"Professional" Practice

Margaret Willard-Traub

The figure of the solitary thinker comprises a most powerful and enduring representation of scholarly life. This is the figure of the autonomous scholar-teacher, whose intellectual sovereignty and productivity, both in and out of the classroom, seemingly rests as much if not more upon untold hours of secluded reading and writing as it does upon building relationships with others—even those others who eventually may comprise important audiences for the scholar's writing and teaching.

Those of us whose experiences inside the institution readily challenge the usefulness of unqualified autonomy as an ideal, simultaneously recognize its appeal. Despite (or, ironically, perhaps sometimes because of) influences such as the political and bureaucratic constraints on scholarship and teaching that scholars like Michael Bérubé, Cary Nelson, and Richard E. Miller have explored; feminist theories and practices examining the role of the 'personal' in professional work; widely accepted educational approaches stressing collaboration and dialogue in learning and teaching; and seemingly daily calls in the media for scholar-teachers to communicate rationales for their work with the public more often and in ways deemed more "accountable," the ideal of the autonomous scholar-teacher, much of whose most important labor occurs outside of collaborative (or competitive) relationships, continues to circulate as a symbol of professional success.

This ideal of autonomy endures perhaps because the vision of relative (if not absolute) autonomy provides academics with what Richard E. Miller would call a "felt sense of distinction" (26); perhaps it endures as well because it comprises, at least for some, part of a legacy and a link to a common, professional past. In any case, at the very least such an ideal operates within the institution like other "subterranean text(s)" (e.g., the text which Linda Brodkey argues leads composition to "abet middle-class illusions of meritocracy" [234]) that "insinuate rather than argue (their) claims" (215). That such an ideal figures strongly in others' and our own perceptions of the profession is evidenced, for example, by the frequency with which "autonomy" is cited by tenured faculty members as one reason for high satisfaction in their jobs (Schneider par. 8).

This text of scholarly autonomy also is powerfully sustained by traditional forms of academic writing that privilege a stance of 'objectivity,' and the development of argument that ostensibly stands outside the shaping influences of social or rhetorical conditions (Gee 63). Such writing follows what both David Olson and James Gee have called an "autonomous model of literacy"—a set of conventions traditionally privileging a writer's explication of logical connections between ideas, while neglecting (or at least de-emphasizing) an examination of the relationship between a writer's subject position and those ideas, or his or her relationships to various audiences.

In recent years, however, a proliferation of scholarly memoirs and other examples of autobiographically inflected scholarship across diverse disciplines in the humanities and social sciences suggests a shifting away in the U.S. academy from scholars' privileging exclusively, in their practices and assessments of writing, this "autonomous" model. Such a trend perhaps also suggests a shifting away from the view that scholars are of necessity professional 'loners,' engaged in work that is optimally solitary. In contrast to traditional forms of academic writing, examples of what I will call more "reflective," academic practice like scholarly memoirs, ethnographies that are 'situated' with regard to the subject position of the writer/researcher, and teaching portfolios, at least in part define themselves against traditional expectations for 'objectivity' that require, for instance, a scholar to adopt a personal detachment from his or her object of study or to maintain a certain distance from potential audiences.

Specifically, I would suggest that such reflective, academic texts emphasize the ways in which *relationships* between writers and their diverse audiences (both those who are scholars and those who are not) are established. Not surprisingly, these texts align themselves with postmodern epistemologies that affirm the multiplicity and contingency of the writing 'self'—acknowledging the 'everydayness' of people's lives (as that is defined by realities of emotion and psychology as well as by material exigencies), and the personal realities of writers and readers in relationship. In this essay I would suggest not that the practice of writing "reflectively" threatens to supplant (or should supplant) more traditional approaches to scholarly writing, however. Rather, I would offer that its most thoughtful examples illustrate how such practice is situated more broadly within an array of causes and effects involved in the current "crisis of representation" endemic to the academy and western culture; and that such practice has the potential for being responsive to history and to the diversity of experience within the current moment in ways more difficult for traditional forms. (George Marcus and Michael Fisher, focusing on the origins and implications of cultural "transition(s)," also argue that broad, historical forces have helped to contribute to a shift in the purposes of academic writing in anthropology specifically, prompting this writing to move away from "explaining changes within broad encompassing frameworks of theory," and toward "exploring innovative ways of describing at a microscopic level the process of change itself" (Marcus 15). As in the case of many of the scholarly memoirs I examine in this essay, this "microscopic" level is often at the level of individual lives and the specific communities and contexts which shape and are shaped by those lives.)

In her collection of autobiographical essays entitled *Crossing Ocean Parkway: Readings by an Italian American Daughter,* Duke scholar Marianna De Marco Torgovnick, for example, theorizes the 'everyday' sources for her authority and knowledge as a scholar, examining what her family history and her childhood growing up in the Bensonhurst section of Brooklyn has meant for her intellectual work. For Torgovnick, Bensonhurst is not only the home of her childhood. It is a place she recognizes as both "choking and nutritive" (11), a place that is also the New York of newspaper headlines, where in the summer of 1989 Yusuf Hawkins is set upon and killed by a group of angry whites. Like Howard Beach before it and Crown Heights after it, this public Bensonhurst will come to signify for much of the rest of the country the intersection of urban violence and racial hatred—a place with a distinct yet terrible 'voice,' othered by its own ability to other a young African American man and the two friends walking with him through the neighborhood that night. Torgovnick herself describes the ways in which her own gender is the basis of an othering within Bensonhurst's Italian American community, and how her hometown becomes for her an object of scholarly—as well as personal—inquiry:

> What has Bensonhurst to do with what I teach today and write? Why did I need to write about this killing in Bensonhurst, but *not* in the manner of a news account or a statistical sociological analysis? Within days of hearing the news, I began to plan this essay, to tell the world what I knew, though I stopped midway, worried that my parents or their neighbors would hear about it. . . . Now, much to my surprise, Bensonhurst—the antipodes of the intellectual life I sought, the least interesting of places—had become a respectable intellectual topic. People would be willing to hear about Bensonhurst—and all by the dubious virtue of a racial killing in the streets. (9-10)

Even though Torgovnick's Bensonhurst presents itself as a "respectable intellectual topic" because of Hawkins's killing, she resists writing about it as such— at least not in the manner in which she has been trained professionally. Instead, she gives us a hybrid text: she briefly provides us with, in the words of my colleague Anne Reeves, a "phantom" treatment of the event as she might have written it, and then goes on to give her audience what she apparently thinks they need to hear, or perhaps at least what she feels she needs to say: "Now, as I write about 'the neighborhood,' I recognize that although I've come far in physical and material distance, the emotional distance is harder to gauge. Bensonhurst has everything to do with who I am and even with what I write" (11).

In this way, Torgovnick's text accomplishes some of what Michael Bérubé identifies as cultural studies' work of "talking back"—talking back to dominant paradigms, "raid(ing) and unsettl(ing) the compartmentalized disciplines of traditional academic study" (138), by replacing a more traditionally framed academic treatment of the events in Bensonhurst with an explanation of the "emotional distance" she has traveled, and the connections between that distance and her intellectual work. This hybrid text not only talks back to assumptions about what constitutes appropriate academic writing, however; it also talks back to assumptions about who constitutes an appropriate—or perhaps inevitable—audience for that writing. For while Torgovnick expresses the fear that her parents and neighbors will react badly to her essay, her anxiety suggests she is inscribing in that essay multiple audiences—composed not only of her academic peers, but of her family and community, as well.

Torgovnick's text, as one example of what I would identify as the most engaging and productive autobiographical writing being produced by scholars today, is also characterized by an inscription and explicit analysis of multiple 'voices' within the text. Such a multiply-voiced text often comprises what Torgovnick herself has called "crossover writing" (*PMLA*, 282), for its ability to establish relationships with diverse, disciplinary audiences within the institution. "Crossover writing" may be a useful term, as well, for thinking through the ability of reflective texts like memoirs also to reach extra-academic audiences. Providing scholars with a means for communicating with audiences beyond the academy's walls, as well as with a means for communicating with audiences inhabiting other academic disciplines and various positions of power within the institution, makes it possible for them to enact an ethics of accountability, for example, to diverse individuals and constituencies both within and outside institutions of higher education.

In the case of scholarly memoir and other 'reflective' academic texts—that is, texts which explicitly examine the subject position of the writer and implications of that writerly position—such communication is achieved through the kind of "heteroglossia" (324) that M.M. Bakhtin describes. Scholarly memoirs thus might be said to comprise an alternative intellectual practice, while also varying (as does all discourse) in the ways in which and degree to which they nurture the "roiling mass of languages" (Holquist 69) and voices of which they are comprised. As a group, these memoirs might be said to privilege the establishing of relationships not only between different voices within the text, but also between the text and diverse audiences without, a practice that enacts both an accountability to and a "responsive understanding" (Bakhtin 280) of the social world.

SITUATING 'PERSONAL' VOICES WITHIN THE INSTITUTION

Such an intellectual practice is embodied in much of the work of feminist scholars across the disciplines. Gesa Kirsch introduces her study of the writing experiences of women scholars in *Women Writing the Academy: Audience, Authority and Transformation* in part by exploring the relation between gender and speaking with an "academic" voice:

> Women who write academic discourse have a different point of departure than men: they first have to establish a place of authority before they can begin to speak and write with confidence. In establishing such a place, women have to challenge old norms and establish new ones; they have to create a space for themselves in an institution that has not always provided space for them.... Furthermore, feminist scholars have pointed out that women's authority is easily undermined because they have to speak—and write—the "language of patriarchy," a language that places men in superior and women in subordinate positions in its vocabularies and representations of everyday phenomena and social relationships. (20–21)

Scholars such as bell hooks, Patricia Williams, Marianna De Marco Torgovnick, Nancy K. Miller and Ruth Behar, among others, also have demonstrated in their scholarly work, much of which draws on examples from personal experience, how academic and professional languages function to place women, people of color, and the poor in subordinate positions both outside and within the academy, albeit in different ways and with different consequences.

Though still too frequently excluded, the voices of these 'others' represented in such scholarly work nevertheless have contributed significantly to a "heightening of debates and stakes involved in writing that is perceived as theoretical" (Lutz 261)—that is, the very writing that is given the highest currency in the institution. At the same time, Catherine Lutz writes that "one effect of the struggle (of women, and men and women of color in the academy) for institutional space and respect may have been an inflation of theory's value even as questions are raised about the dualisms and individualism on which its existence is based" (261). Such an inflation suggests that the heteroglossia of voices emanating from those whose discourses are different from the traditional, "masculinized" (Lutz 249), theoretical discourse of the academy may be as hard as ever for us as scholars to hear.

The kind of "responsive understanding" of the social world which such hearing encourages, however—an understanding that acknowledges the legitimacy and 'logic' of multiple voices striving for equity and defining excellence in multiple ways—is what drives much research in both feminist composition and feminist literary studies. Both fields take as one of their points of departure the (im)possibility of a mix of voices—especially the voices of women, people of color, and working-class people—being both heard and valued within the institution. In her essay "Me and My Shadow," Jane Tompkins articulates this (im)possibility as she identifies herself as, in fact, double-voiced. Tompkins suggests that, by possessing (at least) two 'voices,' the voice of a "critic"-self, and that of a "person who wants to write about her feelings," women academics have a more difficult time achieving speech at all, at least within a professional context.

While Tompkins argues that such diverse voices sound within contexts which are necessarily exclusive of each other because of the hierarchies which inhere in academic discourse and theory, Nancy K. Miller challenges Tompkins's dichotomy by responding, "Do you have to turn your back on theory in order to speak with a non-academic voice?" (5) The very language of even Miller's question, however, suggests the power of dichotomies as she posits two voices, one which is academic and "theoretical," and the other which is not.

Feminist scholars in composition, like Terry Myers Zawacki and Elizabeth Flynn, take yet a different tack on the question of what 'voice' is appropriate to academic writing, as they struggle to find ways to present to students "alternatives to traditional academic discourse," and to help students write "personal-academic" (Zawacki 33) essays—essays that might feature "authentic" voices able to integrate "intuition with authoritative knowledge" (Flynn 429). Lynn Z. Bloom, like Zawacki and Flynn, suggests that finding one authentic, personal voice (845) is crucial if a writer is to accomplish academic work (that is, work involving much debate and innovation) while at the same time claiming political power. Bloom, Zawacki and Flynn echo the notion that there exists an authentic voice which a writer might discover, a notion that Lester Faigley argues commonly operates in scholarly debates within composition vis à vis the view of the individual as "the subject of high modernism: a coherent consciousness capable of knowing oneself and the world" (16). In such a view, a writer's one "authentic" voice might be said to function as a "window" on the self and the world, at the same time it serves as a necessary condition for individual agency.

In any case, this attention paid to the issue of 'voice' in feminist scholarship may be said to represent an anxiety about the (im)possibility of inscribing the personal—which is linked closely to political agency in feminist circles outside the academy—as also part of the intellectual work of scholars and students. Negatively, this anxiety perhaps at times manifests itself in an unreasonable quest for a writer's one, "authentic" voice—that voice which will serve her in accomplishing both the scholarly work of the academy and the political work she might be called on to do outside the academy. Positively, this anxiety has helped drive the proliferation of new forms of academic writing, including that of scholarly memoir.

It is not that the academic trend toward valuing reflective writing offers hope of achieving an 'all-purpose' discourse, fit for purposes both academic and extra-academic; rather, it will be my contention in the rest of this essay that such reflexivity is not beside the point of good academic work, but instead is central to rigorous scholarly practice.

Such a reflexive turn is also part of a wider valuing by society of personal stories, as well as part of a complex dialogue among the voices and life stories which surround us every day. From the floors of national political conventions, to the sets of popular T.V. talk shows, to the halls of the academy, publicly delivered and published reflections about personal lives—some examples of cultural analysis, lavishly textured and insightful; others arguably instances of a more prosaic or self-serving rhetoric—function to persuade, cajole, give testimony to, instruct and entertain a complex array of audiences. Moving along on the social currents created by these stories are voices, highly variegated and kinetic, simultaneously responding to and reshaping each other. And these voices increasingly have made their way into the academy, mixing with traditional voices of disciplinary authority as the canons of many fields have been challenged and disrupted, for example, by the growth of cultural studies, feminist studies and postmodern epistemologies that insist that the 'everyday' and the local are not only valid objects of inquiry, but also valid sources for authority and knowledge.

AN ALTERNATIVE INTELLECTUAL PRACTICE: WRITING TO INTIMATE AUDIENCES

Like Torgovnick, anthropologist Ruth Behar draws on the local and the 'everyday' in order to address multiple audiences. Like much feminist writing, Behar's essay "Writing in My Father's Name" purposely draws attention to its form. Appearing as a series of diary entries, the essay in part chronicles the reaction of a nonacademic audience—her family—to the earlier publication of *Translated Woman: Crossing the Border with Esperanza's Story,* an ethnography which Behar combines with a self-reflexive "shadow biography." A large part of Behar's project in both instances is to illustrate that the forms of academic writing we are most used to seeing, and the forms of rationality this writing represents, are historically constructed, neither universal nor inevitable. And her essay illustrates how this writing has traditionally been constructed: for example, by considering the myriad ways in which patriarchy has affected her own personal life and professional work, she puts into practice Pierre Bourdieu's notion of "epistemic reflexivity," and reveals the "social and intellectual unconscious" of patriarchy "embedded in (the) analytic tools and operations" (Bourdieu 36) of anthropology itself.

Behar treats her relationship with her father, in particular, as an object of scholarly inquiry, an object which she illustrates can lend powerful insights into some of the ideologies that influence how women write, and are written by, culture in the academy. As she chronicles the fracturing of her family and suggests how it is related to discourses like patriarchy and immigration, Behar also acknowledges the multiplicity of her own writing self. Identifying herself as storyteller, anthropologist and daughter, she is writing not only about her parents and how her relationship with them has affected her professional life; in a way, her parents appear as one of the audiences for her writing:

> It dawns on me that I include my parents too much in my professional life. But how could I not? I'm still my father's daughter. I carry his name. And I allow my parents to have a claim on my work. I not only send them reviews of my book . . . I can't stop writing about them. Immigrants succeed through their children; they sacrifice, they invest, so their children will succeed. And the immigrant daughter, who worries about surpassing her parents, keeps trying to include them in her work, to throw a raft their way, so they can sail together on the choppy seas of the academy. (72)

In the context of her self-reflexive writing projects, Behar's relationship with her parents thus serves as an illustration of how—both inside and outside the academy—the pressures of patriarchy compel women scholars to "write in (their) fathers' names" (79). Beyond this, however, the example of Behar's writing might also suggest the gains and the risks involved when a scholar writes both about and to intellectual fathers within the institution, at the same time she is writing both about and to other kinds of fathers (or mothers) beyond its walls—and writing in ways that acknowledge the "claim" these extra-academic audiences have on her work as a scholar.

Behar's use in her writing of the example of her relationship with her parents—an example that helps her to illustrate the impact which cultural ideologies have on her scholarly work—seems, interestingly, to lead her at least in part to the assumption (or perhaps leads her to reveal the assumption) that her parents might share with her and her professional peers the same interests with regard to such an analysis. In fact, an apparent assumption that her parents would want to "sail (with her) on the choppy seas of the academy" collides head-on in her essay with the frustration both of her parents seem to feel because of the ways they see themselves being represented in her "shadow biography":

> *Mira*, I'm going to tell you something, Rutie," my mother announces. "*La mierda no se revuelve, porque apesta.*" Don't stir up the shit, because it will stink. "You know, Rutie, I'm not a typist. *Ya es la segunda vez que los dices.*" It's true, I've twice described my mother in my writing as a typist rather than by her title, Diploma Aide. I try to apologize, but my mother is not done with me yet. "And why did you have to tell everybody your father was ashamed that his father was a peddler in Cuba? That wasn't nice." I wish I could get my mother to understand the poetic logic of my storytelling. "Mami, don't you see? My book is about the life story of a peddler in Mexico. And my own grandfather was a peddler in Cuba, but Papi was always so ashamed of his origins that he couldn't even talk about it. Don't you think that's interesting?" But I can't convince her. Writing about the shame seems only to compound the shame of the shame. (66-67)

In describing this clash of perspectives, Behar takes great pains to insure that her writing 'self' makes itself accountable to the risks involved in writing to extra-academic as well as to academic audiences. She goes on to say that as a consequence of this conflict of perspectives, she has adopted a strategy of "silence, exile, and cunning" with regard to her writing, so she might hide from her father and mother the fact she continues to inscribe "the story of (their) dissolution as a family ever more irrevocably into the academy" (82). Behar's desire to hide her words from a particular, intimate audience is echoed, though not entirely paralleled, in Richard Rodriguez's *Hunger of Memory*. After a confrontation with his own mother about a published account of their family's life, Rodriguez admits he "probably . . . will never try to explain (his) motives (for writing publicly about his personal life) to (his) mother and father" (176). Opting instead to write to "public readers (he) expect(s) never to meet" (177), Rodriguez defines this audience of "strangers" in ways that evoke an "essayist prose style" model of literacy, where the reader "is not an ordinary human being, but an idealization, a rational mind formed by the rational body of knowledge of which the essay is a part" (Gee, 63). Rodriguez thus conceives of his audience vis à vis an uncomplicated, though perhaps not uncommon, notion of the "public reader":

> I write today for a reader who ľexists in my mind only phantasmagorically. Someone with a face erased; someone of no particular race or sex or age or weather. A gray presence. Unknown, unfamiliar. All that I know about him is that he has had a long education and that his society, like mine, is often public (*un gringo*). (182)

Rodriguez's text describes the "public" reader as virtually uncomplicated in subject position, and exceedingly unfamiliar—a 'faceless' reader who could not possibly be more different from his own parents. At the same time, he depicts himself, as the author of his text, as also unfamiliar and, in one sense, as 'voiceless' within the context of his own family:

> I think my mother sensed that afternoon that the person whose essay she saw in a national magazine was a person unfamiliar to her, some Other. The public person—the writer, Richard Rodriguez—would remain distant and untouchable. She never would hear his public voice across a dining room table. And that afternoon she seemed to accept the idea, granted me the right, the freedom so crucial to adulthood, to become a person very different in public from the person I am at home. (189-190)

While Behar, therefore, comes to the conclusion that because of the conflicts it creates, she must exclude (however much she desires to do otherwise) this most intimate of audiences—her family—from her writing, Rodriguez excludes his family as one of his audiences because such an exclusion is "crucial to adulthood," and to the process of becoming a "public" person.

Behar's reasons for the (ostensible) exclusion of this intimate audience is perhaps more akin to Nancy K. Miller's reasons for excluding her father as one of the readers of her own autobiographical essay, "My Father's Penis." Miller's exclusion, like Behar's, is prompted by a concern about the effect her writing ("born of the troubled intimacies of the autobiographical penis and the theoretical phallus" [*Personal*, 146]) might have on the intimate audience that is her father:

> Had my father still been able to read, I would never have written about "the penis." By going public with the details of domestic arrangements on Riverside Drive, I was flying in the face of the parental injunction not to "tell" that had haunted my adolescence and continued well into my adult years; the panic my parents felt that they would be exposed by us; the shame over family secrets. But he was down in his reading to the occasional newspaper headline and, I think, at his end, despite a finely honed personal vanity, beyond caring. He had become no longer himself, and I needed to mourn his disappearance. (146-147)

Miller's exclusion of her father as one of her readers is facilitated by her father's physical decline, the same decline that accounts in part for her "need" to write the essay. And like Behar, this exclusion of one, particular intimate audience is her response to the sense that her writing is "flying in the face of the parental injunction not to 'tell' . . . family secrets."

It may be possible, however, to see ways in which, as a scholar, Behar (if not Miller) both succeeds and fails as she attempts to "hide" her words from the extra-academic audience comprised of her parents. (The French scholar Alice Kaplan and Rodriguez, too, may be said to both exclude and include their families as one of their audiences, an interesting move in the context of memoirs that recount their own exclusions, as children and as adults, by members of their families.) Through her use of dialogue like that above, I would argue Behar's text does indeed inscribe her parents as an audience, and in so doing begins to confront one of the scholarly biases that Bourdieu argues blurs the "sociological gaze," as she begins to examine how her relationships to her family and to her family history have framed her own intellectual work. Such an examination might, in Hans-Georg Gadamer's terms, include both a consideration of the "enabling" and "disabling" biases that such a family history brings to her work as an anthropologist.

But Behar's example, like Kaplan's example in her memoir *French Lessons,* also perhaps illustrates that scholarly autobiography, or autobiographically inflected cultural criticism—like all scholarly writing—is not without its limitations. Like other texts, self-reflexive texts can result in reductive representations of others' subject positions. Owing in particular to what Bourdieu might identify as the "intellectualist bias" threatening to blur the "sociological gaze" of scholars, self-reflexive texts—no more than 'traditional' texts, although perhaps in more highly charged ways—can risk "collapsing practical logic into theoretical logic" (39-40), with the result being a reductive (albeit theoretically 'logical') representation of the actions and attitudes of o/Others, including intimate others. Behar's desire to include her parents on her journey across rough academic waters, for example, as well as her attempt to get her mother to see the "poetic logic" of her writing, may signify an over-identification with these others that in some ways denies the differences in their subject positions. The autobiographical texts I examine here, in other words, vary widely in the degree to which and ways in which they explicitly examine the competitive and collaborative relationships among different subject positions or 'voices' within the text, as well as the degree to which they explicitly examine relationships between such voices and the audiences they inscribe.

Kaplan's memoir *French Lessons,* for example, in articulating an often antagonistic relationship between her own experience with learning French and her students' experiences learning the language, might be said to discourage an examination of the relationship between different 'student' voices in the text. Kaplan's representation of her teaching practice, for example, seems often to involve imposing desire on her students: "I, Madame, have to make their mouths work. I walk up to a student and I take her mouth in my hand; I arrange it in the shape of a perfect O" (134). With her student's mouth in Kaplan's hand, both the student Kaplan once was (a student who learned French by "shaping" her mouth herself, to suit her own purposes in the context of relationships with the friends and lovers described by her memoir), and the younger student sitting before her in the classroom, are at risk of falling mute. Because diverse student voices fail to sound, at junctures such as this in the text there seems to be little room for the kind of double-voiced (much less multi-voiced) discourse that Bakhtin describes, discourse that might be productive of new or alternative knowledge about teaching and learning, for example.

In other words, by not making explicit the ways in which her own learning (through sensual experience) and her students' learning (in the classroom) might intersect as well as diverge, Kaplan's text at times masks the presence of a mix of voices capable of acknowledging the contingency and multiplicity of self, and of the self's relationship with the world. I would suggest that in such moments in Kaplan's text as the one I cite above, these voices and the attendant relationships among (and within) them are hidden from view by a "form of analysis" that is more "conventional" (Holquist 69) than it may at first seem; an analysis that in a sense 'forgets' the material and emotional details surrounding Kaplan's own learning, neglecting the ways in which these contingent details might apply as well (though not necessarily in the same ways) to her students' learning.

While Kaplan's text may thus preclude fuller acknowledgment of the commonalities between her own 'student' subjectivity (or voice) and the subjectivities of her students, Jane Gallop's autobiographical text, *Feminist Accused of Sexual Harassment*, in a sense functions in the reverse. Chronicling her own experience of being a student in college in the early 1970s, and of gaining access simultaneously to feminism, "to real learning and to active sexuality" (5), Gallop goes on to chronicle her experience in the 1990s of being accused by two female graduate students of sexual harassment, and proposes in her book to "produce an understanding of sexual harassment based . . . upon the limit case of a feminist so accused" (7):

> I was construed a sexual harasser because I sexualize the atmosphere in which I work. When sexual harassment is defined as the introduction of sex into professional relations, it becomes quite possible to be both a feminist and a sexual harasser. (11)

Gallop contends that being a "feminist sexual harasser" is a "contradiction in terms" (7), though, because gender is the key factor in a (feminist) definition of sexual harassment (24). Beyond this, however, Gallop's text comprises a challenge generally to condemnations of sexualized relationships between teachers and students, through its examination of her own past, personal experiences with feminism, pedagogy and sex—experiences which she says were "empowering" (43) for her, and which she seems to offer in illustration of their potential benefit for others.

Gallop's use of her own experience, however, may lead her, like Kaplan, to an analysis more conventional than at first it might appear. By neglecting how the details of her own students' psychologies and histories might differ from her own, for example, the potential for a mix of diverse 'student' voices to emerge in the text is diminished, if not erased entirely. Instead, it is Gallop's own 'student' voice that sounds alone, even as it is other students' desires which ostensibly are being articulated:

> Nowadays, women's studies is a lot older and more established; it doesn't feel so much like a bold experiment. While it still is said in women's studies circles that feminist teachers and students ought to have a nonhierarchical relation, ought to work together as sister seekers of knowledge, in fact the relation between feminist teachers and students is not what it was when women's studies was young.
>
> Yet my students still want a feminist education that feels like women's studies did to me in 1971. And so do I, deeply. I want it for them and I want it still, again, for myself. (19-20)

In particular, remembering specific ways in which discovering feminism was for her also about discovering (and feeling) "brave new possibilities" (18)—which included teacher-student sex—Gallop posits her own 'student' subjectivity as "'choke' or origin point" (Lutz 255) for conceptualizing the subjectivities of her students twenty years later.

In other words, Gallop's insistence that it is not necessary for her text to acknowledge in specific ways how her own subject position (past and present) differs from the subject positions of her students, I think bespeaks what Bourdieu has identified as the scholarly bias "more profound and more distorting than those rooted in the social origins or location of the analyst in the academic field"—that is, the "*intellectualist bias* which entices (the scholar) to construe the world as *spectacle*, as a set of significations to be interpreted rather than as concrete problems to be solved practically" (39). As part of a February 1998 electronic exchange on the Pre/Text discussion list, Gallop explains in this way her text's lack of attention to her accusers' subjectivities:

> Because I was not writing about the case in and for itself but only for the light it could shed upon larger issues, there were many things about the case I did not discuss in the book. I chose only to discuss those things, those details that when interpreted could yield wider understandings, understandings that could produce new knowledge ... in the theoretical debates I wanted to enter. Which is why I don't talk about the students. To me the fact that they accused me of things I didn't do is not very theoretically interesting.... It is not unusual for students to find negative evaluations intolerable and to get angry and want to hurt the teacher back. But it didn't seem something that would produce much knowledge. I only could have counteraccused them, written a book about what bad students they were and blind, angry people. I thought that would be tacky, beneath me, so I chose not to discuss that.

In one of her last posts to the list before signing off, Gallop adds an "important, because both obvious and neglected, point about teaching," which may shed some light on why she felt that her options in writing (about the subjectivities of her students) were so limited. As she expresses them, again during the Pre/Text discussion, her reasons seem to have to do with her sense that perhaps relationships between students and teachers are, after all, not the "consensual amorous relation(s)" (57) between two "empowered" (though perhaps differently empowered) individuals posited by her text, but are instead relations between individuals with considerably different amounts and kinds of power and agency:

> All the emphasis on the teacher's power in contemporary pseudo-political discourse on pedagogy neglects perhaps the most essential thing. And something we might not want to neglect in our politics. LABOR. Teachers labor for students. Students do not labor for teachers. Students benefit from our labor; we do not benefit from students' labor.

I would read the scene of work which Gallop sketches out above as one in which the teacher is the subject of high modernism: a coherent consciousness capable of producing knowledge, and of engaging in labor in ways which are not contingent on the collaborative labor of students. In such a scene, one which seems to be replicated in Gallop's text at several junctures, at most a single voice sounds—the voice of Gallop as the teacher.

Behar's desire to include her parents on her voyage through rough, academic waters, too, may be peculiarly academic, and bespeaking the "intellectualist" bias that Bourdieu points to as the central challenge for the scholar aiming to develop a rigorous self-reflexivity. (Pointing to a perhaps parallel, although not identical, challenge confronted by white, middle-class teachers of adult basic education students, Lester Faigley cites Linda Brodkey's findings that "in spite of their energy, dedication, and commitment to universal education, [these teachers] could not admit that their lives were very different from those of their [students] because there was no space in their discourses for the subjectivities that their working-class [students] presented" [35].) All of these examples suggest the difficulties scholars face in order to acknowledge differences in subjectivity between themselves and intimate O/others, including family members and students, an acknowledgment nonetheless crucial for scholarship in which such others figure prominently.

Writing reflectively thus presents scholars with a significant dilemma. For, according to Bourdieu, an "epistemic reflexivity" involves subjecting the social, academic and "intellectualist" positions of the scholarly observer to the same critical analysis as that to which the (constructed) object is subjected, in order to "theorize the limits of anthropological knowledge" (42) associated with the analyst's "membership and position in the intellectual field" (39). Making a distinction between epistemic and textual reflexivity, however, Bourdieu critiques the use of the first person in sociological analysis, and the "postmodern" notion that the writing of a text is itself implicated in the construction of reality. Rather, Bourdieu argues that "it is not the individual unconscious of the researcher but the epistemological unconscious of his discipline that must be unearthed" (41) if the reflexive return is to enable the intellectual to escape the "delusion" (which Bourdieu says is dear to both intellectuals and Westerners generally) of being free and undetermined, while at the same time not encouraging him to fall into "the game of intimist confession" (44):

> Intellectuals are particularly inventive when it comes to masking their specific interests. For instance, after '68, there was a kind of *topos* in the French intellectual milieu which consisted in asking: "But from where are you speaking? From what place am I speaking?" This false, narcissistic confession, vaguely inspired by psychoanalysis, served as a screen in the Freudian sense of the word and blocked a genuine elucidation, that is the discovery of the *social* location of the locutor: in this case, the position in the university hierarchy. . . . I deliberately constructed (the) notion (of the field) to destroy intellectual narcissism and that particularly vicious legerdemain (*escamotage*) of objectivation which consists of making objectivations either singular, and here psychoanalysis comes in handy, or so broad that the individual under consideration becomes the token of a category so large that his or her responsibility vanishes entirely. To proclaim "I am a bourgeois intellectual, I am a slimy rat!" as Sartre liked to do, is devoid of implications. But to say "I am an assistant professor at Grenoble and I am speaking to a Parisian professor" is to force oneself to ask whether it is not the relation between these two positions that is speaking through my mouth. (193-194).

According to Bourdieu, objects of inquiry do not call for distanced observation and theorizing, because such observation and theorizing is impossible: the intellectual has interests which affect how she constructs such objects. At the same time, Bourdieu equates the framing of those interests too individually with "narcissism," and too broadly with an evasion of responsibility, an equation often used by other critics of reflective (scholarly) writing such as Margery Wolf and Daphne Patai.

However, where I think Bourdieu's critique proves inadequate with regard to examples of contemporary, reflective writing like those I have examined here, is in the fact that it does not fully take into account scholarly texts that explicitly address audiences beyond the walls of the university. It is increasingly common to hear academics acknowledge that, for reasons often having to do with political survival, they need to speak to audiences beyond the institution. I would situate many contemporary scholarly memoirs like Kaplan's and autobiographically inflected essays like Behar's along with other reflective, multi-voiced texts such as Patti Lather and Chris Smithie's *Troubling Angels,* within this larger context; as such, these reflective, academic texts necessarily inscribe extra-academic audiences. That these audiences are frequently familial perhaps should not be surprising: the family may very well represent the extra-academic audience which an intellectual knows best, thus not only comprising a focus of both personal interest, but representing as well the concerns of constituencies outside the academy's walls which the scholar may need or want to address.

Attending to such (an) extra-academic audience(s), however, necessitates a more complicated, though not necessarily more narcissistic, reflexivity—focusing on and beyond the writer's social position in the intellectual field, and geared toward an explicit formulation of an ethics for the writing.

Unlike Behar, in her memoir Kaplan includes only fleeting images of her own father, together with a few more, mostly sketchy, representations of other family members. While periodically making observations that connect her school experience with her experience at home ("I had come from a house where the patterns had broken down and the death that had broken them was not understood. Now I loved the loudspeaker and the study hall and the marble floor because they made me feel hard and controlled and patterned" [53]) these brief reflections most frequently elicit only a terse comment from her. Of her sister's objections to her project ("'You're turning the family into a research project.... It's underhanded. And it's cold'"), she says simply: "But I didn't feel cold, I was burning" (202). Such an unelaborated response, including neither a description of her sister nor a description of her sister's specific reasons for her objections (in her "Acknowledgments," Kaplan says only that her sister's "story of (their) family is different" [221]) is another example of how Kaplan's memoir eschews explicit theorizing.

Interestingly it is Kaplan's students, whose appearance is the most prominent element of the book's final chapter, with whom she represents herself finally as communicating best and as having the fullest 'familial' kinship. It is in the classroom, then, that Kaplan says ultimately she feels the least like she is "in exile from (herself)"; and it is in describing at least a few of these classroom scenes that the text includes an explicit and detailed interpretation:

> Then something will happen, in the classroom, and I'll see this French language as essential *in its imperfection*: the fact that we don't have as many words is forcing us to say more. The simplicity of our communication moves us, we're outside of cliché, free of easy eloquence, some deeper ideas and feelings make it through the mistakes and shine all the more through them.
>
> In French class I feel close, open, willing to risk a language that isn't the language of everday life. A sacred language. (210)

If French then is always "not-quite-(her)-own-language," a language with which Kaplan in some ways "gags" (210) herself, she explains it is also a language that allows her to express the "deeper ideas and feelings" that she isn't able to express in English, an expression that perhaps goes against the grain of her desire to forget the past. And it is during at least some moments in class, while she is sharing this "imperfect" language with her students, that such expression occurs.

Kaplan describes just this kind of moment in a passage in the memoir's last chapter, where she describes having assigned her class a novel to read that she felt she didn't really understand: "it seemed too simple and I didn't know how I was going to teach it" (211). In the novel, a crime has occurred in the narrator's childhood; during class, one of Kaplan's students explicates the passage in which the narrator recounts watching adults as they arrive one night at his house. The narrator says he is surprised that after the crime he was not interrogated by the police because "'children watch. They listen, too'" (212). But it is Kaplan's student who, for her, expresses the "deeper ideas and feelings" embedded in the imperfection of this language: "'What he really means to say is that they write. Children grow up and they write about what they saw and heard'" (213).

In one of the most emotionally inflected passages of her book, Kaplan theorizes about this moment in class, seemingly taken aback by the intersections between her own complicated subjectivity (as not only a scholar and teacher, but also a child who watched her father die) and the 'reading' of text and experience which her student brings to the class:

> I cried, not sorrowful tears but tears of happiness from discovering something I hadn't known about before. Why was I so moved by what she said? . . . She had explained to me (the author's) sense of a past that can't be erased but which is always incomplete....
>
> Maybe it was simpler, what moved me. I was thinking about being a child myself and seeing and hearing but not being able to say yet, not having the words for what I saw. Or having them, but no one asked. No one asks the child what is going on, and the child sees, and listens, and engraves those memories and those people one after another in a private language. It's only later—maybe it's too late—that the pain of those memories is brought forward to the present time of writing. (213-214)

Kaplan here both connects the events of her own childhood to this other set of events, events in the classroom, while she also abstracts more generally about the effect on children of the loss of a parent.

Within the memoir and the classroom, therefore, part of Kaplan's intellectual work in (an "imperfect") French becomes theorizing—albeit sporadically—about the effects of her own father's death; as, conversely, does her work in French become part of her emotional experience of his death. In studying and speaking French with her students Kaplan "discover(s) something (she) hadn't know about before"—i.e., that her memoir is in part a record of childhood losses which had been hidden away by her use of French. As readers we know more, finally, of her sense of the personal and professional consequences of having watched and listened while her father died, of having his death engraved in her own private, secret language.

AN UN-'PROFESSIONAL' PRACTICE: TELLING STORIES OF LOSS

Kaplan's memoir therefore explores the imperfections of her experience as a student, scholar, and teacher of French, by portraying—often in exquisite detail—scenes of personal and professional loss. Depicting such scenes may be one of the most controversial aspects of scholarly memoir, for telling stories of loss is an especially rare practice within the academy. Even in the face of a number of contravening tendencies functioning in academic culture, however, the recent field of scholarly memoirs provides us with many different examples of theorizing the intellectual relevance of such stories. Building on the work of Carolyn Heilbrun, I would like to suggest new ways of reading these memoirs and stories of loss, both of which suffer from a relative lack of "critical or biographical commonplaces" that for other kinds of texts have been "elaborated over generations of critical activity" (18-19).

First of the tendencies which make difficult within the academy telling (and hearing) stories of loss, is our impulse as (Western) scholars to dichotomize concerns of a professional, or intellectual, nature, from concerns we might characterize as more personal. Again, this tendency is one which feminist scholars both in Composition and across the disciplines have struggled with for some time now, and from various starting points. Such a tendency is embedded both in the concrete practices and in the discourses of our profession, relying as those practices and discourses do, for example, on thinking through binaries—such as the binary of the 'personal' and the 'professional.' David Bartholomae's "Inventing the University," for example, might be said to invoke such dichotomous thinking (and I acknowledge here the contradiction in my stance, entailing as it does what Andrea Lunsford and Lisa Ede would call disciplinary critique in "traditional agonistic fashion" [169], at the same time that critique is aimed at binary thinking). Bartholomae's essay invokes multiple dichotomies—between student writers and professional writers, between writing in a 'personal' voice and writing in an 'academic' voice—as it argues that "to speak with authority (student writers) have to speak not only in *another's* voice but through *another's* code; and they not only have to do this, they have to speak *in the voice and through the codes of those of us with power and wisdom*"(156) (emphasis mine). The title of Peter Elbow's "Being a Writer vs. Being an Academic: A Conflict in Goals" might be said to invoke a similar kind of thinking, although even as he presents this opposition and the "specific conflicts" it raises in the teaching and designing of a first year writing course, his own text explicitly prods him: "everyone says, 'Don't give in to binary thinking'" (73).

The second (though perhaps not final) tendency within the academy which makes difficult an exploration of the professional and intellectual significance of telling stories of loss is the presumption that loss is unspeakable, a presumption which is perhaps stronger within the institution's walls than it is beyond them. The strength of this tendency may be rooted at least in part in an institutional ideology which posits scholarship as a progressive series of 'gains' in knowledge, an ideology which serves to erase or to diminish an acknowledgment of the losses which are an inevitable part of academic (or any) life. Such an ideology of gain affects our ability to conceive of an individual career—and of the development of professional authority within the trajectory of that career—as marked both by meaningful gains *and* by 'meaningless' losses. Richard E. Miller's analysis of Pierre Bourdieu's *Distinction: A Social Critique of the Judgment of Taste,* has Bourdieu pointing to "the impossibility of radically reforming any highly developed educational system, since that system will, of necessity, be predominantly inhabited by individuals who have profited from that system, who are invested in that system, and whose felt sense of distinction has been established and certified by that system" (26). Yet many of the reflective texts that I examine in this essay—particularly memoirs written by women and scholars of color—describe and theorize instances of professional and personal dissatisfaction, and experiences of exclusion or loss, often at the hands of a system from which these scholars nonetheless have profited and in which they are deeply invested.

I would begin to read such texts as hybrid, incorporating many of the conventions of traditional forms simultaneously with oppositional discourses that challenge various widely-held assumptions about professional life—assumptions not only from which as academics we have profited, but also by which we have been constrained. I would argue that the ideology of gain to which I have referred is just such a constraint, increasing as it does the difficulty of putting into practice a feminist epistemology that affirms the myriad connections between the personal and the professional, and contributing to a feminization in the academy of 'personal' writing—including scholarly memoir—which often is the kind of writing reserved for recounting the stories of loss that we do tell. At the same time, such an ideology may add to the anxieties inherent in professionalization generally, and specifically to the anxieties that are a part of such highly charged "rites of passage" as the job search and the tenure process.

Some of the workings of this ideology of gain are unveiled in a recent article in *CCC* by Andrea Lunsford and Lisa Ede. In a brilliant re-vision of another essay which they had co-authored together a decade before ("Audience

Addressed/Audience Invoked: The Role of Audience in Composition Theory and Pedagogy"), Lunsford and Ede examine what they call the focus on "success in communicating with and persuading others" (173) in academic literacy broadly, and in the rhetorical tradition more specifically. These authors' "self-critique"(168) finds evidence of this impulse toward "success" in their own earlier essay, but avoids the easy tendency toward either/or dichotomizing, "resist(ing) the lure of totalizing, oppositionalizing readings" (169). Instead, the authors reflect on the consequences for their writing of their own "personal identification with schooling," (173) and suggest how their own particular subjectivities were shaped by western individualism and an emphasis on "success":

> Academic good girls, we studied, even excelled, and in so doing we came to associate both schooling and the writing we did in school with a positive sense of self, a means of validation and "success," and of hailing appreciated audiences. So powerful was this identification, in fact, that we recast those painful memories of struggle that we could not repress, reinterpreting experiences that might have led to resistance and critique as evidence of individual problems that we could remedy if only we would work harder, do (and be) better. Such an approach is congruent, of course, with the individualism inherent throughout our culture, educational institutions, and scholarly disciplines, an individualism that traditionally writes the kind of struggles we experienced as students as inevitable, even necessary and salutary, aspects of the western narrative of individual success that (our previous essay) implicitly endorses. (171-172)

Lunsford and Ede suggest that the narrative of individual success which they point to as implicitly operating within their own (previously published) essay, "inevitably, albeit silently, casts misunderstanding, miscommunication, disagreement, resistance, and dissent as failure and, as such, as that which is to avoided or 'cured'" (173-174). In much the same way that the narrative of "success" which these authors point to serves to exclude alternate narratives, so too would I suggest an ideology of gain embedded in academic culture serves to exclude from our consideration a wide range of professional and personal stories.

Many scholars, especially feminist scholars, have acknowledged the need to reflect on and theorize the ways in which personal history and experience shape the 'subject' and the form of professional work, and especially of scholarly writing. One sign of the seriousness—and perhaps again the anxiety—with which scholars have approached this self-reflective project has been the proliferation of terms to describe such critical work: literary theorists Nancy K. Miller and Susan Suleiman have written (about) the uses of "personal criticism" and "mediated autobiography" respectively; anthropologist Behar's "vulnerable writing" has a reflexive quality in common with Linda Brodkey's—and

Mary Louise Pratt's—"autoethnography." Feminist, social theorist Nancy Fraser describes the essays included in her text, *Unruly Practices: Power, Discourse, and Gender in Contemporary Social Theory* as "exercises in *situated* theorizing" (7). Although these terms and writing tasks are various and differently inflected, I would suggest they all signify an alternative intellectual practice which attempts to make sense of the personally situated nature of scholarly work, and to theorize what Gesa Kirsch and Joy Ritchie have termed, after Adrienne Rich, a "politics of location" (7) for that work. Mariolina Salvatori, in a review in *CCC*, describes recent "teacher texts" by Miller, Jane Tompkins and Jane Gallop as constituting a "theoretical phenomenon." Describing these texts as "introspective accounts of how teachers bring their personal and academic lives together as they think about and theorize teaching," Salvatori argues that the "varied nomenclature (of what she calls 'practices of the personal') may be taken to indicate the richness of the genre as a 'category in process' . . . (but) might also be taken as a sign of a certain anxiety about its functions and possibilities" (567).

This anxiety arises in part from the fact that these texts are accountable to a different kind of story than is often told in academia. The 'professional' stories we most often tell ourselves and each other are stories of accretion, stories which elaborate and focus on a progressive accumulation of achievements and gains: gains in knowledge achieved through scholarship, gains in professional status achieved through hard work, gains in prestige. The prevalence and quality of these success stories, and the timbre of the voices which they inscribe, stand in stark contrast to the stories and voices of professional and personal loss contained within scholarly memoirs and other "reflective" academic texts.

In such texts these stories often center on a professional loss, like the loss of a job. *The Cliff Walk* by Don Snyder details his experience of being fired in his third year of a job by a department in the midst of down-sizing. Torgovnick, in her collection of autobiographical essays, *Crossing Ocean Parkway,* describes the circumstances early in her career surrounding her loss of a child, and her subsequent experience of being denied tenure. While Torgovnick sees the two experiences and their consequences as drastically different, she is puzzled nonetheless at how often her colleagues seem to conflate the two. Theorizing that this may have something to do with how the "tenure process is surrounded by talk of 'judgments,' 'destinies,' and 'fates,'" Torgovnick remembers how she, too, had experienced that process as a "sustained attack on (her) identity and self-esteem" (67).

The legal scholar Patricia Williams also examines loss within an institutional context, using an analytic lens trained on how "inept" pedagogies can kill—both bodies and minds—in her memoir *The Alchemy of Race and Rights* (which she subtitles "Diary of a Law Professor). Williams's text comprises an analysis of how traditional legal discourse constructs racial and gender subjectivity as "irrelevant" (100), rendering the concerns of people of color and women, as well as these people themselves, invisible in the larger society. Like Mary Rose O'Reilley's memoir *The Peaceable Classroom*, Williams's text speaks, for example, of the losses incurred by law students when specific forms of assessment and specific pedagogies pretend to rely on neutral or unbiased languages, or presuppose that either students or teachers (or both) possess uncomplicated subjectivities that do not transcend the walls of the institution.

Since Williams's examination and critique of law school discourse hinges as much on her familiarity with her students' experiences—as well as on a reflection about her own experience and family history—as it does on her familiarity with the texts or discourses they encounter, her "diary" is a testimony to her own personal difference. While it might be a contradiction in terms within the context of a supposedly "neutral" discourse to be a "black woman law professor" with a great-great-grandmother who was herself legal property, within the context of her text's discourse her own complex subjectivity is an indispensable resource for critiquing the biases in the law, and the subsequent 'losses' which these biases entail.

In the context of published memoirs, professional stories of loss therefore are often also familial stories, involving intimate 'others' who either were never able, or who no longer are able, to be actual audiences for the text: Williams's discerning of the "shape" of her great-great-grandmother, and of the "hand" (19) of the man who owned her (Williams's own great-great-grandfather); Kaplan's evocation of her dead father, "his image, silent and distant with headphones over his ears, a founding image for (her) own work" (197); British sociologist Carolyn Steedman's evocation of her mother, suffering from an envy that in some ways succeeds in killing her; psychologist Kay Redfield Jamison's description of her father's "black and chaotic moods" (35); and Behar's description of her frequently estranged father. Nancy K. Miller, in the concluding chapter of her book, *Getting Personal*, theorizes her relationship to "the autobiographical penis and the theoretical phallus" (146) in the context of her father's illness and death; and Torgovnick, in the Epilogue of her text, examines her relationship with her father in the context of his final illness and death.

It is striking how often what my colleague Linda Bachman would call the "reflective gaze" around which these scholarly memoirs are constructed belongs, in fact, to an 'other' who is in some way absented or lost—either by illness, death or estrangement. And it is striking as well how often in these memoirs, many written by women who now are established in their careers, that this is an intimate 'other,' a parent, often a father—that parent perhaps most often looked to as a model of professionalism. In an unpublished manuscript Bachman, drawing on the ideas of Peggy Phelan, writes that

> the desire to represent the self in autobiography or performance more broadly emerges from a sense of loss engendered by the inability to see oneself. The reflective gaze of an "other" is therefore the necessary vehicle for autobiographical representation: "one needs always the eye of the other to recognize (and name) oneself ... the external gaze is a compensatory way of returning a failed inward gaze" (Phelan 15).

So perhaps these texts suggest that while autobiographical, or reflective, practices function to (re)conceive the purposes of academic writing—establishing relationships between writers and multiple and complex audiences, supporting the aims of interdisciplinary and disciplinary scholarship, often concerning themselves with issues of social justice and 'public' accountability—at least in part they are also 'personal' attempts to see what can't be seen, to recover what can't be recovered, perhaps even to grieve what has been irrevocably lost.

My own interest in the practice of reflective writing is rooted as well in a desire to acknowledge the part loss has played in my professional life, and how that loss—which has included a distancing from family and friends, and exclusion from the working-class culture of my childhood—has shaped my teaching and scholarship. Turning reflectiveness in upon itself in this way has helped me to see more clearly, for example, how the experiences of students and colleagues as well as those of family and friends, simultaneously converge with and differ from my own—encouraging me to acknowledge all of these different groups as potential audiences for my work. I believe not only has this made me a better scholar and teacher; it has helped me to feel less isolated in my work, and more a part of diverse relationships which make great demands yet offer great intellectual and affective rewards.

I also have learned the value of writing and teaching against an ideal of scholarly autonomy. Richard E. Miller, having summarized Bourdieu's sense of the impossibility of reforming educational systems since such systems are primarily populated by those who are invested in maintaining the status quo, concludes that "it would appear that no academic can escape the allure of this game, not even those overtly interested in fully democratizing current educational practice, since such activists implicitly believe that education is the preeminent site for organizing relationships between individuals" (26). The examples of reflective practice I examine briefly in this essay demonstrate, on the contrary, not only that many academics value relationships as integral to their scholarship and teaching, but also that they believe such relationships are located in various sites not only inside but also outside of higher education.

Unlike more traditional academic prose, these texts summon a language of loss—along with other languages—in order to frame relationships which thus are both personal and professional. In so doing they begin to illustrate how loss is both speakable and unspeakable, within the institution but also beyond its walls; how the complexity of loss can be revealed in the context of a discourse which is multiply-voiced; and how telling stories of loss perhaps opens up new possibilities for speaking to multiple and varied audiences. As examples of scholarly memoir such as those I have examined here speak to multiple and complex audiences—composed of students, of colleagues, and of constituencies outside the academy—they also speak, as Patti Lather might say, with "ears to hear" ("Clarity," 538) the stories of loss these O/others have to tell.

Not alone, but as one practice among many, such speech compels us to acknowledge the connections between the individual and the collective; to examine our assumptions about what kinds of writing do and do not carry discursive authority, and why; to create, perhaps, what Fraser would call "bridge discourses and hybrid publics" (12); and so perhaps, too, to inscribe and collaborate with audiences both inside and outside the academy. Like the audience for this essay, such multiple and complex audiences have much to teach us—including teaching us about how and why to acknowledge the inevitability of loss as well as of gain.

Lather, with her co-author Chris Smithies, has just such a complex array of audiences in mind in *Troubling Angels: Women Living with HIV/AIDS*. The audiences for Lather's and Smithies's text include professional peers as well as women living outside the institution, many of whom are also negotiating—and grieving—the profound loss(es) which accompany illness and death. Lather writes that after the completion of their text, she and her colleague "continue to . . . construct risky practices of textual innovation in order to . . . be of use in a time when the old stories will not do" ("Clarity," 541). We might look to Lather and Smithies, then, as well as to writers such as Kaplan, Behar, Torgovnick, Miller, Williams, and Lunsford and Ede, and to many other scholars writing reflectively across the disciplines, for alternative models of intellectual practice that can begin to fulfill such a need for innovation.

2 IN THE NAME OF THE SUBJECT
Some Recent Versions of the Personal

JEFFREY GRAY

> On hearing that so-and-so was leading a double life, I said with surprise, 'Only two?'
>
> Iris Murdoch

In the past quarter of a century in America, personal accounts have multiplied like Mandelbrot fractals, spreading into spaces formerly inhospitable to them. David Simpson, examining the new primacy of autobiography in *The Academic Postmodern and the Rule of Literature*, notes that personal stories now "pour off the presses, in literary criticism, ethnography, sociology, cultural studies, and philosophy" (23). Two of these areas in particular, cultural studies and literary criticism, might seem unlikely hosts to such incursions. The twentieth century's two chief modes of reading, after all, have had little truck with the personal: the New Criticism studiously ignored subjectivity, while poststructuralism has argued that subjectivity is discursively constructed. Particularly in this latter context, not yet consigned to the museum of critical prehistory, the reappearance of the personal may seem anomalous. Wasn't the author supposed to be dead?

More likely, the author never died at all, but, as Simpson writes, was just put on hold "as an attempted corrective to an entrenched tradition of liberal expressivity" (14). Whatever the case, the Return of the Subject is unmistakable, and several reasons or contexts suggest themselves. First, personal accounts in criticism can be seen as the academic facet of a larger culture of disclosure, whether at the presidential, congressional, or popular level; in television, for example, "true" stories, especially but not only of crime or transgression ("Cops," "The Best of Autopsy," "Survivor," "The Real World," and many others), have been displacing fictions for some time. Second, few serious readers believe any longer in a view from nowhere; the critique of objectivity that began in the sciences early in the twentieth century, achieved, toward the end of it, additional headway from feminism and ethnic studies. In now-familiar postmodern terms, the master narratives of progress and enlightenment have vanished in discredit, opening a large space for the proliferation of smaller narratives (Lyotard).

Third, a de-authored or authorless view of texts undermines the historical impact of writings from socially marginalized groups, writings for which authorship matters crucially. In this connection, a U.S.-centered multiculturalism, which has tended to downplay difference *within* groups, has helped to reinscribe a mimetic theory of representation, a theory within which one *can* speak and represent. In criticism, the Return of the Subject owes much to this latter set of currents and the institutional pressures it has generated.

In this essay, I will point not so much to the presence of full-blown autobiographical accounts in books such as *Wild Orchids and Trotsky*, a collection of essays/stories by literary critics and theorists, nor to numerous writers who have helped to break disciplinary ice by telling stories—Clifford Geertz, say, or Richard Rorty, Stephen Greenblatt, Judith Frank, and others. Rather, I would like to focus on the announcement of "subject position," a synechdochic activity in which the self as a distinguishable entity is displaced by the activity of identity-making, producing not stories but categories of value, what I'll call personal "effects." Before I try to make this and other distinctions, let me offer some background to the discussion.

Many in the fields of multicultural criticism and culture studies argue that, if anything, academic writing is not personal *enough*. In 1996, an issue of the *PMLA* featured a Guest Column of four views and a Forum of twenty-six letters on the place of the personal in scholarship. One contributor, Jane Gallop, argued that the cause for worry is not "scholarship that seems narrowly personal but rather scholarship where the personal does not recognize itself as such and thus passes for the universal" (Letter 1150). For her, as for most of the contributors, autobiographical excess, if it is a problem, is less dangerous than silence as to subject position and the dubious "objectivity" that silence might imply. Gallop does note that "[b]oth excesses contribute to our failure to recognize the extent to which knowledge is entangled in life," but, for her own part, she intends to integrate the subjective so thoroughly that no personal strand can be separated out: "I'm headed for a writing where it would be literally impossible to separate gossip from scholarship" (1150).

In his guest column of that issue, "Against Subjectivity," Michael Bérubé agrees. Using a title that parodies detractors of the trend toward the personal, he offers an argument *not* against subjectivity but only against subjectivity that is insufficiently aware of itself. Like Gallop, Bérubé objects to *omission* of an account of one's subject position. The "worst form of subjectivism" comes in the form of scholars' "projecting their own interpretive idiosyncrasies onto their research while blithely believing that they've finally grasped the object as in itself it really is" (1066).

Indeed that impersonalism worried most of the participants, few of whom found any problem with explicitly personal components of criticism.[1] Bérubé, like Gallop, does acknowledge a potential problem, the danger "for readers, who may view the personal turn as license for reductive conflation of the scholar with the scholarship" (1066) but does not seem to believe that such a conflation, "reductive" or not, is implicitly invited by many if not most scholars.[2] Of course, there *are* specific experiences which strongly condition or even determine scholarship. The question is, which ones?

In other words, it is not a matter of excluding the personal from writing, an impossibility even for those who most insist on that exclusion, but of the ends to which the "personal" is put—that is, of the claims to be made in the name of the Subject. While I will abandon quotation marks following this sentence, my suspicion of the word "personal" is not based solely on the postmodern insight that our subjectivities are continually under construction, even after our bodies are dead and gone. It is rather that the personal as deployed in much current academic writing is *not* personal—that is, not individual, not subjective in so far as subjects are distinct from other subjects, not interchangeable. The personal, instead, is often used strategically and synechdochically. Cathy Davidson writes, in the same issue of *PMLA*, that the Subject is "both individualized and, if it works, generalizable" (1070). She seems to mean by this that in the local we find the universal, but a different meaning may be taken from the phrase and from many recent first-person accounts in scholarly writing. "If it works," what one achieves is a personal *effect* that links the "I" to a collective which becomes rhetorically empowered to the degree that it appears decentered. It is not a matter of announcing *any* subject position but rather certain subject positions and not others. Statements of the personal, then, are not arbitrary announcements of situatedness. They are made for particular reasons and often under particular duress.

The examples that follow have presented themselves in the normal course of reading in the fields of cultural studies and contemporary literary criticism. In order to suggest a continuity and even the beginnings of a typology, I have thought it better to cite several than to isolate a text or two. This need not mean cursory treatment, since statements of position in scholarly texts often take the form of a single paragraph or even a sentence. While the result is inevitably partial and incomplete, I hope to suggest some of the varieties of subject position as set out in contemporary academic writing. I will argue, among other things, that the personal *as individual*, far from being empowered in contemporary discourse, is often associated with guilt and disengagement and is not encouraged but penalized.

PECULIAR SITUATIONS

In her introduction to *Black Noise: Rap Music and Black Culture in Contemporary America*, Tricia Rose writes that her "peculiarly situated identities" are "immensely productive" in helping her read American hip-hop culture. Rose writes that "[s]peaking from my positions as a pro-black, biracial, ex-working-class, New York-based feminist, left cultural critic adds even greater complexity to the way I negotiate and analyze the social world" (xiii). I begin with Rose's statement because it offers a phrase—"peculiarly situated"— useful in looking at several other identity statements, often, like this one, set out in prefaces, and because the categories she invokes are indicative of the kind of subject position announcements I most want to examine here— remembering that the issue is academic writing and not the culture in general, for which a separate argument would need to be made. We might ask first how peculiarly situated these positions are. Some academic intellectuals, "New York-based" or not, may not be ex-working-class, but how many are going to speak from a *non*-"pro-black" viewpoint? How many are not on the Left? How many, who are willing to say so, are not feminist? "Biracial" could qualify, narrowly in New York City, as "peculiarly situated," but to the extent that "even greater complexity" is discernible in the book, why would one attribute it to, say, biracialism, rather than to other factors in Rose's education or sensibility?

I will not be examining preface-book relationships systematically, but let me mention this one so as to try to situate my own criticism. *Black Noise* is an extremely thorough and often insightful book. While it does not describe the formal specificity of rap in the sense of tempos, keys, modes, or rhythms, other than in impressionistic terms, it does scrutinize the technology of production (particularly types of equipment and studio techniques) very knowledgably— one of its chief contributions. So, in saying that there is no particular reason why one would credit Rose's insights or observations to her feminism, leftism, or pro-blackness, I hope to distinguish the critique I'm setting out from critiques of the academy based, as Stanley Fish writes, "on equal measures of ignorance and malice," especially journalistic critiques of the academy's ventures into popular culture—critiques which might characterize a book on hip-hop culture as by definition frivolous. In other words, though I could wish for a world in which I would not need to say this, I look at literature departments' forays into popular culture and music—forays I myself often make—as necessary and salutary. The problem is, rather, that presenting the self as a list of categories has a coarsening effect. The catalogue does not place the self at the center of critical insight; instead, it creates the self as an other, as a set of memberships, parameters of the critical response.

One of the best-known contemporary critics of race and culture—known as much now from television appearances as from her several books—is bell hooks. In her writing, Professor hooks frequently offers first-person accounts in which she, as "an institutionally marginalized other" (*Teaching* 86), is misunderstood or mistreated, or her work rejected by a journal for being too "experimental." She is slighted at a dinner party, detained at an airport by police, or unfairly accused of something (*Black Looks* 174, *Yearning* 23-24, 29–30, among others). In her introduction to *Outlaw Culture*, she writes, "These essays and dialogues represent my ongoing growth as artist, cultural critic, feminist theorist, writer, seeker on the path" (6). Each essay, she adds, "combines the many voices I speak—academic talk, standard English, vernacular patois, the language of the street" (7). Again, we need to ask what cultural capital is being offered here. Surely all writers' work represents some account of their growth as critics, theorists, seekers. All educated persons speak at least the three idioms of the standard, the professional, and the vernacular. Many scholars obviously speak much more divergent languages than these. (Hooks does not speak a non-English language.) Hooks' claims are quite different from Rose's, but hers is, again, the case of a not unfamiliar subject position presented as aberrant, peculiar, and in excess of other, "ordinary" subjectivities—those who aren't seekers on the path, whose work is accepted by magazine editors, who aren't detained at the airport, who speak (presumably) only academese.

In the *PMLA* "personal" issue, Carol Boyce Davies, writes that while not all scholarly endeavors are related to personal experience, hers are. The peculiarity of her situation lies in the fact that "generations of strugglers" cleared the way for her to study and become a professor. Thus, "locating [her]self in history as an active subject is a necessity" (1154). This is not an exceptional narrative—not for African-Americans, where it should be obvious, but not for others either. Thousands of academics are/ have been the first in their families to go to college. Generations of ancestors struggled to produce us all. This reality does not deny Davies' history; it confirms it, but it weakens the argument for specialness.

I will offer only one more "peculiarly situated" example. Caren Kaplan begins her book *Questions of Travel: Postmodern Discourses of Displacement* with the sentences:

> For most of my life, travel has been a certainty rather than a question. I grew up in the state of Maine where the license plates read "Vacationland" and the tourists came and went in seasonal waves. And I have been a tourist myself often enough, looking for some relief from the rooted realities of dailiness. (ix)

Kaplan goes on to explain that she once had relatives in Argentina and still has some in Israel, South Africa, and the United States. She does not claim explicitly that these affiliations authenticate or enhance the book which follows, but *pace* Bérubé, some sort of connection between scholar and scholarship, whether or not invited, is practically inevitable. The problem is that having relatives in other states or countries, or growing up in Maine, are not credentials to support critiques of Euro-American imperialist travel writers in Africa, India, or the Mediterranean.

Kaplan's light remarks about license plates may constitute a trivial example, but that triviality suggests how keenly academics in general—some far more than others, as I explain below—feel a disciplinary pressure to declare a position. Just as deracinated white college freshmen in composition courses that work with the topos of difference have trouble writing that first essay about the "tribe," so many white academics seem to strain to find a credible subjectivity to declare.[3]

It should not escape notice that I have begun with examples from women scholars, three of them African-American (Rose is bi-racial but "pro-black"), who, one might argue, have *had* to make a career out of specialness in some regard. There are institutional constraints placed on non-white literature scholars, often dictating what careers they can or cannot successfully pursue, and penalties for failing to announce ethnicity, of which scholars and writers of color are well aware. If it is true that more non-white than white scholars are introducing the personal, it is also true that autobiographical elements are more often introduced by women scholars than by men, a situation I discuss below. But declarations of peculiarly situated positions are obviously not confined to women or to writers of color.

The options for white academics, however, are limited, as suggested by the last of the preceding examples. And they fall into alarmingly gender-coded categories, the women often apologizing for their class, their privilege, their *embourgeoisment*, and their theory; the men stubbornly refusing to admit those same conditions by pointing up their own non-elitist backgrounds. Barbara Johnson, Elizabeth Abel, Nancy K. Miller, and Jane Gallop, among white female critics writing about black texts, go to such lengths to acknowledge situatedness that they virtually disqualify themselves as critics. Barbara Johnson's article on Zora Neale Hurston, "Thresholds of Difference," begins,

> One of the presuppositions with which I began was that Hurston's work was situated "outside" the mainstream literary canon and that I, by implication, was an institutional "insider." (318)

Moreover,

[I]t was not clear to me what I, a white deconstructor, was doing talking about Zora Neale Hurston, a black novelist and anthropologist, or to whom I was talking....

and

It was as though I were asking Zora Neale Hurston for answers to questions I did not even know I was unable to formulate. I had a lot to learn, then, from Hurston's way of dealing with multiple agendas.... (317)

Johnson goes on to consider possibilities of the interchangeability of outsider and insider, of which Hurston as a participant-observer anthropologist was also aware. Nevertheless, one questions the humility. Johnson's efforts to avoid arrogance result in a patronizing tone that is surely unintended. Would she say of Woolf or Faulkner that she "had a lot to learn" from that writer?

Jane Gallop expresses even more hopelessness about her shortcomings as a white woman critic:

I realize that the set of feelings that I used to have about French men I now have about African-American women. Those are the people I feel inadequate to and try to please in my writing. (qtd. in Abel 477)

Elizabeth Abel quotes Gallop approvingly at the beginning of Abel's "Black Writing, White Reading: Race and the Politics of Feminist Interpretation," where she asks the question,

If white feminist readings of black women's texts disclose white critical fantasies, what (if any) value do these readings have—and for whom? (477)

In a second epigraph, Abel quotes Nancy K. Miller:

I began to wonder whether there was any position from which a white middle-class feminist could say anything on the subject [of race] without sounding exactly like a white middle-class feminist.... the rhetorical predictability of it all. The political correctness.... In which case it might be better not to say anything. ("Criticizing Feminist Criticism," qtd. in Abel 477)

At least one African-American critic has found such approaches problematic. Michael Awkward, in a chapter of *Negotiating Difference,* on white critics and black texts, discusses the Barbara Johnson article, finding it a "more thoughtful and illuminating investigation of the signs 'white' and 'black' than those of her self-referential male counterparts [Fromm, Wesling, and Sollors, discussed earlier in the essay]" (86). However, further along the spectrum of critical self-examination, he finds a more disturbing instance—that of Sue-Ellen Case, who, addressing black women's theater, regrets that any analysis she might attempt is doomed by its inherent, racially determined limitations:

> Because this description of the position and project of women of colour has been written by a white author, the discourse is necessarily distanced from the actual experiences which shape this position.... The distance of the white author from the ethnic community creates a critical absence of ...contacts [with theater companies of women of color] and research opportunities. This distance has influenced all the information in this chapter.... (qtd. in Awkward 88)

Awkward points out that, while preferable to the universalizing moves of earlier, less self-conscious critics, this self-disqualifying approach precludes any engagement at all with the subject matter. It is a "self-protective avoidance of the appearance of white female hegemonic imposition of its own image upon the literature of women of color." Awkward also contends that Case's argument for white limitations is overstated, since "there exist enough critical, historical, and sociological studies of people of color composed by white scholars to undermine Case's claim about the impossibility of white access to non-white" materials (88).

Critical self-interrogation reaches extremes in an article on feminist appropriation of Native American stories, where the author, Victoria Boynton, introduces herself as "Barbie-Tonto":

> How! I greet you as a ripped-off TV Tonto: a white critic with her "Indian" reading. In a word, I am the white character beneath that white word signalling Indian-ness: *How*. In addition, I am Barbie, white doll woman of America, lifting my little pink plastic hand, performing my Indian gesture as I make the word *How* between my little pink plastic lips, cross-talking, pretending it's mine. (53-54)

Boynton does not explain why "Indian," is in quotes while *white* (an unconstructed category?) is not, but that is the least cause for concern. Boynton begins her next paragraph nauseated, she says, with self-hatred: "Race, class, cultural privilege, and personal history gag me as I come to Leslie Silko's writing, a reaction which, in turn, prompts this declaration of *thetos*, this proclamation of my positionality as academic reader. I don't want to colonize through reading. I don't want to steal, appropriate, lay claim to what is not mine" (54).

Guilt this thick overwhelms anything left over or distinguishable as *topos*; certainly, we learn next to nothing about Silko's work. And, although Boynton uses the phrase "personal history," we learn nothing about that history nor about any subject position other than the undifferentiated, *collective* position of guilty white colonialist intellectual, familiar from university classrooms. It would be a relief to find that Boynton's essay was a parody of academic "subject"-anguish, but it does not appear to be.

Nicole Ward Jouve's *White Woman Speaks with Forked Tongue* demonstrates that the trope itself is worth exploring. Jouve explores it through a nuanced, idiosyncratic, *specific* account of growing up in France and Canada. Her beginning might be *de rigeur*—"I belong to the race that has taken a few centuries only to destroy or threaten what it had taken god or nature millions of years to make" (vii)—but she neither claims specialness nor founders in abjection.

Indeed, an acknowledgement of embeddedness and of complicity does not exclude critique and may be made without declarations either of inadequacy or of a peculiarly advantageous perspective. Mary Louise Pratt, in her introduction to *Imperial Eyes: Travel Writing and Transculturation*, writes,

> These projects are both anchored, as I am, in the metropolis; to concede them autonomy or completeness would reaffirm metropolitan authority in its own terms—the very thing travel writers are often charged to do. In writing this book I have tried to avoid simply reproducing the dynamics of possession and innocence whose workings I analyze in texts. The term 'transculturation' in the title sums up my efforts in this direction. (5-6)[4]

This is a well-grounded caution, but Pratt also explains that hers is "a book by an Anglo-Canadian expatriate for whom the openings of the 1960s and 1970s coalesced in an attempt to sustain teaching, maternity, writing, parenting, institution-building, and domestic partnership in the United States" (xii). As with Kaplan's Maine license plates and the example of Iain Chambers cited below, the charisma often attached to "expatriate"—that of artistic or political exile, danger, and exoticism—somehow falls flat when we are speaking of Canada and the U.S., two nations lacking the kinds of relations that call up these rich associations.

Once self-consciousness is introduced, it seems to require a meta-self-consciousness within which it can be understood. Prefatory remarks about subject position, in other words, need context and interpretation. Catherine Keller's preface to *From a Broken Web: Separation, Sexism and Self*, provides an example of the writer who sees the necessity to acknowledge and interpret her own statement of situatedness, even while doing so raises fresh and perhaps unanswerable questions. She writes,

> My being a white North American woman, loosely middle class and eclectically Protestant in background, does not render my vision any more or less truthful than another. But such concrete conditions suggest what I speak from, and so whom I am most likely to address. By naming such conditions I hope to post a few gargoyles at the threshold, warning not to mistake the ensuing generalizations for any all-inclusive truth. (ix)

This is honest and reasonable, and yet isn't the reader capable of making this kind of corrective herself? It would require a naïve reader to assume that a text, especially a contemporary academic text, pretends to offer "all-inclusive truths," even without the author's posting gargoyles. But the self-consciousness *about* self-consciousness is the point here:

> Currently, among white academic feminists, anxious as we are to confess our privilege as well as to fight our oppression, the invocation of our sociological attributes sometimes sounds like a password to political correctness.... Still, it seems worth acknowledging, for instance, that my whiteness is evident in this book, though (or because) I do not thematize race. (ix)

Here is the acknowledgement of the epistemic problem of setting out subject position in the general terms of "white academic feminist." Given the problem, however, one questions the value of making the statement to begin with: If "whiteness" is really evident in the book—and the author claims it is, curiously either *because* she doesn't take up the issue of race or *in spite* of the fact that she doesn't—then, what purpose is served by saying that what follows is written "as a" white woman? To say that whiteness is evident in her book demands some development of what is meant by whiteness, since, while Americans do talk about "black culture," no one apart from the Aryan Brotherhood seems to believe in the existence of a "white culture."

Put in general terms, then, even in the case of a writer who realizes that such positions as "white academic feminist" are not self-interpreting, setting out this statement does seem little more than "a password to political correctness," a means of warding off charges of naiveté. The *specific* terms—Jouve remarks that her entanglement with Greek mythology has something to do with "four formative childhood years in Athens, in plain sunny view of the Acropolis" (ix)— are more useful.

I have said that, under the pressure to declare a viably marginal subject position, white academics have responded along surprisingly stereotypical gender lines. The self-excoriations of Johnson, Abel, Miller, Gallop, and Boynton, for example, are harder to find among male critics.[5] The latter, instead, often either ignore such pressure or react with bravado, constructing their own "marginalized" subjectivities. Harold Bloom invokes his working-class background— "Myself the son of a garment worker...." (23)—in stating his position vis-a-vis the infamous "School of Resentment," his progeny from decades past at Yale. Frank Lentricchia paints himself, in "My Kinsman T.S.Eliot," as a savvy *ragazzo* growing up in an immigrant two-family house in Utica. ("We don't know Verdi or Dante...we never heard of them" [66].) In responding to racist/ sexist/ elitist charges against the poetry of Dana Gioia, the "expansivist" poet Frederick Turner notes on Gioia's behalf: "Gioia, a second-generation Mexican-Italian-American with a Native American grandfather, makes an unlikely 'elitist'" (Turner 813). Turner himself, also evidently under attack as racist and elitist, refers to his Chinese wife and to the question his mixed-race son asks him: "How can *you* be a racist?"

But in rising to the defense, Turner fails to see, as his accusers fail to see, that there is no demonstrable correspondence between private relations and public utterances. That a man marries a woman (or has a mother who is a woman) does not argue either his sexism or anti-sexism. The defense, in other words, is as mistaken as the prosecution: it too trades on a conflation of subject position and ethnic identity. Once accused, there is no defense. Innocence, like ethnicity, cannot be proven by an appeal to experience.

Turner's and Gioia's examples suggest a category that overlaps with, or is perhaps a branch of, the "peculiarly situated" identity. Much has been written about *mestizaje* or *métissage*, but bi- or multi-racialism is only one variety of the "in-between" identity, a position from which one can offer insight into more than one discursive community. A modest but representative example of in-betweenness is Iain Chambers' book *Border Dialogues: Journeys in Postmodernity*, which extends Benedict Anderson's analyses of nationalism (in *Imagined Communities*), taking a wide sweep in its treatment of postmodern elements of New Mexican deserts, England, and Western European cities. The introduction, titled "The Double Solution," explains the "double" view afforded the author by his having lived in Italy:

> Italy has provided me with an important critical counterpoint to a British experience. It has allowed me to look back on where I came from with different eyes and ears....Caught between mimicry, alterity, and ultimately silence, I write from two shores and between two cultures. (12-13)

Even if one subscribes to the idea of an identity constituted and complicated by travel, the claim here seems disproportionate. Many writers have lived abroad for extended periods; whether they should invoke the alterity and authority of "in-between" is another question, especially since both cultures in this case are European, both saturated with the values of capitalism, individualism, and industrialism under investigation in *Border Dialogues*.

A better known and more persuasive example is Edward Said, who writes in *Culture and Imperialism*,

> Although I feel at home in them [the American, British, and French nations], I have remained, as a native of the Arab and Muslim world, someone who also belongs to the other side. This has enabled me in a sense to live on both sides, and to try to mediate between them. (xxiii)

A few pages later, Said adds that

this book is an exile's book. For objective reasons that I had no control over, I grew up as an Arab with a Western education. Ever since I can remember, I have felt that I belonged to both worlds, without being completely *of* either one or the other.... Yet when I say "exile" I do not mean something sad or deprived. On the contrary belonging, as it were, to both sides of the imperial divide enables you to understand them more easily ... these circumstances certainly made it possible for me to feel as if I belonged to more than one history and more than one group. As to whether such a state can be regarded as really a salutary alternative to the normal sense of belonging to only one culture and feeling a sense of loyalty to only one nation, the reader must now decide. (xxvi-xxvii)

The place of Said's work in contemporary cultural and literary studies is so central and familiar that the subject claim scarcely needs to be made. But since Said invites the reader to decide what to think about such a position, we may notice two things. First, that in-betweenness is a positive, beneficial, empowering attribute, enhancing understanding of the worlds between which one finds oneself. Second, and more interesting, that Said continues to see this in-betweenness as aberrant, contrasting it with "the normal sense of belonging to only one culture." But in reality the position Said presents as aberrant is quite normal, particularly so in the discursive community to which Said and his readers belong. An excellent assessment of this position may be found in the *Éloge de la Créolité* by Patrick Chamoiseau, Rafael Confiant, and Jean Bernabé, where the authors point out that the future of the world is Creole, that the child of a German and a Haitian, born and living in Beijing is "caught in the torrential ambiguity of a mosaic identity.... *He or she will be in the situation of a Creole.* That is what we [writers of Caribbean literature] have prefigured. . . . Expressing Creoleness will be expressing the very *beings* of the world" (112-113; authors' emphases). Inaccessible ethnographic interiors may still exist, but *mestizaje* is—and perhaps always has been—the norm of coasts, where we experience our endless interchanges with the rest of the world. But if cultural/linguistic/ideological *mestizaje* is or has become the norm, then who can invoke the authority of in-betweenness? If Difference still needs to be marked against a "neutral" background—whether the latter is seen as whiteness, masculinity, or in this case "belonging to only one culture"—then what happens when everyone becomes Different? We will have to return to this question.

Just as home is no longer a ground against which travel is a discrepant figure, so cultural in-betweenness no longer stands out against a background of homogeneity or rootedness. When Said, in another context, says to Salman Rushdie, "I am—as we all are—a sort of hybrid," he seems to suggest this universality. But, by "all," does he mean "all us postcolonials," or does he mean "everyone"—as in We Are All Postcolonials Now? The latter is the sense in which I read it, a sense for which one finds much support in Said.[6]

An important touchstone of in-betweenness in the past decade has been Gloria Anzaldua's *Borderlands/La Frontera: The New Mestiza*, a book that found its way onto innumerable syllabi, in contemporary literary studies as much as in cultural studies, gender studies, and literary theory. Anzaldua's principal trope—or rather a motif which generates a profusion of tropes—is in-betweenness: "Living on borders and in margins, keeping intact one's shifting and multiple identity and integrity..." is exhilarating, she states in her preface (i). She speaks of "confluent streams," of "life in the shadows," of "juncture" and "cross-pollination" (ii). "Nosotros los Chicanos straddle the borderlands," she says later in the book. But one has the sense in Anzaldua of writing as an attempt to work something out, to make problematic distinctions between unsatisfying categories like *Mexican, Chicano, American*, much as the Caribbean writers of the *Éloge* make them between the terms *Caribbean, American*, and *Creole*. *Borderlands* is full of contradiction—particularly about Mexican-ness as "racial," as "a state of soul," and as "linguistic," falling into one or another version where it suits—but is more credible for that: nothing in her work constitutes a racial or ethnic given, or not for more than a paragraph at a time.

THE TOGGLE SWITCH

My last examples, which show the problems of an emphasis on the collective or representative over the individual or specific, begin to demonstrate a particular maneuver, a movement back and forth between the collective and the individual, according to circumstances. We might call it the toggle switch of multiculturalism, the device of turning on and off the sign of ethnicity. A paradigmatic example can be found in a pair of lines from a poem by Pat Parker, titled "For the White Person Who Wants to Know How to be My Friend":

> The first thing you do is to forget that i'm Black.
> Second, you must never forget that i'm Black. (12)

In these lines, the capitalization of *Black* seems to suggest the continuity of blackness, the small case *i* the contingency of the individual Self. The paradoxical instruction to forget and not to forget offers the possibility of advocating sameness when that functions for moral ground, difference when *that* functions. To argue universalism is, to many in the academy today, to brand oneself as a reactionary humanist, yet to disclaim the continuity of a particular ethnicity or race is a move toward assertion of individual agency on the part of the "Other," which one may applaud, since it does make us all the "same" as regards our rights as individuals. But to work the other side ("never forget"), as

Parker candidly—and *perhaps* ironically—admits to doing, is to assert difference when and only when it serves you.

As a more extended example of this doubleness, Traise Yamamoto's essay "Different Silences" in a volume titled *The Intimate Critique: Autobiographical Literary Criticism* is illuminating. Here I would like to offer a context, since this is a question that has been explored more famously in African-American modernist texts. It is the question of being or not being visible, in situations where neither to notice nor not to notice "identity" is acceptable from the point of view of the seen. Richard Wright, in Paris, described a sense of freedom he had not felt in the United States: on the one hand, it was pleasurable indifference on the part of the Parisians ("He did not bother them! They did not give a damn about him!"); on the other, it was a simultaneous and equally pleasurable visibility (people's stares were "friendly, open, curious" [Webb 247]). But, asking himself which he would choose, if forced to choose, between being ignored or being the object of attention, Wright came down on the side of the visible: "No more fiendish punishment could be devised . . . than that one should be turned loose in society and remain absolutely unnoticed by all members thereof . . . [If they] acted as if we were non-existent things, a kind of rage and impotent despair would ere long well up in us, from which the cruelest bodily tortures would be a relief . . ." (Webb 249).[7]

But what appears a puzzle in Richard Wright (and incidentally in James Baldwin's "Stranger on the Seine") becomes a strategy in Yamamoto's essay, where, as in Pat Parker's poem, neither noticing nor failing to notice is acceptable.

Yamamoto's motif is the sentence with which she begins: "You ask me to speak." The "you," one judges from the incidents, is a non-Asian-American world in which the writer is made to feel uncomfortable. Apparently unconscious of this collectivizing, she inveighs against the "you" which her math teacher deploys to collectivize her ("But you're usually so good at this kind of thing"). Indeed, there are a series of rhythmic accusations against "you," such as "You suggest that housecleaning is a good way to make extra summer money, then say I'm a snob when I tell you that my grandmothers did not clean other women's toilets. . . ." (128). At several points in the essay Yamamoto provides binary choices, neither of which is acceptable to her. There are, for example, "liberal arts folks who ignore or overemphasize 'the Japanese stuff' in my poetry" (130). She quotes Trinh Minh Ha, who describes the ordeal of the Third World woman intellectual, compelled to expose her work to critics who "either ignore, dispense with, or overemphasize her racial and sexual attributes" (Yamamoto133). Yamamoto also writes, "when I tell people I write poetry, they often go on to tell me how much they like haiku, as if it were inconceivable that I might write in Homeric dactyls or Dantean *terza rima*" (130). Thus, to express admiration for Asian forms or themes would be to collectivize the Asian-American writer, and yet to ignore those elements or to expect her to write *terza rima*, would constitute a failure to recognize ethnicity and would also be unacceptable—*more* unacceptable, since her next paragraph begins, "And yet, those particulars [of "Asian-American" experience] are what I respond to when I read Asian American writers."

Her essay ends with the remark that "mine is a heritage that knows the beauty of silence." Such a remark is not necessarily mis-representative, but a writer so self-consciously speaking out of an explicitly stated subject position needs to acknowledge the irony of asserting a cultural continuity that surely would offend—we know because she has told us so—if others asserted it.

Yamamoto's article, nevertheless, provides insight into double-binds for those construed as ethnics in the academy. Obviously, ethnicity is often manipulated from the institutional side. David Palumbo-Liu in an article about representing an ethnic constituency within a literature department, looks at ways in which "individuals marked by racial difference [have] been asked ... to forget the personal as it resides in them as racialized beings experiencing race and at other times not only to recognize the personal as racial but to foreground it particularly in their scholarly duties" (1075). He says that minority scholars are "expected either to dismiss race as a factor despite the reality of the way their race is recognized or to study their race (as ancient culture or contemporary issue) ..." (1075). Thus, "Is the request that I teach Maxine Hong Kingston a sign of the dreaded ethnic ghettoization or a sign of respect?"[8]

But the double-bind can, in Parker and Yamamoto and others, become a sort of disingenuous judo, a power move too little examined, even by those who are learning to use it. In the "personal" issue of *PMLA* that I have noticed in this essay, a young scholar named Sheng-Mei Ma tells how he was denied a teaching assistantship while the non-Asian students "moved on to better teaching positions in the department." He argues that his being Asian doomed him to the demeaning job of media assistant, and that, according to the English faculty, he must have "appeared to belong to an East Asian or comparative literature program," although, for that matter, "comparative literature does not find [Asian] candidates genuine enough either."

Why exactly would any comparative literature department find an Asian student less than "genuine"? And why, at a late-century American university, most of which assiduously court graduate students of non-European ethnicity, would such a student be *systematically* oppressed? The argument gets complicated when Ma confesses that he "toyed with the idea of becoming an Asian American minority" precisely in order to get a job, suggesting that he was aware of the advantages but also that he thought better of it and did not present himself as a minority. But this is not what happened. Originally, he reports, he refused to identify himself as an Asian and spelled his name "Sean Ma," which he thought was an Irish-sounding name. But his professor "set [him] straight," shouting at him in the hallway, "'Sheng-mei, you misspelled your name!'" "When I whispered my motive," he says, the professor chided, "'You shouldn't do that.'" Ma regrets that he never had a chance to thank the professor for teaching him "one of the most valuable lessons I learned in graduate school—my name" (1157-58).

But the lesson he learned was not his name, the importance of which he already seems to have known, but the reality of the market. Ma did get a job and quite a good one. Did he try to get it with a counterfeit Irish name because, as he suggests at one point, the profession prefers Irish to Chinese? In other words, was his whispered motive to enhance his chances in a racist academy, hoping to pass as European, or was it, in a spirit of self-sacrifice, to level the playing field, not to press an ethnic advantage? Though the latter choice is contrary to his interpretation of his demeaning experience as a media assistant, he did not, as it turns out, just "toy with the idea"; he announced—and why not?—his ethnic name. Through all this account, Ma seems unaware of his flipping back and forth between two diametrically opposite versions of ethnicity in the academy, one where it is a boon to be exploited, the other where it is a handicap best concealed. The first of these would appear to be struggling up from its repression, against the complaint, the ignominy of a student who did not get his t.a.-ship.

THE WRITING LESSON

The spelling of Ma's name, not as Sean but as Sheng-Mei, represents a critical moment in identity construction, its writing. In a U.S. institutional milieu, when given the appropriate opportunity in writing, do you or do you not announce ethnicity? Given market realities, I think, of those who can, few do not. Though language is the one thing that can prevent our being reduced to bodies, language is also used to reintroduce the body. Identity cards, passports, birth certificates, and genealogies are among the most authenticating texts we possess. As an example of one of the two most recent horrors of ethnic cleansing,

> [W]hen it came down to the matter of deciding who was a Tutsi, the killers relied first on identity cards, which were introduced by Belgians during this century, and secondly upon knowledge of a person's ancestry. It was after these two lines of inquiry proved insufficient that physical characteristics were used as an indicator. (Fenton)

Benedict Anderson has also used the identity-card example ("Exodus"), as has Gayatri Spivak, whose aged mother, carrying an American passport, breezes through French customs, while Spivak, "Highly Commodified" professor and special guest of the French government, suffers official scrutiny. It is not a matter of color, says Spivak, but of passport ("Postmarked" 90). In the case not of national but of academic and literary borders, the failure to write identity can be a mistake. What began—in feminism and minority studies—as a needed acknowledgement of subject position, problematized or not, has become an institutional directive. There are concrete penalties for failure to announce difference. One of the most compelling poets in the United States today is Jay Wright, who was widely heralded through the 1970s and 80s, particularly in African-American journals. A special issue of *Callaloo* was devoted to his work; he won numerous awards, as well as the admiration of critics such as Harold Bloom, John Hollander, and J.D. McClatchy. But the Yale seal may have been as damning for him as Borges' prize from Pinochet. Most of Wright's books are now out of print, and his work is not included in any of the Norton anthologies, including the *Norton Anthology of African American Literature*, even while poets influenced by him are included. Is there not a relation between this living burial and the fact that Jay Wright seldom allows himself to be photographed or videotaped, and that he writes as much about Southwest Indian roots as about black America? Is Wright naïve to think that his work should stand on its own?

Anyone can quibble about an anthology, but the exclusions in this case tell a story. Henry Louis Gates, Jr., the chief editor, along with Nellie McKay, of the Norton African-American anthology, has long struggled to define black literature in a non-essentialist way. And yet essentialism seems to find its way back into the definition. In 1992, in *Loose Canons*, Gates wrote of the need not to define a black tradition in terms of "a pseudoscience of racial biology, or a mystically shared essence called blackness," but rather "by the repetition and revision of shared themes, topoi, and tropes, a process that binds the signal texts of the black tradition into a canon" (39). At the same time, however, he wrote that we must identify this tradition by moving "inductively, from the texts to the theory" (39). Michael Bérubé has noted how the inductive method suggested by Gates begs the question of how one identifies a "black text" ("Beneath" 223). Black literature, according to the inductive method, would not include, for example, non-black writers whose works may exhibit the same topoi and tropes to which Gates refers. Instead, one would first read texts by phenotypically black authors and *then* decide what the principle topoi and tropes are. If this is to be the method—and why not?—one would presumably arrive, as the Norton anthology does not, at an idea of the black tradition that would include writers as celebrated as Jay Wright or, in a very different sense, Frank Yerby. Yerby was an enormously successful African-American novelist and at one time probably the wealthiest expatriate American author (Coles 1999, 149). Though his novels depict racial problems among black and white expatriates, similar to those explored by James Baldwin, Richard Wright, and Nella Larsen, he disavowed "racially conscious" literature early in his career. At the very least, these writers' absence from Norton should be contrasted with the presence of Queen Latifah or Gil-Scott Heron. But at this point a new series of questions fans out, beyond the scope of this essay: Queen Latifah but not Duke Ellington and Billy Strayhorn? Not Stevie Wonder?[9]

Non-white writers who have failed to identify themselves with collectivities have often suffered infamy as conservatives, apostates, or Europhiles. Richard Rodriguez is seen on the Chicano left as an arch-conservative and is anthologized in freshman English readers with William Buckley, Linda Chavez, *et al*, because he has declared his abhorrence of the "typical" life, because, as he says, "When I rehearse my life, I describe one life only, my own. Richard Rodriguez, not even his brother, not his sisters" (12).[10] Derek Walcott's case is similar in that he has insisted, in a highly nuanced way, on individual agency, has deeply problematized (though never denied) his role as a speaker of or for the Caribbean, and has thus been seen, especially by Caribbean insider critics, as a renegade who has found his niche in the North—this after four decades devoted to creating a theater tradition in Trinidad and, in more recent years, after dedicating his Nobel proceeds to found an arts colony in St. Lucia.

Do white writers of fiction and poetry suffer anything comparable? There are ethnic or national cases in which white writers are asked for fidelity to the group—Seamus Heaney, who used to be criticized for too little addressing the Troubles in Ireland; or Philip Roth, unflattering portrayer/betrayer of the Jews—but generally they are *not* asked. Writers of color, on the other hand, are held accountable to the group and suffer accusations of inauthenticity when they write texts which their critics or the public deem non-representative.

RETROGRADE PAIN

"Everyone's tired of my turmoil," said Robert Lowell in a poem of the 1960s, as his turmoil waxed and his fame waned. Lowell was speaking personally, but he may also have been marking a change in literary tastes and expectations. No one wanted any longer to hear about *individual* problems—marriages, divorces, affective disorders, psychic anguish, material or emotional loss. His students—Anne Sexton, Sylvia Plath, W.D. Snodgrass, and others—extended the "confessional" mode beyond Lowell, a mode that still enjoys currency in popular poetry and music, but is anyone in academic literary studies still interested in hearing a personal account free of collective dimensions?

It is not as though collectivities mean nothing. It is that they mean too much. Blackness takes on meanings in the world which the individual did not intend and over which s/he has no control. Maleness, similarly, is too large a category, too overdetermined, to have specific meaning: it's as if to say "being alive" means something. Its repletion of meaning frustrates interpretation. No one can deny that, in America at least, blackness has had and continues to have negative meanings attached to it, but even those meanings were never exclusive. Like all signs, *black* has tended to a diffusion of meaning. My concern is not only that some of the writers quoted here ignore the specificity and materiality of the personal in order to announce membership in collectives, but that they also ignore the welter of conflicting and overlapping collectivities among and through which one actually lives. Nathaniel Mackey's narrator, in that poet's open-ended poem of identity *Song of the Andoumboulou*, rejects numerous first-person plurals as too suspect, too full of failed promise: "No we of romance we contrived coupling / no nation's we / collectivity's wish. . . ." but, instead: "We / made of how many / who could say?"

How many? The regional we, the we of neighborhoods, the professional we, all the we's of unions and teams and affiliations and affinities (music, sports, religion, politics, even academics!). The affective "we" of empathetic subjectivity—the we's of all the loves possible, in and out of family. These are collectives we move through daily, some saturating our lives more than others. Many can be stronger and more local than race, class, *or* gender. Thomas Wolfe's remark that a French waiter and an American waiter have more in common than a French banker and a French waiter is observable in one's own life, in one's own profession. It is certainly true of musicians and of poets. Watch a Japanese and a Spanish musician interact; then watch a Spanish musician and a Spanish attorney.

To miss these other collectivities and bonds is also to miss the crucial insight that identity is a limitless process of becoming, always in dialogue with otherness, a dialogue much enhanced when investment in a single identity is withdrawn. The painter David Hockney has pointed out that to choose a single perspective is to be dead. To be alive, we must keep displacing perspective. If perspective is fixed, time is stopped, and space is petrified. "To have a fixed point, you have no movement; you are not there, really" (qtd. in Costello 15). One must be willing to engage a wider community of individuals, a wider net of continuities.

The claim for diversity at the heart of multiculturalism continues to be undermined precisely by the insistence on cultural holisms and ethnic continuities, the insistence on borders rather than border crossings, on authenticity rather than on hybridity and agency.[11] Are the border crossers somehow not "multicultural"? The great Chicano novelist Daniel James, the great British novelist Kazue Ishiguro, or the great British novelist Konrad Korzeniowski; the great French poet Edgar Poe or the great French poet Frank O'Hara; the great American novelist Vladimir Nabokov, the great classical poet Derek Walcott, the great Aztec poet Jay Wright, and so on—culture-traitors all? The *Race Traitors* magazine would do well to consider examples other than "whites" longing to be "black." Crossings require sacrifice of the *heimlich*'s complacency; they foster a sharper awareness of the genuinely porous boundaries, if boundaries at all, between cultures.

Finally, speaking "as a" white, black, Chicana, Jew, and so on raises more problems than it can possibly address. If bourgeois individualism has now had the examination it needed, speaking "as a" has not.[12] If the individual subject was problematic and suspect, the collective is no less so. And if we are to speak "as" something, it must be more than a recital of historical/positional categories.

Though discrete human communities certainly treasure continuities, we should consider just how locally constructed our (U.S.) ideas of the collective are. J. M. Coetzee has suggested that Americans may have something to learn from the South African critique of ethnicity. He observes that the idea of "natural" groups seems to be accepted in an unexamined way in the United States, whereas, among the Left in South Africa, there is a strongly skeptical attitude toward the naturalness of groups ("tribes," "peoples," or "races"), and a correspondingly strong deconstructive treatment of the histories and literatures of such groups. This is a natural reaction to having lived for forty years under a regime whose social, educational, and cultural policies were based on the postulate of separate (God-given) groups with separate destinies (Begam 428).

If reinscribing essentialism, as Coetzee suggests, plays into the hands of those who essentialize in order to repress, does not anti-essentialism—one might ask—play into the hands of critics who deconstruct in order to disenfranchise? The question, then, must be how to extend the critique of the Subject without falling into the camp of those who would use it to silence others. Anti-essentialism is suspect among some Left academics, for example, because they see it as a critique exploited by the Right. But one person's anti-essentialism does not spring from the same sources or serve the same purposes as another's. What is needed is an anti-essentialism that subsumes these arguments, one that can account for the uses and excesses of "authenticity" narratives as well as of versions of representation that would reduce all traits and continuities to features of a text.

GENDER AND TRANSPARENCY

I've noted the preponderance of women's names in this essay, about two females to one male. If this should seem askew, consider that the ratio is more than *ten* to one in *The Intimate Critique: Autobiographical Literary Criticism*. Of the twenty-two authors represented, two are male. The editors, apparently finding as I did much more autobiographical criticism by women than by men, offer in their introduction a theory of "male" and "female" modes of discourse—the one formal and hierarchical, the other "open-ended, generative, and process-oriented" (2).[13]

In observing that some women will write in a male mode and some men in a female, the editors are careful to acknowledge the essentializing potential of such oppositions (Ice People v. Sun People?). Does the opposition return us to the disturbing topos examined by numerous feminist critics—the idea of narrative as female, indeed of woman as native, as unreflective "experience," transparent and knowable, opposed to man as knower, as cognitive, inscrutable? Do men theorize, while women write poems and novels?

It is surprising how readily an academic writer can, perhaps unwittingly, submit to a view of Nature as female and Culture as male. Gayatri Spivak has discussed how in the history of theory since the Enlightenment, the chief problem has been that of autobiography, the problem of how "subjective structures can, in fact, give objective truth" ("Questions" 66). In one of the *PMLA* letters on the Personal, Agnes Moorhead Jackson, identifying herself as an "other" in the "white male heterosexual" academy, one "who know[s] from the inside," presents this idea of Spivak's as if it were the *raison d'etre* of the personal in criticism, writing that "our lives are the 'subjective structures' that 'can . . .give objective truth'" (1159).

Jackson does not notice that Spivak is warning us against precisely this reification of native (and female) "experience" as an object of study by male "scientists." Spivak reminds us how the discourse of the "Native Informant" became "objective evidence" in the founding of ethnography, comparative religion, and linguistics. Spivak ends that interview saying

> The person who *knows* has all the problems of selfhood. The person who is *known*, somehow seems not to have a problematic self. These days . . . [o]nly the dominant self can be problematic; the self of the Other is authentic without a problem, naturally available to all kinds of complications. This is very frightening. (66)

How such an explicit warning can be ignored is a mystery. This gendered division of labor (women write novels, men do theory) is not new. In modern culture, as David Simpson has pointed out, sensibility and expression have usually been associated with or allocated to women. Literariness, after all, was thought to consist of fables, poems, and myths, suitable for women and children. Stories must be told by embodied subjects living in history, not by the male founders of global and "neutral" theories, whose own historicity must be downplayed for those theories to be credible. It is with this division in mind that Nancy Armstrong argues that the very notion of modern subjectivity came into being as feminized: "the modern individual was first and foremost a woman" (*Desire and Domestic Fiction*, qtd. in Simpson 95).

To conflate for a moment the issues of gender and ethnicity, consider that, among postcolonial critics, Gayatri Spivak and Sara Suleri frequently announce their problematic subject positions, while Abdul JanMohammed and Homi Bhabha do not. Among white critics in cultural studies, do Andrew Ross or Cary Nelson or Werner Sollors or Frederic Jameson tell autobiographical stories? If not, are they playing the neutrality game so much under antihumanist fire, or have they simply found nothing in the way of birth or upbringing that they can use to authenticate their writing? Significantly, Michael Bérubé, in writing about the centrality of the personal, also leaves out any personal account. He does use a conventional first person, a pleasant, familiar "I." Indeed, Bérubé's recognizable style gives us a person, without our being told his race or gender or his familial or professional struggles. Whatever his reasons, he has chosen to leave those details out.[14]

I think, in short, if someone wanted to do the work of quantifying, s/he would find that male scholars do not insert or assert the autobiographical nearly as often as female scholars do, and that white males, always with exceptions, continue to be the least autobiographical in critical writing. The penalty they incur for *not* announcing a position is negligible or at least milder—accusations of feigned neutrality, universalism, spurious "objectivity"—than that incurred by writers of color, whose failure to mark identity can entail consequences such as I have described above.

THE FUTURE OF THE PERSONAL

Personal experience does not exist in an uninterpretable sphere. To say so is not to deny suffering; instead, it is to assert the one thing that cultural and literary critics are supposed to know: that representations matter, particularly those we make to ourselves. Some people recover completely and even immediately from violence or deprivation; others, who never experienced such traumas, are troubled all their lives. To postmodernize Epictetus: it is a question of how—or even *if*—we read the text of our experience. Leaning over the river of your life, you may see incoherent eddies; or you may see a face. You may decide that face is your own, or you may not.

While many readers now realize that serious thought is not separate from an embodied subject in history, the critique of that subject is certainly incomplete and more necessary than ever. These two realities account for the troubled shift one often notices in contemporary writing between essentialist and anti-essentialist modes, a restless movement between linguistic, anti-transparent positions and the foundation-hungry insistence on subjectivity.

Perhaps one of the reasons this contradiction cannot be worked out is that the discussion takes place within a democratic paradigm. Ethnicity is a contrastive positionality, lived in the meeting of cultures, and often expressed as a figure-ground relationship. In more than a linguistic sense, black has been marked in a white world, female in a male world, short in a tall world (We ask, "How tall are you?"). To take less inflammatory examples, motion is marked in a world where most things appear to be at rest, or irony in a world where "sincerity" is assumed. These latter examples, while less obviously hierarchical than the oppositions of black and white, female and male, illustrate the same problem: if all utterance is ironic, as some critics will say, then there is no irony. If we are all mestizo, then the ground has become as neutral as it was when no one accounted for subject position, when "objectivity" was assumed.

Whatever forms the critique of the subject takes, the personal will survive, in the face of (or the wake of) poststructuralist arguments that subjectivity is discursively constituted. It will do so not by means of explicit positional statements, made under duress to expiate the guilt of achieved individuality, but more likely in the way that the personal has always survived—through what Hans Vaihinger once called the philosophy of "as if." We live *as if* we were not at birth sentenced to death; we speak *as if* language referred to a world outside itself; and we act *as if* we were the loci of coherent subjectivities anterior to our actions and speech. But theorists, at least, should not forget that these suppositions *are* constructed; they should not too easily revert either to the authority of categories or to the authority of experience, whether to convert ontology into epistemology or to move goods in a competitive market.

Some of the most prominent postcolonial critics—Gayatri Spivak, Edward Said, Homi Bhabha, Satya Mohanty, Sara Suleri—have come out in recent years as proponents of something that sounds a lot like liberal humanism ("authentic humanism" in Said, "subaltern secularism" in Bhabha, "post-positivist objectivity" in Mohanty). But a return to humanism need not mean the imposition of the values of one group upon others.[15] Rather, it entails (these critics and others remind us) a settling for the incomplete. Hope of a universal humanism will be compromised by those groups that deny the intrinsic worth of others. An "authentic" or "subaltern" or "new" humanism must be conscious of these perils. Similarly, anti-essentialism need not be discredited because some critics or political figures have exploited it, particularly considering its problematic if not malign alternatives.

The paradox is that what people share is what they cannot share: consciousness, pain, unrecuperable feeling. This unknowability is shared by and among individuals. If consciousness, the place of the subject, cannot be represented in words, yet, in "isolate flecks," as William Carlos Williams said, "something/ is given off." It is given off not so much in statements *about* the self, and least of all in the checking of boxes on a form, as it is in actions, and especially, in this context, the action of writing.

NOTES

I am grateful to Steven Gould Axelrod, Susie Lan Cassel, David Bleich, Julia Fiedorczuk, Melissa Fabros, Felipe Smith, and particularly Dermot Quinn for their suggestions on earlier versions of this article.

1. The twenty-six letters were grouped under two rubrics, more or less "pro" and "con": "The Inevitability of the Personal" (sixteen letters) and "Problems With the Personal" (ten letters). Of the latter, only two, David Simpson's and Terry Caesar's, can be said to question the trend of autobiography in criticism of the last decade or so.
2. See also note 13 below, regarding "The Male and Female Modes of Rhetoric," quoted in *The Intimate Critique*.
3. While I do not want to place quotation marks around every use of "black" and "white," or to say "those construed as white according to local conventions," I use these terms unhappily and under erasure, subsuming and disguising as they do an enormous range of nationalities and identities.
4. "Transculturation," a term coined by Cuban sociologist Fernando Ortíz, means that the peripheral culture selects what it wants from the metropolitan or colonizing culture, not that it merely "acculturates," in the earlier model of cultural transference, absorbing and changing itself helplessly. "Transculturation," is invoked by Pratt not just as an object of study but as a procedure whereby she, as author, may avoid falling under the spell of hegemonic travel texts and thus reproducing or reinscribing their imperial modes.
5. Though less frequent, acknowledgments of limitations by male critics do of course appear. An example is this prefatory statement by George Lipsitz, from *Dangerous Crossroads*: "As a North American limited by the parochialism and prejudices of my life and my culture, I know that my efforts to interpret and analyze political and cultural practices from contexts far different from my own are likely to fall short in ways that I cannot anticipate" (17).
6. In the introduction to *Culture and Imperialism*, for example, Said writes that "all cultures are involved in one another; none is single and pure, all are hybrid, heterogeneous, extraordinarily differentiated, and unmonolithic" (xxv). In "Representing the Colonized," he writes of the need to see Others "not as ontologically given but as historically constituted" and in this way "to

erode the exclusivist biases we so often ascribe to cultures, our own not least."

7. I have discussed Richard Wright's Paris experience in "Essentialism and the Mulatto Traveler: Europe as Embodiment in Nella Larsen's *Quicksand*."
8. This is not the place to take up the question of whether phenotypic markings authorize a person to teach a given subject area, but for many university search committees, they clearly do. See Nellie McKay on the problems created by committees' insistence on ethnicity in African-American studies.
9. Editors Gates and McKay do acknowledge the omission of Jay Wright in this note in their preface:

> With the exceptions of the poetry of Jay Wright, Zora Neale Hurston's *Their Eyes Were Watching God*, and the short fiction of Gayl Jones, which could not be included here for reasons of copyright, our anthology contains the texts that, in the judgment of the editors, define the canon of African-American literature at the present time. (xxxvii)

Jay Wright's work, however, was not excluded for reasons of copyright. After writing my remarks about his absence from the Norton anthology, I learned from a letter from Jay Wright, that Gates and McKay *had* suggested publishing some early poems (two from Wright's first book and a very small one from his sixth), but they wanted none of Wright's more serious work, from the later books upon which his reputation rests. This, at least in Jay Wright's view, still constitutes exclusion, since the conditions for inclusion were unacceptable. The work excluded is work not perceived as "black" according to the "shared themes, topoi, and tropes" which the editors, quite *non*-inductively, consider indispensable; it is also work done in *forms* not conventionally associated with the African-American tradition. These exclusions, obviously, are an editor's prerogative, but so is it a reader's to question them.

The other correction I need to add here is that, while Wright's principal volumes remain out of print, his collected poems will appear in late 2000.

10. See Henry Staten's excellent reappraisal of Rodriguez in the 1998 *PMLA Ethnicity* issue.
11. For a full development of this point, see Susan Stewart, "The State of Cultural Theory and the Future of Literary Form," in the 1993 MLA *Profession*.
12. I take this in part from Nancy K. Miller: "But if 'identity politics' has challenged bourgeois self-representation—with all its unself-conscious exclusions—speaking 'as a' has emerged as an equally problematic *representativity*" (qtd. in Gubar 386). See also Gayatri Spivak: "The moment I have to think of the ways in which I will speak as an Indian, or as a feminist, the ways in which I will speak as a woman, what I am doing is trying to distance myself from some kind

of inchoate speaking *as such*. There are many subject positions which one must inhabit; one is not just one thing." ("Questions" 60)

13. While setting out this opposition as helpful if not definitive, they distance themselves from it by noting that they are drawing on an article by Thomas J. Farrell titled "The Male and Female Modes of Rhetoric." Nevertheless, they do not question it. Quoting Farrell, they say that the female mode "seems at times to obfuscate the boundary between the self of the author and the subject of the discourse, as well as between the self and the audience, whereas the male mode tends to accentuate such boundaries" (2).

14. In another essay and context, however, Bérubé does speak autobiographically, offering a lively account of his coming of age in "Discipline and Theory," his contribution to *Wild Orchids and Trotsky*.

15. Among others who note this, see Tzvetan Todorov, *On Human Diversity*, in which he argues that universalism should not be rejected because of the ethnocentric uses to which it has sometimes been put. Nations have demonstrated (recently, in the case of the French in Rwanda) that actions *can* be taken on behalf of humanity. Moreover, universalism does not in fact *motivate* colonial projects, though it has been used to justify them. Finally, Todorov argues that what is universal is "not one quality or another, but the capacity to acquire any of them."

PART TWO
Self-Inclusion in Literary Scholarship

3 RADICAL INTROSPECTION IN SCHOLARSHIP AND TEACHING

Brenda Daly

My best teaching takes place when I am most attentive to students, when I am fully engaged in listening to and learning from them, when I am talking with them, not at them. Unfortunately, I am not always capable of such deep listening. Students sense this immediately. They may not accuse me directly, as my son has on occasion—"Mom, you're not paying attention!"—but their demeanor changes. It's a subtle thing, but palpable. Over the years, I have come to understand, primarily through the introspective practice of personal scholarship, that I am most attentive to students after first attending to my own needs. As I studied to become an English professor, one of my greatest needs was to integrate my past and present selves, my private and professional selves, my teacher and scholar-selves. I knew, before post-structuralists told me, that the notion of a unified self is an illusion; at the same time, I often experienced this fragmentation as debilitating rather than liberating. When I began graduate school in the late 1970s, I used a private journal to achieve some degree of coherence even as my private life was fragmented by my professional ambitions.

In time, however, my study of feminist theory prompted me to question the necessity of maintaining the boundaries between my journal and my academic essays. If I were to put into practice the feminist credo, the personal is the political, I would have to acknowledge that two topics central to my scholarship, sexual violation and motherhood, were also autobiographical. In order to change the world—along with other feminists—I would have to write transgressively, challenging public hierarchies and practices with stories of their often painful consequences in the realm of so-called "personal experience." At the urging of feminist professors, I began to write such essays in the early 1980s. By early 1990, women students who had read my autobiographical scholarship began asking me to teach them how to use the personal in their academic essays. Initially, I was surprised by their interest in personal criticism; however, I soon recognized that they too felt the need to understand the mother-daughter relationship or, in some instances, recover from the painful effects of sexual violation. As a result, they sought out opportunities to read, reflect on, and write about these complex and sometimes traumatic experiences.

What these women students found—in studies of novels by Edith Wharton, Joyce Carol Oates, Jamaica Kincaid, Jane Smiley, Dorothy Allison, and Toni Morrison—is that autobiographical reading and writing is a complex creative process, at once emotional and analytical. Personal scholarship has also helped these students to heal from personal pain while, at the same time, changing their ways of understanding themselves and the world. I call this teaching/learning process "radical introspection." As James Hill defines it, radical introspection challenges "individualist constructions of pedagogy" and has as its goal "insight toward social action" (18). As Hill says, the concept is rooted in the liberal feminist notion, "the personal is the political," and in "the Italian Marxist Antonio Gramsci's concept of the organic intellectual, and the African American tradition of prophetic Christianity" (Hill 5). Although some academics view the use of the personal in scholarship as a narcissistic, unreflective practice—Dale Bauer claims, for example, that "writing about the personal aims to recapture the immediacy of context and to suggest an authoritative experiential stance but which, no surprise here, seems only to reify the personal" (57)—the practice of radical introspection does not "reify the personal;" rather, it often enables reflective practitioners to move beyond what Maurice Natanson calls "egologic" (quoted in Bleich's *The Double Perspective* 46).

I want to emphasize, however, that radical introspection requires emotional as well as intellectual honesty; without acknowledgment of emotions that many of us would rather disavow—envy, guilt, resentment, shame—the practice cannot succeed. Unfortunately, as Jane Tompkins points out in *A Life in School*, the academy does not encourage introspection. Higher education has failed, she says, to "focus on the inner lives of students or help them acquire the self-understanding that is the basis for a satisfying life. Nor, by and large, does it provide the safe and nurturing environment that people need in order to grow" (xii). Furthermore, as Tompkins argues in "Me and My Shadow," many intellectuals, having been taught that emotions should have no part in the process of acquiring knowledge, fear and disparage emotions. "The strength of the taboo," Tompkins says, "can be gauged by the academician's inevitable recourse to name-calling when emotion, spirituality, and imagination are brought into the curricular conversation: 'touchy-feely,' 'soft,' 'unrigorous,' 'mystical,' 'therapeutic,' and 'Mickey Mouse' are the all-time favorites, with 'psychobabble' and 'bullshit' not far behind" (*Life in School* 214). Indeed, according to David Bleich, "There is an unacknowledged fantasy in the program of cognitive science that intellectual work must be separate from its feelings and passions, must be autonomous relative to its human and social contexts" ("Academic Ideology," 573). Because many academics hold such views, I continue to feel vulnerable when using the personal in my scholarship and teaching; nevertheless, the practice of self-inclusion has helped my students and me to resist and even transform debilitating ways of understanding the world.

In this essay I will give several examples of the process of radical introspection, a process from which the teacher learns as much as the students. The first example comes from my own autobiographical writing. After my mother's death in August 1997, I decided that, rather than attempting to contain my grief, I would continue a project begun before her death: analyzing the effects of my mother's limited education on her life and mine. In an effort to re-understand my mother's so-called "personal" experience of schooling within a broader social, political, and historical context, I read Madeleine R. Grumet's *Bitter Milk,* Carmen Luke's *Pedagogies of Everyday Life,* and Wendy Luttrell's *Schoolsmart and Motherwise: Working-Class and Women's Identity and Schooling,* each of which gave me a new perspective on my mother's education. Here is a brief excerpt from my essay, entitled "Weeping for the Mother":

> Like the stories of working-class women in Wendy Luttrell's *Schoolsmart and Motherwise,* my story is one of "persistent sadness and regret, what Nancy Chodorow calls 'weeping for the mother'" (97). I weep for my mother, a major figure in the story of my schooling, primarily because her life was severely limited by her lack of a formal education—specifically, a feminist education. I do not, however, mean to suggest that my mother was completely unschooled; despite the fact she did not complete high school, she did learn lessons outside the classroom—at home, at church, from television and magazines.
>
> Because I wanted a better understanding of her education, I once asked her what she had read as a child. She answered, "I read little women when I was a teenager. I imagined myself as Jo. I'm going to read it again. Never was anything read to me [at home] as a child. I remember most vividly my Sunday School Pamphlets. I took them most seriously, and Mrs. Schultz, my teacher, made everything come alive for me" (letter, September 24, 1994). Following this brief narrative about her own reading, my mother quickly shifted focus, giving this account of her father as a reader: "I remember being impressed with my Daddy sitting uncomfortably on a kitchen chair, tilted back under a single light bulb—reading far into the nite." Remarkably, when asked about her own reading, she puts the spotlight on her father, a man who, even at the age of 72, she called "Daddy." She's still daddy's little girl," one of my brothers recently observed, with bitter accuracy. Like the working-class women in Luttrell's study, my mother tends to describe men—her father or husband—as school-smart, while discounting her own intelligence. My mother did not believe that the story of her schooling had value, probably because, unlike the subjects in Luttrell's study, she had never had the opportunity to share her story in a classroom setting.

The sharing of such stories would be encouraged in some feminist classrooms while, ordinarily, it would not be allowed. Unfortunately, feminist efforts to allow women to integrate their experiences and their schooling, their emotions and intellects, continue to be misconstrued and devalued by university and college administrators. For example, in Jill Ker Conway's recent memoir *True North*, this former college president explains that she was opposed to the founding of Women's Studies programs because, for one thing, they are based on "specious ideologies about 'feminist' or excessively nurturant teaching styles as a justification for less real research." She continues, "Overly nurturant teaching, from which all overt criticism has been removed seemed to me to run the same danger for the young as permissive child rearing, because both obfuscate the nature of power and thus limit the possibility of rebellion" (218).

Why does Ker Conway assume that feminists would be "overly nurturant," and why does she assume that feminists would "obfuscate the nature of power"? Perhaps some feminist professors do make this mistake; however, since my feminist professors have been both rigorous and nurturing, while also recognizing the need to analyze power relations, it is possible that Ker Conway's view of feminist teaching is based on an unexamined, sentimental view of mothering. The best mothers are not overly-nurturant; instead, as Jessica Benjamin argues in *The Bonds of Love*, they maintain the tension between the demands of self and other rather than simply sacrificing their own needs, boundaries, or expectations. As redefined by Benjamin, the dialogic nature of maternal thinking has important pedagogical implications; nevertheless, we are just beginning to understand why many women experience "an epistemological revolution" (Belenky *et al* 34) when they become mothers. One's world view alters dramatically when it becomes necessary to care for another person—and, at its best, teaching is caring for other people. Nevertheless, many higher education administrators remain suspicious of the goals of supposedly "overly nurturant" feminist pedagogy.[1] Why? One answer can be found in the historical exclusion of maternal thinking from higher education, an exclusion that resulted from the "feminization" of primary and secondary education.

According to Madeleine Grumet, the feminization of teaching during the nineteenth century enabled more women to enter the profession; however, women teachers were discouraged from assuming administrative positions; instead, they were expected to control the children while they, in turn, submitted to (male) administrative control. But most important, schools were organized to encourage the child's identification with the father through a gradual differentiation from maternal nurturance. As a result, higher education came to be defined by the absence of maternal values and practices. As Luttrell points out, "A sexual division of labor is built into the American educational system as its working assumption" (91-91). My mother's acceptance of this sexual division of labor is evident in her assumption that men, such as her father, are school-smart while she, having been a mother all her adult life, is not. Despite the intellectual challenges of nurturing children, my mother holds the view that her "instinctive" maternal practice must remain outside the bounds of formal schooling. So pervasive is this view of mothering—that it is an instinctive rather than a rational practice—that feminist philosopher Sara Ruddick began her book *Maternal Thinking* by asserting that, yes, mothering does require thought. Maternal thinking continues to be excluded from higher education as evident from the continuing exclusion of emotions from most university and college classrooms. As a result, women often experience schooling as a painful process of leaving their mothers behind.

My understanding of this painful loss of the maternal in the academy—and of my own need for radical introspection—was deepened by a former graduate student, DeRionne Pollard, who now teaches writing and literature at a community college in Illinois. In a conference paper Pollard presented at my invitation, she equates the loss of her mother with the loss of her personal voice in academic writing. In the following letter to Pollard, included here with her permission, I respond to her effort to integrate her personal and academic voices which, as she explains, remain segregated in two different papers, one academic, the other personal.

> Dear DeRionne,
>
> I am deeply moved by both your papers, the academic essay, "I Hear You, You Hear Me," and the personal paper, "Mother-Hunger: A Struggle to Find My Voice," which will, I hope, eventually become part of the academic paper. On hearing you say, at the conference here in the fall of 1997, that you had "come to hate writing," I felt such grief and guilt: as your primary writing mentor, I had taught you to hate academic writing. You also said, "Yes, I know the academic language, but I really don't like it. It is so hard for me to translate my voice to paper. Something always gets lost in the translation" ("I Hear" 3).

In fact, when DeRionne expressed frustration with academic writing, I had offered her the opportunity to write a more creative introduction to her thesis, but I did not allow any departure from academic conventions in the remaining three chapters because, I explained, she might wish to submit these chapters as writing samples in her applications to graduate schools. Despite such misgivings, I strive to listen attentively and respond respectfully as DeRionne continues to explain her feelings about academic writing. I reply:

> Your conference paper on the use of personal narratives in the academy has caused me to reflect on and change my pedagogy. In that paper, you state, "This fear of writing has paralyzed me partially because I feel incompetent" ("I Hear" 3). At first, DeRionne, I resisted your harsh self-assessment; I wanted to point out that you are a

> highly competent student who understands theoretical concepts and effectively incorporated them into your writing. In fact, I nominated your thesis for a department award because I felt you had become an excellent writer. How, then, did you came to feel "incompetent"? At the same time, I believe you *felt* incompetent, primarily because I have had similar feelings. Like you, I have sometimes felt that my own voice was "lost in translation" in an academic essay, and like you, I have often questioned my authority as a writer and teacher. Also, like you, I have wondered whether, after taking my courses, students are "better writers" ("I Hear" 2). As a result, I have begun to ask, as you have, "How do I foster a connection between my students' personal and academic voices?" ("I Hear" 3).

As this dialogue illustrates, the practice of radical introspection does not simply "reify the personal," but rather forces me to move beyond egologic: my perception of DeRionne's experience as a student does not match her perception. Initially, I want to defend myself, silencing DeRionne's experience of incompetence by insisting that she accept my view of her as highly competent with theory. After all, my intentions are good: if she accepts my view, she will feel better, won't she? But, reminding myself that the practice of radical introspection must be emotionally as well as intellectually honest, I acknowledge that I too have sometimes felt a sense of loss and self-doubt. Through DeRionne's honest analysis of her own pedagogy, as a community college teacher, I begin to reflect on my own teaching. My letter to her continues:

> Now, as a teacher at a community college, you express fear that your students will lose their joy in writing, just as you did. Speaking of a bright student, you write, "I was so fearful of Cheyenne losing this joy for writing while she was in my class" ("I Hear" 6). But Cheyenne didn't lose her joy for writing; in her final letter to you she wrote: "Our relationship helped me not only because it reassured me that this is what I'm meant to do, it made me feel like there were people out there that care as much about writing as I do. It made me think about my writing with a renewed sense of enthusiasm as well as in a realistic sense. That I shouldn't put so much pressure on myself to be a huge success as a writer, but just to write. And probably the most important thing is to recognize my own voice and to know that I am in everything that I write" ("I Hear" 9). You succeeded, DeRionne: you gave Cheyenne a safe place, in an exchange of personal letters with you, to voice her concerns about your pedagogy, and—most important—her feelings about her relationship with you.

DeRionne has succeeded with her student Cheyenne, whereas I have failed with DeRionne. Nevertheless, because there is trust between us—DeRionne accepted my invitation to present this conference paper, and she is willing to speak the truth to me—I can learn from my past failures; that is, if I can listen and respond without becoming defensive:

At first, you explain, you adopted a pedagogy of distance because "If I wasn't too connected to them personally, if I didn't know enough about them to understand why and how they write, I would be able to maintain my distance which would allow for objective evaluation" ("I Hear" 7). At first you felt that, because you tended "to get too involved" with students, this distancing strategy would enable you to be "fair." I too have felt the necessity of distancing myself from students in order to evaluate their work fairly. But when you say, "If I didn't know them, I wouldn't have to hear them" ("I Hear" 7), I must acknowledge what is lost with the adoption of this pedagogy of distance. Through your exchange of letters with Cheyenne, you came to understand that this distance was consistent with "valuing the academic writing and the academic voice" but at the same time you were "moving away from personal writing" ("I Hear" 7). Why, you began to wonder, were you doing this? To answer this question, you cite the theory of muted groups:

> The theory of muted groups was developed to describe situations in which groups of people are in asymmetrical power relationships) e.g., blacks and whites; colonizers and the colonized). The theory proposes that language and the norms for its uses are controlled by the dominant group. Members of the muted group are disadvantaged in articulating their experience, since the language they use is derived largely from the perceptions of the dominant group.... In order to be heard, muted group members must learn the dominant idiom and attempt to articulate within it, even though this attempt will inevitably lead to some loss of learning. The experiences "lost in translation" to the dominant idiom remain unvoiced, and perhaps unthought. (Crawford and Chaffin 21).

Recalling that DeRionne had read this essay on muted group theory in my seminar, "The American Canon Debate," I felt some relief: at least she had learned something of value from me. But my relief was short-lived because I quickly recognized that by teaching only theory, I had forced her to mute her personal voice. I am unwilling to give up the theoretical; after all, DeRionne is using theory—the theory of muted groups—to explain why the muting of her personal voice in academic writing has caused her to feel "lost in translation." At the same time, our dialogue has prompted me to reflect on my pedagogy. As my letter continues, I ask DeRionne how we might overcome our mother-hunger in the academy:

> I wonder, DeRionne: if we devise a more self-inclusive pedagogy, will it be possible to overcome the mother-hunger we both feel? Do you think that by using the personal in our scholarly writing we might provide our students and ourselves with the emotional nurture for which we hunger? In "Mother-Hunger" you write, "My mother-hunger has immobilized my voice and has rendered me silent. It is like I have cut out my own tongue because I don't want to speak of the pain I feel" (n.p.).

This insight, that the pain of mother-hunger had silenced your personal voice, is of great value. You have articulated a powerful argument for the use of the personal—the emotional, the embodied, the poetic—in academic writing. By censoring this voice, the voice of the mother, academic discourses cut us off, as you point out, from our sustenance, from our linguistic and physical foundations. This, then, is yet another way that the mother—in all her guises—is censored in higher education. Like you, I have found that "mother-hunger is powerful and mysterious;" for example, after becoming a full professor in 1997 I was almost disabled by my disavowal of aspects of my identity associated with the maternal: my body, my emotions, my personal life. As you say, "Mother-hunger creeps up on you. You don't feel her coming, although deep down you know you will have to face her someday" (n. p.). As you say, eventually she "sneaks up on you like a shadow" (n. p.).

After sharing some of my own experiences with this "shadow,"[2] I conclude my letter to DeRionne by describing what her writing has taught me:

> The repression of the personal voice in favor of the theoretical, as I learned from your beautiful essay, "Mother-Hunger," is yet another way in which the academy devalues the maternal. However, I believe that the solution to this problem is not to disavow academic writing, but to integrate our personal and theoretical voices in our scholarship. We must also, as you have taught me, introduce this mixed mode of writing to our students. My failure to introduce you to personal criticism has taught me a valuable lesson: that students have a powerful need, not simply a desire, to integrate the personal voice into academic writing. But I wonder if I have fully understood your experience of being muted in the academy: because you are black and I am white, because you are a lesbian and I am a heterosexual, your experience is also different from mine. In order to continue this exploration of our differences, I am emulating the epistolary pedagogy you employed with your student, Cheyenne. Just as you felt that Cheyenne became your teacher, you have become my teacher. With your help, I hope that my future students will not "come to hate writing" (2), as you have.
>
> With love,

Although I failed to introduce personal criticism to Ms. Pollard, I had begun to teach this transgressive mode of writing to other graduate students, but only upon request and only in tutorials. In the writing of these women students I saw a recurrence of two major topics, both traumatic—the loss of the mother and the experience of sexual violation. These women's self-inclusive academic essays illustrate Shoshana Felman's arguments that "every woman's life contains, explicitly or in implicit ways, the story of a trauma" (16);" they also illustrate Felman's point that the lack of an autobiography is, in fact, the condition of all women. She says,

> In spite of the contemporary literary fashion of feminine confessions and of the recent critical fashion of 'feminist confessions,' I will suggest that none of us, as women, has

as yet, precisely, an autobiography. Trained to see ourselves as objects and positioned as the Other, estranged to ourselves, we have a story that by definition cannot be self-present to us, a story that, in other words, is not a story, but must become a story. (14)

Initially, I resisted the notion that all women are trauma victims because it does not take into account the fact that some women—holocaust or rape victims, for example—suffer much more severely than others. How, I wonder, is it possible to argue, as Felman does, that women, as women, do not have autobiographies? The answer, as feminists have been arguing for some time, is that male-dominated institutions continue to train women to see themselves as "Other." If this training is not completely successful, if a woman's psyche does not come to mirror the militaristic structure of the university, she experiences a sense of estrangement.

Fortunately, the militaristic ideology of universities is now being exposed and criticized. David Bleich argues, for example, that the current grading system enforces a hidden ideology—an ideology based on militarism—that requires the exclusion of feelings. Through hierarchical evaluation of both teachers and students, according to Bleich, the academy maintains its "unacknowledged fantasy ... that intellectual work must be separate from its feelings and passions, must be autonomous relative to its human and social context" ("Academic Ideology" 573). The academy's repression of feelings, along with its emphasis on individualism, creates a competitive atmosphere that makes it difficult for faculty and students to develop a sense of trust. Without trust and a sense of community, individuals feel embattled and isolated. Perhaps, through an exchange of our stories, faculty and students might put aside competitiveness, as DeRionne and I do. Unfortunately, such exchanges are often prevented by the conventions of academic writing. How, in such an intellectual warrior culture, are women students to become "storied selves"? Felman answers that women can do so only indirectly: "by conjugating literature, theory, and autobiography together through the act of reading and by reading, thus, into the texts of culture, at once our sexual difference and our autobiography as missing" (14). If Felman is right, the use of the personal in scholarship is not, at least for women, a self-indulgent practice but, rather, a necessity. In addition, as Felman emphasizes, this act of "conjugating" requires collective action—"together through the act of reading and by reading, thus, into the texts of culture"—of the kind in which my women students and I have engaged.

Unfortunately, traditional grading practices frequently undermine the establishment of trust between students and teachers, and without such trust it is difficult—through this conjugating of literature, theory and autobiography—to transform the texts of culture. Despite this obstacle, my students and I have sometimes managed to create islands of trust, although less often in formal classroom settings, within a competitive university. When a student tells me her story, and I tell her mine—always in the privacy of my office—we are able to begin the work of conjugating, the work of radical introspection. Students often describe this conjugating of literature, theory, and autobiography as a means of "integrating" formerly disparate "voices" or selves. Such claims of self-integration may suggest, at the very least, a lack of awareness of post-structuralists challenges to the notion of a unitary subject; however, these students are not necessarily self-deluded. It is possible, for example, that poststructuralist notions of the self—or "subject"—simply do not apply to women. Political philosopher James Glass makes this argument in *Shattered Selves*, a study of women who suffer from multiple personality disorder, all victims of paternal sexual abuse. Glass concludes that it is irresponsible of post-structuralists to base their claims of fragmented identity on textual examples only; however, despite his commitment to the concept of a core self, he found Julia Kristeva's theory of a "subject in process" compatible with the humane treatment of women suffering from multiple personality disorder. For me, and for my women students, writing personal criticism is a fluid process of *integrating*, not only texts, but also selves (or voices)—personal, social, political.

It was this need to integrate a range of texts and selves that prompted graduate student Sue Woods, after reading my personal essay in *The Intimate Critique*, to request an independent study in autobiographical reading and writing. Because Woods was a mature and intelligent student capable of understanding the risks of such writing, I agreed to mentor her. In the preface to her autobiographical thesis, Woods explains that she had never before "integrated" voices formerly used either in creative writing or literature courses—"the academic/authoritative and the personal/experiential" (29). Even though she found the writing process difficult—there was tension, she discovered, between narrative and analytical modes—she persisted through numerous revisions. Drawing on feminist and Bakhtinian theories of language, she analyzed her experiences of mothering and of sexual violation through their depiction in Edith Wharton's *The Mother's Recompense*. The results were remarkable: after presenting a portion of her thesis at a regional MLA conference, Woods submitted her essay to the editors of *Creating Safe Space: Violence and Women's Writing*, who chose to publish it, along with an essay of mine. Through informal conversations with Woods, women graduate students learned of this new form of academic writing, and they too requested independent studies. Since I was not yet convinced that this transgressive form of writing was safe for students, I continued my practice of teaching personal criticism only at student request.

My next request came from graduate student Angela Larson who, like Woods, wished to explore issues of sexual abuse and motherhood. In the preface to her thesis, Larson explains that she decided to write a personal-criticism after struggling with "intense emotional connections" to Joyce Carol Oates's female protagonist in *Marya, A Life*. She says, "I will never feel complete or whole until I can integrate my abused, private self with my public one" (81). To achieve this integration, or conjugation, Larson analyzed Oates's novel, along with her own experience, through the lenses of feminist and reader-response theories. She writes: "Reading Marya's story has opened my eyes to unknown parts of myself, while using Jean Kennard's bi-polar reading theory has allowed that self-discovery to have focus" (74). Larson regards the writing of her thesis as the first step, the finding of a "safe space" in which to tell her story, in a process of recovering from the trauma of sexual violation. Writing about the experience of abuse by a former boyfriend, Larson asserts, was the first step in saving her own life. Such a claim may seem exaggerated; however, according to psychologist Judith Lewis Herman, author of *Trauma and Recovery*, the act of writing or telling one's story may heal those who have been traumatized by warfare, torture or rape, but only if certain conditions are met: the trauma victim must tell her story, complete with accompanying affect, and in the presence of an attentive and affirming audience. I tried to serve as that attentive and affirming audience for Larson while, at the same time, expecting her to revise in order to achieve the highest quality writing.

As more and more graduate students asked to study personal criticism with me, I gradually acknowledged that, despite the risks, this form of writing was beneficial, not only for women, but also for men.[3] As a result, I began to offer graduate students the option of writing autobiographical academic essays. Creative writer Kim Munger was one of the first to choose this option. Having heard me read an excerpt from *Authoring a Life*,[4] Munger knew that I would welcome an autobiographical-critical approach in my graduate methods course, English 521, "Teaching Literature and the Literature Curriculum." In an abstract for her final paper in that course, Munger defines radical introspection in this way:

> This paper examines . . . the use of the technique of radical introspection to approach teaching Toni Morrison's novel, *Beloved*. It begins with an examination of what it means . . . to cross the boundaries of academic discourse in the disciplines and to take a more personal, introspective approach to reading literature and writing about it. It calls into question the traditional modes of academic writing . . . and suggests the use of radical introspection, a combination of autobiography and reader-response criticism, as a way to de-center the privileged, distanced academic voice and to illustrate how literary texts may take on personal significance for the students who read them.

Munger began her paper by illustrating her own autobiographical reading of *Beloved:* As "the descendent of border-state slaveholders in Chariton County,

Missouri," she announces, she will examine the similarities between the family stories she had been told and Morrison's represenation of the Garner family. Munger suggests that, before assigning the novel, teachers might also engage students in examining their own pasts: "Who are they descended from? Where did their ancestors come from, and when?" (25). She also recommends that teachers ask students to give examples of incidents of discrimination and ostracism in their own family histories, a process that for many becomes an interrogation of their own racial identities, including whiteness.

Following Munger's example, I have also begun offering undergraduates the opportunity to include personal experiences in critical essays. This process began when an undergraduate named Laura Armstrong Randolph came to my office to inform me that she, like two of the sisters in Smiley's novel *A Thousand Acres*, was also an incest survivor. Because of this personal background, she explained, she found it upsetting to discuss Smiley's novel. After revealing that I too was a survivor of father-daughter incest, I asked Laura if she would be willing to a tutorial to study incest narratives. Our goal would be to determine which narratives, in her view, were most honest. Since up to one quarter of the women students in any given classroom are survivors of some form of sexual violation, I explained, I wanted to learn how to be more effective at choosing and teaching such narratives. She agreed to a tutorial in which we would study contemporary novels about father-daughter incest written by both male and female authors. We also agreed that our purpose was not to engage in personal therapy but to participate in a larger feminist project: the work of cultural change.

The results, as I explain in *Authoring a Life*, were even more educational than I had anticipated. Since Randolph was also enrolled in my seminar, "The American Canon Debate," she began to speculate about the relationship between the canon and father-daughter incest. From Christine Froula she learned that, from a feminist perspective, the situation of literary daughters mirrors the relationship of daughters in the incestuous family. This insight prompted Randolph to write a paper arguing that

> the traditional English curriculum has a dramatic effect upon which incest narratives will be considered acceptable. It is highly unlikely, for example, that a narrative of such force as Allison's *Bastard Out of Carolina*, which depicts a working-class victim of paternal incest, will ever be included within the English curriculum. . . . However, the taboo of speaking about incest in the college classroom still exists; therefore, even though the incest narrative may be part of the plot, it is rarely the primary focus of classroom discussion. For example, *The Bluest Eye* is frequently taught; however, attending to other aspects of the narrative, such as its critique of racism, allows the instructor to dismiss, ignore, or make short shrift of the scene in which Cholly sexually violates his daughter, Pecola. (161-162)

In short, although some feminists teach father-daughter incest narratives, we are not always fully aware of how our own race and class identities influence our choices and our pedagogies. A white middle-class teacher might, for example, avoid a working class narrative such as *Bastard Out of Carolina* in favor of the middle-class narrative, *A Thousand Acres,* in which the act of sexual violation is not fully depicted. On the other hand, a middle-class white teacher might choose to teach *The Bluest Eye* so that, by focusing only on racism, it would be possible to avoid even discussing incest. Incest survivors are likely to experience such a pedagogy of avoidance as yet another betrayal by an authority figure.

Despite these and other pedagogical problems—including what now seem to be my own excessive fears about self-disclosure in the classroom—autobiographical reading, writing and teaching have been beneficial to my students and to me. The process of writing autobiographical scholarship has enabled me to externalize and analyze personal traumas, thereby overcoming most of their debilitating effects. In addition, to my surprise and pleasure, my autobiographical academic book, *Authoring a Life,* has attracted readers not only from outside my discipline—such as scholars in creative writing, education and family counselling—but also from outside the academy, such as survivors of childhood sexual abuse and the professionals who work with them in psychotherapy or in chemical dependency programs. This wider readership has given me a sense of community, a kinship that intensifies when survivors respond to *Authoring a Life* by telling me their own stories of trauma and recovery. Through these exchanges of stories, I have come to think of personal criticism as a new form of consciousness raising, a way of putting into practice the old but still important slogan: the personal is the political. Far from reifying the personal, this sharing of *reflections* about our personal experiences, allows us to participate in the ultimate goal of radical introspection: insight toward social action.

NOTES

1. For more on this topic, see Maher and Tetrault.
2. I began to feel the effects of this shadow during the summer of 1997. I was burned-out, joyless, and in constant physical pain from too many hours at my desk. This pain finally forced me to face my shadow-self: in the process of writing an essay called "Our Body Is Our School," I came to understand that, in my personal quest for academic excellence I had, like the university itself, come to overvalue the intellect at the expense of my body and spirit.

Fortunately, through radical introspection, I have come to understand the damaging effects of our current construction of schooling. This essay is forthcoming from Heinemann/Boynton in a collection called *Facing the Shadow in Education*, edited by Regina Foehr.

3. In 1998, a number of male students signed up for my graduate seminar, "The Use of the Personal in Scholarship," (a title borrowed from the *PMLA* forum on this topic in 1996). All responded positively to this transgressive mixed-genre form of writing.

4. On February 18, 1996, I read a portion of a personal essay "My Friend, Joyce Carol Oates," in the *word up!* series sponsored by Iowa State University's creative writing program. This essay, first published in *The Intimate Critique*, became a chapter in *Authoring a Life*.

4 LOSS, MEMORY, AND THE WORK OF LEARNING
Lessons from the Teaching Life of Anne Sexton

PAULA M.SALVIO

Depression is boring, I think,
and I would do better to make
some soup and light up the cave.

Anne Sexton

There seemed to be no standard for dealing with this gifted, ghosted woman.

Maxine Kumin

What is the secret that "oozes from the box?" Deleuze and Guattari suggest "the secret must sneak, insert, or introduce itself into the arena of public forms; it must pressure them and prod known subjects into action."

Thousand Plateaus

PROLOGUE

Anne Sexton was an inspiring, conscientious teacher, a fact that often goes noticed. In addition to her teaching appointment at Boston University, Sexton taught poetry at Mclean Psychiatric Hospital, Colgate University, Oberlin College and Wayland High School in Wayland, Massachusetts. Her collaboration with Herbert Kohl and the Teachers and Writers Collaborative in the 1960s made substantive contributions to revitalizing English education, in part by initiating teaching partnerships among writers, artists and teachers. Sexton is rarely thought of as a dedicated teacher, nor is she immediately associated with the significant contributions she made to Teachers and Writers. Rather, she is most often remembered for her struggles with alcohol and addiction to pills, a mental illness that defied cure, or as a "confessional poet," a category that annoyed and offended her.

When asked about her status as a confessional poet, Sexton explained that she preferred to describe herself as a "storyteller. " Her skill at handling plots and character is evident in the subjects she addressed in her poetry—madness, spirituality, addiction, adultery, death, and the myths encrypted in what she refers to as the gothic New England family romance. Among the most striking trademarks of Sexton's poetry is a cast of personae who expose and question the mass produced images of middle-class women in post World War II America. Typically, Sexton's poetic forays terminate in uncanny images where female bodies are fragmented—a violent breaking heart, a splintered hip, a valley of bones. Sexton replaces images of the content, suburban housewife with "full helpings," as Alicia Ostriker notes, "of her breasts, her uterus, her abortion, her 'tiny jail' of a vagina, her love life, her mother's and daughters' breasts, everyone's operations, the act of eating . . . even the trauma of her childhood enemas" (11, 1982). Each of these images possess a peculiar power that direct her readers away from sentimental notions of home as a place of plenitude. Throughout Sexton's poetry, bodies move toward the edges of life, death, old age, the ends of marriages, childhoods, sanity and love. Kitchens become sites of family constraints and family bonds, spaces where, despite most peoples' preference to avert such issues, the poet inquires into psychic lability and the fallibility of the family.

Yet, despite the substantial collection of lecture notes, correspondences with students and journals that Anne Sexton left behind, the remains of her teaching life have rarely been addressed. In this chapter, I situate Sexton's life as a teacher in the center of what feminist philosophers address as some of the key questions and problems in feminist pedagogy: the problem of navigating the appropriate distance between teachers and students, the relationship between emotional life and knowledge, and the difficult questions surrounding identification and separation in the classroom. This chapter does not offer a biographical portrait of Sexton, rather it literally performs a method of writing auto/biographically in which Sexton functions as an interlocutor or shadowgraph, indirectly illuminating gender, sexual and cultural sediments that influence our conscious and unconscious interests, our scholarship and our teaching. I draw on Sexton's pedagogical documents to test the limits of how much our students need to know about us, what the role of transference and counter-transference plays in our teaching, and what it means for our students to write auto/biographically, beyond the usual story-telling or narration of experience.[1]

Among the key documents that I focus on are the lecture notes Sexton wrote as the Crawshaw Chair in Literature while teaching at Colgate University in 1972. These notes, housed in the Harry Ransom Humanities Research Center at the University of Texas, Austin, suggest that Sexton developed innovative approaches to teaching writing that were performative in structure and drew on one of the privileged concepts in psychoanalysis, that it is the love object that teaches.[2] While Sexton's lecture notes may at first appear as a series of narcissistic acts in which she consistently violates the proper distance between herself and her students, her pedagogy in fact suggests possible ways for educators to compose spaces for learning and teaching that address the half-spoken losses that society and culture fail to address. Sexton did not ask her students simply to listen to her "confessions," nor did she ask them to directly site their losses or "self-disclose" in the seminar room. Rather, she uses a performative pedagogy to indirectly route her students through figures of others so they could more fully apprehend themselves in relation to history and literature. A close reading of Sexton's teaching documents demonstrate that we do not simply come to know ourselves directly, by writing our life, rather we must take indirect routes through the other, through history, literature, and theory, to represent our lives. Through these indirect writing and reading practices we can more fully rethink and modify personal and social expectations. Such indirect routes bring the auto/biographical I to form in ways that can more fully contain the histories and the biographies of those before us, drawing our lives, to paraphrase Virginia Woolf, from the lives of the unknown who were our forebears. The purpose of this approach to auto/biography is not to pass on tradition, but to break its hold over us, and to intervene, as Anne Sexton so boldly did as both poet and teacher, in the transmission of canonic culture.

The losses and ambivalence that Sexton carried into her teaching life manifest themselves in her performative approach to teaching writing and these performances allegorize losses that are deemed ungrievable within our culture. As a young mother, Sexton not only lost her children to the anguish of mental illness, but she writes of abortion and the loss of physical health to cancer, drug and alcohol addiction. Sexton often claimed that her poetry did not replicate her life, but staged it—that it was a public performance of the most prevalent cultural expectations of femininity in post World War II America. The losses that accrue in Sexton's poetry, losses that were not only ungrievable at the time, but often remained unnamable, constituted a part of the prescribed cultural roles for women and children. These losses figure into Sexton's melancholic teaching. In this chapter, I conceptualize melancholia as a lyric lament through which a person protests our culture's narrow prohibitions on who can rightfully grieve and which losses are worthy of recognition.

The lyric turn Sexton makes toward themes of loss is painful insofar as she implicitly attests to the social and psychic threat of contemporary diseases such as AIDS and cancer. Her pedagogy also brings to consciousness what Melissa Zeiger describes as a cultural melancholia that resonates through the end of a century that has repeatedly witnessed unimaginable loss of life, from World War I through the Holocaust and Hiroshima to Cambodia and Bosnia. (see Zeiger's Beyond Consolation). The attempt to represent, in writing or otherwise, memories that we inherit via these encrypted losses can be traumatic, therefore raising questions about the propriety of different kinds of cultural remembrance. Central to this debate has been the question of whether the public exposure of pain and loss is either morally necessary or politically effective. For curriculum studies, a series of questions emerge: In our interactions with the past, what does curriculum remember, repress, or encrypt? How does one enter into an exchange with the past that can negotiate trauma, and at the same time locate the historical specificity of our students?

Drawing on the work of Judith Butler, I argue that melancholia can be a rich resource for teaching and scholarship; it holds nascent political texts which students and teachers can draw upon to re-establish the lines that demarcate psychic and social life, and in turn re-negotiate the personal, social and political prohibitions on grieving. By giving dramatic language to ambivalence and loss, Sexton demonstrates how pedagogy can be used to ritualize melancholy, creating an occasion for teaching and learning that can open texts to meanings otherwise foreclosed upon.

THE ARCHIVAL SITE

Long before her death, Anne Sexton meticulously prepared her manuscripts and letters for the archives so that her work could be reborn into historical memory. She often hoped aloud that her poetry would endure to offer comfort and insight to those who, like her, suffered with the unrelenting pain that dominates people who are afflicted with mental illness and addictions. The archive of Anne Sexton, like the body of Sexton herself, exceeds the limits of a conventional teaching life; it generates a particular form of melancholy that is associated with a life falling apart, a terminal, unrelenting, inexplicable mental illness that resulted in Sexton ending her life by carbon monoxide poisoning on Friday, October 4, 1974, at the age of 46. After returning home from lunch with her close friend, Maxine Kumin, she climbed into the driver's seat of the old red Cougar she bought in 1967, the year she started teaching, and turned on the ignition (Middlebrook, 1991, 397).

It is July of 1994. I am working in the archives at the Harry Ransom Research Humanities Center at the University of Texas, shuffling through some folders that contain correspondences Sexton exchanged with her students. I'm hungry, restless and feeling stiff from sitting all day, so I decide to take a walk. Before I leave, I randomly pull a letter from the file in front of me, skimming through it, planning to return to it later in the day. I note that the letter was written by Chris Leverich, an English major at Colgate University during the spring of 1972, and that the letter is in fact a substitute for the final assignment—an imagined interview with Anne Sexton. In his letter, Leverich details a trail of memories, lost expectations, and emotions that he has kept to himself throughout the term. "In a way, I've fallen in love with you," he writes:

> Of course, it's a fantasy. I know that. Yet, there is something, a force, a charm that is ever powerful and ever attractive to me. So many times I've wanted to be alone with you, to talk to you, to break the formalities of student and teacher.... I guess that's a fair summation of my first feelings toward you: an initial sexual attraction gradually honed into a mixture of respect and admiration. As the semester went on and I got more and more into your poetry whole new horizons opened up before me. I knew I was reading your life and what it was to you. (HRRHC)

Leverich goes on to capture, with tremendous exactitude, the sense of loss he felt for never having really gotten to know Anne Sexton, noting that the end of the term would mark the last time he would hear her voice.

> I sort of resigned myself to never knowing you, even after that little spark flared up in me when you called my name—"Chris". But it seemed like only a reflex action after Bruce said it. Still, I wanted it to roll around over your tongue. I wanted you to say it again in your head and remember it. I couldn't stand that you wouldn't even remember my name someday. Like you said in class about John Holmes: "If you leave someone without having them love you, then you lose them." I knew we would leave that way and I would lose. (HRRHC)

The explicitly sexual content of this letter can be read as an Oedipal narrative—a son's longing for his mother—and contains images of a desire to be devoured (even if in name only). Leverich goes on to fantasize about driving to Radcliffe to meet Sexton's daughter, Linda, where they would talk about philosophy. "But I didn't go. I didn't go because I knew I wouldn't see what I wanted. I wouldn't see a miniature you ... I knew I never wanted Lolita, but Jocasta" (HRRHC). Leverich's desire to know Sexton is, as he notes, a fantasy that I could not help but worry about. On the one hand, I worried about her. To what extent were the images in Leverich's letter symptoms of his desire to swallow his teacher up, a violent fantasy through which to threaten his teacher's identity and claim her for his very own? On the other hand, I worried about Leverich. To what extent did Sexton's memories of sexual distress and loss figure into her pedagogy at this time, mixing in with this student's past, a past wrought with pain and loss that he may very well have been working hard to forget? I began to think about how the encrypted memories we hold of violence, lost ideals, and betrayals are acted out through pedagogy, memories that appear absent but take up an uncanny presence in our classrooms.

Teaching and learning inevitably invoke ghosts from the past, family dramas, and failed romances. Nested in each word Leverich writes, in each scriptural relic, is a personal past that was awakened as he sat in class working with Sexton's poetry, among her poems "The Truth the Dead Know," "Her Kind," "Somewhere in Africa," "The Fortress," "Said The Poet to the Analyst." As a student in this class, Leverich took part in classroom assignments that were performative in structure. "Give me a persona," Sexton asked her students. "Could you write with your mother's voice about her marriage, about her son . . . a woman in church, what is she thinking?" (HRRHC). Leverich writes of the sudden death of his own father when he was eight years old, and his admitted proclivity to "look for a mother and father . . . perhaps that's what I see in you; a woman who is both dominant and passive, at once bold and timid, and even impatient yet understanding."

As I read this letter, I felt as if Leverich had isolated the ache of loss because it was so deeply tied to difficult realities, emotions, and ideas. Such acts of isolation not only numb pain, but they hold it in reserve, blocking it from circulating in our imagination, emotions, initiatives and contacts with other people. The confinement of an unbearable reality to an inaccessible region of the psyche is what Maria Torok refers to as "incorporation" or "preservative repression." Drawing on clinical observations made by Freud and Karl Abraham in 1922 of the increased sexual activity of people who experienced a death in the family, Torok proposes a new category of psychology—the illness of mourning. She argues that the pain associated with loss is not directly tied to having lost a loved one, but rather this pain is associated with the secret that the loss occasions, a secret that she refers to as the "psychic tomb." Torok understood the flow of sexual desire in the face of death as the final, climactic outpouring of love for the departed. Complications ensue, however, when the bereaved is a parent, grandparent, sibling or other "nonsexual associate," because in such cases, sexual feelings and outbursts are personally and socially unacceptable to the mourner; the involuntary effusion of feeling constitutes an event that the mourner cannot make sense of with respect to her or his somber feelings of loss and bereavement. In these instances the affect experienced in the face of death must be kept under wraps, thereby transforming this final outpouring of love into an intrapsychic secret. The mourner sets up a secret enclave, what Torok refers to as a crypt, for the departed love-object, precisely because the survivor is being deluded by society and culture into behaving as if no trauma or loss had occurred.[3] Or, to put this another way, the departed returns to haunt the living because they have not been granted a proper burial. In Torok's view, the shameful, undisclosed suffering of the dead returns to their descendents and unsuspected, the dead continue to lead a devastating psychic half-life in them.

Torok's work emphasizes the ways in which the inherited fears, anxieties and hindered self-fashionings that were unresolved by our decendents are carried into succeeding generations and take occupancy in our lives as memories that are neither fully evident nor fully concealed. This emphasis calls attention to the history of psychic structures, and how psychic traumas and secrets can be inherited rather than strictly tied to individual experience. The concept of the phantom offers us another route into Leverich's letter, a route that brings us beyond reading this document as a letter written by an individual student, to postulating that encrypted in this love letter, this failed assignment, are inherited, secret, psychic substances of his ancestor's lives and that these substances can take up an uncanny presence in the classroom. Leverich's love letter might be more fully understood as an indirect, circuitous outpouring of love, not literally for Sexton, as he told me years later in an interview, but for a beloved aunt who he had lost to drug and alcohol abuse, a woman whose presence he felt in the poetry and teachings of Anne Sexton. The memory traces in Leverich's writing provoke an unsettling disruption in this class, a disruption that was provoked not simply by Sexton's presence, but by the presence of others who are neither fully remembered nor forgotten, neither fully recognized nor ignored (166 in Torok).

"Memory is a sense of the other," writes Michel De Certeau; memories "call out to the other who is absent; they are produced only in a place that does not belong to it,"

> hence [memory] develops along with relationships. . . . It responds more than it records . . . memory leaves its mark like a kind of overlay on a body that has always already been altered without knowing it. This originary and secret writing "emerges" little by little, in the very spots where memory is touched. Memory is played by circumstances, just as a piano is played by a musician and music emerges from it when its keys are touched by the hands. Memory responds more than it records, up to the moment when, losing its mobile fragility and becoming incapable of new alterations, it can only repeat its initial responses (De Certeau, 1984, 86-88).

De Certeau portrays memory as an "anti-museum," that floats and refuses to be fixed in time or space. Pedagogy directs its attention toward remembering and forgetting at every turn; the question that remains is whom do we choose to remember in our classrooms and whom do we fail to address? How do we respond to the memories that are too terrible to disclose? I want to use De Certeau's notion of memory as an 'anti museum' to emphasize the project of remembering implicit in the work of Abraham and Torok. Their concept of the psychic crypt suggests a project of remembering the dead and restoring to memory forgotten and erased persons that harbor secrets and fears that continue to live a half-life in succeeding generations. On one level, the individual example of Leverich depicts how a seminar space might become a site of private mourning. Leverich's memories of loss appear to circulate and flow through his readings of Sexton's poetry, thereby infusing the pedagogical event with the specificity of his own emotions, history, and desires. We might read Leverich's letter as an attempt to articulate strains of feeling that he associated with intergenerational secrets that were unmoored by the poetry of Sexton. The pedagogical project lies in creating occasions, through writing, talking and other acts of symbolization, for Leverich to refine an attachment to the half-spoken losses haunting his personal past and to coordinate these losses with the larger social field. This work is particularly difficult, however, when the losses a person suffers with are not recognized as legitimate and thus not granted public space for articulation.

The melancholic temperament that Torok sought to understand is marked by a loss of address that gives way to an unbounded state in which a person appears to abandon her position as a subject, for she has no addressable other, that is to say, there is no one to listen to her plaints, no one who recognizes her grievances as worthy of attention. In many ways, melancholy bears out the 'crisis of representation' that Simon Watney and Paula Treichler have ascribed to the AIDS crisis. Both Watney and Treichler speak of the human devastation incurred by the AIDS epidemic, as well as the rage at injustice that it demands. In her study of AIDS and breast cancer elegies, Zeiger points out that the work of Watney and Treichler emphasizes the profound difficulty of "producing an adequate discursive response to something as ideologically dense and resiliently irrational as AIDS discourse has been. Because hatred of people with illnesses, and of gay men and women, is naturalized at so many levels, discursive refiguration has had to take place in moral, emotional, sexual, metaphysical, aesthetic, and political terms" (Zeiger 21). If a crisis cannot be named or represented, then how can it be taught? If the only modes of representation available to us as teachers function either to sensationalize and thus diminish human suffering on the one hand, or to disassociate people from daily experience and therefore from the human on the other, then we slip into a pedagogical narrative that disassociates itself from the life of feeling and the needs, desires and vulnerabilities of the body. Melancholia inevitably poses questions about the difficulties of representation and the sense of despair that can be associated with establishing modes of address when what people long to write about can place them in jeopardy, compromise their safety, or position them as a contaminant among their classmates. Nested in these questions are other questions about memory, remembrance and separation—not simply the final separation between the dead and the living, but also a wide range of disconnections between persons who are "well" and "sick", emotionally stable and unstable, intellectually worthy and unworthy, excessive and productive. What degrees of distance do we keep between the living and the dead? How do we remember those we have loved and lost?

Many of the poems Sexton wrote and taught in her classes contain themes of loss and mourning and attest to the psychic and social threat of cancer, early sexual distress, addictions and madness. Maxine Kumin remembers Anne Sexton in her early years as a poet, working strictly with traditional forms, "believing," writes Kumin, in the value of their rigor as a forcing agent, believing that "the hardest truths would come right if they were hammered to fit " a stanzaic pattern, a rhyme scheme, a prevailing meter ("Reflections" in Anne Sexton, The Artist and her Critics, 1978, p. 104). Sexton often spoke of writing poetry as a form of psychoanalysis that could create coherence out of the disjunctive, fragmented experiences of psychic lability that came to take possession of her. For a time, the dramatic situations Sexton rendered in her poetry functioned as an effective methodology for inquiring into memory and grief. In "Briar Rose", a poem from her 1971 collection, Transformations, she renders a searing representation of sexual violence:

>Each night I am nailed into place
>and I forget who I am.
>Daddy?
>That's another kind of prison.
>It's not the prince at all,
>but my father
>drunkenly bent over my bed,
>circling the abyss like a shark,
>my father thick upon me
>like some jellyfish.

Here, Sexton uses vivid images to convey how sexual assault functions to eradicate identity, "I forget who I am," resulting in a form of amnesia that effectively takes a victim's life, "nailing her in place", imprisoning her, stripping her of will and agency. Throughout the time Sexton wrote poetry—from 1957 when, at the suggestion of her psychiatrist, she enrolled in a poetry workshop taught by John Holmes at the Boston Center for Adult Education, to the time of her death in 1974—Sexton used writing to "make a new reality and become whole . . . When writing," Sexton explained, "it is like lying on the analyst's couch, reenacting a private terror, and the creative mind is the analyst who gives pattern and meaning to what the persona sees as only incoherent experience" (quoted in Middlebrook, 1991, 64). While teaching at Colgate University during the spring of 1972, Sexton described the tight lyric form as a cage in which a writer could put wild animals in, a means through which to "make a logic out of suffering . . . One must make a logic out of suffering or one is mad." She asserted, "All writing of poems is sanity, because one makes a reality, a sane world, out of insane happenings" (HRRHC).

Yet the memories of loss that Leverich inscribes in his letter and Sexton in her poetry did not simply surface because they willed them to, just as I cannot simply summon up my own memories and set them in the syntax of an essay. Women, marginalized people, and those who have endured trauma cannot write from memory, argues Shoshana Felman, for our auto/biographies are comprised of precisely what our memories cannot contain, or hold together as a whole, although our writing inadvertently inscribes it. While the historical conditions that constituted trauma for a white middle-class woman such as Sexton are not equatable with the historical conditions of people who have endured generations of colonization, in both cases the structure of trauma works to obliterate an addressable other. Felman finds that memories can only surface and circulate vis à vis a process through which we access our stories indirectly—by conjugating literature, theory, and autobiography through reading, writing, and, I will add, history and performance, and in turn reading into the texts of culture our difference(s) as missing, absent, lost.[4] This approach to writing, reading, and teaching auto/biography requires that we are united with the lives of others, not by a synthetic understanding, but whereby one person's concerns are meaningful to another and these concerns return to us an unexpected revelation, desire, or insight in our own life.[5] The letter written by Leverich was just one artifact that returned an unexpected insight. As I re-read his letter, I remembered a scene earlier that term, long before I had left to make the trip to Austin, Texas, a scene that reminded me that Sexton was indeed perceived by many as a teacher perpetually in error.

THE RETURN OF AN INSIGHT

After I had received the news that I was awarded funding from the University of New Hampshire to travel to the archives, one of my colleagues came up to me in the hallway. He made it quite clear that he thought the university was wasting its money on this project. "My wife wondered," he told me with a laugh, "why you would want to study someone who was not only crazy, but who slept with her students? And what has this project got to do with teaching and teacher education anyway?"

At that moment, I became acutely conscious of how precarious Sexton's status as a teacher would be. It is one thing to write about mental illness and loss as a poet, but to teach in the throws of profound melancholia, anxiety, and alcoholism is quite another. It became evident that the remains of Sexton's teaching life were quite troubling, for the images that surfaced when I proposed that her teaching life be remembered, that we might even be instructed by her pedagogy, were those of a woman in ruins, untrustworthy, and strange. The ghost of Sexton, as teacher, exists at the border between convention, rationality, and madness. As I approached Sexton's life as a teacher, I felt myself writing and teaching from a vulnerable position. I began to loosen my grip on the sense of command and authority I brought to the archive. In retrospect, I remember this encounter in the hallway because, as much as I wanted to deny it, my colleague's questions were questions I had harbored all along. The letter written by Chris Leverich was but one relic that provoked my own anxieties to surface, anxieties that I had managed, up until now, to ignore.

I have since learned that much of what remains of Sexton's teaching life represents excessive sexual violence, anxieties, fears, and desires to remember and be remembered, all of which will not remain repressed. To consider bringing these excesses into the realm of education is to threaten the meticulous work that is being done by mainstream culture: (1) to solidify normative notions of what it means to be a good teacher and a good student, (2) to possess emotional stability, and (3) to determine which bodies and bodies of knowledge are most worthy. Sexton is the symptom that signals the (failed) repression of the infectious, melancholic teacher; she is the non-normative teacher who is believed by many to lack academic taste and who, as my colleague demonstrates, can function as a foil for educators to declare themselves "dissimilar" to her excessive, tormented pedagogy. After all, educators worth their salt are prudent and straightforward.

AN AUTOBIOGRAPHICAL FRAGMENT

Anne Sexton appears as an uncanny interlocutor through whom I have begun to approach unresolvable questions about memory, knowledge, and the body, questions that were fused into my teaching life from the very start. I began to teach in 1981, the year my father began to suffer with esophageal cancer, a disease that is aggressive and for which there was very little curative treatment. Esophageal cancer does not strike out randomly, rather it is selective, primarily afflicting people who are addicted to alcohol. One morning, early in December, after my father had just returned home from a month-long stay in the hospital, I sat at the kitchen table with him, not knowing what to say, yet knowing I had to say something, for he had arrived, we were told, at the limit of his life. And what was left for him to do he had to do alone. "Does it terrify you to know you will die soon?" I asked him quietly. "Alone into the alone," he quoted from C. S. Lewis. He said it felt like that. And, how improbable that it should be otherwise. Long before my father had died, he felt cut off from us, and it was not simply the certainty of his death that made this so. Nor was it the fact that as a doctor, he knew all too well what the months ahead would hold, his biggest fear being that he would suffocate to death.

My father suffered with severe melancholia that took hold of him at unexpected times, thrusting him into painful silence, isolation, and despair. He drank, I think, to ease an unrelenting anguish that he never spoke of but that intruded on him throughout his life. I could tell you that like many men growing up during the depression and World War II, my father learned to believe that drinking was a part of being a man. I could tell you that like many men of his generation, drinking was tied to rituals that bound people in rites of celebration, mourning, friendship, romance, and religion. But such a narrative departure into cultural history would only serve as a defense against the pain, loss, and sense of betrayal that came to feel so familiar to me as a child. For me, liquor was never endowed with romantic or sacred properties. Rather, in my mind, it was nothing less than a lethal substance my father used to commit a slow suicide.

How could a devoted doctor knowingly and most deliberately disease himself? How can a person who excessively diseases himself so skillfully offer others a cure? I was left with unresolvable questions that I could not put to rest, and for which I could find no meaningful allegorical equivalents or redemptive possibilities. The losses that I accrued through my father's life and death—a sense of abandonment, betrayal, a severed attachment—are among the encrypted details that seep through my pedagogy and my scholarship.

My father's life and death taught me to be skeptical of knowledge. Not only are skeptics determined to avoid confusion, but they are also fond of delay and doubt. They harbor suspicions about forming attachments to concepts, persons, and beliefs. Perhaps this is why the null hypothesis always intrigued me—it offers a method through which to claim an attachment and then delay commitment through methods of deliberate disavowal. The art and science of a democratic education offered me processes through which I could put my skeptical temperment to use. The scientific method of John Dewey subordinates transmitting the past to creating a future that is distinct from the past (see Dewey, 1984). This method of inquiry is described by Horace M. Kallen as one that 'makes precept a function of practice, exalts variation over repetition, encourages the free co-operation of differences to displace the regimented reproduction of identicals, prefers the doubt, the enquiry, the experiment of competitive cooperation of the sciences to the obedient and unquestioning rehearsals of dogmatic faith' (360 in Hook)—all problems that we struggled with in our Catholic household. "One can never know," my father's father would say as he read the newspaper in the evening, sitting on the terrace, drinking a glass of wine.

But the truth is that the feelings of skepticism that flooded our home were more akin to a kind of wholesale mood of exaggerated distrust and an unexpressed yearning not to repeat the past than they were to the disciplined forms of scientific inquiry that my father found so compelling. I could write a narrative history of my family's skepticism for you. I could write about the ambivalence my paternal grandfather felt about educating his children—skeptical as he was of the educational value of academic knowledge, both wanting and not wanting his children to secure academic degrees, feeling torn, possessing, despite his lack of formal education, an enormous appetite for the lyricism of Dante, Leopardi, Puccini. I could go on to link my family's proclivities to doubt our lovers and to scrutinize our politics, religious faith and one another to philosophical traditions that scrutinize the sanctities of faith and hope.

And I could render scenes of teaching where skepticism seeped into my classroom, touching my curriculum entirely. But such a move, once again, would only serve as a defense against a more profound lesson my father handed down to me, for the practice of skepticism was not the most memorable lesson I inherited. From my father, I learned that knowledge and the body are often at war and, despite our apparent mastery of knowledge, our bodies too often remain vulnerable. In seeking knowledge, we are really seeking insight into what to do with our bodies, for teaching and scholarship are inevitably about decisions of the flesh.

In looking back, I learned to recognize that in the throws of illness, loss, or during a crisis in meaning, there are prohibitions placed on the expression of weakness, fear, and pain. But perhaps more importantly, I have come to understand that the shameful, undisclosed suffering of the dead, suffering that could not be expressed, returns to their descendents and unsuspected, this suffering continues to lead a painful half-life in them. Thus, the undisclosed suffering of my father, made manifest in his acute melancholia, lives on, haunting me in unsuspected ways, slipping into my pedagogy uninvited, compromising my capacity to refine my attachments to memory and history. From this point of view, a dividing line no longer falls between my father's life and death. His life and death can flow together, repeating and reinforcing each other vis à vis my teaching life.

In the narrative account I offer, I turn to teaching as a consolation for my loss, and this turn exacts a serious price. Not only do I position myself as a vulnerable daughter who inherits a scholarly and pedagogic project from her father, but by using pedagogy as a consolation for loss I displace my sense of abandonment, betrayal, and outrage rather than working through it.[6] My loss registers in strikingly apparent ways. For example, in the books that I choose to read with my students in courses I teach in curriculum studies, literacy, and

English education. Among them, *Missing May* by Cynthia Rylant, *Krik? Krak!* by Edwidge Danticat, *My Brother* by Jamaica Kincaid, *Fugitive Pieces* by Anne Michaels. Each of these stories portrays profound loss, from the death of a beloved aunt and a brother, to the horrific loss of life endured by the people of Haiti, to the brutalities of World War II. These books function like urns, holding loss, keeping it in place. As my students and I read *Krik? Krak!* events that we have failed to learn about claim a presence in the room, a presence that demands that we speak beyond our means. Yet, to what extent do we use this book to console ourselves after learning of the U.S. involvement in Haiti and the horror of living under the brutal threats of the Tonton Macoutes? Do the routes that we take through Danticat's book only function to offer my students a narrative adjustment to loss, a consoling sign that enables each of us to adjust to the injustices that Danticat writes about? Do these consoling signs in turn distract us from properly re-membering the dead? The historical figures in these stories are not easily quieted by the official discourses of momuments and memorials. In her analysis of *Shot in the Heart,* the account by Mikal Gilmore of his family history and the execution of his brother, Gary Gilmore, Leigh Gilmore emphasizes that "trauma causes history to erupt from its manageable confines. In this context, the dead are no longer persons who lived in the past, but angry, bitter, and mournful ghosts. The dead in this construction refuse to do the work of history, which is to stay buried, in effect, to 'be' the past, and to maintain the rationality of time as past-present-future. . . . The dead return because they were not properly buried" (5). To address trauma in the classroom raises several questions posed by Gilmore, including how the dead will permit and be permitted by the living to live on. Such questions invariably pose rhetorical challenges that are directly tied to melancholia, for melancholia is brought about by a 'failed mourning,' a failure that torments the melancholic by stealing speech because the losses that she has endured are not deemed grievable by our culture, and therefore they cannot be spoken aloud.

In *The Psychic Life of Power,* Judith Butler elaborates on the ways in which melancholia works as a lyric lament to protest our culture's narrow prohibitions on who can rightfully grieve, and which losses are worthy of attention. Following Butler, I want to argue that melancholy can be a rich resource for teaching and scholarship, for it holds nascent political texts which students and teachers can draw on to redraw the lines that demarcate their own psychic and social life, and, in turn, renegotiate the personal, social, and political prohibitions on grieving. The pedagogy of Anne Sexton offers us insight into how poetry and writing can be used to renegotiate these prohibitions, particularly the lecture notes she wrote while teaching at Colgate University during the spring term of 1972. These lecture notes provide a more complex way of putting melancholia to productive use in the classroom, offering us insight into the ways in which we might use poetry, performance, writing, and reading for learning about the transitions necessary to life, grieving being one among many of the vital transitions we can work through.[7]

THE MELANCHOLIC PEDAGOGY OF ANNE SEXTON

Throughout Sexton's pedagogic documents are moments in which she directs her students' attention to social issues pertaining to the suffering, violated entity Elaine Scarry has termed "the body in pain."[8] The bodies in Sexton's poetry are most often women's bodies—one freshly scarred from a hysterectomy, a dying woman who is incontinent, a young girl giving up her baby, a daughter refusing to grieve—who speak to the reader through dramatic speech. While much of the subject matter for Sexton's poetry came directly from her own life and times, she also transcended these biographical details, shaping them into art forms that spoke to a vast audience about the silent anguish felt in many post World War II households, testifying, in other words, to the discontent felt in the bourgeois American family.

When writing poetry with her students, Sexton asked them to use the force of dramatic consciousness to engage in composition processes that demanded what Sexton described as a "total immersion of you into the subject." (HRRHC). In her poems, as she tells her students, we have the poet as actor:

> Wearing different faces; the young girl running from her lover ... the unknown girl giving her baby up so intensely, so close to the bone ... we have the seamstress bitter and gnarled over her sewing machine, spitting bile onto the zippers and we have the young lovers, the young girl specifically with her adulterous moment trying to marry for a moment at least some happiness (HRRHC).

The acts of total immersion that Sexton engaged her students in often began with the invitation to "write a short poem, a character sketch using a persona ... become that person, put on that mask." The methods of dramatic introspection and incorporation that Sexton used to write poetry and to teach writing are strikingly akin to those used by actors as they work to build their characters. Nowhere are these methodologies more evident than in the notes she wrote for a course she taught as the Crawshaw Chair in Literature at Colgate University. The Crawshaw Chair required a long, weekly commute from Sexton's home in Weston, Massachusetts, to Hamilton, New York. Sexton was required to teach two days of classes back-to-back, a writing workshop for about ten students in the evening, as well as a lecture course on poetry in the afternoon. During the time Sexton commuted from Weston to Colgate, she often complained of feeling anxious to the point of nausea. Much of Sexton's teaching was accompanied by stage fright and uncertainty, and there were many bad days and fears of failure.

Leverich describes Sexton as a shy, sensitive person who, on certain days, would sit at her desk in class, chain-smoking cigarettes, croaking out words between drinks of water. She seemed to him a desperately lonely creature. At the same time, there was a force, a charm, that was ever-powerful about her. She was both bold and timid, dominant and passive, even impatient, yet understanding (HRRHC).

In a conversation I had with the chair of the Department of English at Colgate, Bruce Berlind, he recalled the difficult weekly routine of picking Sexton up at the airport in Syracuse, driving back to Hamilton, New York (frequently singing songs from the 40s), and, the next day, driving back to the airport where she boarded a small plane for Boston. They co-taught the poetry workshop, and Sexton taught the lecture course alone. The lecture course, entitled "Anne on Anne," co-designed with Berlind, was composed of a series of eleven lectures for a small group of English majors. Berlind describes this course as a "course in herself."

> Its structure was simply linear, beginning with Bedlam and coming up-to-date. The lecture component of the classes was minimal. Mostly the classes were discussion sessions based on the students' readings of her books, copies of Anne's drafts of many poems, and copies of various interviews and reviews of her work. The "first-person presence" was, of course, at the center—although Anne often claimed that the I in poems dealing with her affairs was a fiction (Personal correspondence, 1996).

The aim of this course was to engage students imaginatively with the writing life of Anne Sexton by studying and then performing the interpretive methods she used to write poetry. Gathered together in Lawrence Hall, room 320, students would sometimes inhabit the poetic form of a Sexton poem and then extend it, at times changing the content, but miming the metrics. Sexton openly invited her students to study along with her what she referred to as the tricks, flaws, and false starts that a poem undergoes before it reaches its final, published form. Throughout her lecture notes are meditations on poetry, mini-lectures, and classroom assignments that suggest that Sexton was not satisfied with having her students talk about poetry. Rather, she demanded that her students inhabit poetic forms and take on personae. In Lecture I of the Crawshaw series Sexton read the following statement by one of her critics: "Anne Sexton's poems, for example, create largely the world of her persona, the I of the poems, which undergoes a continuing development and is clearly related intimately and painfully to the poet's autobiography." She, in turn, responded to this statement by stating that

I would like for a moment to disagree. It is true that I am an autobiographical poet most of the time, or at least so I lead my readers to believe. However, many times I use the personal when I am applying a mask to my face, somewhat like a young man applying the face of an aging clown. Picture me at my dressing table for a moment putting on the years. All those nights, all those cups of coffee . . . all those shots of bourbon at 2 a.m . . . all this applied like a rubber mask that the robber wears (HRHRC).

Like Sexton's composing processes, theories of melancholy evoke acts of incorporation, skin, and the personal and cultural objects we endow with meaning. In ways akin to a method actor, the melancholic incorporates the beloved; she takes them in as idealized, demonized, in some cases, exoticized, others. In his 1917 essay, "Mourning and Melancholia," Freud argues that when a person has lost someone he/she loved, the ego incorporates aspects of the lost other into its very structures, thereby "sustaining" the life of the bereaved through acts of imitation. "By taking flight in the ego," writes Freud, "love escapes annihilation." Yet this escape from annihilation comes at great cost, for the incorporative strategies used by the melancholic function to disavow the loss and to deepen the grief.

These incorporative strategies are an effective means through which to remake the ego into the person who has been lost. It is in this sense that the melancholic bears a resemblance to a method actor, for her body becomes a double body, skilled at reproducing the gestures and being of some other person, a lost love, a charismatic leader, the ethos of a nation (see Phelan, 1993, 172). The language that Constantin Stanislavski used with his actors during rehearsals is replete with the language of incorporation and is useful for understanding the strategies used by the melancholic. In *Building A Character*, Stanislavski documents a young actor's discussion of the process he used to create the character of a man who possessed distinctly different characteristics than himself. He writes:

[A]s soon as I was in this other man's skin, my attitude towards you (Stanislavski) underwent a radical change. . . . I enjoyed looking you full in the face in a brazen way and at the same time felt I had the right to do it without fear. Yet do you believe I could have done this in my own person? Never under any circumstances! In that other person's skin I went as far as I liked, and if I dared do that face to face with you I should have no compunction in treating the audience across the footlights in the same way. (p. 27–8).

The capacity to cross the boundaries of skin into the character of another, and to do so with intention, caution, consistency, and to keep within the boundaries of the character, the play, or the "given circumstances" is work the actor, unlike the melancholic, is adept at. The melancholic does not exert agency over her desire to transpose the ego of the bereaved into her own. And while both the actor and the melancholic may be skilled at transposition and incorporation, the actor retains these incorporative strategies as techniques, while for the melancholic these strategies serve to chisel away at the ego, resulting in a profound sense of ego loss.

Jacques Hassoun characterizes the melancholic as the eternally ravished one, the passive victim, who is depleted of drives and thus incapable of investing anything in the social world, sinking deeper and deeper into a desperate, endless recitation of complaints that are directed at unnamable, ungrievable losses. About social and institutional life, writes Hassoun:

> Confronted with the enigma that the Other's violence poses, the subject—here brought to subjection—finds himself somehow confronted with an absence of otherness. Where all the components of the social bond should be—audible, comprehensible—suddenly what looms up instead is a surprise that can only alienate the subject (Hassoun, 7, 1997).

I find Hassoun's portrait of the melancholic troubling, however, for he casts melancholia as a passive state wherein a person is utterly stripped of agency and will. Returning to Freud, I found a somewhat different portrait, for the plaints and endless lyric laments of the melancholic proceed, according to Freud, from an attitude of revolt, a mental constellation by which a certain process has become transformed into melancholic contrition (1989, 169–70). I want to proceed from the position of revolt and lyric lament that characterizes much of Sexton's poetry to the place of her pedagogical performances. As I do so, I want us to keep in mind that while the melancholic is overpowered, she refuses to be tamed (see Fanon 1965).

APPARENT CONFESSIONS

On the one hand, Sexton appeared to engage in self-conscious confessions in the seminar room, displaying her own raw and visible wounds to the academy. Confessions work to enlist the sororial and fraternal sympathies of the listener so as to exonerate the sinner and, in turn, to efface the differences between them. The confessional narrative casts Sexton as the victim, and through the medium of narrative, she passes her guilt on to her students and readers. After all, we may very well summon up some sympathy for Sexton, secretly finding that we are more like her than we dared imagine, and, out of our own unexamined anxieties, we might very well exonerate her.

Sexton openly admits to "doing reference work in sin," and to using her place at the podium to seek "an appeal before a trial of angels" (HRRHC). In one of her lectures at Colgate, she brings her students back to the scenes that inspired her poem "Flee on Your Donkey." Sexton begins this lecture by telling her students that they will learn things that "no one else in the world knows" from looking at her worksheets. Back at the scenes that inspired this poem—a poem that would take Sexton from June 1962 to June 1966 to complete—students learn of Sexton's desire to flee not only life but madness. She confesses that this is "a poem that everyone told me not to publish. It was too self-indulgent, it was material I had already gone over. And yet, I hadn't told the full story of my madness. I hadn't talked about fleeing it as well as fleeing life" (HRRHC). Her lyric laments persistently invoke the bodies of women who are confined, maimed, dying, contemplating suicide, melancholic, medicated, or penetrated without consent.

Yet, while Sexton appeared at every turn to confess her life repeatedly and unabashedly to her students, positioning herself as an apparent victim,[9] her lyric laments and apparent confessions come from a mental constellation of revolt that is characteristic of melancholia. This melancholic revolt is manifested both in the trope of the mask that appears throughout the Crawshaw Lectures and in her parodic sensibilities. Sexton insisted on the fictive character of the I in her poems and explained to her students that, in the case of her poetry, "I am often being personal but I am not being personal about myself." Sexton's parodic sensibility functions to undermine the normative order of "performing confession" in the academy. Parody need not be comic. Derived from the Greek parodia, parody is a countersong, a neighboring song (see Crapanzano, 1990, 144).

Like melancholia, parody is structured in ambivalence, for it too has the paradoxical capacity both to incorporate and challenge that which it criticizes. There is a paradox inherent in the incorporative tactics of Sexton's composing processes: she simultaneously incorporates loss or lack in her body and disincorporates the authority of the master by wearing her wounds, to paraphrase Franz Fanon, on the surface of her skin like an open sore—an eyesore to the colonizer.

The losses and ambivalence that Sexton carried into her teaching life manifest themselves, I believe, in a specifically performative approach to teaching writing. Put more directly, the performativity marking Sexton's teaching documents is drenched in melancholia, and these performances allegorize losses that are deemed ungrievable in academic institutions where grief is preempted by the absence of cultural conventions for avowing loss. I do not intend to suggest that all performative pedagogies are manifestations of trauma, but I do want to argue that there is social value in framing performative pedagogy as a structure of address that is directed toward loss. This value is articulated in the following passage by Butler: "Insofar as the grief remains unspeakable," writes Butler, the rage over the loss can redouble by virtue of remaining unavowed.

And if that rage is publicly proscribed, the melancholic effects of such a proscription can achieve suicidal proportions. The emergence of collective institutions for grieving are thus crucial for survival, for reassembling community, for rearticulating kinship, for reweaving sustaining relations.... What cannot be avowed as a constitutive identification for any given subject position runs the risk not only of becoming externalized in a degraded form, but repeatedly repudiated and subject to a policy of disavowal (Butler,1997, 148-149).

By giving dramatic language to ambivalence and loss, Sexton demonstrates how pedagogy can be used to avow a broader range of subject positions in the classroom. Her use of performance accommodates the double-ghosted bodies that are housed in the melancholic. Performative modes of address have the capacity to bring about dialogue with the phantoms we hold, precisely because in performance, the body is metonymic, of self, of characters, of voice, and of personae. As I said earlier, what marks the melancholic student is a loss of address, an unspeakability that is not a symptom of thoughtlessness, or "retrieval problems," but rather a symptom of what cannot be spoken in school. In my case, I failed to locate a narrative structure through which I could speak of and grieve my father's self-abuse and my sense of abandonment. Consequently, I used teaching as a means through which to compose a narrative that could contain my loss. This move, however, only served to harbor the not fully confronted phantoms or secrets from my earlier family history. The figure of Anne Sexton is but one example of an historical figure to whom I turned in order to establish an addressable other through which I could work through the losses that were encrypted in my pedagogy. In this sense, we might think of Anne Sexton as a mask through which I could approach the secrets of my past about the claims addictions made on my family and how these secrets exert their influence on my pedagogy. What remained half-spoken in my life prevented me from using language in conventional or normative ways. Thus, the mask constitutes another kind of expressive contract, it organizes an/other operation of language.

Students who get lost in their own circuitous speech can often establish an object of address through the spatial registers characterizing the mask and the image or through the fragmented, associative narratives of juxtaposition. Because performance is contingent upon physically establishing an addressable other, an audience, and crafting a character and a point of view (subjectivity), it offers a viable means through which to introduce the Other into pedagogy. In this sense, pedagogy can ritualize melancholy by creating an occasion for writing that is open to ambivalence and can, moreover, allow the writer to link melancholia to a larger historical field, which would open texts to meanings otherwise foreclosed.

The approach to remembering I call for requires that we create exchanges between the ghosts and the living, thereby transforming losses that await articulation into meaning. This work is delicate; it calls for a logic that Peggy Phelan describes as moving us beyond the Euclidean plane, for ghosts defy the laws of "proof," and hence they are likely to be subjected to dismissal and doubt (1993). The melancholic cannot reproduce or prove the presence of the Object she longs for, but if, through writing and other forms of representations available through the expressive registers of theatre, dance, the visual arts, and music, the melancholic can remember by generating personal meanings, details, and associations, then she can restage and restate the effort to remember her loss. In this way, she can learn how loss can acquire meaning, and potentially generate recovery, not of the departed, but of herself, as the person who remembers.[10]

If I began this chapter in the archives in Austin, I want to end with a phone call to Aspen that was prompted by the letter I found in the archives. In February 1998, I interviewed Chris Leverich. Leverich remembers Sexton as fragile and sickly, suspicious, her eyes glazed over with tranquilizers. "I felt that she was working hard to get through the class. She was so terrified to be there, and you could see the terror in her body. At the same time, she was profoundly insightful, perhaps the finest professor I've ever had." When I asked Leverich what price he exacted as a student in her class, he told me that "Anne Sexton's teaching triggered for me a deep channel of emotion and areas of thought which were oftentimes frightening, so much so that I would push them aside. I've looked at these emotions for brief moments of time, but they trigger feelings beyond grief and sadness. Sexton wrote and spoke to us about her deepest emotional and social involvements, and she taught me to address mine." Leverich's memories suggest that Sexton's pedagogy of masks offered her students opportunities to approach, in some instances to wear, the masks of an Other. Such an approach to teaching and learning can create possibilities for teachers and students to re-draw the lines demarcating their own psychic and social life, and, by doing so, to renegotiate the personal, social, and political prohibitions on grieving.

NOTES

I wish to thank both the University of New Hampshire for funding this project through a 1994 Liberal Arts Summer Faculty Fellowship and the University of New Hampshire Center for the Humanities for a Gustafson Fellowship during the spring of 1998. Versions of this essay were given at the

Conference on Curriculum Theorizing, Bloomington, Indiana, 1998, at the Narrative Conference in Evanston, Illinois, 1998, and at the American Educational Research Association Conference in San Diego,1998. I would also like to express my gratitude to Rachel Trubowitz, Mary Rhiel, Elizabeth Lane, John Erni, Lad Tobin, Madeleine Grumet, Toby Gordon, Peter Taubman, David Bleich and Diane Freedman for reading earlier drafts of this work. I also want to thank Jenny Marshall for the patience and sensitive insights she offered during the final preparation of this manuscript. Finally, I am indebted to Bruce Berlind for offering me his memories, his time, and his rich, personal collection of Sexton's teaching materials.

1. This essay portrays an example of what Leigh Gilmore refers to as the "autobiographical demand," a form of critical life writing in which the demands of autobiography, the call to tell my story, and the demands of biography, the call to tell your story, coincide. Gilmore argues that the auto/biographical demand presents a narrative dilemma because it both divides and doubles the writer. At the moment that I begin to tell the story of Sexton's teaching life, aspects of my life surface and demand articulation. These demands provoke a sense of instability in my writing and pose emotional and rhetorical constraints that auto/biography manages by mingling a range of forms: biography, memoir, autobiography, poetry, the essay and theoretical writing. Throughout this chapter, I draw on Gilmore's concept to explore the ways in which the auto/biographical demand places in relief the double bind faced by a writer who inherits the unavoidable tasks to speak for the dead and to properly address a traumatized past that is unspeakable because it remains shrouded in shame. The dead, Gilmore goes on to remind us, make demands on the living, they surface in our dreams, our current relationships, through writing, teaching, and scholarship. But in order to understand these demands, the writer must distinguish between her story and theirs and in so doing, must navigate through the delicate tensions that are inherent in the narrative structure of auto/biography—the tension between telling stories and sustaining family loyalties, articulating family secrets and properly mourning a traumatized past (see Gilmore).

2. Throughout this chapter, I draw on teaching documents that are housed in the Anne Sexton archive at the Harry Ransom Research Humanities Center at the University of Texas, Austin. When referring to these materials, I use the abbreviation HRRHC.

3. Abraham and Torok develop the concept of "cryptonymy" to reconfigure the Freudian notion of the unconscious as a psychic crypt, a kind of tomb or vault harboring the not fully confronted "phantoms" or secrets from the analysand's earlier family history. For more on the concept of the fantome and cryptic incorporation, see Peggy Kamuf, "Abraham's Wake," Diacritics 9,

no. I (1979): 32–43 and Nicholas Rand's translator's introduction to The Wolf Man's Magic Word, "Toward a Cryptonymy of Literature." Also, for further commentary on Abraham and Torok, see Esther Rashkin, *Family Secrets and the Psychoanalysis of Narrative.* Princeton University Press. Princeton, New Jersey, 1992. Also, for a discussion about the implications melancholia has on student writing and the difficulties students face in locating an object of address when writing about loss see Hallet (1999).

4. Madeleine Grumet discusses the epistemic and pedagogical implications of composing educational autobiography by conjugating theory with literature, history, and other people's stories in "Scholae Personae: Masks for Meaning."

5. For an extensive discussion on the concept of a "return of a difference," see Elizabeth Ellsworth (1997), *Teaching Positions.*

6. To 'work something through' is to re-possess or reclaim emotions that we have become estranged from; this work makes present that which was otherwise encrypted or buried in the past so that it can in fact be felt as emanating from one's own person, one's own body. Thus, 'working through' memories entails the gradual knowing of the disaffected material that comes from our own being. In his essay, "Remembering, Repeating and Working Through," Freud describes this process as one which must "allow the patient time to become more conversant with this resistance with which he has now become acquainted, to work through it, to overcome it, by continuing, in defiance of it, the analytic work according to the fundamental rule of analysis" (volume twelve, *Standard Edition of the Complete Psychological Works of Sigmund Freud*, ed. and trans. James Strachey, p155).

7. Throughout this essay, I characterize Anne Sexton as a melancholic writer/teacher. Although Sexton's mental illness was never defined during her lifetime, psychologist Kay Redfield Jamison maintains that if she were living today, the case for manic-depressive illness would be very strong. Not only does Sexton have a strong family history of mental illness and suicide, but her symptoms—pronounced swings and lability in mood, expansiveness, impulsivity, altered sleep and energy patterns, anger, seasonal variations in mood—are all highly characteristic of manic-depressive illness. So, too, are her alcoholism and the worsening, rapidly cycling quality of the course of her illness. Sexton's "hysterical" symptoms may very well have been a manifestation of the emotional extremes and lability that go along with manic-depressive illness. Women who have affective illness not uncommonly are diagnosed as "borderlines" or "hysterics."

With this said, I want to emphasize that throughout this chapter I use the term melancholic to evoke more than a congenital disease caused by a biological endowment gone awry, or a "brain problem." I do not wish to deny the biological dimension of melancholia, rather I wish to argue that melancholia contains the possibilities to articulate more fully the boundaries between psychic and social life, and, like every human emotion, it offers us the opportunity to gain insight into self and Other. Sadness, writes Michael Vincent Miller, informs us that the loss was important; "anger alerts us that the person in our path is an obstacle. Depression can be the most chastening state imaginable: it throws us back on our deepest sorrows and feelings of helplessness. What it may tell us about our limitations, our fears of abandonment, failure, death, ought not to be narrowed too quickly to a matter of neurotransmitters flowing between synapses" (see Miller in Hassoun, viii–ix).

8. See Elaine Scarry (1985). Scarry not only explores the political implications inherent in the inexpressibility of physical pain, but she explores the role of the imagination in coming to terms with the limits of language, arguing that 'the human being who creates on behalf of the pain in her own body may remake herself to be one who creates on behalf of the pain originating in another's body; so, too, the human beings who create out of pain (whether their own or others') may remake themselves in a way that distributes the facts and responsibilities of sentience out into the external world'(pp. 324–5). Scarry's theory of making offers important insights into the potential implications of Sexton's poetry, suggesting that her imaginative work as a poet, teacher and playwright distributed unspeakable facts and responsibilities of sentience into an external world in an effort, not only to articulate loss, but to move away from pain, towards the boundaries of self-transformation.

9. Diane Wood Middlebrook is cautious about concluding that Ralph Harvey, Anne Sexton's father, made sexual advances toward her. However, Sexton's memories of this abuse do surface in her psychiatric tapes and in her work. Middlebrook writes, "Was Sexton's report a memory or a fantasy? This question achieved great importance in her therapy, and in her art, but it cannot be answered with certainty. The evidence for its actuality lies chiefly in the vividness and frequency of her descriptions during trance states. Moreover, Sexton's symptoms and her behavior—in particular, the dissociative states that were so prominent a feature in her case, her tendency to sexualize significant relationships, and the fluidity of the boundaries she experienced between herself and other people—fit the clinical picture of a woman who has undergone sexual trauma. From a clinical point of view, her doubts about this memory were not evidence that it did not happen" (57). Middlebrook goes on to note that Sexton's accounts did vary and that her memories of abuse surfaced in therapy when she was reading and writing about incest, especially during active work on a play that had, as its central conflict, an incestuous episode. "As Sexton frequently commented," notes Middlebrook, "once she had put a memory into words, the words were what she remembered. Thus she could give dramatic reality to a feeling by letting

it generate a scene and putting that scene into words for Dr. Orne while in a trance" (57). Dawn Skorczewski however, notes the danger inherent in questioning the evidence of such abuse, arguing that to suggest that Sexton merely dramatized her memories through her art is to align ourselves with patriarchy. For a substantive and moving discussion about the educative value of teaching incest narratives, see *Authoring A Life,* by Brenda Daly.

10. In *Unmarked: The Politics of Performance,* Peggy Phelan elaborates a form of remembering that does not seek to reproduce the lost object but rather rehearses and repeats "the disappearance of the subject who longs always to be remembered" (147). The crucial point underlying Phelan's argument is that to simply describe what or whom we have lost does not reproduce the object, rather these descriptions remind us how loss acquires meaning and can indeed generate recovery, not of the lost object, per se, but for the person who remembers. The economy of performance spurs memory on, encouraging memory to become present, yet these memories cannot be contained or controlled.

PART THREE
Teaching and Scholarship Face to Face

5 "KNOWLEDGE HAS A FACE"
The Jewish, the Personal, and the Pedagogical

Susan Handelman

> The ultimate conflict in the classroom is who we are when we encounter and are swallowed up by the artificial world of academia, our fleshly selves slumbering in hard chairs, and how does this strange ritual come to mean anything to us. Our private lives occur in terrifying places where we grapple alone with the impossibility of certitude or peace. Teaching these conflicts means addressing that, opening the windows of academia and letting life seep in like air.
>
> *Abby Bardi, graduate student*

> The movement of Eros and the movement of the mind cannot take place separately, converging only at the end. In the person, the student, they interact and interpenetrate. They must be treated so in interactions with a person. They must be moved together.
>
> *Joseph Schwab*

> Our Rabbis taught: If one sees a great multitude of people, one says, "Blessed [are you God] who is wise to secrets." Just as all their opinions are different from each other's, so too their faces are all different from each other's.
>
> *Talmud Brakhot*

FINDING A VOICE

I am not quite sure know how to begin this essay. A book whose subject is "the place of the personal in the academy" is bound to raise so many rhetorical expectations. I imagine my readers eagerly anticipating liberation from dry impersonal, academic prose, and wondering what secrets might be revealed. So I ask myself: Which rhetorical form should I use in this piece? Must it be a monologic narrative? Could I write it as a dialogue or letter? But which "I" do I present here? What will be my persona?

I am comforted to learn that the word "personal," is derived from "persona," which in turn designates the "mask" used by actors in ancient Greek drama, the *dramatis personae* who spoke through it: *per* + *sonare*, "to sound through." Let me continue to take refuge in etymology and philology as I try to find my voice, my way of here "sounding through the mask." The word "voice" itself comes from *vocare* and is connected to "vocation," derived from the Latin *vocatio:* a "bidding, an invitation, a call, a summons." So vocation is a profession as a "calling." Here I begin to recognize connections between the personal and the academy ... if one views the academy as I do, as truly a "vocation," a "calling." Needless to say, this sense of profession as a calling to "service," as having a moral and even religious component, has been obscured by the more contemporary meaning of "professionalization." Today, the term connotes the achievement of technical skill, specialized theoretical knowledge, and admission to an elite community of self-governing practitioners.[1]

Being "professional" is also commonly taken to mean being able to remove one's own "personal" prejudices and emotions from the task at hand. Yet a "professor" is also defined as one who "professes": from *pro-fateri*, to "declare loudly," publicly; one who "makes open declaration of his statements or opinions, one who makes public his belief." "Con-fess" and pro-fess share this same Latin root; so one also "professes one's faith, love, or devotion." I am intrigued by the way this etymological chain of connections moves so swiftly into the theological—to the extent that even the word "Parson," (the representative head of a parish church) appears under the entry for "personal" along with the "Three Persons of the Trinity"; "Divine being, hypostasis."[2]

I have to stop. The dictionary supplying these definitions has now taken me into the heart of Christian theology, supplied me quotes from Chaucer, Milton, Dryden, Shakespeare, and the New Testament. But one of the central concerns of my academic (and personal) life has been finding and hearing the "Jewish voice." And being caught between voices: the voices of my secular, elite Ivy League education, and the voices of Jewish tradition: the clamorous, argumentative voices of the Talmud, the creative, ironic story-telling of the Midrash, the rapturous voices of Jewish liturgy, the deliberative voices of Jewish philosophy, the lyrical, yearning melodies of Hassidism.

Contemporary literary theory has enabled me to read these classical Jewish texts in new ways, and in my previous academic work, I tried to reveal some of the underlying Jewish strands in that theory itself. Yet I have written by "sounding through certain masks" and not others. Early in my academic career, I felt compelled to write in a certain way, as I myself became professionalized, entered the ongoing conversation in the field, mastered its lingo and codes. In mid-career now, I have acquired a sense of how quickly the theories, topics, and interests of what we in literary studies often refer to as "The Profession" change. Those exciting, radical books about "Structuralism in Literature" from my graduate school days are now abandoned in a remote corner of my bookshelves. I sometimes wonder how soon it will be until those new volumes which took their place on the main shelves—on body studies, queer theory, post-colonial and cultural studies—will become their dusty, neglected neighbors.

It's not surprising to me, then, that the recent move towards "personal criticism" was spearheaded by mid-career, highly successful and well-known literary critics who had previously been engaged in the highly theoretical discourse of the 1980s. Like Cultural Studies, the turn towards "the personal" both continued and reacted against those modes of criticism. But I suspect that the shift in these critics' perspective also has to do with the changing course of inner life as one matures in years. I know that "inner life" is not exactly an *au courant* theoretical term; and I don't remember any academic preparation for dealing with the kinds of unexpected turns one finds oneself making in one's self-definition as a scholar, colleague, or teacher as one progresses in a career. Like several other of my contemporaries, though, I find our previous ways of writing, teaching, and talking about literature to be unsatisfactory and constraining.

And so I have refocussed my earlier highly abstract theoretical work in deconstruction and hermeneutics, to a concern with the ethics of criticism, and an intense interest in pedagogy.... an interest that was always implicit in my work, but not able to find open expression.[3] I have returned to that older meaning of "profession" as "calling," and it is much more the question of what are we "called" to do in the University with our students that preoccupies me now I seek also to hear my students' voices in a different way. For I keep finding that they—in their resistance and awkwardness and naiveté and freshness and unprofessionalized sense of things—are often more provocative, unpredictable, and challenging than many of the latest new theories or interpretations.

READING AS CALLING TO EACH OTHER

I also take with me from Jewish tradition a deeply-rooted sense of teaching and learning as "holy" and "redemptive" endeavors, and of being bound to a three-thousand year old community of memory, study, and practice which has endured the vicissitudes and traumas of history. I write this essay in the city of Jerusalem, on a special Fellowship for educators from around the world. And I partake here of the "quiet revolution" occuring in women's access to the most rigorous and advanced forms of traditional Jewish learning.

In Hebrew, the word for "calling"—*kriyah*—is also the word for "reading." In this sense, reading is not just a matter of "textual "or "cultural" analysis. It is a voicing, calling to the other, a being called to account, a summons to be present. From my previous academic work on the great modern Jewish philosophers Franz Rosenzweig (1886-1929) and Emmanuel Levinas (1906-1994) and their relation to literary theory, I have seen how Western culture, too, has to be "called into account" by Judaism. Rosenzweig and Levinas both came out of the monumental German-Jewish tradition of philosophy, and abandoned the project of constructing grand theories, meta-narratives of knowledge long before the familiar contemporary postmodern critics we all customarily cite did so.

Rosenzweig also left a brilliant career in the German University to found an Institute for Adult Jewish Education in Frankfort, but all too quickly died from amyotrophic lateral sclerosis (Lou Gehrig's disease). He continued to write, translate and teach as his physical capabilities diminished solely to the ability to blink his eye. Levinas emerged as one of the most influential philosophers in post-War France after surviving in a prisoner-of-war camp, and losing many relatives in the Holocaust. His work helped inspire Sartre to engage in phenomenology and Derrida to critique ontology. Above all, Levinas called philosophy to account and placed ethics prior to metaphysics. He also had dual pedagogical career, engaged both as a French University professor and a teacher training young French Jews at the preparatory school of the Alliance Israelite Orientale. He too, wrestled with the problem of being, as he put it, a Jew "speaking Greek," the language of the academy and of philosophy.

I also wrestle with this problem and I, too, sympathize with Rosenzweig's departure from the suffocating German academy of his time to become another kind of "Teacher"; yet I am not ready to abandon my career in the University. But I do hope university learning can be changed, and believe that Jewish models of study and commentary have much to say to educational reform. Ultimately, what I learn from Jewish tradition is that "texts" are not only, nor primarily "books"—or "cultural practices" or "discourses" or "ideologies"—but ultimately "Teachings" (this is the root meaning of the Hebrew word *Torah*, used to refer to all the biblical and rabbinic literature). For me now, hermeneutics or cultural studies or political critiques or pedagogies of the oppressed are not, in the end, enough to encompass the meaning of "teaching" ; on the contrary, there is a sense in which "teaching" instead encompasses them. Or as Rosenzweig writes:

> Literature is written only for the sake of those who are in the process of development, and of that in each of us which is still developing. Hebrew, knowing no word for "reading" that does not mean "learning" as well, has given this, the secret of all literature away. For it is a secret, though a quite open one, to these times of ours—obsessed and suffocated as they are by education—that books exist only to transmit that which has been achieved to those who are still developing" ("On Jewish Learning" 216)

I have spoken here of "teaching" and of "voices,"but so far carefully avoiding the word "God." Needless to say, the relation of the modern University to religion is vexed. As I leaf through the pages of the most recent *PMLA*, and its book ads, I wonder: Should I instead talk about these "Jewish voices" in terms of "hybridity "and "alterity" and "marginalization" and "diasporic ethnicity" or the "symbolic construction of the Jewish body" or "cultural and discursive practices?" Perhaps were I at another stage, I would find this language and its rousing calls for liberatory practices more useful, but now I seek to let the sounds of a Jewish voice be heard differently—differently even from standard "Academic Jewish Studies," which itself has always had a complex relation to the University.

Moshe Idel, the preeminent living expert on Jewish mysticism has recently argued that the conception of Jewish learning as "experiential, transformative and intended to go beyond the strictly mental level" was marginalized in much foundational academic Jewish scholarship.[4] This was due in part to the culture of the nineteenth century German University in which modern academic Jewish studies was born. Idel argues that Torah study, however, was never seen solely as matter of content, or the amassing of knowledge; it was not even ultimately about "knowing," but the changing of one's way of life. Even the "Book" itself, in much of Jewish thought was seen as only one step on a long trajectory of performative religiosity; learning, in other words, was instrumental and "knowledge,"(though of course important) was not its ultimate purpose.

Traditional Jewish modes of learning, moreover, attempted to bring people together into what Idel calls a "sonorous community"—a "sound community." In traditional Jewish study and reading, the text is activated by being sounded out orally, loudly vocalized, sung, exteriorized. This practice rested in part on the view that since language mediates the experience of God, words become forms of power. Shouting out the sacred text also created an external reality that encompassed all those together in study . . . just as God creates in the Bible by "calling"—*kriyah*—not by fiat. (This understanding of study was especially prominent in Hassidism and Kabbalah.) "Learning," concludes Idel, is "entering an ambience as much as it is an acquiring of knowledge" and we need to be cautious in overemphasizing the purely mental aspect when we describe the historical phenomenon and practice.

The traditional *Beit Midrash*, "House of Study" was, and still is today, a place of clamorous noise, quite unlike the hushed university library. One of the traditional modes of study which is still quite alive in *yeshivot* (advanced Jewish religious schools), and which I have personally most loved, is to learn orally with a fixed study partner—*hevruta*—with whom one intones the text aloud, line by line, and engages in vigorous questioning and argument about its linguistic nuances and meaning. A passage in the Talmud *Kiddushin 30b* describes that relationship:"R. Chiya bar Abba said, even a parent and a child, or a teacher and his student who are studying Torah together . . . at first become enemies of one another—but they do not move from there until they become devoted friends of one another." That is, the passionate debate at first makes the study-partners opponents; each disputes the other's interpretations as they seek to fathom the meaning of the text, each bringing his or her own background, associations, experiences, questions. Nevertheless, they are engaged in a collaborative enterprise, in a face to face intimate dialogue. Out of this intense reciprocal interchange, hierarchical relations dissolve, and they become in the end intimate friends.

In their analysis of the sociology of the *Beit Midrash*, where a large community of study partners sit and learn in the same room, Moshe Halbertal and Tovah Halbertal note that the volume and gesticulations of all these pairs together create a physical choreography of bodily movement, voice and noise, a kind of "acting out of a page of Talmud." The students, that is, are enacting the voices of the same rabbinic sages whose own debates with each other constitute the pages of the Talmud the students are studying. At the same time, the students are also interpreting this "script ; it becomes a text and drama at one time. This approach to the text is non-chronological; all the previous commentators printed on the pages of the Talmud, dating back a a thousand years and spanning the entire Jewish diaspora, are taken up along with the current students in a kind of a contemporaneous conversation, a discourse above time and place (Halbertal).

The technique of learning in small groups or pairs has been rediscovered in the past few years by educational theorists, who now call it "co-operative learning." Its advocates support their work with epistemological claims that all knowledge is in fact, social, dialogic, communal. They offer abundant evidence of the pragmatic effectiveness of co-operative learning and its success in creating classroom community, a truth I can affirm from my own use of these techniques in my classes.

What further, I wonder, might models of "sacred learning" have to say to the "secular" University, and how could they be used in non-dogmatic ways? Especially when we in literary studies tend to talk about everything in our "discourse" of ethnicity, multi-culturalism, alterity, and critical pedagogy except God and religion. A recent story in my Smith College alumna magazine about "religion on campus" quoted a student who said: "It is harder to come out as a spiritual person than as a lesbian here at Smith (Fisher, 12). In an ironic way, "spiritual persons" have become "marginalized" "silenced" voices in many classrooms. Yet the "postmodern" world is indeed a post-secular one as well, and the old dichotomies between "critical thinking" and "religious belief," or "science" and "religion" are just as outmoded as those between "subjectivity" and "objectivity."[5] In sum, I agree with Mary Rose O'Reilly who writes: "The question for me is, how do we teach people who are profoundly, and even stubbornly, spiritual brings? I think we assume that spiritual beings is the last thing they are (because it is on of the last things they will let us know" (138).

It is time for a personal anecdote. A brilliant honors student in a recent senior seminar of mine told me she was having great trouble choosing a topic for her honors thesis. She wanted to write, she said, with an ironic half-smile, on "The Meaning of Life." Her advisor, however, discouraged her and said, "Why does it always have to be about you?" She said to me wistfully "Maybe there's something wrong with me, but I always want to see how it relates to my life. I was assigned to write a paper for my American Literature class on 'Financial Exchanges in *Huckleberry Finn*' But I'm just not interested in that." In other words, our students, too, are desperately trying to find their "personal place in the academy." This student does not see the world as entirely "produced and constructed by material, historical factors, in a network of political and economic exchanges" . . . and neither do I.

How, then, can students like this feel more at home in the University? Can and should we also attempt to help our students in their spiritual struggles, which they often keep so hidden from us and from the classroom but which are so much a part of how they try make sense of the world? As a very bright undergraduate once poignantly and somewhat bitterly said to me: "You professors here in the University pull out the rug from under us—and we never even had a floor." So true: we contemporary academics, especially in literary studies, often describe our pedagogical and intellectual goals in terms of "critique, subversion, interrogation"—or what Lionel Trilling felicitously called "the unmasking principle" that has influenced intellectuals since the French Revolution. Marx and Freud, Trilling wrote, "taught the intellectual classes that nothing was as it seemed, that the great work of intellect was to strike through the mask" (Dickstein, 1998). That wonderful phrase comes, of course, from one of Captain Ahab's grand anguished speeches in *Moby Dick*. It also re-echoes the etymology of "persona": can we ever *strike* through, or only *sound* through? What are the pedagogical consequences of these attempts? And how can our students' *resistance* to our work also teach us? As the Talmud says, "Much have I learned from my teachers, even more from my colleagues, but from my students, most of all" (*Ta'anit 7a*).

KNOWLEDGE HAS A FACE

"As the Talmud says." With that phrase, I revert to one of my most comfortable Jewish voices; citing a classical rabbinic text and commenting in the margins . . . with the adverb "as" signaling a commitment to the text before the moment of analytical questioning, debate, and interpretation. There is a way in which I would probably be most "personal" here if I assumed that rhetorical role of rabbinic-style commentator on a Jewish text. For I must say I am not entirely satisfied with my "voice" in the sections I have just written. My resort to English philology and etymology was a way of historicizing the words dealing with the "personal" and the "professional," in order to open them to the traces of other meanings inscribed in them. Of course, I also wanted to find a shared language with my readers, and try to move a theological discussion to common ground.

I would be equally uncomfortable, though, with a purely "confessional voice," or an autobiographical narrative. The individual "confessional" voice is not such a major part of classical Jewish discourse, in part because Judaism is not a "confessional" faith dependent on an individual's affirmation of certain dogmas, or a conversion experience, but instead a covenental membership in a People with a collective history, fate, and destiny. Even on Yom Kippur, the Day of Atonement, the holiest day of the year, the numerous "confessions" of sins in the liturgy are said in the collective: "*We* have transgressed, *we* have betrayed, *we* have robbed, *we* have slandered," and so forth. My sense of myself as a Jew, and my voice as a Jew is indeed at its most "personal" when it is most bound up in that collective and transhistorical "sound community" of study-partners and interpreters who shout and sing out and wrestle with the sacred text together, who argue and laugh together, celebrate each other's sorrows and joys together through the liturgical cycle of the Jewish year, which itself recapitulates and re-enacts the dramas of Jewish history. As the biblical scholar Michael Fishbane once remarked, the most "authentic" Jewish literary genre is, perhaps, the *anthology*—a simultaneous compilation of diverse texts, voices, sources. That is the way the Bible, the Talmud, Midrash, halakhic codes are constructed—as massive anthologies . . . the collective voices of scores of generations superimposed on each other, jostling each other on the page, calling to each other.

Even amongst the Jewish mystics, there is a paucity of personal, confessional experiential accounts, especially compared to the Christian tradition. I have no space here to analyze further why that is so, or attempt a "history of the self," or the notion of "peoplehood," or the rhetoric of commentary in Jewish thought. If I think, however, about resources in Jewish thought and literature to examine the "personal" and its relation to contemporary teaching and scholarship, I go back again to Rosenzweig and Levinas, who model for me a way to exist as a Jew in the modern Western University, and to some key passages in the Bible upon which they have commented, foundational texts familar to all.

The well known early chapters of the Book of Genesis describe the creation of the first "person," Adam. In the Hebrew Bible, "Adam" does not initially signify a proper name; it is a pun on the word *adamah*, "earth, ground," and so signifies "the earth creature." Nor does this word in itself signify a gendered creature. In one of the classical midrashic (rabbinic exegetical) readings of the creation of Adam, this "earth creature" is described as a kind of androgyne with "two faces" (*du-parzufim*) which are positioned away from each other, one in front and one in back (*Ber. Rab.* 17:6; *Berakhot* 61a). God's splitting of this double-faced creature into two, and turning the faces so they could see each other, is also the origin of "male and female." This reading is based on interpreting the Hebrew word *tzela* in Gen.2:22–23, usually translated as "rib," in another possible sense: "side." On another level, one could say this midrash also teaches that human identity is from the beginning "bifurcated": "identity," *"personhood" come only when one faces the other.*[6] Indeed, the word for "face" in Hebrew, *panim* is a plural noun which takes a plural verb. Its verbal root, *panah,* means "to turn towards." The living face is never still and singular; it is always a moving, changing set of gestures, expressing/concealing turns of feeling and thought. The Hebrew word for "innerness," *pnimiyut,* is also derived from *panim.* The face is physically the distinctive mark of our individuality, the most "personal" aspect of ourselves Yet, paradoxically, we cannot see our own face directly.

The face also acts as an interface between self and world. What it means to "face the other," and what it would mean for *"knowledge itself to have a face"* are central issues for both Rosenzweig and Levinas. And, I would add, *for any teacher, for any pedagogical scene.* I have finally found here, I think, a Hebrew counterpart to the English word "personal." I want to use this notion of the "face" to guide the rest of my thinking in this essay about the meaning of the "personal" in the academy. In that way, I hope to sound my "personal" Jewish voice, and perform a Jewish mode of study while trying to clarify our larger collective professional and pedagogical goals in the University. In much of my past research, I engaged in meta-theoretical analyses of rabbinic hermeneutics; here I also want to enter "inside" that exegetic process itself. Yet like Rosenzweig and Levinas, I aim to move dialectically between "inside" and "outside," to illumine what in Jewish tradition speaks to all of us, Jews and non-Jews, professors and students, persons of faith and atheists.

After completing his philosophical magnum opus *The Star of Redemption,* Rosenweig wrote and taught very differently. In a letter to his fiancé in 1920, just before he became ill, he said: "You see, I can no longer write a "Book"; everything now turns into a letter, since I need to see the 'other" (in Glatzer, *Rosenzweig,* 90). That indeed was the inevitable rhetorical and pedagogical consequence of the philosophy he formulated in the *Star,* the last few pages of which end with a vision of truth itself as a "countenance," a face (*Star,* 418–24).

For what else do we mean by the "personal" than to "give a face" and voice to something? For knowledge to be "personal," in this sense, would not mean for it to biased, confessional, ideological, but on the contrary to have a "face"—that is, to be turned towards another, vulnerable and susceptible to the face of the other, in all her or his particularity ... an address to the other. This position would imply a similar foundational pedagogical stance.

Another way Levinas, and Rosenzweig articulate that stance phenomenologically, and the meaning of the "personal," is through the expression "Here am I" (*hineni* in Hebrew; *me voici* in French), which is also the response of the biblical heroes in climactic moments of their being summoned: Abraham to the sacrifice of Isaac (Gen 22:1); Moses to the burning bush (Ex 3:4); Isaiah to his prophetic call (6:8).

Instead of evasion and blame, "Here am I" should have been Adam's response to God's question "Where are you?" in the Garden after the first sin (Gen. 3:9). Rosenzweig interprets God's question here as God's own quest for the "you"; this address is a kind of indefinite deictic which opens the possibility for an other to be constituted who can freely confront God as an "I." Comments Rosenzweig: "The I discovers itself at the moment when it asserts the existence of a Thou by inquiring into its Where" (*Star* 175.) But the answer *hineni*, the opening of the concealed isolated, locked self, comes for the first time in the biblical narrative only later in Gen 22:1 when God calls out to Abraham before the sacrifice of Isaac, in the vocative, in direct address, not with an indefinite "you" but with his proper name, "Abraham!" That is, in all Abraham's non-conceptual particularity and individuality, and in love for his singularity: "Now he answers, all unlocked, all spread apart-all ready all soul 'Here am I.' Here is the I, the individual human I ... wholly receptive" (*Star* 176).[7] Deborah Kerdeman (1998), using Gadamerian hermeneutics, argues that indeed education should not focus on "self-understanding" through the question "Who are you?" That assumes the self could be reflected upon apart from the situated relationships in which self-understanding is constituted. In the existential hermeneutics of Gadamer, "self-understanding is rather constitutive of our being, an indication of how we are situated in relation to people and events ... an expression of practical engagement that illumines and shapes our moral orientation. The key question for Gadamer thus is not "Who"? But "Where? Where are we? We're always someplace. Are we present? Or are we hiding?"

For Levinas, influenced by Rosenzweig, "Here am I" is a phenomenology of the self answering the violence of philosophical ontology. Over and over again in his philosophical work, the word *I* comes to mean *"here am I"* answering for everything and everyone—a self constructed not out of "ontological presence" but ethical responsibility, as a "reason beyond the cogito." This "I" is not a manifestation of "innerness" but an extra-version a breaking out of the narcissistic, enclosed self to be exposed and vulnerable to the other, to the extent that one becomes completely responsible for the other. Or as Levinas puts it: the "here am I" is a kind of bearing witness, the self at the service of others "without having anything to identify myself with but the sound of my own voice or the figure of my gesture—the saying itself" (*Otherwise Than Being* 149). The "calling" of the face of the other is met by the sound of my voice, saying "here am I for you."

Behind his emphasis on this term is Levinas' own bitter experience as a Jew in France during World War II, and the transformation of his former teacher Heidegger into a Nazi sympathizer. So it is also precisely the phenomenological *impersonality* of "Being" in Heidegger, that spurs Levinas to link neutrality to indifference, and ultimately to violence and murder. This position underlay Levinas' critique of all anonymous and impersonal structures of thought including Structuralism, and its descendants. Neither was the answer the existentialist emphasis on the cry of the subjective self, for he viewed the ego in its natural state as self-enclosed, self-interested and violent. This is a complex philosophical discussion which I have explored in depth in *Fragments of Redemption*. Here, though, I'm more interested in how it all relates to pedagogy in the contemporary University.

TEACHER AND STUDENT: A RELATION OF TWO FACES

> As waters [reflect] face to face, so is the heart of one person to another.
> *Proverbs 27:19*

One way a text is "made personal" is by being embodied in the living voice, face, and being of the teacher in dialogue with the student, and the students with each other. This mediation is a key pedagogical aspect of the hermeneutics of the tradition of rabbinic interpretation in Judaism—also called the "Oral Torah." The Oral Torah is the record of the collective voices of the teachers and their students through the generations as they debate and perform the meanings of the teachings, and search out what rabbinic tradition calls the "seventy faces of the Torah." It began to be written down in the early centuries of the Common Era, and includes the Talmuds, midrashic literature, legal codes and analyses—all that is not explicitly written in the Bible. Oral Torah is also invented and continued every time we in turn read, teach, argue over, and interpret these texts, find a new face in them. So I have often thought it would be more appropriate to calls Jews the "people of the Mouth" rather than the "People of the Book." Even the Hebrew language is written without vowels; in the very act of reading it, one must vocalize the words, even if only mentally supplying the vowels that make the words have a sense .

I spent a great deal of intellectual energy in my first book, *The Slayers of Moses,* trying to understand the creative freedom of rabbinic interpretation, and its wondrous exegetical extravagances. I linked that hermeneutic to the creativity of contemporary secularized Jewish interpreters from Freud to Derrida. But I missed this key pedagogical link: "Oral Torah" attains that creative and interpretive freedom because it is a lived teaching and not only a book or a system of signs. It is mediated and embodied by the relations of teachers and students who literally breathe voice into and give a face to the written text in the context of a community of memory, obligation, and practice. In this light, one can understand some of the many poignant Talmudic stories and Jewish laws that compare a person to a *sefer Torah,* a Torah scroll. Says the Talmud, for example:" A person who is present at the death of someone, is obligated to tear his clothes [a sign of mourning] To what is this similar? To a Torah scroll that has been burned." (*Shabbat 105b*).[8]

I want to move into another kind of "Jewish voice" now, and turn from Rosenzweig and Levinas the university philosophers, to Rabbi Nachman of Breslov, a remarkable nineteenth century hassidic Rebbe. In addressing the ruptures modernity had brought to the Jews, he wrote not only commentaries, but also parables, stories, and songs and was one of the sources for modern Hebrew literature. The relation between a hassidic Rebbe and his disciples was particularly intense, and led R. Nachman to intriguing reflections on the nature of the teacher-student relation. R. Nachman especially stressed the importance of *seeing the face* of one's teacher rather than only reading the teacher's writings, or hearing from another person what the teacher has said:

> Know: one who has the eyes to see, can see and recognize in the face of the student who his teacher was, even if the student only saw him once, for "Who is like the wise man and who knows the interpretation of a thing? A person's wisdom makes his face shine, and the boldness of his face is changed [Eccl. 8:1]." And therefore when the student receives the wisdom of his teacher, he receives his face [*kabbalat panim,* a pun on the phrase "welcome"]. And for this it is necessary to look in he face of his teacher at the time when he is receiving his wisdom, as it is written [Isaiah 30:20]: "And your eyes shall see your teacher" [referring to the messianic era and vision of God]; for wisdom is in the face, as explained above, and therefore, when one looks in the face of the student, one can know who his teacher is. (*Likkutei Moharan* 230)

In the next quote, this "teaching" relation is inscribed as well between friend and friend.

> One has to make limpid and clear one's face, so that each person can see his own face in his face as in a mirror, until, without rebuke or preaching, his friend will immediately repent over his deeds, just from looking into his face. For in looking

into the other's face, he will see himself as in a mirror, how is own face is sunk in darkness." (*Likkutei Moharan*, "Tefillah L' Habbakuk." 19)

What possible translation of these passages is there for the University? What further could we understand as the relation between knowledge and the face? Perhaps that the "face" here signifies something about the *relation between* student and teacher over and above the *content* transmitted, the way in which any true wisdom is ultimately inscribed in a human relation and is not simply a "text." The way the teaching ultimately comes from the teacher on a level deeper than pure intellect, and beyond its verbal representations. The way in which the teacher embodies the knowledge in an act of giving forth to the other out of desire, and connection. That the moments of illumination a student has are when she or he discovers his or her "own face" through the face of the teacher, which means that the face is not a simple mirror which passively reflects a similitude but refracts back actively. And this requires not imitation of the teacher, but the work of the student, who senses the need for inner change. Likewise, to "receive the face" (*kabbalat panim*) is not a passive act. "Reception" and "reflection" here are modes of self- transformation. This "mutual seeing" is the opposite of the one-sided, eagle-eyed view of the Hegelian philosopher who observes all from above, or the sinister all-seeing gaze of the Foucauldian Panopticon, or a rapacious, objectifying sexual gaze. Nor, could the "virtual, electronic face" of a teacher in the video version of "Distance Learning" fully express it. There is something in the living face that eludes this capture. (Redefining knoweldge as a relation to an other rather than a reflection of some independent, essential substance is, of course, a paradigmatically postmodern epistemological position.)

One could try to translate these passages in psychoanalytic terms. Arthur Frank, in an essay on "Lecturing and Transference: The Undercover Work of Pedagogy" also asks what induces people to attend lectures in person, when reading a written text is so much more efficient. He insightfully analyzes the latent desires of audience and lecturer—and by extension student and teacher—in this living pedagogical situation. The ritual and celebratory nature of the occasion, of course, draws the attendees. The auditors further believe they can somehow glean more by contact with the personal presence of the speaker. The actual text of the lecture, he then suggests, is in reality only a pretext—just as the manifest content of a dream, in the Freudian paradigm, is the screen that allows latent meaning to be transmitted. In the same way, the pedagogy of the lecture is highly personal, but the lecturer for the most part conceals that element and purports to be coolly only transmitting knowledge and information. Like the dream, then, "the lecture works precisely by *concealing* the personal essence; stated another way, the personal element is effective only *if* it is concealed" (30).

The same holds true, Frank argues, for the student-teacher relation which he also configures in terms of the Freudian notion of "transference" in psychoanalysis. "Transference," simply defined, is the unconscious projection of desire and fantasy by the analysand onto the analyst; "counter-transference" is the unconscious projection of the analyst onto the analysand. The student (like the analysand, or audience at a lecture) projects the teacher as the one who possess the Truth, or in Lacanian terminology, the Subject-presumed-to-know: "I do not mean the truth of the subject matter of the course, but rather the supposed truth of the lecturer herself and the truth of the students themselves" (31). Inevitably, then, the teacher/lecturer/analyst is also the "one who never says what they want him to say":

> I propose that the desire of the students is for the speech of the animator's self—not the spoken text the animator presents (that is only the price of admission), but the *speech of what animates* the text. For structuralists (if there are any left) the subject may be dead, but for students, the key to ideas is in the biography of the thinker. This principle of truth deriving from life experiences pervades students' relations not just to those they study but to their teachers. (30-31)

Since this autobiographical speech is concealed and never fully given, the desire of the student is stimulated by this lack: "What this desire is for, insofar as desires are ever *for* anything, is for the subject-presumed-to-know to reveal herself in some exercise of authority." The key to successful psychotherapy, however, is the conscious understanding, working out, and resolution of the transference. Frank argues that the role of the educator parallels that of the good analyst, who understands that the issue is ultimately not her or his own self-revelation but rather querying the analysand: "What do you want from me" and "What should you expect from yourself": "The essence of what I call moral education is this capacity for self-reflection: to become moral beings we must see our actions as they are seen by others." (32–33). Citing Irving Goffman, he adds that this kind of moral education can't be "taught"; it can only be modeled during teaching: modeled not as a method of scholarship or knowledge, but rather as "a mode of how to handle oneself in the matter of one's own claims to position" (34).

Compare R. Nachman again: "One has to make limpid and clear one's face, so that each person can see his own face in his face as in a mirror, until, without rebuke or preaching, his friend will immediately repent over his deeds, just from looking into his face. For in looking into the other's face, he will see himself as in a mirror, how is own face is sunk in darkness." On the one hand, this, too, could be a kind of "transference relation": without speech, one's silent face, made limpid and clear," "without rebuke or preaching" enables one's friend or student to sense her own lack, and stimulates her desire to transform herself. The analogy goes only so far, however, for R. Nachman implicitly also reminds us that to make one's face limpid and clear involves one's own moral-spiritual work .The classic injunction to the psychoanalyst to make her face a "blank screen" is not the same as shining visage emanating from a lived wisdom that has left its luminous trace on the body. I, too, still believe in a truth deriving from life experiences, (and from texts) written on the face. And I also identify with that student of mine who still was half-hoping, to find "The Meaning of Life" in what she was reading. What was she really asking of me? What was my responsibility for her?

Martin Buber, in his eloquent essay "The Education of Character" describes a moment in a teacher's facing a group of typically unruly and resistant students:

> But then his eyes meet a face which strikes him. It is not a beautiful face nor particularly intelligent; but it is a real face, or rather, the chaos preceding the cosmos of a real face. On it he reads a question which is something different form the general curiosity: "Who are you? Do you know something that concerns me? Do you bring me something? What do you bring?" (112)

Do not our students come to us "in search of their face," and do we not need to bring them something more than the negative moment of undoing our authority? Do we not promise them something by our very act of standing before them? What do we owe them?

For Buber "Education worthy of the name is essentially education of character" (104) which does not mean *giving instruction* in ethics. He argues that only the whole being of the teacher can affect the whole being of the students, and often this happens when the teacher has the least thought of affecting the students. Yet Buber urges the teacher to will to take her part in the stamping of the student's character, along with all the uncontrollable multifarious influences that are inevitably affect students lives. For Buber, "great character" is a person who in "every living situation" acts out of a "deep readiness to respond with his whole life, and in such a way that the sum of his actions and attitudes expresses at the same time the unity of his being and its willingness to accept responsibility" (114). Buber envisions a "rebirth of personal unity, unity of being, unity of life, unity of action" to move "beyond all the dividedness of individualism and collectivism" and which is the way also towards genuine community (116). In an era where absolute values have been destroyed, he says, an educator can begin by fostering the student's painful sense of lack of this unity, nurturing it into a desire, and showing students some glimpse of that unity, as far off as it might be,

In our fractured postmodern era, especially in literary studies, we rarely hear words such as this; we tend to stress instead rupture, divided selves, fragmentation, the dark binds of power and ideology, the difficulty of "agency." We begin with lack but often do not move far beyond it, "pulling out the rug when they never even had a floor." We cannot return to a naive innocence, but Buber's vision is a kind of needed pedagogical counterbalance which also, I think, describes the deeper yearning of students, the moment when their faces are open to ours.

What, I wonder further, is pedagogical desire? Who gives and who takes? What do we yearn for in wanting to teach and wanting to learn? How do we keep this yearning, this dialectic of giving and receiving from becoming manipulative and degraded? In an intriguing essay entitled "Eros and Education" Joseph Schwab also traces the vicissitudes of Eros and argues that education cannot separate the intellect from feeling and action. "Eros, the energy of wanting, is as much the energy source in the pursuit of truth as it is in the motion toward pleasure, friendship, and fame, or power." For Schwab, the teacher's task is to locate those objects to which "youthful Eros" readily attaches, and then direct it to more enduring objects. Eros, he points out, is first located and activated by "a certain face-to-face relation between teacher and student," an interpersonal relation involving a reciprocity of evocation and response (109-110). Schwab means this quite physically and concretely, and supplies a vivid and subtle picture of classroom dynamics:

> If in the first moments of the first meeting of a new class, the teacher's gaze wanders first to one, then to another and another of the anonymous faces before him, those faces which are not readable yet as to promise and performance, and if, in this wandering inspection, two or three students answer his regard in a way which signals to them their curious awareness of him as a person, a start has been made. The person who is thus aware of me is a person of whom I become aware. The wandering movement of my eyes is stopped. They return to him or her. From an anonymous sea of faces, from the mere collective, individuation has begun; the "class" is beginning to be "persons." The teacher thus answers the awareness he feels in the student; he examines more closely the person who has signaled interest in him. In reciprocity, this new inspection is no longer felt by the student as mere curious awareness, but as awareness of himself as a person. More, the student feels his own movement from item to individuality, from anonymity to personality. And he is grateful (110–111).

Eros at bottom for Schwab is a "desire for selfhood: To experience another's recognition of one's self is to receive reassurance of that self's existence." That initiates further growth and gratitude, which the teacher also in turn experiences, knowing that she is needed and useful. And in the end, the teacher "wants to convey not merely what he knows, but how he knows and how he values it. He wants to communicate some of the fire he feels, some of the Eros he possesses, for a valued object" (124).

GIVER AND RECEIVER: CONTRACTING THE SELF

Or, I would add, as the Talmud puts it, "More than the calf wants to suck, the cow wants to give" (*Pesachim* 112a). That relation of suckling infant to nursing mother is also a not-so-simple dynamic of desire. Who indeed "initiates" and "controls" the relation, the mother or the infant? Many texts and stories in Jewish tradition use the feminine imagery of nursing to describe not only the teacher-student relation, but the relation between text and interpreter. Among the most extraordinary is the following Talmudic statement: "Why were the words of Torah compared to a nipple? Just as with a nipple, whenever an infant fondles it, he finds milk, so it is with the words of Torah— whenever a person ponders them he finds relish in them" (*Eruvin 54b*).

There is also way in which the desire of the infant to nurse activates the milk of the mother, and the way the desire of the student to learn activates the desire of the teacher to teach. To use kabbalistic terminology, the "receiver" [*mekabel*] activates the "bestower"[*mashpia*]. The tension between withholding and giving, holding on and letting go is also itself key to the pedagogical act. In Jewish mystical tradition, the relation of "bestower" and "receiver" is itself an ever shifting dialectic of desire and fulfillment, meeting and separation that is seen as structuring the entire creation—from the most interior fluxes of the divine godhead, to the relation of the divine and the human, human and human, male and female, and so forth. Kabbalistic texts describe the initial act of creation not as an overflowing self-expression of the divine, for that would have left no place for the other, and for a separate finite world. Instead, there was a primal "self-contraction," by God, a *tzimtzum*, a "concealing or withdrawal" of the divine light in order to leave an "empty space." In that space, however, remains a "trace" [*reshimu*] of the divine. And in that hollow, the world subsequently begins to develop (as in a womb) as further divine contractions and emanations are projected into the void. In a sense one could also say that "self-contraction" is really the secret of human relations, and of ethics: I let go and make space for the other person.

Many chassidic and kabbalistic thinkers also understand this cosmological withdrawal as a paradigm of pedagogy, and vice versa. The analogy is made to the teacher who also has to make a number of contractions and concealments, in order for her or his thoughts to be apprehended by the receiver. For if the teacher would try transfer her or his ideas directly on the level s/he conceives them, that student would be overwhelmed. As R. Yosef Yitzhak Schneerson

(1880–1950) puts it, in order for the student to absorb the influence of the teacher, the teacher must first entirely "remove the light of his own intellect, and conceive an intellectual light that is on the receiver's level." The concealment, however, is ultimately for the purpose of revelation, just as the *tzimtzum* is made for the purpose of a new independent creation.(Schneerson, 21).

This dialectic of revelation and concealment would be another way of analyzing "sounding through a mask," or the role of masking in being "personal" in teaching. The "concealment" of *tzimtzum*, however, is a "masking" not for the purpose of manipulation, or a postmodern play of surface mirrors, but an ascetic-ethical-spiritual gesture in which one limits oneself, in which one moves out of one's own position into the position of the other. I indeed use this model to instruct me in my own teaching, conceiving of my role less as expansive self-expression but as leaving a "trace" (*reshimu*) of myself in the space I create for my students, a trace that hints, points, invites, but does not compel. (Thus also my reluctance to write a highly "confessional," autobiographical narrative here as well.) Students should also have the freedom to withhold their personal beliefs. But the larger lives we all live should be felt at the edges, indicated, traced.[9] R. Nachman further understood in his own brilliant way that this act of emptying out is also deeply productive for the teacher. For in the act of teaching, of comprehending and giving of knowledge, the teacher, so to speak, "empties" herself of her knowledge," and so creates an open space within herself that enables entirely new knowledge to enter her mind. The bestower becomes the receiver.

Ultimately, this concept of *tzimztum* and necessary contraction reminds me of what my many years of teaching experience have also led me to conclude: *that one can never really teach anything "directly."* The teaching that is truly received and absorbed by the student is done via indirection. And the arousal of the desire to know itself also comes so often through indirection, through a lack which prompts desire, through a glimpse of a trace which tracks a glimmering light. Indirection, as R. Nachman understood so well, was also the secret power of stories. Stories, he said, help people who have "fallen asleep," who are sunk in an existential darkness and lack of awareness to awaken and, as he puts it, "find their face," without the light overwhelming and blinding them. Stories "garb" and "enclothe" the light so it can be received, enable the sleeper to awaken gently, like blind person healing and slowly coming to see illumination (*Likkutei Moharan* "Patakh. R. Simon" 60)[10]

Maria Harris, in *Teaching and the Religious Imagination,* has also described teaching-via indirection using Kierkegaard's idea of "indirect communication." In indirect communication, the communicator's intent is nevertheless to "confront the hearer in a way that enables the hearer to discover that a rigorous demand is set before her or him," an "existence possibility" that forces the reader to choose her relation to the communication (positive or negative). In so doing, the hearer chooses her own subjectivity. This is not a choice for or against the "subject matter" as a system of clues, but the *relation toward* that possibility or subject matter. The hearer does this through a "double reflection: through apprehension of the form presented, and through approbation of the form in relation to the self" (66). Ultimately, then the student/hearer is aroused "not only to *do* something (or be something or dream something, or await something, or allow something to happen) but to recognize that one is morally, ethically religiously *called* to do something" (69).

LETTERS: SEEING THE FACE OF THE STUDENT

I cannot conclude this essay without at least offering a glimpse of some of the faces in my classroom, and of modes of teaching I have tried to develop to "see the face of the other." In the end, for me it all comes down to what occurs in the classroom, when teacher and students meet "face to face." Jane Tompkins says it well when she writes that despite all our professed academic goals of critical thinking, or social change, or transmission of cultural heritage, or professional training,

> I have come to think that teaching and learning are not preparation for anything but are the thing itself.... The classroom is a microcosm of the world; it is the chance we have to practice whatever ideals we cherish. The kind of classroom one creates is the acid test of what it is one really stands for. And I wonder, in the case of college professors, if performing their competence in front of other people is all that amounts to in the end. ("Pedagogy," 659)

For all the proclamations of contemporary cultural and postmodern theory abut the social and dialogical nature of knowledge, and how knowledge is created through the conversations we engage in with communities of interpreters, and for all our idealistic talk about the University as a "community"—all too often, the academy is lonely, fragmented, and anxiety-ridden place for both faculty and students. A philosophy professor friend once bemoaned to me that he could not find a community in which he felt at home: his only real "community" are the people for whom he writes his academic essays, and who come to the conferences he runs. But that is an *audience*, not a community. Despite our attempts to create classroom and University "community," we often are really only "audiences" for each other' s monologues.

Like Rosenzweig I find it harder and hard to write "books," and more and more use an epistolary mode in my teaching and writing in order to see the face of the other. It was one of the students in a graduate seminar I offered on the topic "Literary Theory and the Teaching of Literature" who spurred this change in my teaching She pointed out to me that the " memos" I had asked all the students in that seminar to write to each other about the micro-teaching exercises that each did for the class, had become wonderfully interactive letters. She persuaded me from then on to stop having students write "journals" in my classes, and convert to a form of "communally published letters." I am eternally grateful for this advice to Mary Alice Delia, whose dissertation, *Killer English: Postmodern Theory and the High School Classroom* (1991) includes an excellent chapter on letter writing.

This practice radically changed my teaching and the dynamics of my classroom; students write with a rare creativity, eloquence, and passion, and form closer relationships amongst themselves. The rhetorical form of the letter frees the writer to choose her or his persona and is, of course, a way of simultaneously "sounding through a mask," and "facing the other," a way of revealing and concealing at the same time, without coercion. The writer can be as intimate or as distant, as analytical or as emotional, as direct or indirect as she or he chooses. I ask each person to read his or her letter aloud, and I, too, write along with everyone. In the end, this letter writing makes every one a participant, gives everyone a voice and a face, even those who are shy or afraid to speak.[11]

That frustrated student who had wanted to write her Honors Thesis on the "Meaning of Life" wrote the following end-of-the-semester summary letter to our "Bible as Literature Class":

Dear Class:
We've chatted long and hard about the Old Testament and discovered more ways than I thought possible to look at it. We talked of good and evil and love and humanity, and almost all of creation. We've looked at families and gender and cycles of forgiveness. And perhaps some of us are in agreement with Jan's statement about the Bible, that "it is not supposed to make sense." But that's exactly why it does make sense. We can look at it from any angle and see a semblance of ourselves in its reflection of the world. We find connection (and in a small way, comfort) by that recognition. And that's the marvel. That's why so many millions of people have turned to it, and continue to turn to it,

While I started out the semester asking, "What is the meaning of life?" and I'm not necessarily any closer to the answer, I've learned more ways to search for it . . . it comes down to us to judge ourselves.

We may all be "tools" in a master plan. Or there may truly be free will. We may all be doomed to isolation and failure—no character in the entire Bible exists without suffering, and an occasional mistake. Even the "upright and blameless" Job must bear his share. Whatever the truth of reality is (which we have no way to ultimately determine) it is only ourselves that we can hold accountable . . . We lose things when we lose track of ourselves. The Bible is one way of finding ourselves. Our connections with the characters, our instincts to fill in the spaces by relating what we would feel or think, that is what provides meaning, what unifies us all as humans.

We often cannot make sense of the data of our lives, because like Jacob who doesn't know how to reconcile himself with what he's done because "he's done something that is greater than his awareness of himself. He has moved into his destiny" (Hugh O'Donnell), we cannot always see past our present knowledge to the changes that are occurring in our being. We can only take Pam's interpretation of Eve to heart and realize that not just the serpent, but God and ourselves are "necessary to the realization of our purpose: to live."

"We can look at it from any angle and see a semblance of ourselves in its reflection of the world": her words uncannily echo the key trope I have been working with here all along. In this class, not only the text, but each of us was a kind of refracting mirror which allowed her to see a "semblance" of her face—and to connect with the faces of others.

THE PASSING OF TEACHERS AND STUDENTS

These letters often forged deep connection between myself and many of these students. In the cycle of teaching and learning, though, the student and teacher often reverse roles, and ultimately have to part from each other. Mary Alice Delia, the graduate student who inspired me to use letters in the classroom, and who became my dear friend, was an award winning High School teacher whose battle with leukemia forced her to retire early, until the end came in November, 1997.

Ironically, the day before Mary Alice passed away, I was talking about her creativity as a teacher to a colleague in Jerusalem while we were examining texts from Jewish tradition about various forms of leave-taking, and about teachers and students. We were again looking at that greatest teacher in the Bible, Moses, and the way he responds to God's telling him that the time has come for him to leave the world, and reiterate he will not be able to go into the Promised Land. At the very end of the Book of Deuteronomy, Moses has to accept this decree and make arrangements to pass his teachings and authority on to his student and successor, Joshua. There are many intriguing *midrashim* which creatively expand on this narrative. In many of them, Moses protests, argues, and refuses to accept God's pronouncement that the end has come. In one of the most extraordinary, Moses again asks God for the chance not to die and God tells him:

> "This is how I have decided, and this is the way of the world: each generation has its interpreters, its economic guides, its political leaders. Until now, you had your share of service before me: now, your time is over and it is your disciple Joshua's turn."
>
> Moses answered, "Lord of the world, if I am dying because of Joshua, I shall go and be his student."
>
> God replied, "If that is what you wish to do, go and do so."
>
> Moses goes to become Joshua's student, conceals himself at door of Joshua's tent and listens to him teach, but suddenly the methodological and pedagogical rules of wisdom are taken from Moses and he no longer understands. The children of Israel plead with him to teach them the last words of the Bible, but he says, "I do not know what to tell you," stumbles and falls. And he then says to God, "Until now I asked for my life, but now my soul is given to you." (Midrash *Tanchuma*, end of *V'Etchanen*).

In this midrash, in order to hold on, Moses is willing to abandon his role as teacher and become his student's student. But that perhaps is the way of any great teacher. Both the way a teacher begins to learn how to be a teacher, and the way a teacher ends her career as a teacher.

So, finally, I often wonder what indeed does remain of all the classes we have prepared, committee meetings attended, writing we have read and published, and students we have taught. I will remember Mary Alice as much as, if not more than, the books and lectures I have written and heard. For in the end, what are they all about but to facilitate each other's illuminations, to recognize and confirm each other's faces? So I end this essay with these reflections not to depress or sadden, but to help us remember the preciousness of our lives together in the University, and the shortness of the time. The writer Grace Paley once said: "To me teaching is a gift because it puts you in loving contact with young people." As I think back on my life in academia, perhaps that what will be what most endures.

NOTES

I would like to express my gratitude to the Mandel School for Advanced Professional Educators in Jerusalem where I was a Jerusalem Fellow from 1997–1999 for the time and support needed to write this essay. I am equally grateful to the many friends and colleagues in Jerusalem, who stimulated my thinking about this topic, helped me formulate ideas and track down sources, and who represent to me what Jewish learning, superb pedagogy, and humanistic education are all about: Rav Daniel Epstein, Melila Eshed- Hellner, Walter Hertzberg, Menachem Kallus, Rav Marc Kojovsky, Daniel Marom, Simi Peters, Jeffrey Saks, Ora Wiskind-Elper, Sassona Yovel, Noam Zion, Aviva Gottlieb Zornberg.

1. See Lee S. Shulman, "Theory, Practice, and the Education of Professionals." *The Elementary School Journal* (98:5):511–526. That turn of the century "ideology" of professionalism, writes Shulman, valued the technical "objective" and "scientific" but also had an equally strong moral and "service" aspect which we need to recover.

2. The dictionary I refer to here is the online http://www.dict.org which is the DICT Development Group: Online Dictionary Query, a database of several dictionaries. I also used the online Middle English Dictionary http://www.hti.umich.edu.

3. My earlier books were: *The Slayers of Moses: The Emergence of Rabbinic Interpretation in Modern Literary Theory*, and *Fragments of Redemption: Jewish Thought and Literary Theory in Scholem, Benjamin, and Levinas*. Recent work on pedagogy includes: "The Torah of Criticism and the Criticism of Torah: Recuperating the Pedagogical Moment," in Steven Kepnes, ed. *Interpreting Judaism in a Postmodern Age* (New York: New York UP, 1996): 221–242; "Dear Class," *Essays in Quality Learning:Teachers' Reflections on Classroom Practice* in Steven Selden, ed. (University of Maryland, IBM Total Quality Learning Project, 1998):17–32;"' We Cleverly Avoided Talking About God': Personal and Pedagogical Reflections on Academia and Spirituality," in *Courtyard: Jewish Theology Seminary* 1:1 (1999); "Emunah: The Craft of Faith," *Crosscurrents: Religion and Intellectual Life* 42:3 (1992): 293–313.

4. Moshe Idel, "Models of Learning in Jewish Mysticism," unpublished lecture to the Summer School of the Institute for Advanced Study, Hebrew University, Jerusalem, June 26, 1998.

5. For more on the relation of the modern secular University and religious issues, see works such as Parker Palmer, *To Know as We are Known: Education as a Spiritual Journey* (San Francisco: Harper San Francisco, 1993); Jane Tompkins, *A Life in School: What the Teacher Learned*, (Reading, MA: Addison-Wesley, 1996); Mark Schwen, *Exiles from Eden: Religion and the Academic Vocation in America* (NY: Oxford Univ P, 1993).

6. This precise formulation comes from my friend and colleage Simi Peters.

7. God again asks a similar question to Cain: "*Where* is Abel, you brother" (Gen 4:9) In response, comes the famous rhetorical question: "I know not. Am I

my brother's keeper? There is an implicit textual connection with the "where" question addressed to Adam, and the two non-answers—between the inability to face one's own actions and the inability to face the other . . . resulting in murder. Following the narrative logic of the Bible in the early chapters of Genesis, perhaps we could say that the original "personal identity" question is not, "Who are you" but "Where are you?" . . . where are you situated in relation to others, present or hiding?

8. See the excellent analysis of Martin S. Jaffee, "A Rabbinic Ontology of the Written and Spoken Word: On Discipleship, Transformative Knowledge, and the Living Texts of Oral Torah," *Journal of the American Academy of Religion* (65.3): 526-549. Jaffee insightfully analyzes the dialectic of Oral and Written Torah in terms of the "face-to-face encounters" of the rabbinic teacher-student relation, and the sense of teacher as "living text" to be decoded and recomposed by the student for his or her life.

9. I thank R. Zvi Blanchard for helping me formulate the relation in this way.

10. I am grateful to Ora Wiskind-Elper for her kind personal assistance in helping clarifying R. Nachman's work for me, and aid in tracking down sources. See also her book on R. Nachman, *Tradition and Fantasy,* p. 220 and her entire Ch 2, "Telling Tales, or the Physic and Metaphysics of Fiction."

11. See also Wayne Booth's well-known essay "The Rhetorical Stance." Booth points out that most college students have no sense of a real audience when they write, nor can they find the proper tone of voice—for after all, the reader is the instructor with the red pencil and grade book, and that is not a "real" audience. So students write in the pedantic, disembodied voices that suppress any personal relation to the reader, or between the writer and the subject, and lose any sense of what the writing is *for.* In *Writing Teacher's Source Book,* ed G. Tate and E. Corbett. (New York: Oxford UP, 1981).

6 "WHO WAS THAT MASKED AUTHOR?"
The Faces of Academic Editing

Louise Z. Smith

To what extent and in what ways is academic editing personal? It might look objective. Since 1980, *PMLA* has had a policy of author-anonymous and referee-anonymous (or "blind") review of manuscripts. Submissions must exclude internal tip-offs as to their authors' identities, so that referees can focus on what's said rather than on who (or whose protegé) said it. Referees' identities, too, are withheld from authors: no rewards, no reprisals. The object is fairness. Recently, though, *PMLA*'s editorial board considered doing away with anonymity. With signed submissions, so goes the argument, established authors will not have to bother with the long, drawn-out process of review and revision some see as "brutal," but will get into print as quickly as if their articles had been commissioned (Shea). As for unknown authors, good luck. *PMLA* has maintained anonymous review. But even *with* it, you can't entirely eliminate the personal in academic editing.

The four participants in *PMLA*'s "Guest Column: Four Views on the Place of the Personal in Scholarship" (1996) concurred that "the personal" inevitably shapes literary scholarship. Of course, literary editors have famously imparted their personal imprints: Gordon Lish substantively "changed some of [Raymond Carver's] stories so much that they were more his than Carver's" (Max 34). *The New Yorker*'s Harold Ross and William Shawn employed dramatically differing though equally influential editorial personae. Although Shawn's persona seemed "an inspired sort of doing nothing, of just letting a piece run" (Mehta 71), his tastes governed which pieces ran. (In contrast to Shawn, unduly assertive copy editors have damaged literary manuscripts [Higgins, Becker]). Editors of life writing, too, acknowledge personal factors; if editing is hard when they have "to drag the mere truth out of some notable who is swollen with self-importance," it is "even harder when the editor [knows] the author" (Davison 92). Over the past twenty years, even the relatively objective field of textual studies (which compares textual variants so as to arrive at a "standard edition")—has "reapportion[ed] textual authority . . . from a monovocal . . . toward a [democratized] polyvocal" entity in which many personal agendas must be negotiated (Pettit 252; Tanselle). I know of no one so far, however, who speaks of a profoundly personal enterprise that also shapes scholarly discourse: journal editing.

Having edited *College English* between 1992 and 1999, I now have a fuller understanding of "academic discourse." What finally gets into print by no means represents it. Only editors know the broad spectrum of submissions, and if we sent *every* submission to referees, they'd be justifiably furious with us for wasting their time. Each published article bears the personal imprints—in both substance and style—of author, referees, and editors engaged in often highly personal processes of negotiation. An article is a polyvocal text, though its author finally bears responsibility and authority. Moreover, behind each *un*published manuscript stands a person who very often, in one way or another, is isolated. That person needs an editor's serious reading perhaps even more than a regularly published author does. Corresponding with both published and unpublished authors was a major part of my work as editor. An editor does not necessarily just sift submissions and publish some of them, thumbs up, thumbs down.

If they ever think about it, readers may find my editorship impersonal. (Quiz: Name the current editors of *PMLA*, *CE*, and one journal in your special field. Gotcha? Donald Gray's term as *CE* editor ended in 1985, James Raymond's in 1992, but in 1999 I still get forwarded letters addressed to each. Journal editing is a bastion of anonymity.) Until now, I have chosen to remain pretty much behind the scenes except for a few 4Cs and NCTE panels. Don't expect a searing exposé here, either: in what follows, disguised details protect confidentiality. Behind the scenes, though, the personal inevitably enters in many ways. It shapes the development of published articles, shapes editorial policies, and—for better or worse—shapes the professional lives of both obscure and established authors, as well as of editors themselves.

THE PERSONAL IN MANUSCRIPT DEVELOPMENT

My editorial term fortunately coincided with the decline of theory-speak and the ascendency of a more personal, down-to-earth voice. Richard Larson, who edited *College Composition and Communication* from 1980 until 1986, valuably advised, "Don't try to make everybody sound alike." To make room for individual voices meant, ironically perhaps, allowing some authors to continue using post-structuralist terminology, though I asked them to tame it by explaining a concept in fairly ordinary language and then giving the special term in parentheses. Every profession from English Studies to Dairy Science has its own lingo, after all. A letter-to-the-editor complaining about the term "phronesis" got no editorial sympathy (or space in *CE*), since the article's explanation had been clear. How come some English professors balk at learning new words?

What kinds of personal criticism to publish in *CE* was, for me, an intriguing question. Personal criticism is usually all about the pronoun "I"—how I read this, how I came to understand that, how I changed my mind about the other. Personal criticism has been identified as "the witnessing 'I' of subjective experience," and it has often been associated with feminist writing produced for particular occasions (Miller 14). A good example is Adrienne Rich's famous speech, "When We Dead Awaken: Writing as Re-Vision," which she gave at the MLA conference in 1971. Rich saw herself as "asking women's questions, bringing literary history and criticism back to life in both senses" (33). And she saw herself as searching for "ways ... in which the energy of creation and the energy of relation can be united" (43). Personal criticism took courage. In *The Last Gift of Time* (1997), Carolyn Heilbrun looks back twenty years to when she wrote *Reinventing Womanhood* (1979). The book

> represented, in its introduction, what was for me *a remarkable act of bravery*; it *still* seems brave to me upon reflection. In this current age of memoirs, detailed recollections, and the publication of one's most personal ordeals and imaginings, *my need of the courage required to speak personally and of my family in the late 1970s must seem quixotic, if not deluded.* (193, my italics)

In the tabloid-besotted 1990s, it was easy to forget what courage personal criticism demanded of Rich and Heilbrun, and their historical moment in early feminism is in any case long gone. Now we can readily acknowledge that Rich's questions are not exclusively "women's questions," and that the challenge of uniting the energies of creation and relation is not only women's work. In 1942, Alfred Kazin praised Edmund Wilson because

> At a time when ... the very exercise of criticism seemed peculiarly futile and isolated, Wilson continued to write ... [as, in Saint-Beauve's words] a "naturalist of souls," a critic in whom judiciousness and sympathy became illumination.... In [the 1930s,] an age of [Marxist] fanaticisms and [New Critical] special skills, he stood out as the quiet arbiter, the *private* reader of patience and wisdom whose very skill gave him a *public* importance. (447-448, my italics)

Perhaps it is no accident that Wilson's dedication of *Axel's Castle* takes the form of a personal letter addressed to Christian Gauss, a letter that says "I have wanted to dedicate [this book] to you in acknowledgment of the kindness and instruction which, beginning at college, have continued ever since...." What kind of "you" might Wilson and Kazin, Rich and Heilbrun have in mind in envisioning their readers? In working with manuscripts, it seemed to me that the implied listener in personal criticism is a "you" rather than a "they" and that we need to distinguish the "you" of strong personal criticism from the "you" of merely cathartic personal criticism.

The implied listener in personal criticism definitely is a "you" rather than a "they," because personal criticism firmly embraces the essay form, as distinct from the article form. In an article, a relatively disembodied writer addresses a remote audience—"they" who must be convinced. *New Literary History* editor Ralph Cohen illustrates the point by quoting Paul de Man's account of fruitlessly seeking unity among a collection of his own articles (which he calls "essays"):

> The fragmentary aspect of the whole is made more obvious still by the hypotactic manner that prevails in each of the essays taken in isolation, by the continued attempt, however ironized, to present a closed and linear argument. The apparent coherence *within* each essay is not matched by a corresponding coherence *between* them. Laid out diachronically in a roughly chronological sequence, they do not evolve in a manner that easily allows for dialectical progression or, ultimately, for historical totalization. Rather, it seems that they always start again from scratch and that their conclusions fail to add up to anything. (qtd. in Cohen 1)

Such a disjunction is the antithesis of personal criticism—and of the essay. The article writer presents an airtight case: the facts and the very best way to interpret them, a way that overcomes all potential counter-arguments and emerges as unanswerable: "So there!" In each new article, de Man seems to me to be saying, the disembodied argument begins "from scratch" because it must stifle the embodied person—that potentially trouble-making person who knows firsthand where the flaws and counter-evidence are buried so as to make the argument "closed and linear." If the real embodied person were allowed to speak his mind more fully, there *would* be some continuity from one argument to the next. On the other hand, in an essay—as in a personal letter that makes its recipient "feel addressed" (Koppelman 76) and invited to answer—a speaker more candidly acknowledges troublesome factors, addresses a nearby "you" listener, explores some of the facts and offers an interesting—though not airtight—interpretation of them to which "you" responds with gestures of intimacy—a nod, a glare, a raised eyebrow, and so on. Ironically, even while the participants in *PMLA*'s Guest Column affirmed "the personal" in scholarship, none addressed the others as a listening "you"; each was writing an article, not an essay.

As I have recently suggested, an essay makes "you" feel addressed by employing the deictic relationship between "I" and "you" that Montaigne coined in discovering

> that he is neither the source nor the location of deixis. He cannot construct stable distinctions between object and subject.... He can produce only a record of ... shifts, uncertainties, and displacement. (Kittay and Godzich 206-07)

The "you" he addresses in ordinary language (not Latin) is thus not a stable and remote entity (like the King or the Cardinal), but a nearby listener whose moment-to-moment reactions affect how "I" speaks and what "I" speaks about—the "shifts, uncertainties, and displacements" that a real person experiences but that a de Manian arguer suppresses in the interests of airtightness. Three centuries after Montaigne, Bakhtin elaborated this deictic when he spoke of the "surplus," meaning the shared but differing perspectives that result when "you and I" are together, each looking over the other's shoulder and seeing something the other cannot (Morson 53). At such proximity, each of us is "answerable" to the other, not because of systems (such as "class") but because of our concrete acts with other real individuals in ordinary life (Morson 114-15). The "surplus" embodies the ethical relationships that Kittay and Godzich explain linguistically as "spatiotemporal coordinates of the act of utterance" (19). One could say that Bakhtin's notions of "answerability" and the "surplus" are ways of naming this intellectual intimacy (Smith "Prosaic").

Today's "personal criticism" produces mixed results, some strong, others merely cathartic. Essays of strong personal criticism vigorously address a friendly and respectful reader (Germans would say, a *Sie*), whereas cathartic essays address an intimate (a *Du*) (Smith "Make"). Cathartic criticism addressed to a *Du* can be illustrated by a 1993 essay called "Breaking Silence: *The Woman Warrior*," in which the critic confesses,

> [A]fter I was divorced, sometime before the saving decision of Roe vs. Wade, I measured my security by my ability to afford an abortion. Even as a graduate teaching assistant, I kept enough money in my savings account to allow me to travel outside the United States should I need one." (Garner 122)

Sentences like those do nothing to illuminate *The Woman Warrior*. Instead, they distract us by testifying to the author's personal association with No-Name Woman, an association about which nobody cares except the author's intimates—the relatives and friends who share a personal relationship with her. Diane Freedman, editor of the volume that included Garner's essay, told me that when her students read it, they remarked that Garner had not written personally *enough*. Enough for what? To me, their reaction illustrates how easily the line between personal *criticism* and personal *exposé*—what Heilbrun above calls "the publication of one's most personal ordeals and imaginings"—may be blurred. In another example—from a critical essay on narratives of Western families by Tillie Olsen, Meridel LeSeur, and others—the author muses, "I can remember the pain I felt when I first wrote that final sentence two years ago" (Graulich 186). Again, the spotlight is redirected from criticism of the works themselves to an exposé of the author's experience of writing about them, implying that her pain of authorship is somehow comparable to the suffering portrayed in the narratives: a mawkish analogy.

CE submissions that aimed at catharsis were not published. One such submission claimed that its author "felt violated" when her dissertation director stole her citation. The rape metaphor neglected how people who had experienced literal rape might feel in reading it. Another submission recounted how a writing group helped its members to recover from a natural disaster. When it was rejected, the author retorted that only an insensitive editor could fail to sympathize with their pain—as if sympathy were the main criterion for publication. These examples illustrate a self-indulgent personal criticism that seeks authorial catharsis more assiduously than it does illumination of texts and issues. In short, the deixis involved in such cathartic criticism places "you"—*Du*—too close to the author, so close that the listener is caught up in the speaker's Montaignean "shifts, uncertainties, and displacement." At such close range, there's no room for the listener to look over the speaker's shoulder and see the Bakhtinian surplus. Instead of Bakhtinian "answerability," the self-indulgent speaker elicits Rogerian echoing: "You felt violated?" This foreshortening results in the listening *Du* seeing almost the same things the speaker sees, risking a kind of rhetorical solipsism. Self-indulgent personal criticism addresses readers *as if* they were the author's intimates and thus falsifies intimacy. The "you" it addresses is a phoney: am I supposed to say, "I'm sorry"? How sorry *am* I, really, or is that just a sweet nothing, after which I go about my business? Susanne Langer's description of some expressivism as "a frozen tantrum" (26) comes to mind.

In editing *CE*, I avoided the cathartic *Du* and turned to the strong "you"—*Sie*—of the best personal criticism: *about* but also authentically, "answerably" *to* a person, one who owes the speaker nothing morally or emotionally—only friendly intellectual attention. Mina Shaughnessy provided a model for *Sie* when she recalled sitting at her desk at CUNY in 1977, "reading and re-reading the alien papers, wondering what had gone wrong and trying to understand" (*Errors* vii). Without claiming to feel my eyestrain or asking me to feel hers, she made me feel addressed and able to look over her shoulder so as to develop and challenge her work (cf. Lu, Hunter). Ten years later in 1987 Jane Tompkins's manifesto of personal literary criticism, "Me and My Shadow," appeared in *New Literary History* (how jealously I wish *CE* had had the opportunity to publish it!). Some paragraphs portray the scene of writing (Jane sits stocking-footed at her desk) and address her colleague as "you" or "Ellen"; others portray Tompkins's work impersonally and speak of the same colleague as "she" or "Messer-Davidow." To undermine "the public-private hierarchy" in academic discourse, Tompkins quotes Hawthorne's advice: authors should imagine that "a friend, a kind and apprehensive, though not the closest friend, is listening to our talk" (170), and that is the kind of reader she addresses: *Sie,* not *Du*. Feeling addressed, I thought, "Maybe after—if?—I get tenure I'll dare to write like that." Shaughnessy's preface and Tompkins's essay are models of strong personal criticism.

Similarly, Patricia J. Williams in 1991 wrote an account of how she transformed an experience recorded in her personal journal—her rage at a white clerk's prolonged refusal to unlock a door and admit her into a women's clothing shop—into a law review article. Near her essay's conclusion, Williams achieves the union Rich imagined between creation and relation, the private and the public. She moves from a private reflection—on the power she felt as the sole audience for her father's poems—to a public reflection on race and gender:

> My power was in living the lie that I was all audiences [of my father's poems]. My power was in the temptation to dissemble, either out of love or disaffection. This is blacks' and women's power, I used to think, this power to lie while existing in the realm of someone else's fantasy. (707)

Williams's intimate family members are by no means the only "you" to whom her personal reflections are addressed. Both Tompkins's and Williams's stories of writing achieve intellectual intimacy between the storytelling speaker and *Sie*. This is what cathartic criticism, limited by *Du*, merely claims. Yet, there is an element of celebrity journalism in these pieces of personal criticism: if Tompkins were not well-known as editor of *Reader Response Theory* (and as Mrs. Stanley Fish), or if Williams could not subtitle her book *The Diary of a Law Professor*, could they risk self-revelation with quite the same confidence that readers would find their private lives interesting?

Self-revelation without self-indulgence characterizes *CE* essays I published by Carol Deletiner, Richard Miller, Paul Kameen, Kurt Spellmeyer, Ruth Spack, and Nancy Welch to name just a few. Here are some examples. Dan Morgan's student confesses to murder, and from grappling with how he should respond personally and professionally, Morgan concludes that students' "extreme" situations *"reflect what has been occurring in our society at large"* (324). Dana Elder transforms a "prose poem addressed to my parents" into a public meditation on social class in the academy (Elder 570). Pauline Uchmanowicz calculates her double-time career as a part-time instructor in terms of "dog years" and finds pedagogical riches in correspondence between students in private and public colleges (Uchmanowicz). Jerry Herron recalls writing of Walter Pater's "arrival at Oxford [as] typical of a more general arrival, which the university made possible . . . ," and then remarks, "This passage has a lot more to do with the wishful transformation of somebody like me . . . than it does with Walter Pater. . . ." Herron's experience of "turning against where [he] had already been" is not only personal, but also a "turning against history" that may characterize "ambitious Americans" as a class, people with "an urge to belong and not to belong" (930-934). Just as he says after reading a poem, "it was so good to be written to" (937), *CE*'s readers might feel he was writing to us as his *Sie.* Linda Brodkey wishes "everyone were taught to write on the bias" because language without a bias "is only words as cloth is only threads," and because writers cannot avoid bias simply "by recast[ing] their first person claims into the third person" (546): the personal is inescapable. Revision entails many personal elements, and not one single *CE* submission was published without revision—almost always substantive. To define the border between editing and co-authorship is a special challenge, learned mostly by trial and error. It often began with my trying to understand why two referees had rendered conflicting advice, to help an author decide which of their suggestions to heed or ignore, and to consider what suggestions I could usefully offer. How could I help an author to address both specialists and generalists, to acknowledge opposition without sacrificing her own stance, to integrate further research without losing focus on his original question? How could I help an author to organize more clearly and less repetitiously, to introduce and conclude more engagingly, to boil down stylistically—without ending up sounding like me? Would an author receiving my five-page single-spaced revision letter full of questions and suggestions—along with half the manuscript's sentences restructured and condensed—just pack up and take the work elsewhere? That happened once. Authors did not accept every suggestion, nor did I expect they would. For me, *the* great pleasure of editing was to talk over what an author's idea was and how best to get it across. To see me through occasional bad days—hazy, hot, and humid days when editing felt like doing somebody else's laundry while my own piled up—I kept a "kudos" file full of letters saying "Thanks for helping me figure out what I had to say." In 1997 I wrote such a letter to *Mosaic* editor Evelyn Hinz in gratitude for her extensive work on a manuscript I had submitted—the best support my writing has ever had. Every published *CE* article entailed many personally negotiated questions, but you might find examples of them tedious. Besides, they are confidential.

THE PERSONAL IN EDITORIAL POLICY

An editor's personal preferences can shape a journal in matters ranging from insignificant to crucial. An editor can design a journal's look and feel, can revamp its features, and can control the much more serious matter of anonymous or signed review. I changed the first two as little as possible. I maintained anonymous review—fiercely! Even so, no matter how carefully guarded the identities of authors and reviewers are, eventually an editor cannot help but find out. Fierceness notwithstanding, the personal then enters into manuscript selection.

An editor might use a journal's design as a way to express her personality, kind of like wallpaper. Oh boy, I fantasized, now *College English* can have cat cartoons and a centerfold "Theorist of the Month." But I never thought the journal belonged to me personally. Asked in 1991 to redesign the cover, I replied "What's wrong with the blue stripes?" NCTE answered, "We always redesign for new editors." After my "But why spend the money?" repeatedly failed to persuade, I finally suggested, "OK, how about the letter E in various fonts flying through a window, suggesting the varieties of English Studies to which the journal is open?" Still blue and white.

Nor did I feel it was up to me to change the features (which earlier editors had kept consistent). Yes, *CE* would continue to include lyric poetry, which enabled the journal to be literary in brief, offered pleasure to readers and, frankly, provided flexibility in spacing copy. No, I would not add an editor's column, since I wished neither to opine eight times a year nor to explain how each issue cohered; *CE* would speak for itself. Yes, *CE* would continue to ban footnotes, even though I personally prefer them (Thompson). *That* decision, though, was a mistake: footnotes can provide readers with access to the origins and trajectories of a discussion, a valuable function for a journal whose over 15,000 member subscribers span a great many specialities. I compounded the mistake by believing that fairness demanded consistency throughout my editorial term. In not changing the journal's design and the features, I did not of course avoid "the personal." Some of my characteristics—thrift, respect for precedent, preference for staying in the background (oh well, *and* fondness for blue and white)—invisibly shaped these early decisions and the discourse resulting from them.

The most important editorial policy was to maintain anonymous review. This policy hadn't been broken exactly, but it had been a little bit bent by guest-edited issues. Even if a "call for papers" precedes these, guest editors *may* end up quietly commissioning contributions. Then fairness diminishes. Avoiding guest-edited issues, I nevertheless retained the clearly labeled "Editor's Choice" and introduced the occasional "symposium" among experts whom I obviously had invited. By and large, however, I resisted Stanley Fish's view that author-anonymity is neither feasible nor desirable. For Fish all editing is personal: famous authors' manuscripts are *ipso facto* significant, as are their protegés' to a lesser extent, whereas unknowns' manuscripts require the advice and consent of the most famous referees willing to evaluate them (1985,

1988). However, I believed that Fish's view confused ideological with personal identity, over-valued the latter as constitutive of scholarship, assumed that reputation is self-maintaining, and—all or nothing—found anonymity undesirable unless it could assure a perfectly objective process (Smith "Anonymous").

In order to maximize *im*personality, our practice at *CE* resembled the *PMLA* practice to which Fish objected. I commissioned book review essays by experts whose own scholarship had earned them the right to evaluate that of others. Otherwise, our staff logged in each manuscript anonymously, making sure to conceal any internal reference to the author's identity (including institutional affiliation). Anonymous log-in applied even to manuscripts whose authors I had invited to submit revised and expanded talks given at MLA, CCCC, and other conferences; issuing about 75 invitations annually, I had no trouble forgetting who had given which talk. I read every manuscript and conferred with the associate editor(s) on whether to seek referees' advice. We then made up a list of possible referees. Only after that did we learn its author's identity, a necessary step in order to avoid selecting the author or the author's colleague as a referee. To the staff's amazement, my list of potential referees for a manuscript as-yet-anonymous to me often included its author's name. In fact, that is how I learned that a scholar's reputation is not self-maintaining. We readers were sometimes taken aback to discover that a piece we thought unworthy of even of being refereed, much less accepted—or that seemed likely to need very extensive revision—was in fact the work of a well-known scholar. One of my least favorite tasks was to write rejection letters to these scholars, especially when they were also my friends. On the other hand, we sometimes found that a manuscript publishable with little revision was the work of an as-yet-unknown graduate student.

*Im*personality with regard to manuscript selection was the goal—but not the means—of author- anonymous and referee-anonymous review. The personal enters the review process because potential conflicts of interest among an author and referees must be minimized. This is harder than it looks. In the small world of scholarship, it is possible to know who teaches in an author's department and appears regularly with the author on conference programs. But it is impossible to know who may have read a manuscript already for another journal, who may have heard the piece at a conference, what other social relationships may link author and referee, and who may accurately guess the author's identity. Of course an editor seeks unbiased referees—what would be the point of sending a manuscript to a referee whose approval or disapproval one could anticipate? But an editor remains at the mercy of individuals' professional integrity, which I assure you is unevenly distributed. At the high end is Heather Dubrow, whom I invited to referee a manuscript because she had established her expertise in its subject by guest editing a special issue of *PMLA*. When she received this manuscript, however, she recognized it as a submission for that special issue, one which she had admired but finally could not include. I said that that didn't matter. She wrote a detailed, positive report with valuable advice, and the piece appeared in *CE*. At the low end is a referee whose name I will not mention. An author asked her friend at another university to read a manuscript in draft; by coincidence, *CE* later asked the same friend to referee the piece, and without disqualifying herself, she trashed the manuscript (bringing up issues she had never mentioned to the author). No one would ever have discovered the conflict of interest except for a *terrible* clerical accident (the only such we know of) in which the referee's name was left unconcealed when *CE* transmitted the referee's report to the author. That was the end of their friendship, and of my respect for the referee. It took two acts of fate to make the personal visible—glaringly—in this ostensibly impersonal process.

Other personal factors can color an anonymous review process. Referees are selected because they have published scholarship in the field to which an author seeks to contribute—*and* because they can be counted on to deliver a detailed, constructive review on time, a personal quality that an editor discovers only through experience. Some very famous and busy referees took time to compose detailed and constructive reports for which the authors and I are deeply grateful; whether these referees ever contacted the authors once their manuscripts were published I have no idea. If not, the connection remains invisible.

Another personal element is that a referee may sabotage or promote an author's challenging or applauding the arguments that that referee has established. However, an editor can usually avoid that referee only if he or she appears in the author's works cited list. Unlisted but similarly situated referees cannot be avoided because no *CE* editor can possibly know all the networks of alliance and enmity in every scholarly speciality. The editor of a specialized journal or a newsletter might have a somewhat better chance at guessing who might recognize an author's identity or have an ax to grind, and so on. Also, referees may use a manuscript as a springboard for their own ideas, ignoring what it does say and competing rather than collaborating with the author.

Still another factor that compromises even anonymous review is that today's reviewer may be tomorrow's reviewee (Patten 100), a consideration that may have prompted a doctoral student to volunteer to review his dissertation director's latest book for *CE*. (Or was he just green?) Moreover, I believe one earns the right to review others' work by making one's own scholarly mark first. The butter-up factor is one reason why referee-anonymity is just as important as author-anonymity. In the interests of consistency and fairness, I even declined referees' requests to be identified to authors so as to collaborate, reasoning that their collaboration could grow after a manuscript was published.

Personal circumstances—especially impending tenure decisions—also can affect objectivity. An assistant professor's request for speedy review can be ethically accommodated. But what about the author, invited to revise a refereed manuscript, who told her tenure committee that it had been accepted—and then later, when the revision turned out to be weaker than the original and was rejected, enlisted an advocate to twist my arm? An amusing instance of attempted interference came from an irate participant in the University of Texas's culture wars during Linda Brodkey's days as writing program director. Having heard of her *CE* article "Writing on the Bias," he threatened me with a lawsuit if I published anything more about the UT situation. How easily he might have discovered that "bias" referred to cutting cloth, a metaphor in Brodkey's literacy biography.

A final personal element was my reliance on readers to realize that the views expressed in any given article were not necessarily those of "the management." I never felt that *CE* belonged me; rather, it ought to represent the interests and demographics of a very large and diversified professional organization. I tried to make sure that *CE* included authors representing various kinds of academic institutions and ranks, as well as races, ethnicities, and religious and sexual orientations. Only once in seven years did an author claim ethnic discrimination as the cause for rejection of a manuscript. I told the author that the manuscript simply wasn't done well enough for *CE*. (When my stuff gets rejected, is it because an editor has found it too smithily bland, too Z-fully mysterious, too tall?) Thus, while *CE* included my interests (such as reception studies, forms of poetry, non- and *echt*-canonical authors in balance, applied linguistics, and deafness), it also included articles that were not of particular interest to me and, frankly, some that I heartily disagreed with (for instance, Alan France's critique of David Bartholomae and Anthony Petrosky's *Ways of Reading*, which I consider The Great American Textbook for composition). Politically, I hoped that some readers would find me too conservative, others too liberal. They did. The late Thelma Atkins, a part-timer at UMass/Boston who had been a USO tap-dancer, often reassured her students, "If I insulted you today, don't feel bad. Soon I will have insulted everyone." A good motto for me, I thought.

All in all, the personal element of manuscript selection involves how such matters as the clarity and consistency of editorial correspondence, as well as the timeliness of decisions and of publication, affect authors' and referees' careers and reputations. The *im*personal, it turns out, cannot entirely avoid depending upon the personal.

CORRESPONDING WITH UNPUBLISHED AUTHORS

Does an editor read all the submissions, or just the better ones chosen by staff readers? Who writes the rejection letters? To what extent are they boilerplate? The answers to these questions have a lot to do with an editor's personal characteristics. If you decide to read all the submissions and write the letters, you're going to have less time for professional reading or playing the piano or. . . .

CE publishes roughly 10% of submissions. I decided—in retrospect, perhaps with excessive idealism—that the best I could do was to read the other 90% just as seriously and to write some individual comments to the authors. (Except for a one-semester sabbatical, when Associate Editor Gillian Gane was in charge, I did this.) In time I learned to adjust my comments to the seriousness of the submissions. The few frivolous submissions received short notes: a high school student's "A" paper, an unsolicited review sent in 1991 of a single book published 1986, a software ad thinly disguised as an article, a short story, an after-dinner speech to a town reading group—all manuscripts whose authors had obviously never looked inside the journal. In June, 1992, two poems arrived with a cover letter written on three-hole lined paper, which I'll lightly paraphrase (so as to avoid tracking the poet down for permission):

> I am a young man who has moved out of his parents' house and has written many great poems, of which one has been published in *Dude* magazine. . . . It would be very much appreciated if you published one of the following poems in your mag. Like any other professional writer, I expect to be paid if published. The first poem was written in '91, and the second was written last week.

Authors like this one received letters suggesting as gently as I could that they try another publisher.

Most rejected submissions were serious but inadequately researched. Since lazy people do not write manuscripts, I reasoned that the authors were isolated in one way or another. Some taught in colleges geographically remote from good libraries and inadequately supplied with electronic resources. Some lacked colleagues working in the same field, who could give their manuscripts preliminary readings. Some faced overwhelming workloads. Some authors confined their research to outdated sources or read too superficially, thus remaining unaware that their points had already been made. In contrast, other authors summarized research so thoroughly that they never got around to saying what made their own work newsworthy. Or they acknowledged having nothing to add to a professional discussion but, nevertheless, hoping that readers would like to know how they saw it. They were addressing *Du*, not *Sie*. Some authors represented others' work inaccurately, as saying what it would be convenient for their own arguments if it had said. And some manuscripts suffered the same ills that English 101 papers are heir to: vagueness, windiness, repetition, and convolution affecting everything from sentences to paragraphs to overall structure—none of it beyond my willing editorial help if the idea itself warranted refereeing. These authors were all writing uphill and deserved encouragement. To read their work attentively and offer some detailed comments or suggest some further reading—and sometimes to remark on interests and experiences we shared—were ways in which my rejection letters could modestly counter their isolation and foster their professional growth, and—a little at a time, I hoped—the growth of the profession. One thing no editor ought to do, however, is to name another journal that would be just right for the rejected piece; although I gladly published a few castoffs from *PMLA, Profession,* and other journals (and noticed some of *CE*'s rejections in print elsewhere), I never welcomed the task of disappointing the false expectations other editors raised, however well-intentioned. Instead, authors' own research ought to show them which journals publish in the fields to which they seek to contribute.

Some well-established authors of rejected manuscripts really ought to have known better. The prize for sentimentality went to a famous author who described taking students to spend a day in jail so that they would know what it's like to be incarcerated: the absurdity lay, of course, in the fact that the incarcerated do not go home at the end of a day. The prize for boneheadedness went to the faculty member who had her entire seminar submit papers; reading through these anonymously logged-in submissions, I increasingly wondered why so many in a single batch dealt with such similar questions—only to retrieve their cover letters and discover that the students had been sent to *CE* in search of a second set of paper comments! ("Editor goes on six-state murder spree!") Then there were the two senior authors who persuaded their graduate student to withdraw an accepted manuscript from a book-in-progress and send it along with their two manuscripts to *CE* as a three-part package. Since that would have amounted to their guest-editing a special issue, I let the three know that their manuscripts would be refereed individually. Referees recommended rejection of the graduate student's work, which I agreed was weak. I accepted the other two manuscripts, but rather than leave their protegé in the lurch ("All for one! One for all!"), the two senior authors withdrew their work. Months later they relented, *CE* published their articles, and eventually *CE* also published an entirely different manuscript by the graduate student. Another well-known author's manuscript required extensive revision, on which associate editor Pat Wright and I labored for days; on the morning when Pat was finally about to mail copy to the printer, he was eating breakfast and browsing through another publication when his eye fell upon an article by the same author, including—oh, no!—a very long passage corresponding word-for-word to part of *CE*'s copy. Of course, we had to pull the whole article and substitute another, wasting all our work and scrambling to meet the printer's deadline. Confronted with the double submission and narrowly missed copyright infringement, the author answered unapologetically, "But I <u>want</u> to publish it in *CE*. The circulation is so much larger." Each of these vignettes shows personal motives that remain invisible in published academic discourse. Thank goodness such situations are unusual.

Editorial correspondence includes personal moments as sad, bizarre, and funny as any other part of academic life. An established scholar urged me—purely on his say-so, never mind the scholarship—to write on behalf of his friend at another university who had been denied tenure and to get my friends to do the same. An unknown author accused a *CE* author of repeating the unknown's ideas expressed some years before in a graduate seminar they had taken together. A famous author charged that in rejecting his submission I was part of a cabal. When a submission that relied upon caricature was rejected, its author retaliated with Xeroxed copies of several already-published articles setting forth the identical caricature—but with differing examples: a kind of self-plagiarism. An author's name appeared on each page of a submission (against the rules on *CE*'s mast page), so we cut it off before reviewing it; not having kept a copy, the author insisted that I retype it. I rejected a humor piece, thus convincing its author that I had no sense of humor—or had lost it since *CE* published another humor piece years before. And so on.

ME AND *MY* SHADOW

What does it mean to me personally that I am *CE*'s first woman editor? When my gender is no more noteworthy than my being the first Dutch-American editor, or the tallest, feminism will have accomplished one of its goals. For years women have made such significant contributions to the English Studies profession, that my relatively small role in the 1990s seems to me quite ordinary—and it's very good to be able to say that. In 1998, a freelance writer's informal survey of editorial correspondence concluded that male editors value competence, autonomy, and achievement, whereas female editors value nurturance, collaboration, and understanding (Thomson). He presents his results lightly, and I do not want to make too much of them except to say that they not only reify outdated gender stereotypes—the (male) ethic of justice and the (female) ethic of care, as if we could have one without the other—but also contradict my experience of having my work edited by *Mosaic*'s Evelyn Hinz and *CE*'s Donald Gray, who both value all those qualities.

Am I just a cog in the profession's publication machinery? Faculty hired in the 1950s and early 1960s might finish their dissertations after they became tenured, whereas today's young faculty complete theirs—and often publish several articles—before getting their first jobs. At places where tenure once demanded an international reputation, it now must be intergalactic. Tabloid scholarship sells increasingly well because "as a credential for tenure or promotion at a real college or university," such work is "transgressive"; the background of traditional scholarship gives such work its point (Dowling 121-124). As the young publish more, so must the gray—or forego merit raises. Ernest Boyer's 1990 report to the Carnegie Commission revealed that 47% of professors thought that publications were merely counted (not read qualitatively). And 45% felt that pressures to publish detract from teaching. Yet of twenty-five reasons to publish given by James Axtell, Kenan Professor of Humanities at William and Mary, fifteen are personal (Axtell 5, 9-15). His last, most emphatic reason is that "publication of scholarship . . . is a form of teaching in itself" (16), and I believe that *CE* is especially attuned to that connection. To publish in *CE*, with its broadly conceived orientation towards teaching, might help win tenure and promotion in some institutions—and place one below the salt in others. In my early years, *CE* became my favorite journal because its articles closely linked knowing, understanding, and *doing*—though only occasionally transgressing. Ideally, every *CE* article helps readers teach with greater understanding of English Studies (even if they do not teach the particular subject—or with the particular critical concepts—at hand). It will be up to others to judge the extent to which we achieved this ideal.

The most personal element in academic editing is the professional friendships built through correspondence and amongst the staff. How often have we thought, "Why even ask so-and-so if s/he is willing to referee a manuscript when s/he is in such demand as a speaker and writer?" only to receive a cheerful "Sure, send the manuscript" followed in due course by a thoughtful, detailed, and collaborative referee's report. How often have I mailed one of my mega-revision letters and then regretted some lapse in diplomacy, only to hear from the author, "Thanks, I needed that!" Our profession is rich in generous good will, much of it given quite invisibly—all far less colorful than some of the situations described above—and almost always proffered in a friendly, respectful way to *Sie*.

In the transition from James Raymond's editorial term to mine, he advised me, "Hire people who can do things that you can't." Office manager Anita Anger kept us organized (in seven years, we misplaced one manuscript), helped me find the right tone of voice in difficult correspondence, and particularly nurtured our interns in learning the ways of professional life. Associate editor Pat Wright fiercely perfected every detail (insisting, for instance, that the printer's software could print a really *good*-looking Old English ash for John

Niles's *Beowulf* article [December 1993]), and he put together the symposium on teaching literature in the composition classroom (March 1993). Associate editor Gillian Gane fiercely got the graphics just right (for instance, in Andrea Lowenstein's article on teaching *Maus* [April 1998]), and she put together the symposium on English Studies at the millennium (July 1999). The beautiful young people who have been our interns have gone on to careers in music, social services, public relations, publishing, academic administration, and secondary and college teaching. At the end of my seven years, I felt grateful to have edited *CE* yet completely ready to let it be someone else's turn, anticipating continuing associations with those colleagues I now not only write to but also talk with as *Sie,* and especially with the staff: all harmoniously *Du.*

PART FOUR
Teaching and Scholarship Public and Private

7 AUTOBIOGRAPHY
The Mixed Genre of Private and Public

Madeleine R. Grumet

As the social structures of affiliation become more abstract, more diverse, or distant, we find ourselves dashing headlong in retreat to symbols of connection that are increasingly familial—and defensive. Baseball, that great repository of nostalgia, has, for a long time stood as an icon for the intimate and enduring relations of small town life. *Bring the Dodgers back to Brooklyn!* And even I, who forswore the sport after the Dodgers left, worry that the Yankees will move to New Jersey. If the Marlins could move from obscurity to the playoffs through the purchase of "free" agent Livan Hernandez for 4.5 million dollars, then maybe like the rest of our culture, the slowest game in the world is speeding up.

But it is the freedom of Miriam Carreras, the mother of Livan Hernandez, and their reunion that provided the excitement for the '97 World Series and its narrative. Livan, who defected from Cuba to Mexico in 1995 "made eye contact with his mother for the first time in almost two years," just before the game started. Just two days before the game, Miriam Carreras had received an emergency visa from the United States Interests Section in Havana, promoted by Florida's Governor Lawton Chiles. In sunny Florida, basking in warm waters of the post Cold War world, absent an evil Empire, Castro steps up to the plate first as the villain of the piece and then, with Governor Chiles, as guardians of the mother and child reunion. It is a reunion that thrills the Latin American immigrants in the Miami bleachers as well as retirees in their Florida condominiums pining for their children, still ensconced in Cleveland and Pittsburgh. This year we were mesmerized by another parent child drama in the reclamation of Elian Gonzales by his father from his Miami relatives after his mother drowned during her flight from Cuba with Elian.

The call of home, sounding through sports, politics and media was projected on to the best seller list in 1997 in the novel, *Cold Mountain*, the saga of a reunion of lovers, and reunions between them and the land? Ada, a city girl from Charleston, living in rural North Carolina during the war learns to put down her books, her music, and drawing pad, for agrarian self-sufficiency. Her reunion with the earth is paralleled by Inman's journey away from the war, back to his home and her:

> Bleak as the scene was, though, there was a growing joy in Inman's heart. He was nearing home; he could feel it in the touch of thin air on skin, in his longing to see the leap of hearth smoke from the houses of people he had know all his life. People he would not be called upon to hate or fear. . . .It was to Cold Mountain her looked. He had achieved a vista of what to him was homeland. He looked out at this highland and knew the names of places and things. He said them aloud: Little Beartail Ridge, Wagon Road Gap, Ripshin, Hunger Creek, Clawhammer Knob, Rocky Face. Not a mountain or watercourse lacked denomination. Not bird or bush anonymous. His place. (281)

In *From Where We Stand,* Deborah Tall offers us a fascinating history of nostalgia:

> The word was coined in 1678 for the disease of homesickness. Its symptoms included insomnia, anorexia, palpitations, stupor, and the persistent thinking of home. Nostalgia was described in European medical encyclopedias up until the nineteenth century as fatal . . . Armies were frequently beset by the malady, leading one Russian general in 1733 to announce that "any soldier incapacitated by nostalgia would be buried alive." (121)

Tall comments that the meaning of nostalgia has shifted from being a primarily geographical disease to a psychological one rooted in time, the loss of home collapsed into a yearning for the past, particularly childhood. The field of education has been beset with nostalgia as Allan Bloom and company have attacked our contemporary diversity with idealized versions of their intellectual histories.

The politics of reunion haunt our work as well as loss of place, loss of relationships and loss of symbols for and of connection, are powerful and pervasive themes in curriculum and in the autobiographies and ethnographies that speak of the experience of education.

What are our attempts to recuperate our losses in our work as educators, as teachers, as researchers?

I have thought for a long time that both parenting and education inevitably involve this project of recuperation. To live with children or with students of all ages is to revisit the processes of one's own formation. You hear your mother's voice sail right through you in moments of frustration or worry: You got in at 4 a.m. and you're going out again? You worry that they will not secure the approval you sought from your father or your uncle. You stop yourself from grabbing them off diving boards, off horses, and elections platforms. You wince when they commit your particular brand of indiscretion. There iterations are exasperating, inevitable, and beautiful. They are the mimesis that extends the dance of families through time. In the intimate life of families, between each day's waking and lying down, we walk, and talk, and eat, we stand and dodge and dream together and maybe we plan and promise, graceful or clumsy, light or plodding, we dance the gestures of our parents and grandparents with our children. And even when we buy new dancing shoes, no taps for me, we liken our new dance to theirs.

Schooling, on the other hand, offers us more distance, if we would take it. It provides the stage for the same transferences as the kitchen and the living room, but the players are different, and if we are fortunate, more various. They have their own moves. The family personae are all there, costumed in the characters of the play of school, waiting to be performed, but schooling is lodged in the liminal space between the family and the workplace, and it is the privilege and responsibility of schools to offer teachers and students opportunities to play with the relations rather than to repeat them obsessively and slavishly. Because no families are ever exactly alike, not even happy ones, this gathering of students and teachers from many families invites us to write the story of coming to form once again, redefining the goals of development and the paths we will walk to reach them.

I do not say that schools are a *tabula rasa* for our imaginings of new ways to be human together; they mimic other institutions, churches and synagogues and mosques. Malls and factories, hospitals, museums, and internment centers. School time is still modeled on the labor needs of an agrarian past, school space on pews facing an altar. For few of us are these schools strange. They may be sad, but they are familiar and invite collusion with the politics of power contained in the architecture, and their rituals. Nevertheless, strong as these patterns of school culture may be, and as vulnerable as we may be to the *mise en scene* of our early hopes and disappointments, I can not believe that they exert a mystification equal to that of family life.

Because curriculum gives a name and form to what goes on in schools, to what they are supposed to be about and to the relationships and interactions that support and result from this purpose, it gives us a way to name the past and the present. Genres of curriculum operate in schools the way they do in literature. The familiar form, whether it is the lesson plan or the one-act play, provides what Frederick Crews calls a countercathected system, "a coded assurance that psychic activity will be patterned and resolved along familiar lines" (20). Because the genres of the classroom are more deliberate, because they are created and sustained in public by debate and negotiation, their function and effects (even when produced by manipulations calculated to dominate and deflect other constituencies) may be more visible to us than the forms and relations that contain our lives in families.

It takes a long time for new genres of curriculum to take hold. We are still experimenting with cooperative learning as if it were an unstable element, threatening to blow up in our faces with any prodding or poking. But the genres that we employ to study schooling are more dynamic. In the mere 25 years since William Pinar and I published *Toward a Poor Curriculum* in 1976, urging recourse to autobiographical investigations of educational experience, autobiographies, memoirs, recollections of all sorts have proliferated. The call of narrative is so strong and pervasive, that we even find it projected in a *New York Times Magazine* Section advertisement created for that great recollector of *le temps perdu*, Ralph Lauren:

> Only in America. Plaid flannel shirts, soft and worn. Jeans that are broken in, unbridled, no restraints. Clothing with the kind of honest, timeworn patina once achieved only through years of wear. Each piece is a rugged individual. There are clothes that tell a story, rich in atmosphere and character.
> Double RL by Ralph Lauren

The Marlboro man has traded in his smoke for a madeleine.

Let me recover, briefly, the genres of autobiography in my own work, for it has moved from a phenomenological inquiry to a feminist project and now is heading back to its origins.

When I try to remember what I was up to in 1975 I think that I was literally trying to change the subject of educational research. Research in the early 1970s was still dominated by quantitative studies. Analytic philosophy dominated foundations studies. The appeal of autobiography in education was the call of the humanities, specific, detailed, and organized to express the subjectivity of the learner. Phenomenology provided both goal and method. If there was a project of recollection it was the reflexive turn that recuperated the moment of intentionality; it was the desire to catch oneself in the act of thought, rushing like Sartre's wind through consciousness toward the object of interest. I never knew whether to call what I did research or pedagogy. When I worked with students it was pedagogy. When I wrote about the work it was research. As I responded to student narratives with questions, the functions of research and teaching blended. Ten years ago, I described working with a student's narrative this way: "She writes as an artist, rid of all preaching. I read as a scientist looking for the meanings both common and uncommon. My reading of her text must enter its world. I join her in a hermeneutic stroll, meeting the relatives, the neighbors, locating the object, educational experience within her horizons, her body, her language. She joins me on an epistemological perch, from which we survey the territory that she has traveled" (Grumet 1990, 120).

Over the decades that I did this work, I rarely taught a course without asking students to write three autobiographical narratives that re-presented their experiences of the phenomena we were studying. I didn't care whether these experiences they recounted had ever really happened, because I was not interested in their psychology. I was not trying to find out why they thought as they did or what events in their lives had made them the personas they were. I was interested in what and how they thought about the world, and I was interested in asking them to think about this thought. In that way the inquiry became more philosophical and phenomenological than psychological or sociological, for it was about meanings, not causes. An interesting project for people who want to teach other people about the world, don't you think? But I did not ask them to tell me what they thought of education, and the last thing I wanted to know was their personal philosophies of education. That invitation would have elicited the latest piece of popular psychology, or the old formulaic homilies that were substitutions for thought. My own scholarship involved investigating taken-for-granted assumptions about education by offering reading of narratives that challenged them and, reciprocally, of bringing questions to the narratives provoked by educational theories.

The narratives were not limited to stories of schooling. Narratives of educational experiences addressed mundane experiences like walking the dog, traumas like car accidents, adventures in mountains, on oceans, in foreign countries. Stories were told about love and crime and birth and death. The pedagogical motive was constructive, however, as well as descriptive, for students were always asked to bring these narratives into another conversation. Thus, the grand narrative of the course would include philosophical texts of Plato, Dewey, and Sartre, or literary autobiographies of Benjamin Franklin, John Stuart Mill, James Baldwin, or Sylvia Ashton-Warner. The task was not parallel play; it required them to blur genres, to challenge their narratives with these other readings and to challenge the assumptions and assertions of these other texts with their readings of their own stories. The final paper was, in my view, a linguistic bridge from the symbolization of experience they had called private to the ways of knowing we call public.

It is telling that whereas the word *public* functions as a noun in this phrase and in everyday speech, the word private rarely is seen as a noun outside the context of this opposition, except when it refers to a military recruit, or as a euphemism for genitalia. It is characteristic of our gendered society that the private should function as an index to unnamable contents, an adjective to an absent noun. Feminism has taken up the task of naming the private, taking an inventory of its contexts, and of exploring the relation of this category to the public, its putative antonym. Because schooling and education are the processes through which persons move from the domain of family—the private, to the domain of work and knowledge—the public, the experience of education has served to strengthen the opposition of these categories. Once feminists had revealed these categories as cultural constructions, rather than natural or universal necessities, feminist educators began to address the ways that schooling and informal education could undermine, rather than strengthen, this opposition and provide continuity and reciprocity between public and private experience.

The struggle to connect public and private labor mirrored the project of consciousness raising that developed in the Sixties and the Seventies, expressed in the women's movement's slogan "the personal is the political." In professional meetings and in everyday life, women met to speak and study what had been kept secret in their lives. The history, function, and cultural processes of the separation of the public and the private were explored in the significant works of Dorothy Dinnerstein, Nancy Chodorow, Jean Bethke Elshtain, and Mary O'Brien, between 1976 and 1981. The psychoanalytic and object relations theories, as well as the scholarship in political economy developed in this era moved the feminist analysis of educational experience from the liberal emphasis on rights and power to the discussion and analysis of desire. Influenced by Lacan, this analysis lodged power in the imagination, believing that it accrued to certain people or to people who were male or tall or mature because of the projections of others, as they associated power, privilege, superiority, and resources to be associated with men and not with women. As analysts studied the motives for these attributions, consciousness raising invited women to come together in their everyday lives to talk about their lives and to see how they had been complicit in the arrangement that oppressed them. The autobiographical voice was invited not only to speak in public of the experience considered private, but in the process of that speaking which served to resymbolize experience, to formulate a story and a theory that would extend the knowledge and experience of private life into the public life of communities, knowledge, and government.

In my own work the feminist projects invited me to recuperate the discourse of reproductions for education. The arrogation of that word—reproduction—to the neomarxist critique of the ways that schools extended the means and methods of production, has dramatized the extent to which reproduction, a theme in human consciousness, has been effaced in educational theory and literature. *Bitter Milk: Women and Teaching* (University of Massachusetts Press, 1988), my book that grew out of this discourse raised a number of questions about the experience of reproduction, of being a child of one's parents, or a parent to one's children and about the relation of these experiences to the ways we work with other people's children. The book raised questions about the motives that we bring from those experiences to our work in schools and universities, projects of differentiation that have led us to repudiate what we know in favor of the abstractions and canonical texts we find in school. The phenomenological project joined an analysis of identity, for what it meant to be a man or a woman has a great deal to do with how human beings think about and experience our worlds. Our sex endows each of us at birth with a set of possibilities related to our anatomy, our hormones, our capacity to procreate. These differences between men and women assume different meanings in different times, different cultures, in different families. Just as the small child learns to discriminate mama from the lady next door, learns not to run into the street, and learns to tell a dog's bow-wow from a cat's meow, that child is also learning that he or she is male or female, and what being male or female means to people with whom he or she lives. Because knowing is always situated, sexuality, class, race, religion, ethnicity are all necessarily themes that shape our attention to a world that is the object of intention and desire.

It was important to me then, as it is now, to bring the autobiographical voice into the theoretical discourse of *Bitter Milk*. It was important to resist the impulse to hide my femaleness, my motherliness, so that I would pass. I was afraid that by relinquishing the distanced stance of an abstract supposedly universal speaker (otherwise read as male) I would trivialize the work, consigning it to *Good Housekeeping's* compendium of women's confessions. I was afraid that if I mentioned the birth of my children, the life of my family, the text would be taken as a call for a return to compulsory heterosexuality and nuclear families, as it was read by a number of feminists and young women who understood the women's movement as liberating them from having to identify with procreation and child rearing. One journal's referee rebuked me for telling my middle class story here and there without including as well the stories of women of color, women of poverty. He was not, I believe, concerned about the exclusion of the narratives of women of wealth.

Some of those who welcomed the presence of narrative in the text wished that I had not contaminated it with educational theory. They liked the image of my working at the dining room table, but didn't want to plow through my ideas of what that all had to do with Piaget or Lacan or object relations theory. In elevators at the American Educational Research Association's annual convention, people would read my name tag and tell me about their dining room tables and the birth of their children, but few commented on the book's thesis that our education work is motivated by our desire to contradict our relations to our children and our own parents, relations profoundly influenced by our sex and gender. Well, it was an academic convention.

When that work was first published, first as essays, later as a book, the act of mixing genres was still pretty unusual in professional scholarship. Some feminist literary critics such as Elaine Showalter and Jane Gallop provided models, but educational texts tended to be either anecdotal or theoretical, not both, and rarely both working off each other. I have taken some time to talk about the style of this text for it is the ambiguity of style or double discourse, if you will, that, for all of its ambiguity, I miss in much of the contemporary work in educational narrative.

Before I lodge my complaint against the current rise of autobiographical studies in education, let me celebrate some of its achievements. The feminist project to bring women's voices into public discourse and to broaden that discourse to include accounts that had been silenced by the private/public split and the privileging of male discourse has been and continues to be important. There is now an extensive, persuasive, and poetic literature that testifies to the exclusion of women's experience, and particularly of our domestic experience from the texts and glossaries that constitute the disciplines of knowledge. In literature, in sociology, in anthropology, in philosophy, psychology, history, physics, biology, political science, women's standpoints are those which honor the material, concrete particularity of everyday life and honor the connection and intimacy between those who share the actual time and space of everyday life. The power of those who bear the babies and nurture them, who order the provision of food, decide what is clean and dirty, who wash the sheets and care for the aged is palpable. Repressed, this creativity has been repudiated by the myth of immaculate conception, the myth of menstrual contamination; it has been inverted into violence and destruction; it has been appropriated by abstract disciplines of knowledge, bureaucratic systems and the projection and collection of things calls property. We are still in the midst of that wave of revelation, and it is interesting to speculate about the degree to which these narratives have influenced changes in policies and law that address domestic violence, abuse, divorce, and sexual harassment.

Over the last decade, the literature of women's experience has been enriched and differentiated by texts detailing the lives and experiences of teachers and students of color. In *Learning From Our Lives* (Neumann and Peterson), Gloria Ladson Billings describes the efforts of Gloria Hull, Patricia Bell Scott, and Barbara Smith to create Black Women's Studies, a discourse situation apart from white women's racism and black men's sexism, a discourse dedicated to revealing the relatedness of race, class, and gender within and outside the academy. In the same volume, Martha Monteiro-Sieburth speaks to her Latina experience, the importance of language communities, and the importance of standpoint discrimination, insider/outsider perspectives on education and research.

Autobiographical writing became one strand in the project to dignify the professional work of teachers during the last decade. Teachers' narratives were elicited in order to display the complexity, ambiguity, creativity, or teaching. Narratives were elicited as well to convey the loneliness, frustration, and subordination of teaching. Bringing teachers together to write and to read each other's texts reinforced the collective creativity of the Bay Area National Writing Project as well as the calls for creative responsibility in the work of Maxine Green's existential challenge, Donald Schön's well received construction of the reflective practitioner. Janet Miller worked with teachers to elicit their understanding of their work, interested in building school communities from groups of teachers whose reflections would generate a common project. Connelly and Clandinin approached autobiography as a method to encourage teachers' reflexive grasp of their teaching, the ways they understood and constructed curriculum within the context of the school.

Teachers' narratives were elicited to provide the processes of community, literature, and knowledge that would remedy the sexism, classism, and downright sadism that had consigned the knowledge of teachers about children, knowledge, instruction, the politics of schooling and community to girl talk, rushed conversations in the halls, the lounge, long conversations over the phone, late at night. Let me make it clear that I am not denigrating the function of this writing or of its community building. It has brought some of the energies of consciousness raising to the communities of teachers and contributes to the ongoing work to recognize the dignity and challenge of this work.

But now, as I leaf through the articles, book titles, chapters of education literature I feel as if I am drowning in narrative. I, Miss Subjectivity of 1978, find myself scanning the memoirs, rushing past gritty scenes of urban density, languid landscapes of rural loneliness, skimming accounts of inspiring mentors, desperate differentiations. My eyes move up and down the pages seeking that shibboleth of poststructural criticism, the generalization. What's the point, I want to know. What can we make of this? What difference does it make to education? Maybe my impatience comes from this work I remember doing, administering a school of education in Brooklyn, New York where there is, to put it mildly, a lot to do. Maybe, as I age, ricocheting between the deaths of my mother and older colleagues, I am losing existential courage, knowing that I too will disappear into the moments and particulars, I seek the comfort of the large idea, the marker, so long live this, and this gives life to thee.

I am not alone in my resistance. Poststructuralist critics of autobiography have expressed their suspicions of all these scribbling selves, challenging the spurious unity of the narrating self and its linear psychology. Accompanying the logic of its narrative, is, they assert, a naïve conflation of viewpoint and truth, as if the risk of confession and the discomfort of disclosure were sufficient to confirm the veracity and authority of its judgments. This critique challenges the reliance on reflexivity that came to dominate the discourse of teacher education and development in the 1980s, as well as educational research in the 1990s. Lacking theoretical scaffolding as well as identification of educational aims, reflexivity, on its own, can dwindle into the paralysis of infinite regression or self-absorbed trivia. In response, feminist educators have pointed to the irony that postmodernism arrived to erase the speaking self just at the moment when women had seized the podium (Brodbribb). This sardonic observation is accompanied with a serious concern that the activist and political expressions of feminism will not survive the assault on the psychological self, which for all of its suspect cohesion, sustains the public identity and commitments capable of, and necessary for, social action.

Education is about social action. We teachers and teachers of teachers are different from our brothers and sisters who pursue the disciplines of history and sociology, of anthropology, of philosophy, and literature without the educational prefix. We cannot ignore the implications of what we study for the events that are taking place in schools across this country as we read and write, interview and teach, as we visit schools and communities, archives and malls.

Autobiographical theorizing suits an educational arena that finally, in the words of Jerome Bruner, has recognized that "domain specificity [is] the rule rather than the exception in logical development [and] that the achievement of knowledge [is] always situated, dependent on materials, task, and on how the learner understands things" (132). For Bruner, it is the narrative construal of reality that can constitute accounts of situated learning. He argues for the isomorphism of the narrative and thought, and offers nine universals of narrative realities. It is his assertion of these universals that interest me more than their particular qualities. If we can recognize the structures of narrative, then we may examine the processes of our own subjectivities and of the education that has contributed to their shaping. Anna Neumann provides us with an instance of this awareness as she offers us readings through thee separate narratives related to her mother's experience of the Holocaust. One narrative is Anna's, recollected from family knowledge. Another encodes her mother's answer to questions in a family interview, and the third is an account that her mother produced in a document that was part of the process of applying for reparations. Neumann tells her reader that with each telling of the story, her understanding of her mother changes, and their relationship deepens. Neumann asks how these stories, told and untold, have not only shaped the consciousness of this woman but also structured the relations within her family. Judith Butler has argued that it is the performance of the narrative that constitutes our identity, and if we understand that performance as generated outside the fact of writing in the lived and discursive conventions of our many communities, then these performances can help us to understand our own educational experiences and those we design for others.

Nevertheless, we are still nervous about holding the conversations that would help us to make some collective sense of these narratives, instances of what Seyla Benhabib calls "situated criticism." We are worried about offending each other. If a text is an expression of identity, then what is it we criticize when we find it boring, or offer an interpretation that is not the author's, or take issue with the way that someone has constructed the narrative of her or his own formation? And if that formation is situated explicitly as an expression of gender or ethnicity, how can we take issue with its assertions, if we do not share those characteristics. Our narratives have estranged us because they are defensively declarative. They preclude engagement and conversation. Their confessions display an intimacy that their rhetoric forbids.

Benhabib suggests that our postmodern passion for situated criticism (and I would add our avoidance of engaging each other's narratives) expresses our nostalgia for home, "for the certitude of one's own culture and society in a world in which no tradition, no culture, and no society can exist any more without interaction and collaboration, confrontation, and exchange. When cultures and societies clash, where do we stand as feminists, as social critics and political activists?" Benhabib asks (227). In *Situating the Self,* Benhabib articulated the concern that I am addressing here by calling for a conversation across narratives which she names "interactive universalism": "the practice of situated criticism for a global community that does not shy away from knocking down the parish walls." She describes the sometimes necessary exile of the social critic, outside the walls of the city, for "if cultures and traditions are more like competing sets of narratives and incoherent tapestries of meaning, then the social critic must herself construct out of these conflictual and incoherent accounts the set of criteria in the name of which she speaks. The hermeneutic monism of meaning brings no exemption from the responsibility of normative justification" (228).

From what ground can the critic of an autobiographical or situated text speak? If Benhabib places herself outside the walls of the city, McClaren places himself inside the walls, adopting the guise of the flaneur, to which he attaches a marxist eye. He offers us a text interrupted with journal entries from Paris, West Hollywood, Mexico, East Berlin, and Rio de Janeiro and asks whether we can "use new ways of organizing subjectivity to create a self-reflexive social agent capable of dismantling capitalist exploitation and domination" (228).

I too ask the questions that McClaren and Benhabib raise as they try to find a place for themselves as readers of culture. They seek a position from which they can make judgments and comparisons, and a place from which their understanding can project ideas and plans for a better world. I think that the position of critics is that of the reader and that the object of the critique is not the other, a hypostatized version of difference congealed into another person, but the text's display of subjectivity making sense of the construction of subjectivity. Bruner associates this process with metacognition: the object of thought being thought itself. Nevertheless, in our anxiety about identity and in our political correctness, we resort to Crews's anaesthetic criticism, "looking for motifs, inconsistencies, but avoiding the experience of being alone with a text, acknowledging its hold over us" (20). Crews sees every text as a negotiation between the fantasy of an infantile appetitive imagination and the compromises effected between those wishes and constraints of culture, achieved by a negotiating ego. These strike me as the struggle of education in a democracy, the struggle to construct a common conversation about what is possible in this place and this time for the great diversity of people who live in this community. What Crews's position returns to us is a glimpse of subjectivity, historical, embodied, but still making things up.

That is what I think autobiographical texts do: they make up stories, selecting this episode, eliminating that one, exploring this moment in details, but glossing that. They structure the accounts into fictions of causality, with beginning, middles, and ends. They attempt to capture us, as readers, by attracting our sympathy, or shocking us into admiration, or humbling us by revealing our ignorance. They invite us to abandon ourselves to their worlds, that easy reunion again, or they hold us at a distance, proclaiming their distance and inaccessibility. They insinuate multiple references or meanings or stay tight to one horizon in diction and cadence.

Bruner reminds us that when conflicting construals of reality are brought into confrontation, what is at stake is more than a theory or a finding; perhaps it is a way of being in the world. But he reminds us also that there are privileged forms of confrontation, intimate friendship—psychoanalysis, for instance, "where *prise de conscience* is the objective of the whole exercise" (Bruner, 148). To capture consciousness, to understand it, is, in my opinion, the point of educational studies; consciousness is consciousness of the world and understanding that relation of knower and known is what our work is about. If the discourse of identity and education will continue and flourish, we will need autobiography to continue to proliferate and differentiate itself, hospitable to authors who will speak from the many places and positions that this wondrous world provides. We will also need autobiography to blur genres with curriculum criticism and foundational studies so that the particularity and process of an individual's coming to know the world can be in continuous discourse with the world that presents itself to our experience.

Marilyn Brownstein offers the work of Virginia Woolf and Walter Benjamin as exemplars for this conversation with a person in the world. Woolf's *Three Guineas*, and in Benjamin's *A Berlin Chronicle* each portray an instance of what Brownstein calls a catastrophic encounter, a moment of vulnerability and ambiguity that is sensuous, embodied, and profoundly implicated in the social and ideological structures of their lifeworlds. These moments capture the contradictions that bind the speaker to the situation and generate questions about the world within which this encounter is nested. Two instances of this approach in our work come to mind. One is Jane Adan's book, *Children in Our Lives*, where the narrative of a child's dilemma is exquisitely investigated as it reveals the interpenetration of a child's construal of reality with those of the adults who care for him. Another is Wendy Atwell-Vasey's *Nurturing Words: Bridging Private Readings and Public Teaching*. Atwell-Vasey brings object-relations theory to teachers' narratives of their own conflicted and ambivalent reading experiences to understand why teachers who love to read would embed books within curriculum that discourages the intense experience of texts that these narratives convey.

Maybe the reunion of Livan Hernandez and Miriam Carreras was one such moment of critical encounter, when they were reunited by the economic and political interests that had separated them. How would they tell that story? And how would you read it? In each case there is a double tension. There is tension in the original narrative and there is tension on the part of its interpreter/critics, who meet the text with body and soul, credulity and incredulity. For finally, the position of the critic/reader/interpreter is not a problem of placement, inside or outside the city walls, but engagement. Rather than parallel play, we must write narratives that pose a question about our experience in the world and invite our readers to join us in the exploration that results. It is a generous and humble act that displays one's own vulnerability as writer and reader. The research of such an autobiography is indeed a reunion as the writer recuperates a wish and the struggle to negotiate its satisfaction in the world. It is a reunion when the reader following the arc of the writer's question recovers a world worth knowing.

8   THE SOCIAL CONSTRUCTION OF "EXPRESSIVIST" PEDAGOGY

Karen Surman Paley

In his introduction to *The Art of the Personal Essay*, a nearly eight hundred page anthology from the classical to the contemporary era, Phillip Lopate writes, "The personal essay is the reverse of that Chinese set of boxes that you keep opening, only to find a smaller one within. Here you start with the small . . . and suddenly find a slightly larger container, insinuated by the essay's successful articulation and the writer's self-knowledge" (xxviii). This capacity of the personal essay to open itself up, the way it relies on an implied induction to be realized in the mind of the reader, makes it a versatile genre that can embrace many modes of discourse and can communicate a social significance that extends deeper than the folds and crevices of one human navel.

I want to affirm the value of personal narrative, of writing about the self in the context of family or community, in a climate in which it has come under sharp criticism by social constructionists and Marxists. The tendency to view essays about the self as "inconsequential," to borrow a word from Susan Miller, outside the classroom overlooks the fact that, for example, the family system is a site both of individual development and political consciousness. It is often the place where individuals experience abuse and oppression. Familial mistreatment may establish a tolerance for and lack of questioning of racial, class, or gender oppression outside the family. Those who want to frame their composition classes with a cultural studies approach but who diminish the importance of family-based narratives are overlooking the connection to the very cultural studies they imbue with such significance. Students usually feel both welcome and important when we invite them to write about life experiences (ones they feel comfortable making public). By either excluding or quickly jumping over these types of essays, I think that some compositionists fail to see how the family might function as one of the many capillaries through which power and powerlessness circulate. Or, as Bonnie Sunstein and Elizabeth Chiseri-Strater put it, "To understand someone's culture, we often need to understand the person's family, too. Through the individual we come to understand the culture, and through the culture we come to understand the individual" (216). The Chinese boxes open either way.

Disrespect for people of color and for people of different religions was something I learned from my mother, long before I went to school, watched television, or read the newspaper. By the same token, I learned about gender roles by watching my father go to his retail business seven days a week and my mother work in the home even after there was almost no work left to do there. Adrienne Rich tells us, "[My father] demanded absolute loyalty, absolute submission to his will. In my separation from him . . . I was learning in concrete ways a great deal about patriarchy, in particular, how the 'special' woman, the favored daughter, is controlled and rewarded" (650). Ideology is wrapped up in the family system and, in many cases, these systems are impacted by a variety of unhealthy behaviors including substance abuse. Those who attempt to diminish the importance of family-based stories or sever these stories from the political beliefs of their students miss out on their pathos and intellectual energy and fail to help these students make important connections between their personal lives and the society at large.

Social constructionists who do make use of autobiographical writing may do so in a way that seriously constricts its expression. Categorizing the personal essay as "sentimental realism," David Bartholomae called the genre "corrupt" in 1995 (71). Apparently attempting to repair it, in the fifth edition of *Ways of Reading* (1999), Bartholomae and co-editor Anthony Petrosky continue to include autobiographical writing assignments.[1] However, the assignments in "Autobiographical Explorations" are not spontaneously written narratives which might be guided by the false purposes of "display or self-promotion, or to further (rather than question) an argument . . ." (802). Unless student writers follow the editors' assignment guidelines, they are at risk of "produc[ing] each week only more of the same, the same story written in the same style" (803). Instead, in the book's introduction Bartholomae and Petrosky direct the student "to imagine [his] own familiar settings through the images, metaphors, and ideas of others" (4) and this directive is later mystified as free topic choice. The clause "you can write about anything you want" (804) is qualified by the parenthetical statement "(but you would be *wise* to stay away from childhood experiences and to stick with more adult experiences") (emphasis mine, 804). The ruling out of childhood experiences as topics is not explained; the student whose mind did drift there might feel ashamed, as s/he has been judged as not "wise." Neither do Bartholomae and Petrosky see any need to explain the ban. Using a pedagogy that is at once classical in its imitative purpose, and controlling in its injunction to avoid childhood occurrences, the editors seek to shape the representation of experience with models they feel are appropriate. "[Y]our job in this assignment is to look at your experience in [Richard] Rodriguez's terms, which means thinking the way he does, noticing what he would notice . . . seeing through his point of view . . ." (805). Why can't students frame whatever experiences they select in the way they choose, and then write a revision framing it from Rodriguez's perspective?

The purpose of this essay is to critique the misrepresentations of pedagogies that affirm the teaching of personal narrative, misrepresentations that are based largely on published writing as opposed to classroom observation. The case against "expressivist" pedagogy derives from written discourse outside the classroom, in texts such as Peter Elbow's *Writing without Teachers* and William Coles and James Vopat's *What Makes Writing Good*. As Thomas Newkirk writes, social constructionists' objections "proceed in an empirical vacuum" (89). Through excerpts from Kathleen Cassity's unpublished ethnographic study of Peter Elbow, who is largely regarded as one of the founders of "expressivist" pedagogy, I will complicate the assumptions of what can transpire in a classroom identified with this pedagogy.

In the last ten years, social constructionists like Lester Faigley and marxist James Berlin have launched a campaign against what was once seen as a progressive movement in education. Social constructionists, according to Patricia Sullivan, "regard knowledge as a function of language, as a product of consensus achieved through communal discourse, and [the theory] locates the 'real' in a web of social interactions and symbolic transactions" ("Social" 950). In *Fragments of Rationality, Rhetoric and Reality,* and *Rhetorics, Poetics, and Cultures,* Lester Faigley and James Berlin construct an image of those they have come to label "expressivists." As Thomas O'Donnell puts it, these constructs "become unrecognizable (to me at least) as anything expressivist teachers are actually invested in" (425). For example, it is as if "expressivists" are so naïve as to believe that the authors of personal narratives are unquestionably writing *in propria persona*. Somehow we are so passionate in our beliefs that, like the Maoris in the film *The Piano,* we confuse drama with real life and jump on stage to prevent a villainous murder.

I will examine the way Faigley and Berlin discuss "expressivism" in their own texts. This critique will take us through major issues in composition theory today: coherence of the self, "authentic voice," the social significance or insignificance of writing about the self vis-à-vis the family or community, and whether the purpose of peer groups is to reinforce "the private vision" of the individual writer or to construct meaning and purpose in community.

WHAT IS AN "EXPRESSIVIST"?

While I have chosen to use the word "expressivist," I might have easily chosen any number of other words. In a review of three teacher texts, Mariolina Salvatori writes,

> [T]he practices of the personal go by many different names, often used as if they were interchangeable: personal criticism, autobiographical criticism, narrative criticism, personal narrative, self-writing, life-writing, auto-graphy (Perrault), confessional

criticism (Veeser), rhapsodic criticism (Lentricchia). Although such a varied nomenclature may be taken to indicate the richness of the genre as a "category in process" (Perrault), or its need and right to self-definition, I suggest it might also be taken as a sign of a certain anxiety about its functions and possibilities" (567).

I concur with Salvatori: the sheer circulation of so many synonyms or near synonyms may be indicative of anxiety about the personal in the academy. On the other hand, the multiple names may reflect the versatility of the form itself.

Let me offer a working definition of "expressivist" pedagogy. Influenced by James Britton's notion of expressive discourse, "expressivist" pedagogy is a theoretical bent that affirms the use of personal narrative without necessarily saddling it with the kind of constraints indicated above in *Ways of Reading*. Personal narrative takes the writer's own life as its focus. It involves the use of a narratorial "I" which seems to be the actual voice of the person who writes. Sometimes the narrator may appear to isolate individual consciousness and sometimes s/he may represent the self in one or more social contexts, such as the family. The narrator may or may not explicitly link the particular situation with those experienced by others. Additionally, the pedagogy many include many forms of academic discourse, including a range of first-person writing. For example, Lad Tobin, Director of Freshman Writing at Boston College, is identified with "expressivism." He reports that by the winter of 1997 he had studied about 650 syllabi for courses in which nearly 10,000 students have been enrolled. Only 25% of the assigned writing in his program falls into the genre of personal narrative. The rest of the assignments would be considered cultural criticism, argument on public issues, and response to texts. Yet he qualifies his comments by reminding me of the kind of hybrid papers he sees in the freshman writing program at Boston College where elements of personal narrative mix with exposition or argument in the same paper.

FAIGLEY: THE SELF IN DISCOURSE

In 1992 the University of Pittsburgh Series in Composition, Literacy, and Culture published Lester Faigley's *Fragments of Rationality: Postmodernity and the Subject of Composition*. In 1994 it received the Outstanding Book Award from CCCC for making an outstanding contribution to composition and communication studies. It contains such an impressive body of knowledge about the history of composition, post-modern thought, linguistics, and computer assisted instruction that, had I been a member of the Outstanding Book Award Committee along with Alice Gilliam, Cheryl Glenn, Betty L. Hart, Frank Littler, and Charles I. Schuster, I might have concurred with the decision. And I might have done so despite deep reservations about the chapter entitled "Ideologies of the Self in the Writing Classroom."

In this chapter, Faigley uses a postmodern orientation to deconstruct the merits of the personal essay in the writing classroom. According to Faigley, this genre proclaims "the existence of the rational, coherent self and the ability of the self to have privileged insight into its own processes," (111) both of which are questioned by postmodern theory. "Expressivist" writing is guilty of what Catherine Belsey calls expressive realism, a naïve assumption that language is somehow ahistorical and apolitical, that it provides a transparent window into the empirical world (112).

Faigley is also troubled that the field of composition shows signs of being biased toward personal narrative. Despite a broad range of contributing faculty to William Coles' and James Vopat's *What Makes Writing Good* (1985), a collection of what these professors felt to be excellent responses to their assignments, the bulk of the writing samples are personal experience pieces. "Not one essay resembles the frequently assigned 'research paper,'" according to Faigley (120). Moreover, when writing teachers use "authentic voice" as an assessment criterion, they assume the reader can "distinguish the true self" (122). Faigley argues that because of the unconscious, we cannot know if something is being repressed and, therefore, we cannot assess the sincerity of the writer (127). Additionally, the apparent freedom students are given to choose autobiographical topics in writing classrooms conceals "the fact that these same students will be judged by teachers' unstated assumptions about subjectivity and that every act of writing they perform occurs within complex relations of power" (128). In short, the contributors to *What Makes Writing Good* do not explore the institutional context of personal narratives "and how that setting is implicated in the production of 'honest' and 'truthful' writing" (129). They naively assume that the rhetorical situation is neutral and that the pressure of representing oneself to an authority figure has no impact on the content of these essays.

In spite of this avalanche of arguments, it is to Faigley's credit that he sees some value in personal experience essays. He tells us, "The many varieties of autobiographical writing have provided sites for resistance to dominant discourses...."(129). However, I am surprised that, given his support for cultural studies, Faigley does not elaborate on the phrase "resistance to dominant cultures" or provide any examples of such writing. Personal narrative has been historically associated in this country with African Americans and with women who are writing against oppression and producing what Foucault has called subjugated knowledge. Additionally, essays about what Faigley calls "difficult family situations" can also resist dominant discourses (121). In fact, I read narratives about childhood abuse as acts of resistance against an oppressive and unhealthy power structure within the culture of the family, one that may mimic capitalist relations of power and authority. In critiquing the limitations of Freud's discussion of his "hysterical" patient Dora who was distressed by her father's affair with her governess, Catherine Clément describes his "ideological misunderstanding" in *The Newly Born Woman*. "The family does not exist in isolation, rather it supports and reflects the class struggle running through it" (152). In the same text, Helene Cixous describes Dora as "the one who resists the system . . . It is the nuclear example of women's power to protest" (154). Faigley's limited reference to this type of writing is puzzling.

In my critique of Faigley's chapter, I want to comment on his preference for a certain type of research essay as well as his assumptions about a unified self and "authentic voice" in "expressivist" pedagogy. In the process I will point out gender bias in Faigley's lack of intellectual respect for a particular student essay.

Faigley is disappointed in the overrepresentation of personal narrative in the selections in *What Makes Writing Good*. He writes,

> [T]he range of contributors is not matched by a similar range of student writing. By my count, at least thirty of the examples in the collection are personal experience essays—twenty of them autobiographical narratives—and several of the remaining eighteen include writing about the writer. Only four examples are in the genre of professional writing (two letters and two reports). Four examples briefly discuss works of literature, but there is no literary analysis paper of the kind described in rhetoric texts. Only two essays present sustained analyses of other texts . . . Not one essay resembles the frequently assigned "research paper." (120)

Faigley has a clear vision of what he refers to as "the frequently assigned 'research paper.'" Since there are no essays that resemble it, but there are many that feature or at least contain "writing about the writer," it follows that Faigley does not consider that the personal figures in "the frequently assigned 'research paper.'" Perhaps he is correct. If he is, then Jeanette Harris may be wise to promote hybrid texts that combine expository prose with the writer's experience in order to avoid "the anonymous sterility that frequently characterizes discourse that is exclusively based on information" (187). She is not alone.

In the eighteenth century, George Campbell taught us that the audience requires some kind of gratification or it will cease to pay attention. "[N]othing tends more effectively to prevent this consequence, and keep our attention alive and vigorous, than the pathetic, which consists chiefly in exhibitions of personal misery" (113). In the nineteenth century rhetorician Alexander Bain admired elements of poetry in historical writing. He writes, "There is always a powerful attraction in human personality—man's interest in man" (176). He praises Plato for "reliev[ing] the severity of philosophical discussion with touches of general human interest. Plato adopted the form of the Dialogue to introduce the action and re-action of personalities . . . The debate is interrupted by dramatic displays of personal feeling" (202).

In the last decade many scholars have advocated creative nonfiction that blends first person singular narrative in with more traditional exposition. For example, Mathew Wilson describes a required course he taught in research writing. "The texts were interesting and 'relevant,' the students earnest, the class discussions lively, and the papers uniformly dull" (242). Not only were the papers dull, but they were imbued with the positivist notion that we can ascertain objective truth. In these papers there is a denial of ambivalence and no discussion of the act of writing itself. "Most college research writing involves 'carting dead bones from one graveyard to another'" (247). Thus, if it is the case that what Faigley calls the "frequently assigned 'research paper'" is author evacuated expository prose, we are encouraging the production of very modernist texts that assume the possibility of objective truth. I will return to this point.

Why is Faigley so intellectually unhappy with personal narratives? His thinking rests on one of the now almost foundational "truths" of postmodern thought: there is no such thing as a rational, coherent and unified self, the persona that is always already in personal narrative, according to its critics. Personal essays that exhibit rational, coherent, and unified selves constitute a naïve ignorance of both the complex human consciousness and the social context of the writer and his or her persona.

There seems to be a double standard in his analysis. In his book *The Performance of Self in Student Writing,* Thomas Newkirk comments on a contradiction or what he calls "a strange schizophrenia" regarding narrative in English departments. "On the one hand, [English Departments] are built upon the narrative—it should come as no news that students become English majors to get academic credit for reading narrative fiction. Yet in writing classes there is a sense that narratives are relatively easy to write and academically suspect" (20).

Moreover, while devaluing a rational, coherent, and unified self he sees in student texts selected as examples of good writing by many of his colleagues, Faigley apparently values such a persona in academic writing. More specifically, nowhere in his book, *Fragments of Rationality,* does the narrator, Lester Faigley, actually present a fragmented consciousness. The argument and point of view are consistent and clear throughout. Faigley celebrates the postmodern notion of the self in his title yet the celebration is not actualized in his writing. Why is it permissible to present oneself as rational and coherent in one mode of discourse but not another? Why can Faigley present a rational, unified coherent persona in an expository book on composition, but students who do so in personal narratives and professors who affirm these essays are missing the latest boat in terms of theory? Eleanor Kutz, who offers ethnography as an alternative to the traditional research paper we assign our students, describes the voice in one student's ethnography. "This is not a distanced academic voice, and it does not pretend to an objectivity that would always remain unrealized" (355). There is such a presumption of objectivity in *Fragments of Rationality.*

I wonder, too, about the representation of "expressivist" pedagogy as an open invitation to produce testimonies of coherent selves. Times may have changed the positive regard for a unified persona during the seven year lapse between the publication of *What Makes Writing Good* and *Fragments of Rationality,* but perhaps not. What I can say is that I was involved in two English departments that social constructionists would not hesitate to call "expressivist." I was a graduate student at the University of New Hampshire for over a year and a lecturer at Boston College for six years. During my employment at Boston College, I taught seven sections of the Freshman Writing Seminar and two sections of Prose Writing. I have been to many staff meetings where we discussed sample student papers. One problem we have attended to is the personal narrative that reveals some rather disturbing circumstances regarding a family member but closes with an often pat, unsubstantiated conclusion that undermines the very testimony of the narrator. It is not atypical to read such a paper with an ending, "But I know my father loves me" or "I love my brother in spite of it all." The majority of composition faculty I have known at these two "expressivist" departments admire ambivalence and unresolved conflict in the character of the narrator in personal essays.

What many of us may share with the contributors to the Coles and Vopat collection is an acknowledgment of honest voice, one that hints at integrity (Faigley 121). However, respect for a voice that has integrity does not imply belief in "the true self," but instead demonstrates the persuasiveness that accrues to a narrator who achieves ethos. It is a staple of Aristotelian rhetoric to have the speaker convey ethos, i.e. to appear credible, moral, honest. When an evaluator labels a text as "honest," "authentic" or written with "integrity," in my opinion it is a strong indication that the narrator has convinced the audience of her reading of a situation. She has persuaded. In fact, I would argue that *the logos of expressive discourse, of personal narrative, is its ethos.* As Aristotle puts it, "the speaker's *character may be called the most effective means of persuasion he possesses*" (emphasis mine, 1329). I read Aristotle as saying that the audience is persuaded because of the credibility of the writer. When Faigley dismisses the notion of "authentic voice" as a belief that the author is writing *in propria persona,* he is confounding an alleged naivete of the "expressivist" reader with the ethos of the writer.

Yet how can we determine the credibility of the author when we have author-evacuated prose, the kind of prose that is currently the standard of credibility in academia? If we take into consideration Faigley's approval of Greg Shaefer's essay, "Thucydides: The Historian as Creative Artist," along with his disappointment with personal experience essays, we can conclude that he prefers author-evacuated prose. Faigley compares Shaefer's well-written expository piece with Norma Bennett's personal narrative about her family. Faigley asks his audience, "[W]hy is writing about potentially embarrassing and painful aspects of one's life considered more honest than, say, the efforts of Joseph Williams's student, Greg Shaefer, who tries to figure out what Thucydides was up to in writing about the Peloponnesian War?" (121).

Shaefer has been directed to "compare and contrast the first two speeches in Thucydides' *History*" (Coles and Vopat 305) and that is precisely what he does. His essay is lucid and well argued, but ventures no opinions. Schaefer writes, "The Corinthian argument failed because for an imperial power like Athens, justice is not a very strong controlling force," (309) but we do not know where he stands in either the dispute brought before the Athenians or in regard to Thucydides' representation of speeches he never heard.

Norma Bennett, on the other hand, does take a risk. She chooses to write an essay which exposes her family to the public eye in response to an assignment by Erika Lindemann that does not ask for any kind of exposure. "The assignment asks you to write an essay that is primarily descriptive but that makes its point by comparison and contrast." When I read Faigley's summary of Bennett's essay before reading the essay itself, I imagined the piece to be maudlin and self-pitying, and I imagined that the narrator was so upfront with her emotional pain that I would feel embarrassed reading it. I felt contemptuous toward her mother and repulsed by her father from his reconstruction. After reading the essay itself, I no longer feel any of these things. Here is Faigley's summary:

> Norma Bennett's paper is a narrative of a summer vacation spent with her two divorced parents who now go to different resorts. Her mothers [sic] wears her PTL ("Praise the Lord") jacket (in the days before Jim and Tammy Bakker's fall) and spends much of her day sleeping or sobbing. Her potbellied father also spends much of the day sleeping-passed out drunk on the beach with a twenty-five-year-old woman in a white string bikini while Norma babysits for the woman's young child. I have a great deal of sympathy for students like Norma Bennett, who must cope with difficult family situations as well as the pressures of college.... (121)

After reading Faigley's representation of the Bennett essay, I have negative feelings toward her mother who is a member of the religious right and who sleeps and sobs most of the day. Yet my experience of this woman is different when I read Bennett's own account. While her mother's religious affiliation does emerge in the text, the description does not play on any anti-fundamentalist biases of the reader. Norma's mother rises before dawn each morning to walk to the beach and collect shells. "My mom . . . praises God for his magnificent creation, and photographs her favorite sanctuary" (Coles and Vopat 159), activities that feel decidedly ecumenical to me. Moreover, there is no indication that, as Faigley puts it, "she spends much of the day sleeping or sobbing." Norma tells us only that when her mother returns from the beach, "her eyes are watery, her cheeks are red, and her nose is runny. I'm not sure if it's because of the cold wind outside or if she's crying about my dad again or if she's been overwhelmed by the presence of the Lord. Maybe it's all three." (159). Faigley condenses Norma's speculation to one word, sobbing, thereby reducing the representation of the mother from a spiritually active person who is experiencing an appropriate grief reaction, to an emotional mess. In doing so, he short-circuits the kind of compassion we feel for her after reading Norma's account. Nor do we have any evidence that she spends much of the day sleeping. Norma writes, "I give her a hug and grumble about getting up. She laughs and teases me about being lazy. My mom won't go out on the beach in the middle of the day. She goes back to bed while I go lie with my friends. Late every afternoon, just before dinner, we go out on the beach together, carrying sand buckets and shovels. Like a couple of kids, we sink down in the sand and start building a castle" (159). Because Norma's mother goes back to bed in the morning and does not go out on the beach in the middle of the day, Faigley assumes she is the "lazy" one. In the absence of any account of her activities, probably something that Norma herself is not privy to, he concludes that she sleeps away the day.

I am troubled by Faigley's representation of this woman. It leads me to identify against myself as a woman. Drawing on a theory of Judith Fetterley, Patrocinio Schweickart puts it this way: "Androcentric literature . . . does not allow the woman to seek refuge in her difference. Instead, it draws her into a process that she uses against herself" (42). After reading Norma's essay, I realize I had been drawn into collusion with Faigley, that I had adopted a contempt for Norma's mother and other women who are working through losses, a contempt that borders on misogyny.

Faigley reads Norma as writing about "potentially embarrassing and painful aspects of [her] life" (159) but I do not feel her embarrassment, I do not think she burdens the reader with her pain, and I do not think she asks for our sympathy. She treats both of her parents with respect, something that may be hard to do in relation to a father who does appear to "spend much of the day sleeping-passed out drunk on the beach with a twenty-five-year-old woman in a white string bikini" (Faigley 121). Yet Norma does not display this kind of contempt for her father either. She concludes her essay:

My Dad yells and says for me to look after David [his girlfriend's son]; they'll be back late. Tears come to my eyes. Dad has *lost his sobriety*, his family, and his God. I wonder how long it will be before his foundation is washed away, and his castle is level with the sand.

I love my mom and my dad both. My dad has many friends and many good times, but he is too miserable to enjoy them. My mom is a loner. She has quiet times and peace of mind. As I look at my own life, I search for a castle—up high, away from the shoreline—far away from the destruction of the tide. (emphasis mine, Coles and Vopat, 160)

I feel the narrator's pain here but I do not feel her reaching out for pity from the audience. There is maturity and an ethos evident as she stands apart from her parents wanting none of the "destruction of the tide" in her life. She writes that her father has "lost his sobriety." Faigley and other readers may be unaware that she is using what ethnographers call "insider language" from Alcoholics Anonymous, bringing not embarrassment to the story but a view of her father as a man with a disease who has gone into relapse. I believe she maintains her father's anonymity in print by not being more specific. What "lost his sobriety" means in this context is that he was abstinent from alcohol for a period of time in AA, but that he lost that abstinence and the peace of mind that can come from working the program's suggested steps. I feel only her sadness at this relapse.

Perhaps it is Faigley who feels embarrassed by the story. The absence of any sort of self-reflexivity in this particular chapter further weakens his arguments against autobiographical writing. Edward Said advises theorists to declare their personal investment in critical projects. Influenced by Antonio Gramsci, he suggests that we develop a consciousness of who we are as products of "the historical process to date." These processes have left many marks but no inventory. "'Therefore it is imperative at the outset to compile such an inventory'" (qtd. in Said 25). I wish Faigley had done so.

THE BERLIN WALL: IS WRITING A PRIVATE VISION?

Many of us who teach writing have been influenced by a taxonomy of the field of composition established by James Berlin. Berlin shapes a history of what he calls expressionism beginning in the early part of the twentieth century but with historical roots in romanticism and further back in Plato.[2] "The ideal of liberal culture indirectly encouraged the development of expressionistic rhetoric through its philosophic idealism and its emphasis on the cultivation of the self, both derived from its ties with Brahminical romanticism" (*Rhetoric and Reality* 73). Berlin's reasoning is slippery here. By declaring an "indirect" link between "expressionistic rhetoric" and "the ideal of liberal culture" with its "philosophic idealism and its emphasis on the cultivation of self," two characteristics derived from romanticism, Berlin makes these characteristics of liberal culture appear to be attached to expressionistic rhetoric. The indefinite pronoun "its" is used three times in the sentence further blurring liberal culture/romanticism and expressionistic rhetoric.

What Berlin calls expressionism is almost always associated with notions of encouraging the student to develop his or her own "unique self" in writing, writing that avoids and even disdains connection with the material world. This disdain for the external world is nowhere documented by Berlin but is apparently to be taken on the good faith of the implied reader who is willing to accept the connection to Plato[3] Berlin refines his view over the course of four frequently cited articles or books, sometimes referring to his earlier publications as the only evidence for arguments in later works. These are "Contemporary Composition: The Major Pedagogical Theories" (1982), *Rhetoric and Reality: Writing Instruction in American Colleges, 1900–1985* (1987), "Rhetoric and Ideology in the Writing Class" (1988), and *Rhetorics, Poetics, and Cultures* published posthumously in 1996. Publishing his view over a fourteen-year period, Berlin had plenty of time to see if his conclusions were being practiced in classrooms. If he had, he might have seen a range of pedagogies, some more overtly sociopolitical than others depending on the comfort level and belief system of the teacher. As it is, Berlin limits himself within the methodology of his own choosing.[4]

Furthermore, Berlin seems to either ignore or misunderstand the importance of group interaction in process pedagogy. As Peter Elbow puts it in the introduction to the twenty-fifth anniversary edition of his first book, *Writing without Teachers*,

> A highly respected scholar and historian of composition, James Berlin, does write briefly of my epistemology, but it's hard to believe he looked carefully at what I wrote. For he says that I am a Platonist who believes that knowledge is totally private, whereas I make it clear that both the teacherless class and the epistemology of the believing game can only function as group processes, and that their validity derives only from people entering into each others' diverse and conflicting experiences. *I argue specifically that the meaning of any spoken or written discourse is entirely dependent on groups and communities* (see p. 156 for what I wrote). The teacherless class and the believing game are completely undermined if one tries to function solo. (Emphasis mine, xxvi–xxvii.)

Elbow's notion of meaning making discourse communities does not sound so different from what Berlin calls epistemic rhetoric. In *Rhetoric and Reality*

(1987) Berlin tells us, "The epistemic position implies that knowledge is not discovered by reason alone, that cognitive and affective processes are not separate, that intersubjectivity is a condition of all knowledge, and that the contact of minds affects all knowledge" (165). Thus, for both Elbow and Berlin, meaning making is a social process.

In "Contemporary Composition" (1982) Berlin lays out a taxonomy that basically remains the same for him in later publications, although he does revise the names. Berlin expounds on the Platonic vision, how the "ultimate truth can be discovered by the individual, but cannot be communicated" because it is "beyond the resources of language" (771). Berlin sees the interactive group process in expressionism as similar to dialectic but its purpose is not to construct meaning or knowledge. "The purpose is to get rid of what is untrue to the private vision of the writer, what is, in a word, inauthentic" (772).

In *Rhetoric and Reality* (1987) Berlin takes a harder line on this type of group process. "For the expressionist, solitary activity is always promising, *group activity always dangerous*" (emphasis mine, 145). Berlin does make an attempt to undercut this essentialism by allowing for "varieties of expressionistic rhetoric" (145) including a few that approach epistemic. "[I]n this view language does not simply record the private vision, but becomes involved in shaping it" (146) But alas, this group of expressionists also runs amuck "because it denies the place of intersubjective, social processes in shaping reality. Instead, it always describes groups as sources of distortion of the individual's true vision, and the behavior it recommends in the political and social realms is atomistic, the individual acting alone" (146). Among the expressionists who follow what he calls the "latitudinarian" view are Ken Macrorie, Donald Murray, Walker Gibson, William Coles, Jr., and Peter Elbow (146). Berlin's conclusions are as inflammatory as they are unsubstantiated.

After closely studying Berlin's text, I do not find any support that these five men either view group process to be dangerous or recommend acting alone. There are only two references to the expressionists and group processes, or what Berlin calls editorial groups, in the section. He writes, "[T]he purpose of editorial groups is to check for the inauthentic in the writer's response (Berlin, "Contemporary Response") (152). His source for this conclusion lies not in any of the five expressionists he called our attention to, but in his own prior article. I might add that neither does he offer the reader a page citation from this article. The second and final reference to editorial groups is in relation to Elbow or, as he puts it, "Elbow's camp," and it concludes the section.

> It is not surprising, then, that Elbow's version of the editorial group was influenced by the methods of group therapy and of the encounter group (121). Finally, at the start of this discussion, I said that Elbow's approach is not overtly political. In the last

analysis, however, for Elbow as for other expressionists, the personal *is* the political—the underlying assumption being that enabling individuals to arrive at self-understanding and self-expression will inevitably lead to a better social order. (154-5)

While Berlin does refer back to one thing he said at the beginning of the discussion, that is, Elbow's work not being overtly political, he does not refer back to his initial inflammatory remarks, "For the expressionist . . . group activity is always dangerous . . . The behavior it recommends in the political and social realms is atomistic, the solitary individual acting alone" (145-6). Berlin has not provided one shred of evidence for these initial assumptions. The notion that the personal is political has become something of a slogan in various theoretical circles, most noticeably some feminist ones. Berlin does not agree with his own definition of what the slogan means, that individual change precedes social change. Moreover, he seems rather obtuse about the workings of "the editorial group" and the process of meaning making that goes on in it. Of course these groups make meaning and they are, in their own right, discourse communities. Even if he is correct and some "in Elbow's camp" saw their purpose as solely to help the individual clarify and strengthen her writing, that does not mean that they encouraged an atomistic life style. I find the opposite to be true: by sharing one's work in a safe community where there is both encouragement and constructive, non-shaming critique, there is a breakdown of individual isolation.

Even more importantly, these groups have the potential for creating bonds across racial and class lines. In my ethnography of Boston College, *I-Writing: the Politics and Practice of Teaching First-Person Writing*, a white teacher develops a relationship with the only student of color in her course that is strong enough to help the student workshop an anti-racist essay and become an active member of the community. In another instance, when one of my students workshopped an essay about his aging grandmother, he and several other students in the class became emotional. Because they were in the same developmental stage, many of the students were facing similar losses, including one student who had just learned the evening before that her grandmother did not have long to live. Berlin advocates "intersubjectivity" (*Rhetoric and Reality* 165) in the construction of knowledge, but "it is important to remember that *inter*subjectivities require subjectivities, and vice versa" (Cassity 179).

Berlin reduces the dialectic in expressionist editorial groups to one function: "to enable the writer to understand the manifestation of her identity in language through considering the reactions of others—not, for example, to begin to understand how meaning is shaped by discourse communities" (153). What kind of meaning gets credit for being shaped in discourse communities in the Berlin worldview? He never specifies. When students come together to help each other write more forceful essays about racism on campus or about the loss of a loved one, isn't this making meaning within a community? Doesn't this kind of bonding break down the distrust, cynicism, and competitiveness that accrues in academia, a bonding that could carry over to all kinds of collective support, whether for "overtly political" causes such as organizing to stop the spread of racist graffiti or for overtly personal causes such as supporting one another through loss?

In *Romancing Rhetorics,* Sherrie Gradin takes on the false binary personal/political with her neologism "social-expressivism" and provides a different rendering of the legacy of romanticism than Berlin does. She tells us that "expressivist theory evolves from a tradition [romanticism] that recognizes the economic, social, and political conditions of existence," but acknowledges in response to Berlin that "the practitioners of expressivism can certainly fail to incorporate this tradition into their pedagogy" (109). There are, as Berlin himself tells us, "varieties of expressionistic rhetoric" (145). Perhaps some classrooms are less overtly political than others depending on the degree to which individual practitioners are comfortable with the potential for heated debate. Individual differences not withstanding, these do not constitute a concerted and monolithic theory either of avoidance of such issues or infatuation with "the private vision."

In "Rhetoric and Ideology in the Writing Class" (1988) Berlin argues that "the ruling elites in business, industry, and government are those most likely to nod in assent to the ideology inscribed in expressionistic rhetoric" because it reinforces "individualism, private initiative, the confidence for risk-taking, the right to be contentious with authority (especially the state)" (487). Furthermore, Newkirk sees a logical fallacy underlying one of Berlin's conclusions, namely that expressionism nurtures the capitalistic spirit in its students. He faults Berlin for making similarity appear to be causation. Referring here to *Rhetorics, Poetics, and Cultures* (1996), Newkirk writes,

> To paraphrase Berlin, there are attitudes and values fostered in expressionist pedagogies that *resemble* those that a capitalist system seeks to foster in consumers (the self-gratifying enjoyment of "choice") and in entrepreneurs (private initiative). Because of this similarity, expressivist teaching causes students to enter happily and even successfully into that system.
>
> This argument is so loose that it could easily be used against the cultural studies approach [of Berlin and others]. One could easily imagine how corporations could profit from the critical skills students develop when they "problematize" seemingly self-evident arguments and positions" (89).

Because two things appear to be alike, it does not follow that one causes the other. Newkirk does not see how Berlin has proven that expressionism fosters an accommodation to capitalism. I would add that any pedagogy that results in grading students, ranking them in their class, and providing the basis for records that go out to future admissions officers or employers is part of capitalist relations of power and authority. Grading and ranking trigger competition whether you are teaching the canon, grammar, personal narrative, or some form of cultural studies in which students are encouraged to see how representations of the empirical world in the mass media work to maintain a class system (as Berlin suggests in two model courses in *Rhetorics, Poetics, and Cultures.*) Most teaching in our system perpetuates divisions and hierarchy.

In *Rhetoric, Poetics, and Cultures*, a book that was published posthumously in 1996, Berlin does not explicitly debunk expressionism, but he does come to a surprising conclusion. There is only one reference to expressionism and it is indirect. The proposed course "Codes and Critiques" is put forward as a foil to an unnamed but behind-the-scenes pedagogy. He uses some coding himself here that the Berlin reader should have no trouble recognizing. "Unlike classrooms that insist that each student look within to discover a unique self, this course argues that only through understanding the workings of culture in shaping consciousness can students ever hope to achieve any degree of singularity" (124). Berlin advocates singularity, a word that means being one of a kind or having a trait marking one as distinct from others. It is surprising that Berlin's goal is for the individual to see herself as "distinct from others" as it seems to represent the very "private vision" this cultural critic argued against over a fourteen year period.

IN SITU: THE POLITICAL ELBOW

Berlin and Faigley have perpetuated a characterization of a certain type of pedagogy that has come to be known, largely through their efforts, as expressionist or "expressivist." I have found their arguments to be frequently unsubstantiated and misleading. By way of contrast, I want to turn now to the only ethnography, to my knowledge, of the work of Peter Elbow. Reading Kathleen Cassity's study is a way to get a sense of the culture of Elbow's section of English 100: Expository Writing, a required course for incoming students; it brings us closer to lived experience than either critical commentary on texts or generalizations about imagined classrooms. The study was conducted at the University of Hawai'i in Manoa during the spring of 1996, the year Elbow was a Visiting Professor. As an MA student, Cassity had an opportunity to take a course with Elbow and then observed his Expository Writing class as the basis for her MA thesis. He had been looking for someone to give him feedback on a new grading contract he was implementing that semester.

Like myself, Cassity is troubled by the association of "process/expressivist" approaches "with rugged individualism, with naïve and simplistic concepts of 'self,' and with epistemological frameworks that shortchange social, cultural and historical contexts" (15). She ultimately finds in Elbow's teaching something that looks like the radical approach of Henry Giroux, "border pedagogy." Giroux believes we should give students more opportunity to write about their own personal experiences with and emotional reactions to issues such as race rather than have them only "articulate the meaning of other peoples' theories" (Giroux 11).

The focus of Cassity's ethnography is Elbow's grading contract. In this contract the student could choose what grade s/he wanted based on workload. Many students found the workload necessary to achieve an "A" to be burdensome even after he modified it twice. My interest in her study, however, is in the evidence Cassity provides for her initial statement that the representation of "expressivist" pedagogy as shortchanging social, political and historical registers is false.

Issues of race and ethnicity are prominent. Of the nineteen students in Elbow's class, Cassity reports that fifteen are Asian, Pacific, or mixed ethnicity and four are Caucasian (9). Six of the fifteen students raised in Hawai'i indicated that their primary language is Hawaiian Creole English or pidgin (7). In one of many lively group discussions observed by Cassity, the students complain about the perception of Hawaiians by outsiders.[5] "People are so stupid, they actually think we live in grass shacks and stuff . . . You tell them you go to the University of Hawai'i and they're, like, surprised that people in Hawai'i even *study*" (65). Their discussion reminds Cassity of her graduate seminar in colonialism.

The first written assignment began with a freewrite on "any aspect of your group identities" (70). Of note is the fact that the assignment does not encourage students to write about their individual, unique identities. After the freewrite became a homework assignment, it was then to be revised into a more public form. Students would pair up and their collaborative projects were to include library research. Sue, a shy eighteen-year-old Chinese American, read her paper aloud in conference. When asked to write about her "group identities," Sue selected the topic of racism toward Chinese people.

> She discusses the slurs used against those of Chinese descent in Hawai'i and recites one of the derogatory rhymes she heard other kids chanting when she was little, rhymes feeding into the stereotype that the Chinese are "cheap." Breaking away from her text, she tells Peter as an aside, "I don't really believe it, you know."
>
> "Right," says Peter. "But it's sort of like some of the rhymes black kids have had to hear—some of the slur—nowadays it's outlawed, but you've still heard it. It's still in there." (70-1).

The discussion here is not about one private experience but the more general experience that people of color face.

The use of Hawaiian Creole English or pidgin surfaces in the class. Cassity does not address the theoretical influences on Elbow here, but from what I can see of his pedagogy, he is in line with suggestions made by both Lisa Delpit and Eileen Oliver. Delpit tells us that "each cultural group should have the right to maintain its own language style." However, we must tell students that "there is a political power game that is also being played, and if they want to be in on that game there are certain games they too must play" (292). They must learn the dominant register both to understand and to change the power realities (293).

Elbow apparently values both native and the dominant dialects. Cassity demonstrates the pedagogy here through Elbow's work with Kerry. This student was worried that her primary language is non-standard English. Here are some excerpts of either oral or written dialogue between student and teacher on the subject.

> Kerry: I'm afraid my pidgin English will get in my way. You didn't write anything about pidgin English on your contract.
> E: Feel free to write in pidgin.
> ...
> E: (responding to an essay written in multiple linguistic registers) I like the pidgin section a lot. In my view, it's important to learn to write in it. As you say, it's YOUR tongue, your "mother tongue"—and so it's got the most "juice" in it—and you can put the most of YOU in it. You need to write in standard English; but it's my belief that your standard English might improve if you let yourself sometimes write in pidgin.
> K: (responding in a process letter) I am very pleased that you don't discriminate against my language.

Cassity tells us that Kerry received an "A" in the course, even though she had said at mid-semester, "I give up." "The more Elbow not only accepted but encouraged Kerry's 'mother-tongue,' the more she wrote in both Standard English and pidgin" (141). Language is clearly an aspect of group identity for Elbow and his students.

The issues of ethnicity and gender emerge with an apparently defiant young man named Gary. Cassity describes a conference.

> Gary interrupts again, launching into another monologue. Peter urges him to talk to his collaborator. "If you want to make these arguments about gender and ethnicity, if you want to say all these don't affect who you are, I want you nevertheless to take account of the fact that it looks to a lot of people like they do. I want you to take into account the opposite point of view"... I wonder if [Peter] feels frustrated as I do. If so, he doesn't reveal it in either his facial expressions or body language. (74)

I do read frustration in some of Elbow's written comments as he challenges viewpoints he disagrees with. He writes to Dave and Brad: "When you talk about the rise in wages for women compared to men, you forget to mention one little fact: that women still get paid *much less* than men for the same work!" (89). To Karen and Gary, he writes, "There's something quite weird about your paper. *Every example* of racism that you talk about is an example of thinking or behavior by members of a targeted group, blacks or Hawaiians. *Nowhere in your paper* do you ever give an example or seem to acknowledge the more pervasive racism of groups with more power . . . as though you think only blacks and Hawaiians are racist. Did you mean to do that?" (89). To Adam and Mark, he notes, "You make a bunch of statements that are kind of illogical—that no one you know is gay. (You better not be so sure.) That everyone you know who is gay is messed up. (I thought you didn't know anyone.) That once someone is gay you can't see them the same. (Well how can you trust your perception when you know you go into this gear?)" (90).

In spite of Elbow's disagreements, he is still able to make positive comments on some aspects of each of these essays whose perspectives clearly trouble him. However, Cassity informs us that to Adam and Mark (who wrote on homosexuality) "the best he can come up with is 'I'm glad you enjoyed working together—and that you did substantial re-arranging and changing'" (90). From her perspective, he was struggling to find something positive here.

Let us recall that Elbow and other white people were in the minority in this classroom. After reading the first draft of this summary of her work, Cassity, who is herself of mixed ethnicity, responded, "Obviously, if you come cruising in here with a white superiority attitude, you will soon be cruising back out, probably with a black eye. Peter was well liked by his freshman students so I think that says a lot about what kind of attitudes he displayed in class toward differences."

After having had this privileged peek at a small slice of Elbow's teaching practice, I can only conclude that race, gender and sexual orientation are fair game for this "expressionist's" classroom. Not only does Elbow appear not to find the last word in any private vision, as Berlin has repeatedly told us, but he seems to have no inhibition whatsoever about challenging his students' visions when he disagrees with them.

REPRESENTATIONAL PSYCHOTHERAPY

Is it possible to change? Can we stop playing Extreme Representation?

When a composition teacher who aligns herself with Bartholomae, even insists that everyone use *Ways of Reading* in her composition program, read an early version of this essay, she asked me to make light of the ways "expressivists" have been represented. I did not then and I have not now.

We live in a world that fibrillates daily with ethnic conflict (and the outbreaks would be even more plentiful if many of us stopped sublimating our xenophobia with sports team fanaticism) and I see a version of this type of destructive Othering in the discipline of composition and rhetoric. (My guilt does not elude me; I, too, sublimate my introjected racism with sports mania and I have broken some kneecaps in this essay.) We have to stop and look more precisely at what our colleagues are saying in print and how the text is dramatized in classroom practice. I am not asking naively, "Why can't we all just get along?" but rather I am saying, "Let us look more carefully before we write each other off."

Revising concepts of a lifetime is not easy. I am a Jew currently teaching in my second Jesuit university. "Now you've gone too far," (says my diseased mother from her grave) as I conduct an ethnography of a class in Liberation Theology taught by Father Tom, a real priest. We talk, we argue, I notice things that strike me as anti-Semitic in the reading, he says they are not meant to be. Why do I bring this project up? Because immersing myself in the theology of another religion no longer produces a sustained flinch. After seven and a half years, I no longer feel the horror of centuries of pogroms and forced conversions and exterminations with each annunciation of the word "Christ."

Can we stop our theoretical flinching in composition? Can we stop kicking our colleagues to the curb? Perhaps we can think of such a change as a lesson in what Robert Schreiter calls "intercultural hermeneutics" in his book *The New Catholicity*. In Schreiter's discussion of the differing needs of a speaker and a hearer, he offers the example of a missionary couple who went to North India to evangelize. Unfortunately they owned a cat, an animal the villagers associated with witches. "[T]he appearance of the missionaries' pet cat caused the evangelistic message to be lodged near witchcraft in the hearers' world, rather than near salvation" (35). Just because some composition teachers valorize writing about personal experiences, it does not follow that economic, ethnic, and religious differences are reduced in status in our classrooms and in our students' texts..

I have analyzed commentaries by Faigley and Berlin that were based on "expressivist" texts. In an effort to encourage a larger project in composition studies, where theorists take a look at the opposition's classrooms before publishing critiques that then become hypostatized as actual situations, I have borrowed from an ethnographic study of someone who has become associated with "expressivism." It has been my intent to disrupt the essentialized misrepresentation of those teachers who encourage both personal writing and writing that would be seen as cultural criticism. O'Donnell argues that "expressivist bashing" (423) has flourished perhaps because of a failure on the part of expressivist teachers to articulate the theories underlying their practice" (425). It is my hope that this essay will enter a gradually growing body of work by researchers such as Kathleen Cassity, Thomas Newkirk, Sherrie Gradin, Thomas O'Donnell, and Christopher Burnham, who are taking the time for some needed theoretical clarification.

NOTES

1. According to Karen R. Melton, the Director of Marketing for Bedford/St. Martins, more than a quarter of a million copies of *Ways of Reading* had sold as of December 2, 1999. This total "makes it one of the most successful readers on our list (an impressive feat) and in the industry as a whole."
2. W. Ross Winterowd traces a similar genealogy. "Plato represents and is the father of a tradition that sees the goal of composition as helping the writer develop his or her own 'voice' or expressivity, just as Aristotle is the ultimate source of composition as entering a discourse community" (xii).
3. Susan Wall points out that Berlin's critique of expressionism emerges from his responses to scholarly texts and not from "qualitative research that might contextualize expressivism in specific teaching situations." There is a certain irony in a social epistemic critique which fails to examine context because of "its own theoretical claim that discourses . . . are socially constructed and politically interested, shaped by specific and historically contingent material circumstances" (252).
4. Again I am not alone in my objections to Berlin's work. Cassity notes that, writing in 1987 (*Rhetoric and Reality*), Berlin only comments on Elbow's first book *Writing without Teachers* (1973) and ignores *Writing with Power* published in 1981. Wall argues that "in the expressivist works [Berlin] critiques (publications of the sixties and seventies), the authors do not generally define the self as isolated or knowable apart from language. . . ." (241).
5. In contrast to Berlin's characterization of Elbow's groups, Cassity writes, "The small groups were not designed for the purpose of assessing any writer's 'authenticity' or 'sincerity'; instead, the techniques of showing, telling, summarizing, pointing, and relating 'movies of the mind' (all described in *Writing without Teachers*) allowed for reader response and negotiation of meaning between readers and writers" (171). In short, they were dialogic.

9 LIFE WORK THROUGH TEACHING AND SCHOLARSHIP[1]

Diane P. Freedman

> Writerly writing is personal writing, whether or not it is autobigraphical.
>
> *Marianna Torgovnick*

> "I learned that what I have to say is valuable in and of itself and does not need to be generalized into obscurity."
>
> *Susan Krieger, quoting a student*

> One must ask whose privacy we really protect when we deny students the right to address these [personal] topics, and whose interest it serves to maintain the traditional taboo on these topics.
>
> *Cinthia Gannett*

One appeal of the personal voice in academic writing is its flexibility, its accessibility, and potential literariness—that is, its reliance on rhythms and word music, imagery, specificity, allusions. Another is its capacity for principled disclosure—of research goals and practices, of researcher stakes, of implications for problem, field, and author. That is the aspect I am interested in as a researcher, as a writer, and in my graduate courses in autobiographical scholarship. But the aspect on which I will focus here is the capacity of personal classroom writing—personal responses to course readings and disciplinary issues and the use of personal forms—to negotiate the divide college students often feel between school and work or school and home, their writing and their caring, their knowing and their being. Allowing our students, for a time anyway, to posit connections, can encourage discouraged and dislocated students, give them a way into the disciplinary conversations that might otherwise daunt and distance them.

When I invoke the personal as pedagogy, stance, or style, what I am really endorsing is connection, between student and subject, teacher and student, reader and writer, student and student, coursework and the work of the discipline and the world. I'm not asking for easy writing with pat or unambiguous conclusions about life or intellectual problems. No, the "personal" is a multipurpose route or ruse that invigorates academic learning, academic publishing, our various disciplines. Many disciplines have been "getting personal" in various ways. Postmodern versions of selfhood posit its constructedness in and through discourse, including the "I" voice of a discourse that, in a more innocent time, seemed private, deep, authentic. Now to speak of the personal "always already" means to ask for a poetics of the personal and to recognize its rhetoricity. We know even our *freshmen* (emphasis on fresh) come to us socialized and not "pre-sexual" or "pre-economic," such that even when writing emotionally or narratively about immediate or past personal events and feelings they write out of ideas and with discourses formed or inflected by others.[2] Moreover, to quote Jane Tompkins, "What is personal is completely a function of what is perceived as personal" (36). Tompkins acknowledges that "what we are really talking about [may] not be the personal as such, what we are talking about is what is important, answers one's needs, strikes one as immediately *interesting*. For women," she believes, "the personal is such a category" (36). All of this is to say that so-called personal writing is also inevitably varied, complex, and likely in flux even within one writer's experience.

In my classes and in this paper, I build on the pedagogical work of David Bleich, Norman Holland, and other early "subjectivist" teachers or reader-response theorists in composition and women's studies, including Louise Rosenblatt, Charles Moran, Anthony Petrosky, Nancy Hoffman, Jean Kennard, Suzanne Juhasz, Patsy Schweickart, and Jane Tompkins, among others.[3] I also draw on postmodern debates and the educational approaches deemed "applied" or "service-learning." Personal scholarship teaches that knowledge work involves the whole person. Axel Nissen, in a special *PMLA* issue on the personal, writes, "The will to know, which is at the base of all scholarship, is located not only between the ears but equally under the sternum and in the crotch. Intellectual curiosity, love, and desire are intimately intermingled in our work as scholar" (1149). And service-learning teaches that education does not come in isolation; it involves the whole community.[4] These theorists seek not *just* the personal, nor just anything else, but a comprehensive pedagogy that goes beyond a goal of disinterested, hands-off intellectual activity.

Such a pedagogy underscores what many teachers of writing and literature and especially many women teachers know, that students are unavoidably bringing their personal lives into their academic work, the classroom space, and their conversations with teachers and peers. One response is to draw out the personal connections and develop them as scholarship—or as material recognized as interfering with student understanding of a text and its critical reception to date. If the personal is to remain in the final draft of a paper, it must serve to illuminate the text or issue under discussion; if, on the other hand, to quote Douglas Atkins, "the experiencing, responding critic is not interestingly and effectively represented . . . why [would] anyone else want to read him or her or . . . be expected to do so?" (97). The classroom permitting experimental critical writing and encouraging service-learning projects can help students find academic work more rewarding, bring student work closer to the "masters" and models students usually study, connect home life or past life with school life, and join one person's "unique" experience with that of a larger community group.

Besides encouraging students to explore personal and associative responses to academic texts and issues, I encourage students to take classroom work into the field (an effort aided by large bulletin-board or career-center lists of organizations seeking volunteers, intern-for-credit programs, and the many new state and university organizations for public and community service). A disclaimer: this work has been done and much more extensively by those more skilled in ethnographic work and who teach more writing courses or service-learning-based courses than literature teachers like myself. While I have a good background in and a degree in teaching writing (and another in creative writing) and all courses in my present department are termed "writing-intensive," I was hired most recently as an "Americanist" with special expertise in contemporary American literature, especially poetry and autobiography. Students in my classes are invited but not expected to write personal criticism. And although I have been appointed by the Governor to the New Hampshire Commission for National and Community Service, and while I do encourage all of my students to consider undertaking community service related to writing and literature, I do not *require* that the "project" component of each of my courses consist of service—it may instead involve music and art or independent research. Nonetheless, I will share some student testimonials regarding reading and writing personally, offering them against a backdrop of important work and debates in autobiographical scholarship—the subject area about which I can claim greatest knowledge. As Joseph Boone has written, "While the proliferation of autobiographical narratives by scholars is a significant development, the role that the personal plays in pedagogy is equally important" (1153). Indeed, self-inclusion has become a valued scholarly genre, one that both authorizes and learns from its use in composition and lit.-comp. classrooms.

Most of us are familiar by now with the genre of autobiographical or interactive scholarship and the experiments in the personal voice and blurred genres it offers and advocates.[5] It is most widely practiced in literary studies. Specialist in African-American literature Claudia Tate sees "no boundary between our scholarship and our political commitments" (1148). Michael Berube, English professor and one of the new "Public Intellectuals" writing and speaking (even on the radio) for a broad audience, answers critics of the new subjectivity. Berube refuses to see "personal narratives as some kind of generic violation of scholarship in the human sciences," adding,

> as long as the scholarship in question concerns humans and is written by humans, readers should at least entertain the possibility that nothing human should be alien to it.... In fields like history, anthropology, sociology, or literary study... the interests of the observer are an integral element of research, so much that to ignore those interests is to run the risk of pretending (or at least assuming) that the human sciences might aspire to the accuracy of the physical sciences if only humanists (and antihumanists) would conduct human sciences without hermeneutics. (1065)

Some investigating or practicing "personal criticism" set it against postmodernism, feminist theory, or post-structuralism (in the name of the everyday, of writing pedagogy, of accessibility and anti-elitism), but most recognize that its current growth is very much a part of or in keeping with feminist critical, theoretical, and pedagogical practices not to mention postmodernism. Sociologist Laurel Richardson aptly assesses the current situation in *Fields of Play: Constructing an Academic Life* (1997), announcing, "Today, the domininant intellectual context challenges... all claims for a singular, correct style for organizing and presenting knowledge." In her book, Richardson offers conversational writing, an ethnographic drama, and poems, among other experiments. To Richardson, president of the North Central Sociological Association, a personal, creative, and non-authoritarian approach is appropriate in academia today. She confesses heretical leanings and a "penchant for mingling the personal, the political, and the intellectual" (12). She borrows from anthropologists, who describe the present as a period in which we have the loss of authority of a "general paradigmatic style of organizing research" (Marcus and Fisher 1986, 8; qtd. in Richardson 13), and observe that "ideas and methods are freely borrowed from one discipline to another, leading to a 'blurring of genres'" (Geertz 1980, qtd. in Richardson 13).

Indeed composition and literature teachers now also speak of, demonstrate, and offer courses in the blurring of genres. (Tom Romano offers such a summer course in the Reading and Writing Program for teachers held at the University of New Hampshire, where Pat Sullivan and I each offer similar courses in academic autobiography during the year; at other campuses, Brenda Daly, Madelon Sprengnether, and Olivia Frey have taught related courses as well.) Richardson, like others, perceives that

> the loss of grand theory has affected all the disciplines, although their responses have differed. In literary criticism, literature is aesthetically equivalenced [such that writers on literature, or deconstructors of literature, are on par as *writers*].... In law, critical legal studies... abrogates the legal reasoning model (Livingston, 1982). In

philosophy, the principles of uncertainty and contextuality undermine the possibility of universal systems of thought (Rorty, 1979). In physics and mathematics, the focus is on the inelegant, the disorderly, indeed, even "chaos" (Gleick, 1984). In sociology and other social sciences, sociological production, like other human productions, is seen as socially produced (cf. Fiske and Shweder, 1986). (13)

Since professionals in these various fields have questioned grand theory and passive-voiced, author-evacuated prose and science envy, it is not misleading to our students to have them write differently and expect that their work can still be taken seriously or lead them to the fields or grad programs of their choice.

Nellie McKay, renowned scholar and editor of African-American literature, concludes, "I am convinced that the personal voice, used seriously and responsibly, has an important role to play in the education of young people" (1155). Of course, personal and experimental essays, the memoir, the confession, and so forth have long writerly histories. "If I tell how I chose this topic, what serendipitous encounter with book or friend put me onto this approach" and so forth, George Wright insists, he is "only following lines laid down by Augustine, Montaigne, Coleridge, Keats, Woolf [and many others]" (1160). In the eighteenth century, George Campbell said of persuasive writing, "passion must also be engaged" and "Nothing . . . keep[s] our attention alive and vigorous [more] than the pathetic, which consists chiefly in exhibitions of personal misery" (113, qtd. in Paley 17). In the nineteenth century, another rhetorician, Alexander Bain, praised Plato for his relief of "the severity of philosophical discussion with touches of general human interest. . . . The debate is interrupted by dramatic displays of personal feeling" (202, qtd. in Paley 17). Jules Lemaitre and Anatole France "defended the free play of the appreciative mind," the basis of the "impressionistic" criticism much maligned by the "New Critics." In 1910, J.E. Spingarn described such critics as being sensitive to impressions, capable of expressing themselves well, and (thus) producing new works of art in response to the sensations generated ("The New Criticism" 5). If accused of straying from the work of art, these critics reply: "Do not deceive yourself. All criticism tends to shift the interest from the work of art to something else" (Spingarn 7). In the 1960s, Irving Malin and Irwin Stark extolled the work of Jewish-American critics writing against New Critical tenets. In *Breakthrough: A Treasury of Contemporary American-Jewish Literature,* they explain:

> Many of these [anthologized] critical essays emphasize the value of suffering. In this, they are noticeably different in temper from the pure, scientific, rather aloof criticism of the "New Critics" who avoid committing themselves to any real understanding or sympathy. . . . The refreshing quality of American-Jewish criticism lies precisely in this involvement with passionate spiritual questions, which is certainly a more

humanistic involvement than close scientific explication. This is not to say that American-Jewish critics are merely impressionistic—they think as well as feel. (18)

A decade ago, I noted that blurred or mixed-genre texts have been "produced and theorized by feminists, deconstructors, French psychoanalytic critics, reader-response critics, and composition teachers, not to mention past poet-critics from Sir Phillip Sidney and Walt Whitman to W.E.B. Du Bois, Gertrude Stein, and Charles Olson along with anthropologists Clifford Geertz, James Clifford, Renato Rosaldo, George Marcus" (*An Alchemy of Genres* 83).[6] Today's alternative forms also have echoes of nineteenth-century women's work in such "nontraditional genres" as sketch, letter, diary, newspaper column as well as of the testimonial mode of slave narratives.

In terms of the personal as pedagogy, however, let us only go back to the early twentieth century for now. Drawing on James Berlin, Karen Paley reports, "in 1928, Richard Reeve encouraged the use of dreams for invention in writing personal essays. In 1932, J. McBride Dabbs had his students keep journals and made their texts the central reading of the class. In 1938, Edith Christina Johnson saw writing as a way to form identity and gain self-knowledge" (Paley 42). Also in 1938, Louise Rosenblatt brought out *Literature as Exploration*, the text that gained great critical attention when it was reissued in 1976. Rosenblatt had asserted that "the reader counts for at least as much as the book or poem itself . . . through books, the reader may explore his [or her] own nature," and "just as the author is creative, selective, so the reader also is creative" (Rosenblatt 42).

Back in the 1970s, when I was an undergraduate, Cornell University offered many sections of a freshman writing course entitled "Writing from Experience." I myself taught "Writing Family Histories" in Cornell's "Experimental College." As a graduate teaching assistant at Cornell, however, I assigned my students in "Film and Rhetoric" and "Practical Prose" only academic writing exercises—summaries, analyses, reviews. At the University of Washington, in a writing program under the direction of Charles Schuster, I taught several courses (expository writing, writing about literature, essay writing) in which personal essays served as models for student writing. In the advanced writing courses, in particular, my students modelled essays on those in Robert Lyons' collection *Autobiography: A Reader for Writers* (Oxford, 1977), Nichols's *Writing from Experience* (now out of print), or David Cavitch's *Life Studies: A Thematic Reader* (St. Martin's, 1986).

Even traditional composition classes, taught in the modes (description, narration, classification, comparison and contrast, process), like those offered (including by me) at the State University of New York in Cortland in 1979, relied on personal narratives, although students were to "progress" from these chronologically arranged essays to argumentative essays organized by the reasons offered in support of the thesis that appeared in an opening paragraph. But by the time I taught "expository writing" at Washington and at Skidmore College (as an assistant professor) feminist-theory groups discussed essays in feminist theory and pedagogy; friends and colleagues shared their syllabi and writing exercises—the personal was the political, and it was in. Composition and Gender Studies conferences had sessions in which the evocative and nuanced personal narrative ultimately was celebrated as a possible capstone project of a course rather than considered an easy, throwaway, warmup exercise to be used only in the beginning of a course. Paley describes a class she taught at Boston College in which several students wrote moving personal essays and others wrote more conventional academic essays. A student who did the latter "apparently did *not* find writing narratives to be easy. In fact," writes Paley, "he found it to be more challenging than writing papers about the thoughts of famous philosophers" (my emphasis; e-mail excerpt, 19 February 1999). Rather than a copout genre, the personal essay or the hybrid personal-scholarly essay requires practice and antecedents. Moreover, it is a real genre called for across the disciplines and in the "outside world" though perhaps rendered predictably and poorly in some places.

Wouldn't it be a delight if those college and graduate-school admissions essays were truly evocative and interesting? What about cover letters in job-application packets? Grant and TA applications? Letters of welcome to new students, stockholders, or community members? The question is not whether real writing or real scholarship is personal. It is inevitably so, as most of the twenty-six contributors to the *PMLA* Forum on the subject and others attest. Moreover, I accept what Bleich in 1978 found to be a basic principle:

> an adolescent student—ages 12 to 22—is intensely preoccupied with his [or her] own person—physically, psychologically, and socially. He[/she] shares in common with people of all ages a fundamental concern about the relationships and people in his[/her] life. These preoccupations and concerns are the key to bringing out a new, serious awareness and understanding of the role of emotional life in intellectual development. (18-19)

It is inevitable that much if not all scholarship, student work, and real-world writing is personal. I've elsewhere asserted that "joining the personal and professional, analysis and emotion, 'self' and other," personal scholarship "powerfully connects readers to texts, to their own writing, to our own (if previously unacknowledged) critical process, and to one another" ("Autobiographical Literary Criticism as the New Belletrism" 12). The questions then become:

when and how the personal should be given expression in a scholarly text (Nissen 1142); are there more or less productive ways of getting personal (Gallop 1150); must an openness to personal writing mean a naive acceptance of the notion of a rational, coherent, and unified "self," a notion critiqued by postmodernists and thought to inhere in all personal writing; and how can a teacher avoid getting overly involved in or upsetting students' emotional lives when personal, even passionate, essays are permitted or solicited.

EVERYDAY WRITING AND TEACHING: PERSONAL NARRATIVES

I begin this next section with a braided epigraph, a student taking off, in a personal-scholarly way, from a writing theorist's ideas:

> One idea that Farrell discusses is . . . that the "female" mode is more relaxed for both the writer and reader [because] it comes close to "recreating the process of thinking as it normally occurs in real life" (910). Everyone has a "real life," and every day of this real life people think (even though we often wish we could avoid it). Since this idea is so universal, I think that writers should use their "every day" mode of thought to structure their writing and thus allow themselves, as well as their readers, to relate to their work. As a writer trained in Farrell's "male mode" [that is, "logical, controlled, framed, and contained" as opposed to "open-ended, generative, and process-oriented" (910)], I . . . distance myself from my work. This is very unnatural and tedious. However, I think that by using my "I" voice and being able to retrace my thoughts on the page, I can be more free . . . as a writer.
>
> Cory, undergraduate student

An important and inevitable cautionary note is sounded fully by Brenda Daly in the following passage from *Authoring a Life*. Daly is thinking about fiction and personal narratives detailing childhood sexual abuse, including her own:

> The decision to speak or write autobiographically must be made again and again. As each situation arises, we must ask: What is the nature of the constraint? What are the risks of speaking openly? Who benefits from my silence? Who benefits when I speak out?

Now to my own real life, my teaching life.

I had been carrying around a folded departmental envelope daily for nearly a year on which I'd recorded my telephone authorization code—as a faculty member I get a code and department stationary—only to realize suddenly one day that the envelope had first been someone else's, an unknown, ungendered student whose "to do" list (jotted on this very envelope) had included: Freedman's office, thank you note to Jill, condoms, and call Mom. What message about my *calling* was I to read in the envelope then?

Is the year it took me to notice all that a measure of the level of faculty-member-student disconnect even a personally-oriented teacher like me sustains? Am I just one among hundreds of faculty members intent on his or her private code, secure that an envelope with a departmental address is necessarily one of her own? Or does the overwritten envelope signify that students and teachers are in fact on the same page and that it is every day about the body? Teachers in my department (English) have always taken into account student needs overtly and because literature and writing have healing effects. But as student needs grow every day more apparent and psychically acute, must our pedagogies grow ever more personal? What would that mean? And how can we avoid overwhelming students and ourselves by our classroom modes and materials? Dan Morgan, in "Ethical Issues Raised by Students' Personal Writing," describes well the situation (which has intensified since Bleich described the preoccupations of adolescent students, just as some think the period of adolescence has lengthened into what was formerly adulthood):

> A teacher's responsibilities always did entail more than content expertise and classroom management, always did include listening, encouraging, mentoring, and even, occasionally, some degree of informal counseling. But we now live in a time when many more college students have "special needs," when we see a much higher proportion of students who have led nontraditional lives, a larger number of what I call "broken wing" students. And so, our roles have of necessity become even more time-consuming and challenging. (139)

More and more students remain on campus more than four years or begin college after age eighteen. Most at my campus work, often at more than one job, sometimes more than forty hours a week, while taking a four-course academic load. A good proportion are first-generation college students; several have told me their parents cannot read. Many students everywhere today are also victims of some kind of abuse or of "everyday" accidents, errors of judgement, loneliness, or intellectual isolation.

I know this not because my students have appeared in the hallways drunk or stoned or weeping or otherwise marked as troubled. I know it not because of articles like Morgan's or Bleich's early book or what I learned in TA-training or in new-faculty orientation, but because of what my students say and what and how they write. Especially, I venture to guess, in the American-literature, writing, and women's-studies classrooms, perhaps also philosophy, psychology, and sociology courses, student self-disclosures have increased in and through writing. Whatever the complex cultural forces at work, the result is that more of our young people have had difficult, even traumatic, experiences, and those experiences are erupting in college classrooms, whether disclosure of them is sanctioned or not, overtly related to course materials or not. It is no accident that at the same time, we have a "memoir boom"—the increasing publication not just of tell-all tv-talk-show-like narratives, but literary memoirs and "self-inclusive" or "personal scholarship." Subject matters previously taboo are no longer so; either we are a culture no longer in denial or more and more of the world's citizens are traumatized. One of my graduate students, who is also an instructor of first-year composition, deems our entire culture a traumatic one, by which she means nearly all of us are touched by traumas— our own or others. Dan Morgan offers ways of perhaps heading off excursions into the personal in composition class (tightly assigned topics, a greater concern with audience and purpose, announcing a lack of preference for papers dealing with past or present illegal activities, eliminating personal narratives). But they're not necessarily desirable—even to him—and certainly not foolproof; Morgan acknowledges students will still find ways to write what they want. Instead, our curricula and methodology in the university classroom can—*should*—reflect an awareness of the students' inner and everyday lives without overwhelming ourselves or our students. One's innermost experiences and values are fair grounds for teaching and research, and classroom learning is enhanced by acknowledging inevitable and necessary connections between life and learning. In fact, the prevalence of new experiences and new genres means we have more pedagogical and socially-grounded writing options to explore with our students.

How can we build bridges between the major (for which we teachers have too often served as Major General) and the student every day—whether traumatic or more happily connected to the figures inscribed on the coveted envelope: "Mom," "Jill," and the lover implied in the jotted injunction to [buy] "condoms"?

I certainly do not propose that we should all get re-degreed as counselors or install couches in our offices or even that we should spend more time just chatting with students during our office hours or on e-mail. I argue for the cultural and ethical work of facilitating lifework through coursework, the writing and reading of personal-scholarly narratives. Nearly all disciplines offer narratives. However, many scholars have pointed out that we sanctify the study of narratives as perhaps the chief coursework of the literary studies field, for example, and yet cordon off the narrative mode from further application. Thomas Newkirk comments on the "strange schizophrenia" regarding narrative in English departments: "On the one hand, [English departments] are built upon the narrative—it should come as no news that students become English majors to get academic credit for reading narrative fiction. Yet in writing classes there is a sense that narratives are relatively easy to write and academically suspect" (20). I consider it no crime to let students respond in kind. Even "in atomic physics," according to physicist Franz Capra, "we can never speak about nature without, at the same time, speaking about ourselves" (*The Tao of Physics*). While there is theoretical justification for this reflexivity in the work of so- called "expressivists" such as Donald Murray, Peter Elbow, Lad Tobin, and Newkirk; reader-response "subjectivists" such as Bleich and Michael Steig; feminist critics such as Louise DeSalvo, Adrienne Rich, Michelle Cliff, Jane Tompkins, and Brenda Daly; in the new "ecocriticism" practiced by Scott Slovic and Ian Marshall;[7] and others, a case can also be made on the basis of the experiences and writing of college students. In the end, I do not suggest that everyone should or can regularize the use of personal narratives in the classroom, just that linking course work to life has been of major and increasing importance for students *and* scholars. It has helped bring students into positive relation with one another as well as all facets of their educations. It has produced "good," "close," and "strong"[8] readings and powerful and eloquent writing.

As an example, an undergraduate student, Kelly,[9] discovered writing about and reading literature was not only significant for herself, but, she imagines, for her classmates and other readers, "I hope my sharing ... can encourage or uplift you or maybe make a difference in your life. If I didn't speak, that would be a burden. I believe it is wrong to hoard things to yourself that have the potential of encouraging others." Erica invoked poet Muriel Rukeyser when she opined, "However confused the scene of our life appears, however torn we may be who now do face that scene, it can be faced, and we can go on.... Poetry helped me to face the scene when my life was confused."

Classmate Lolly agreed, "There is a sense of connection that I feel when I read and analyze different literary works because in everything that I read I find a connection within it to my own being." Literature continues to be what educational theorist Paula Salvio terms a "technology of self." For most college students the dynamics of any classroom and discipline are a technology of, guide to, and test of selfhood. And the inverse is true: through the self or personal experience students access and create disciplinary knowledge.

Neither the emotional intensity of some student narratives nor the questions, cautionary tales, and postmodern denials of agency have made me abandon the comprehensive curriculum that relates the personal to the academic. Kate Redfield Jamison, a psychologist who writes of her own mania, depression, and psychosis in *An Unquiet Mind* (1995), announces perhaps an extreme view: "I have no idea what the long-term effects of discussing such issues so openly will be on my personal and professional life, but, whatever the consequences, they are bound to be better than continuing to be silent" (7). I cannot but share her position based on faith, student and professional testimonies, and contemporary literary and pedagogical theory.

At the outset of her book *Vertigo: A Memoir*, published in 1996, literary critic Louise DeSalvo writes:

> Without books, without talking about books, where would I be now? . . . would I have created a life for myself so different from my mother's, from my sister's? Filled with pain, yes, but not disabled from pain as they were? I don't think so.
>
> Books were, at first, solid objects to hide behind. *Hawaii, The Brothers Karamazov, Exodus* were substantial books I could get lost in, safe screens to prevent me from watching my family. Something to hold in front of my face so I could not see what was happening. . . .
>
> Events in books became a universe against which to measure what I was living through, a world through which I sought understanding. . . . (6-7)

She concludes, "It is as simple as this. Reading, and writing about what I have read, has saved my life" (7).

Many of us in the profession agree. Sometimes reading or writing narratives whose themes are the very things that cause one's pain is even more useful. It is worth noting that DeSalvo's testimonials on the life-saving effects of both pleasure reading and scholarly writing come in the wake of one of DeSalvo's most poignant undertakings, a book about the relation of Virginia Woolf's early sexual abuse to her later life and work. DeSalvo further confides:

> When I started my work on Woolf, I did not realize how similar her family was to mine—did not know my sister would kill herself as Woolf had; did not see depression as the core of my mother's life as it was the core of Woolf's and her mother's; did not realize that I, too, would fight depression; did not see that we were both abuse survivors. And that I would learn, through studying her, the redemptive and healing power of writing. (11)

The reciprocal and layered process of discovery depends on such identification, conscious and unconscious.

In anthropology, Ruth Behar calls the making of such connections between one's life and one's work, "vulnerable" anthropology, emphasizing, "Vulnerability doesn't mean that anything personal goes. The exposure of the self who is also a spectator has to take us somewhere we couldn't otherwise get to. It has to be essential to the argument, not a decorative flourish, not exposure for its own sake" (14). In this era, she argues, "we need other forms of criticism, which are rigorous yet not disinterested; forms of criticism which are not immune to catharsis; forms of criticism which can respond vulnerably, in ways we must begin to try to imagine" (175). Laurie

Stone, author of *Close to the Bone: Memoirs of Hurt, Rage, and Desire*, offers a similar view of what makes memoirs "literary" or successful instances of cultural autobiography:

> [Their authors] are vulnerable on the page, digging at their actions and emotions.... They are interested in their layers, their ambivalences, their irresolvably mixed feelings.... All the rage, self-pity, and self-importance have been spent.... What's left is a voice that may once have told its story as a weeper but now knows, ineluctably, it is threaded with comedy. (B9)

Student work increasingly too exhibits this wonderful layering. Moreover, students writing for self-analysis and self-help have usually begun this process and the making of the literary before we meet in the literature classroom. They merely extend it in the presence of contemporary narratives that serve as models of thought and expression. I teach with the expectation, now, that difficult themes will emerge sometime in the semester, in reading, perhaps discussion, often in conferences. *But I'd rather have them emerge in the writing than in conference alone.*

For those students for whom or for those topics for which writing personally is not a welcome possibility, students and syllabi offer other strategies—such as visual narratives—for relating course materials, the class, to life. Projects have included painted and dyed triptychs, a quilt of the bedding that dates back to early scenes of incest, photographs of a consoling and invigorating network of wooded trails. Other students, working in community-based programs, have helped men and women to read or to prevent or deal with sexual harassment or sexual abuse. Still others read to local children in schools and daycare centers, offering children more of the literary solace on which they remember having so depended. These are academically legitimate narrative interventions as well, especially when they are further described in term-end journal entries or classroom presentations consisting of personal stories and visual aids.

Newkirk sensibly insists that:

> writing situations can be therapeutic precisely because we [teachers] don't act as therapists ... In fact, the therapeutic power of such writing may be the experience of having it treated as "normal"—that is, writing that can be responded to, critiqued, even graded. Writing may have healing power because it represents a *third* part of the relationship; it is an artifact, a construction, a relatively stable representation of experience. (19)[10]

The text and the writing are stays against confusion. Writing about Ann Petry's short story "In Darkness and Confusion," a graduate student in

"Autobiographical Scholarship" addressed her new understanding of the riot at the center of that story, moments of intense rage in her own life, and the central role of literature in life:

> I know that rage destroys both its object and its host, and I have used the study of rage in literature to prevent my own hatred from destroying me. It is not a coincidence that I was depressed for months before that night when I attacked my father, nor is it a coincidence that William [from the story] was stifled in his dismal surroundings.... After encountering rage within this story I realized that it was possible to discover literature that deals directly with my own problems and concerns.... This threefold nature of literature is essential to an understanding that human emotions and the human condition are best comprehended *when studied simultaneously through individual, private, public, and artistic means.* If I had not discovered that literature can be therapeutic, my own pain and anguish would have remained buried within me and would have boiled to rage again sometime in the future, just as my inability to speak initially brought upon my rage. (my italics)

After teaching the graduate seminar, I developed an undergraduate seminar, "Poems and Essays that Matter." This course acknowledges student wariness and concern about the use(s) of literature from the beginning. The course description, which begins with an epigraph by contemporary New York poet Sharon Olds, follows:

> English Major Seminar: Poems and Essays that Matter
>
> For twenty years I've lived in New York City on a block with two "heroin hotels"—a lot of middle-of-the-night screaming, cop cars, loud radios, and over the years occasional singing, laughter, and gunshots. So I'm often hearing sounds of suffering, and seeing its signs. Deep down, I have a fear that poetry is useless, I guess I mean *my* poetry is useless, a self-indulgent activity—that it's obvious I should, instead, be holding infants in a hospital orphanage, or working at a good kitchen for the homeless. Other times I feel extremely lucky to be able to spend time on what I adore doing and need to do. But it's obvious that a worker at a shelter for battered woman, or a tutor in a ghetto, is a more useful member of society.
>
> And yet my wild hope is that poetry somehow, secretly, matters as much as anything.
>
> Sharon Olds
>
> With opportunity for student input, but with an emphasis on recent U.S. women writers, this course will focus on poets and essayists of political, personal, formal (stylistic), or local importance to course participants. Students will work on their own poems and essays that matter as they consider—as subject matter, inspiration, and models of good writing—poems and/or essays by Adrienne Rich, Patricia

Williams, June Jordan, Annie Dillard, Edna St. Vincent Millay, Wendell Berry, Nancy Mairs, Alice Walker, classmates, UNH faculty members, and other suggested activists, feminists, ecocritics, and literary critics and theorists whose writing moves us. There will also be guest visits by UNH faculty members; student-led discussions; outside poetry readings; special projects, field work, or service work.

Directly or indirectly, this course may answer such questions as: Why study literature? How do we define the literary? Why write? What might we do with an English major? (Or a Women's Studies major or minor with an interest in writing?) What will we choose to read and write in years to come? Where might we find what we want and need? What literature have we previously found inspiring, important, irresistible? Why? What might we share with friends, parents, children, and/or the larger community? What else constitutes current issues and debates in literary studies and its value for teachers and students and the country at large?

Three books and a packet of readings were required, though students collectively decided which readings would stay in and which go out for classroom discussion. To these we added other student-recommended contemporary U.S. poems and essays that fell under one or more of the three course rubrics.

Writing on poems or essays of nature and place, Erica described poems in relation to her past depression, illuminating both:

> It seems as though that whole time was Frost's "Desert Places." I had always loved the soft "s" sounds, thinking of them as replicating fallen snow. But now I understood the last lines, "I have it in me so much nearer home/To scare myself with my own desert places." I also understood why Frost's woods are "lovely, dark, and deep."

Helped by a second look at the literature and by others' personal-literary essays, Erica identified and communicated to others her situation and that of the poems, understanding them both more than she might have previously.

Lana, who made a quilt of her childhood blankets, was also able to write "Deconstructing the Bed," emulating and empowered by course reading. She explained:

> My bed is a metaphor for my disease. My dis-ease is the covering over of painful memories. Each night, I slide into bed between sheets that are as old as I, and a pile of blankets I've been collecting since those sheets were purchased. They are meant to cover something huge, something unbearable, something so ugly it must be concealed. In my bed, I suffocate under my own attempts to heal, which are really only attempts to avoid naming an unutterable thing—the abuse I suffered at the hands of my father from the time I was three to the year of my parents' divorce, abuse that is best described by the following poem, based on Joy Harjo's poem "I Give You Back"[11]:

I BRING YOU FORTH
I deliver you, my lustful and vengeful
child. I deliver you. You will be the symbol
of muted words, brought forth in a scream of
pointed blame.

. . .

I bring you forth to the naked children
who were made ugly and seductive creatures
by ignorant fathers, and voiceless mothers.

. . .

[The bed] is on a pedestal, it is a sacred space, and yet it is a detestable thing, a corner of the room blazing in lust and blood and fire, and all the things from which we are taught to avert our eyes. . . . I've been covering a scar with gobs of makeup which have made their own mess.

. . .

Somewhere beneath
this expression
I am not afraid.

Lana detailed the influence of Harjo and of autobiographical scholarship on her work, sharing her foreword and her mixed-genre autobiography in the seminar as well as at a year-end departmental conference, by which time the piece had become part of a portfolio, creative and research-based, that constituted a senior honors thesis.

Like several students in classes taught by Karen Paley, several of my students turned their private or hybrid discourses into public documents or presentations. Paley reports that one student wrote an essay regarding campus security at another university in the form of a written complaint; she mailed the letter to officials there. Paley herself published an essay about how one student's experience of harassment became the subject of a class, and the letters classmates wrote became public documents in the struggle against racism on her campus.[12] Some students had essays accepted in the campus publication *Fresh Ink*, a juried collection of freshman essays passed on to the next year's freshman. Some are even reprinted in the college's alumni magazine, circulation 130,000 (35). Paley notes too that three essays from her advanced writing seminar are being considered for publication in that magazine, and they are all first-person narratives (whose topics speak to outsiders and well as community members: drinking, losing grandparents, a visit to Auschwitz). She concludes, "When such essays emerge from the process writing classroom into more public domains, the discourse is not as contained as [some detractors] claim [personal writing] is" (35).

For another of my undergraduates, writing was at times a substitute for complete (which, to her, meant oral) disclosure, and she was not yet ready to have her academic work in classes outside the seminar be joined with this special kind of writing: "Writing is my chance to say what I can never say in real life. I have all these thoughts and ideas in my head that are never expressed verbally, so I have to write them. Otherwise I might go crazy." But this very private sentiment was one shared during peer-critique sessions in the seminar—as if to disturb again the false or provisional line between inside and outside, private and public.

Other students also might not have made a formal presentation of their personal or hybrid personal work or published their work, but at term end they made their essays available to classmates through the library Reserve Desk. They claimed to find the class assignments good practice for reading and writing sensitively in other contexts, and they linked even their practice work to professional writers and writing. Marianne reported:

> This is what I try to accomplish with my personal writing. It is not very productive in the sense that there is no real goal. I don't know where I am going with it. I have not written a complete, finished poem or a complete work of short fiction since I was a little kid.... My writing is what Natalie Goldberg would call practice. I like to think of it as an exploration of myself.

Chris found words to name her writerly version of Du Bois' double consciousness:

> I am a writer with two voices. But I am now more aware and appreciative of both voices. After reading Farrell's and Frey's pieces, I now recognize the difference between my "male" and "female" modes, my "direct" and "indirect" voices. Both have their advantages and disadvantages. Both play important roles in my life, professional or personal. Perhaps with my new awareness, I will be able to enjoy both styles more and exploit better the advantages of both.

Chris moves back and forth between modes and genres, a versatility I encourage in even the most autobiographically inclined students, and this dynamic is both socially potent and socially dependent. It is in the company of others' stories and voices that we acquire the skills we need—creative, stylistic, interpretive, attitudinal—to make writing matter in life and school.

Kelly writes in several places about the pedagogical and healing effects of inter-animated, facilitative narratives, taking off, again, from an observation of Farrell's, when she states:

> I suspect that the female mode can be learned but cannot be taught. Is faith something that can be learned but cannot be taught? Is high school writing? Would my

friend's comment about fellowship in suffering have meant anything to me at all if I was not learning something about pain and suffering for myself? [She was ill while her friend had lost her husband to cancer.] Is that what teaching is—what learning is? Making things be or bringing things to such a personal level that the student feels or begins to feel some connection with what I'm saying? How do I do that? Then I thought about the difference between learning something and being taught.

I'm left-handed and have always wanted to learn to crochet, but I've only ever known women for some reason who were right-handed and said they couldn't teach me. Then, just recently, I had two different right-handed friends attempt to show me the process. With one, I was taught. With the other, I learned.... [Patty showed her an old-fashioned handout, while Lynn told her that her left-handed grandmother had taught her to crochet by sitting across from her and providing a mirror-image for her to see.]

So what was the difference? Both friends wanted to teach me, both were sincere, but when I sat next to Patty and watched her show me the stitches, I could think only of my inept hands and her nimble fingers. When I sat across from Lynn, I listened to her story.

What students need to know and how can often be found in everyday, "personal," language and spaces, classroom or kitchen. Kelly, whose father cannot read, taught the next semester in a local elementary school and compiled a scrapbook of poems about the experience. Then she served as a literacy volunteer, was nominated for a student service award, and is currently completing her education while teaching literacy and literature in a local prison. She argues that being able to write personally and analytically gives her a combined sense of herself as writer, editor, teacher, and scholar.

Models and open-ended assignments, careful editing, and peer review move students toward what Behar and Stone and other academics and general readers prefer. Others might object that the domestic spaces explored are too dangerous—or dull. But these are strong students, supported by strong texts. Four from the undergraduate seminar subsequently completed undergraduate theses and supported one another in a writing group. Two of the graduate students wrote personal M.A. theses. Against the worry that these writings are sub-standard or non-standard, one might counter that "vulnerable" or personally-inflected writings are becominly increasingly numerous and well respected, and few classroom papers are or ought to be published, even the objective, unemotional ones. Either there will be time, there will be time, for decisions or indecisions, before the taking of a toast and tea, or, once off to graduate school or teaching or business writing, our students will continue to balance anew the personal and professional, private and communal. Two of the undergraduates are already enrolled in graduate programs welcoming their creative criticism, and several more continue their service work reading to children and helping them improve their reading and writing.

"In telling what feels like one's own unique story based in childhood trauma, the writer can be propelled into producing a highly political narrative," Paley asserts. She quotes Bonnie Sunstein and Elizabeth Chiseri-Strater approvingly: "To understand someone's culture, we often to understand the person's family, too. Through the individual we come to understand the culture, and through the culture we come to understand the individual" (206; qtd. in Paley 2). The personal is inevitably shot through with the social.

Norman Holland speaks of "another kind of productivity" than the conventionally academic: "the writing of things that are pleasures to read," adding, "How do you evaluate a personal essay? You evaluate it as you would evaluate any essay" (1147). In answer to the question, "Why now?" He suggests:

> Could it be that a growing number of academic critics are realizing that academic writing about literature or "culture" has lost political support by cutting itself loose from the concerns of ordinary people? There in the back of the bus are some nonacademics who might just support the NEH, the NEA, tenure, or better salaries for teachers—if they could figure out how our essays matter. In this harsh time, could we be returning to the battle cry of another harsh time, the sixties? To *relevance?* (1147)

I shall close by quoting another undergraduate student's recent testimony. Domenica Gorini writes of the relevance of Alice Walker's words in "Saving the Life That Is Your Own." She echoes and enhances our understanding of not only Alice Walker's words but of "personal" writing:

> Walker ends her essay by stating, "It is, in the end, the saving of lives that writers are about" (14). Writing has saved my life, given me a sense of accomplishment—writing has allowed me to sleep at night by giving me a way to deal with the world around me that seems too complex and harsh at times. Reading authors like Walker has also saved my life, by opening the door to worlds I would have never known, feeling and ideas I thought I bore alone, as well as providing hope for a better world, but most of all, a better me.... To be a writer is to be an investigator, one who is willing to search for what is being longed for or answers to endless questions....
>
> Writing has permitted me to "inquire further" (as in Anne Sexton's poem for John Holmes) into what might be viewed as shameful or crazy. Writing has helped me understand my human experience as a white, middle-class American, a young woman facing adulthood, an Italian, a Catholic, a feminist, ... environmental activist, and seeker of joy.

NOTES

1. I wish to extend my thanks to the many persons whose work and support have helped me in the completion of this essay and motivated my teaching, among them David Bleich, Karen Paley, Rachel Trubowitz, Brenda Daly, Martha Stoddard Holmes, Paula Salvio, Laura Duhan Kaplan, and other writers cited, my students in English 697 and English 935, and Brian and Abraham McWilliams.
2. Here I agree with Karen Paley's critique of Susan Miller's claims in *Textual Carnivals* about the classroom community of the beginning student (Paley 34).
3. See, for example, Bleich, *Subjective Criticism* (Baltimore: Johns Hopkins UP, 1978) and *Know and Tell: A Writing Pedagogy of Disclosure, Genre, and Membership* (Portsmouth, NH: Boynton/Cook/Heinemann, 1998); Holland, "Transactive Teaching: Cordelia's Death," *College English* 39 (Nov. 1977): 276–85 and "The Inevitability of the Personal," *PMLA* 3.5 (Oct. 1996): 1146–47; Rosenblatt, *Literature as Exploration* (New York: Appleton-Century, 1938; MLA, 1976); Moran, "Teaching Writing/Teaching Literature," *CCC* 46 (Dec. 1984): 756–66; Petrosky, "From Story to Essay: Reading and Writing," *CCC* 33 (1982): 19-35; Hoffman, "Reading Women's Poetry: The Meaning of Our Lives," *College English* 34 (1972): 48–62; Kennard, "Personally Speaking: Feminist Critics and the Community of Readers," *College English* 43.2 (Feb. 1981): 140–45; Juhasz, "The Critic as Feminist: Reflections on Women's Poetry, Feminism, and the Art of Criticism," *Women's Studies* 5 (1977): 113–27; Schweickart, "Reading Ourselves: Toward a Feminist Theory of Reading," *Gender and Reading*, ed. Schweickart and Flynn (Baltimore: Johns Hopkins UP, 1986) 31–62; Tompkins, "Me and My Shadow," *The Intimate Critique*, ed. Freedman et al (Durham, NC: Duke UP, 1993) 23–40, and "Criticism and Feelings," *College English* 39.2 (Oct. 1987): 169–78.
4. Debra Nitsche-Shaw, citing Ernest Boyer, in her *New England College Service-Learning Guidebook* (Fall 1997) 1.
5. For fuller definitions and examples, see Diane P. Freedman et al., eds., *The Intimate Critique: Autobiographical Literary Criticism* (Durham, NC: Duke, 1993); Nancy Owen Nelson, ed. *Private Voices, Public Lives* (Denton: U N Texas P, 1995); Judith P. Hallett and Thomas Van Nortwick, eds., *Compromising Traditions: The Personal Voice in Classical Scholarship* (New York: Routledge, 1997); and H. Aram Veeser, ed. *Confessions of the Critics* (New York: Routledge, 1996).
6. See Sidney, "An Apology for Poetry" (1595); DuBois, *The Souls of Black Folk* (1903); Whitman, Preface to 1855 *Leaves of Grass;* Olson, "Projective Verse," *Poetry New York* 3 (1950); Geertz, "Blurred Genres," *Local Knowledge: Further Essays in Interpretive Anthropology* (New York: Basic, 1983) 19-35; Clifford,

Writing Culture: The Poetics and Politics of Ethnography (Berkeley: U California P, 1986); and Rosaldo, "Grief and the Headhunter's Rage," *Culture and Truth: Renewing the Anthropologist's Search for Meaning* (Boston: Beacon, 1989).

7. See, for example, Murray, *Write to Learn* (Fort Worth, Texas: Holt, Rinehart, Winston, 1989); Elbow, *Writing Without Teachers* (New York: Oxford UP, 1973); Newkirk, *The Performance of Self in Student Writing;* Tobin, *Writing Relationships* (Portsmouth, NH: Heinemann/Boynton- Cook, 1993); Haroian-Guerin, ed. *The Personal Narrative: Writing Ourselves as Teachers and Scholars* (Portland, ME: Calendar Island, 1999); Steig, *Stories of Reading: Subjectivity and Literary Understanding* (Baltimore: Johns Hopkins UP, 1989); DeSalvo, *Vertigo: A Memoir* (New York: Penguin/Dutton, 1996); Cliff, "A Journey into Speech," rpt. in *Multicultural Literacy,* ed. Rick Simonson and Scott Walker (St. Paul: Graywolf, 1988) 57–81; Tompkins, "Me and My Shadow," rpt. in *The Intimate Critique: Autobiographical Literary Criticism,* ed. Diane P. Freedman et al (Durham, NC: Duke UP, 1993) 23–40; Daly, *Authoring a Life* (Albany, New York: SUNY P, 1998); Slovic, *Seeking Awareness in American Nature Writing* (Salt Lake City: U of Utah P, 1992); and Marshall, *Story Line: Exploring the Literature of the Appalachian Trail* (Charlottesville: UP of Virginia, 1998).

8. These are traditional attributes of good, traditional literary criticism. For a fuller discussion, see Frances Murphy Zauhar, "Creative Voices: Women's Reading and Women's Writing," in Freedman et al. 103–116.

9. All students are identified in ways they chose to be were I to quote, with their permission, from their work—by first name, first and last, or by pseudonym.

10. See also Tobin, *Writing Relationships* (Portsmouth, NH: Heinemann/Boynton/Cook, 1993), and Salvio, "Student Autobiography and the Project of Self-Creation," *Cambridge Journal of Education* 20.3 (1990), for instance.

11. "I Give You Back" appears in *She Had Some Horses* (New York: Thunder's Mouth, 1983) 73–74.

12. See Paley, "Writing and Rewriting Racism: From the Dorm to the Classroom to the Dustbowl," *JAC* 16.2 (June 1996): 285–296.

10 PERSONAL EXPERIENCE PAPER

RACHEL BROWNSTEIN

> Taste and Good Taste have become so separated from active human senses, and have become so much a matter of acquiring certain habits and rules, that Wordsworth's attack [on them] is still relevant.
> *Raymond Williams*

PART 1

Keith says he thinks Jane Austen is "naughty"; Sarah purses her lips. He draws big gay quotation marks around the word with his gay voice, reminding the class that nice as pie though he is he's also naughty and knowing; she looks demurely down through the bottoms of her bifocals, quietly amused, refusing to meet his campily candid blue gaze. There is a sense, in the room, that the bartender and the schoolteacher—members, this semester, of my graduate seminar—are playing themselves to an audience of intimates, like the amateur actors at Mansfield Park. Both of them are sure they understand Jane Austen, sure she would have understood them. Each is one of those "true admirers" who read Jane Austen cherishing the happy thought, as Katherine Mansfield put it, "that he alone—reading between the lines—has become the secret friend of their author" (qtd. Booth 265). For both of them, it is as if (in spite of the notorious failures of her biographers) they know Jane Austen personally, know—in spite of her careful, cagey obliquities—what she really thinks. (People tend not to read Tolstoy, or even Henry James, in quite this way.)

As often in a graduate seminar, more is at stake than interpreting a text: for the dramatic moment, lives seem to be, or at least lifestyles. Keith is about twenty-five, with a shaved head, a leather jacket, and three graduated gold rings in one ear; Sarah, more unusual, is over fifty. Keith has been provocatively maintaining all term that Jane Austen's notoriously chaste novels are all about sex, sex first of all: sex is their "ground," he says excitedly now, and as he interlaces his long white fingers he explains it's in everything in the novels, it can't be separated out, because it isn't "just sex, by itself," which is what's so very good about it, so, well, sexy. It's clear to me that sober-suited Sarah thinks Jane Austen is (like her) beyond sex—and so very good precisely because she transcends it. Sarah cannot speak compellingly here as a member of a marginal group, the way queer Keith does; the others aren't eager to agree with her, his party being much more exciting; but I personally have considerable sympathy for Sarah's position, being closer to her age than Keith's—also distracted by the vagrant thought that it's easier to come out as gay, in the late nineties, than menopausal.

But no one here is coming out, around Jane Austen of all people: Keith is merely claiming the novelist for his party (the transgressives) as Sarah is claiming her for hers (the ironists). Appropriation is what literature students engage in these days, illusions of objectivity having been put away. For their separate reasons, Keith and Sarah treasure Jane Austen's skepticism about the gendered status quo. They share her acute sense of what's socially appropriate in looks, behavior, bearing, being—and the as acute sense of being themselves, personally, both more and less than what is generally expected. "Personally," that is, in the near-archaic sense of that word which signifies the person or the body: the aging woman, the gay man, hear their own odd inflections echoed in the voice of George Austen's not-handsome, not-rich, but extremely clever younger daughter. Keith is correctly costumed for his role as Sarah is for hers, and just like her in his love of decorum and the pleasures of parsing epigrams. He too prefers the oblique, wrapped-up, and elliptical to the explicit, bald, and blatant; he finds it more sexy, as I do. That's why they're both here in my classroom reading between Austen's lines instead of Blake's or Bronte's or Ellison's. Jane Austen might have called it a matter of taste—a perfect word, with its (sexy) suggestion of talents of the tongue that tongues can't articulate.

No theorist, the top-ranking genteel lady novelist of all time cuts a figure in the conversation about taste that has been going on from Hume and Addison through Wordsworth and Ruskin to Raymond Williams and Pierre Bourdieu. She has been widely considered an avatar of taste at least since the beginning of this century, when a representative American critic wrote flatly, "The appreciation of Miss Austen has come to be one of the marks of literary taste" (qtd. in Southam 7). In spite of the recent feminist emphasis on her professionalism, most of her true admirers have been unable to shake the first impression made by her brother Henry's influential assertion: "She became an authoress entirely from taste and inclination. Neither the hope of fame nor profit mixed with her early motive." (Austen V, 6) By naming "taste" and "inclination" as two different things, Henry Austen begins to suggest the distinction and the connection between Definition 6 of *taste* in *The American Heritage Dictionary,* "A personal preference or liking," and Definition 7a, "The faculty of discerning what is aesthetically excellent or appropriate." He points, as well, to 7b, "A manner indicative of the quality of such discernment." Implying links between feeling, intelligence, and manner—between the senses, the critical mind, and appearances—the sequence of definitions might have been conceived by Jane Austen herself.

By signing her novels "A Lady," she lent herself to being read as an arbiter of taste—as the proper lady who, as Mary Poovey and others have pointed out, ruled the drawing rooms of England where propriety (along with civility, and civilization itself) was being defined. For women like the historical Jane Austen—landless and portionless members of the gentry with tenuous tantalizing connections to the aristocracy—claiming distinction by making distinctions was a way of life. (Latter-day English professors and graduate students may be in a somewhat analogous position: witness Keith and Sarah, both of them working hard at low-prestige jobs, both of them tuned in to the intelligence-taste-superiority nexus, each on the *qui vive* to note the other one's gaffe or lapse.) In Jane Austen's England, as people with new wealth and works of art and leisure aimed to ape aristocrats, there was a question of whether true distinction was based on blood or something more ambiguous that was then (with another nod to the body) sometimes called breeding. Clever or artistic people could stake a claim to personal superiority on a (tasteful) display of their taste in clothes, furnishings, feelings, personal habits, and/or in music, drawing, and poetry. Class and its markers concern the characters in Austen's novels; the plots pivot on lapses of taste, and the people tend to be anxious about how their taste measures up to the very best people's, and to pride themselves on how it surpasses that of the vulgar. A glance at some uses of the word in one Austen novel suggests her awareness of the range of its meanings.

Taste is sometimes fairly value-free, simply personal inclination: Lady Russell, in *Persuasion,* has "little taste for wit" (*P,* 27); because they have similar tastes, Admiral and Mrs. Croft are happily married. More often, *taste* means *good taste,* a positive aspect of genteel femininity. Anne Elliott is distinguished by "the fastidiousness of her taste" (*P,* 28); she has "a mind of taste and tenderness." (*P,* 84) (The alliteration associates the mental faculty with the emotions, or sensibility.) Seven years before the action the novel chronicles, Anne's taste overcame her tenderness when Lady Russell convinced her, against her inclination, not to marry Frederick Wentworth because the sailor was socially inappropriate for a baronet's daughter. Taste is socially conservative, being the ability, as Bourdieu writes, to "sense or intuit what is likely . . . to befall—and therefore to befit—an individual occupying a given position in social space." (Bourdieu 466) But Austen's language characteristically registers and seems to embrace opposite meanings: *taste,* a mark of high civilization, is also a nearly physical feminine attribute that makes a woman attractive to men. The narrator explains that Anne, in early youth, was "an extremely pretty girl, with gentleness, modesty, taste, and feeling," perfectly suited to match the dashing Wentworth, whose more masculine attributes are "intelligence, spirit, and brilliancy." (*P,* 26) Elsewhere *taste* is not gendered but simply sexed: back on shore years later,

Wentworth is described as "ready to fall in love with all the speed which a clear head and quick taste could allow" (*P,* 61). Taste sexily mediates between the poles of maleness and femaleness as the less than masculine Captain Benwick, who has "considerable taste in reading," influences bumptious Louisa Musgrove to develop into "a person of literary taste, and sentimental reflection" (*P,* 167).

Literary taste, in Jane Austen's novels, is a sure sign of sensibility, a quality of mind and heart that can be excessive and debilitating but is also civilizing. Her reading heroines are the ones whose color changes most often, Marianne Dashwood and Fanny Price. (Jane Austen always lays snares for would-be generalizers: bookish Mary Bennet, who recites by rote from the readings assigned to girls, lacks both tact and taste.) The aesthetic faculty seems to be socially benign, but it can nourish a preference for luxury and excessive pride in the distinctive, distinguishing signs of membership in the upper class. This is true in the case of Anne's snobbish father and older sister, whose desire to "reduce their expenditure, without involving the loss of any indulgence of taste or pride" (*P,* 10) motivates their move to Bath. Too-fastidious taste can produce those overly nice distinctions that embarrass even devotees of Jane Austen. Comparing Mrs. Musgrove's tolerance for domestic noise to Lady Russell's for the street noise of Bath, the narrator disdains both: "Every body has their taste in noises as well as in other matters; and sounds are quite innoxious, or most distressing, by their sort rather than their quantity." (*P,* 135) The show of distaste for noise of all kinds—the implicit boast of delicate, distinguishing, and therefore distinguished superior ears—is nearly offensive. Worse yet, good taste borders on bad in the scene where Anne and Wentworth try not to laugh at fat Mrs. Musgrove weeping over the death, years ago, of her son: the hardhearted attack on maternal feeling distresses many twentieth-century readers. "Personal size and mental sorrow have certainly no necessary proportions," the narrator elegantly and wickedly intones. "A large bulky figure has as good a right to be in deep affliction, as the most graceful set of limbs in the world. But, fair or not fair, there are unbecoming conjunctions, which reason will patronize in vain—which taste cannot tolerate—which ridicule will seize." (*P,* 68) We have come full circle: far from taming and civilizing unruly individualizing passions, taste here leads to an anarchic giggle that threatens mannerly self-control. Tellingly, it is a response to a body.

Wordsworth worried whether taste was active or passive; Jane Austen's critics attack her for being conservative, judgmental, coercive. "Taste classifies, and it classifies the classifier," writes Bourdieu (6). Jane Austen's novels are fun for graduate students to analyze; developing a taste for them, one develops a taste for making distinctions, and a more developed taste for distinction itself. Austen's distinguished prose may make the students in my seminar find less complex and nuanced texts too boring and bland; by over-refining their taste, it may even make them unfit for ordinary writing, noise, behavior, society. What price refinement? We don't ask; we take the risk. Talking about *Persuasion* and manners and language and what Keith calls sex, which is to say ourselves, we are having a very good time—in spite of the fact that graduate students today are in no position to linger over what suits their taste and inclination, or to write without the hope of fame or profit. Seminars like mine have no clear, direct relation to the academic work of teaching composition or literary history, or publishing scholarly papers that spell out meanings (we enjoy the process of teasing them out). Would Keith and Sarah and the rest be better off doing—and reading—something else? Are we, in this seminar, open to the charge of escapism that is so often leveled against amateur readers of Jane Austen's novels? Am I wasting their time?

Could be. The most successful of my students will write persuasive papers that consider Jane Austen's relation to the jurists and journalists and poets and playwrights of her time, and/or to the theorists of ours—some of whose language is (if for different reasons) as dense and demanding as hers. Will they be betraying their personal stake in interpretation, their giddy, charged excitement about tiny shifts and slippages of meaning? And what of the others who are unable to stake out territory of their own in the well-tilled terrain of Austen studies? Will they be equipped to move over—as one is encouraged to do, now—to the less interesting language of Mary Robinson and Charlotte Smith?

PART 2

> [T]he question is ... not only how to understand and with what to connect Austen's morality and its social basis, but what to read of it.
> *Edward W. Said*

People read and study what other people have written in order to situate themselves among others, to gauge and locate and define more precisely their own feelings and experiences, some say their humanity. ("I'm back in school only to find out who I am," a student confided recently, as if no one had said that before.) It is not a matter of being narcissistic or solipsistic or simply self-involved. To put ideas and feelings into language is to put them into a shared social world; to see how the best writers deploy words is to learn what can be expressed. When high school seniors argue about why Hamlet dilly-dallies, their own fears about taking action are discernible in the things they say. Some readers are turned on by finding that in its very difference and distance, formality and dignity, Shakespeare's dialogue or Jane Austen's speaks to (and about) them; others prefer the writing of a lyric poet or a contemporary memoirist who is more concerned with the solitary self. But no matter what text you talk about in an

English class, a teacher always aims for personal reactions: it's a sign you have sold the book. And in the process of exchanging responses to a book everyone has a chance to discover something new.

I was initially annoyed by the sweet young undergraduate who smugly argued, in one of the first classes I ever taught, that Jane not Elizabeth Bennet was her favorite character and the heroine of *Pride and Prejudice,* being prettier and nicer than her sister. I despaired of a reader so blind to the shape of the book. But Linda's discomfort with Elizabeth's wit (and perhaps with mine) ended by taking the class in a useful direction. The same sort of thing happened in another class, when John, also an undergraduate, startled me by arguing the novel was really about Mr. Darcy, who had nothing on his mind but relationships and arranged everyone's lives in the end. Linda couldn't see herself in Elizabeth; John, brought up to believe that men went to work while women were in charge of family life, envied Darcy's leisure as well as his power. Decades later, I remember their distortions of the novel, which led me to tell the class about Austen's condemnation of most (pretty, nice) novel heroines, and her admiration of Richardson's *Sir Charles Grandison,* a novel about a heroically domestic man. My students' misreadings taught me something. But mostly clearly, I recall the drama of their charged, barely articulated discoveries about themselves.

Teaching *Mansfield Park* to undergraduates in Brooklyn, one semester in the early eighties, I was forced by my students to look harder than I ever had before at a minor moment in the plot—Edmund Bertram's response to his sister Maria's engagement to Mr. Rushworth. "Edmund was the only one of the family who could see a fault in the business," Jane Austen writes apropos of Maria's having closed the marital deal in her father's absence; "but no representation of his aunt's could induce him to find Mr. Rushworth a desirable companion. He could allow his sister to be the best judge of her own happiness, but he was not pleased that her happiness should centre in a large income; nor could he refrain from often saying to himself, in Mr. Rushworth's company, 'If this man had not twelve thousand a year, he would be a very stupid fellow.'" (*MP,* 40) The punch line, for most readers, makes you forget what goes before. But Teresa, the cleverest young woman in my class, wanted to talk more about what she called Edmund's self-absorption and his passive complicity: taking up what had seemed to me a marginal point, she insisted that he should have intervened and told his sister what he thought of her fiancé. Popular magazine articles about "co-dependency" were in the background of her indictment of the hero who Jane Austen is said to have admired above all her others (except Mr. Knightley); still, Teresa was feisty, fiery, and eloquent. Her passion provoked tall, taciturn Steve to rise to the defense, not exactly of Edmund but of Rushworth. Maria, he insisted, should be allowed to marry as she chose. As the debate heated up uncomfortably, pitting the rights of stupid people against the responsibilities of those who can identify them as such, I tried to change the subject and bring the conversation round to what then seemed to me an important theme of the novel. I pointed out that when Sir Thomas Bertram comes back home and meets Mr. Rushworth, he takes it for granted that Maria is marrying for money, complacently telling himself she doesn't have "strong feelings," which is Jane-Austen for sexual ones. Tender Fanny Price, I observed, who blushes easily and refuses to give up her tenacious love for Edmund, does have strong sexual feelings—of a different quality than those of Maria, who flirts adulterously with Henry Crawford while she's engaged, and runs off with him after marrying Rushworth.

But my students were less interested in distinctions among forms of female desire, which is what my fellow feminist literary critics were talking about in the eighties, than in the morality of marrying for money's sake and matrimony's, which is openly discussed in every Austen novel as desire is not. There were two reasons for this: first, they were unsophisticated readers, better at noticing the said than the unspoken; and secondly, Brooklyn in the eighties, as regards what was said and left unsaid, was just like Hampshire in Jane Austen's day. These young people could no more talk *about* than *during* sex, for them a furtive, rebellious, ecstatic, or drunken release from consciousness into the purely physical. On the other hand, they did have a lot to say about marriage and money. I let them say it. As the conversation raged it became clear that there was a personal matter at stake. To my surprise but nobody else's, Steve finally admitted to the group that his own sister had just gotten engaged to a rich man, a nice guy but nothing special, and that while he personally didn't think she really loved him he also didn't think there was anything wrong with her marrying money and having a big diamond to show for it. Teresa indignantly insisted that Steve was morally obliged to ask his sister to think about whether she really loved the man; he maintained that it wasn't his business any more than it had been Edmund's. But he left the room dropping a remark about maybe having a little talk with his sister that evening.

On my way home on the subway, I thought about how good the class had been and how close, in spite of everything, the discussion had come to the important themes of *Mansfield Park*. We had begun to consider the theme of permissible and impermissible intimacies, which is first broached when Sir Thomas Bertram meditates darkly about "cousins in love." We had come close to the theme of exogamy versus the countervailing pull of the familiar and familial; and we had dealt with the theme of the responsibility of brothers and sisters for one another, and raised the question of whether we are not all brothers and sisters. (Critics would develop these themes in interesting ways in the next several decades.) I congratulated myself on orchestrating the interaction, around common concerns, of ethnically diverse people (Teresa was Hispanic, Steve Jewish) who ordinarily wouldn't meet or talk like that, outside the classroom. Basking in rather presumptuous contentment, I thought about how literature (and English classes) could alter lives for the better (Steve would finally talk to his sister). But I was under no illusion that I'd created lasting enthusiasm for Jane Austen's novels. Maybe Teresa, who was in the throes of a long engagement, would develop a taste for canonical literature—which might alienate her from the sweetheart she'd been going with since high school. All the others would leave at the end of the semester with perhaps a tiny bit of cultural capital they could conceivably parlay into cash and nice things—big diamonds, maybe, that were not in the best taste. Reading and discussing Jane Austen was no more likely to advance these students in life than to radicalize them.

On the other hand, it might begin to make them look harder at words and people, and to talk more together about what matters. Our discussion of *Mansfield Park* had led to an exchange on a deeper-than-ordinary level; analyzing the motives of Jane Austen's characters had led the students to talk to one another more directly, more seriously, passionately, personally, than they habitually did. Real talk doesn't happen among most friends and families; in most people's lives today, there is a dearth of what Anne Elliott, in *Persuasion,* calls "good company, the company of clever, well-informed people, who have a great deal of conversation." (Even in Jane Austen's time that was hard to find: Mr. Elliott—ironically, the villain of the piece—corrects Anne, saying "that is not good company, that is the best" (*P,* 150). People in the habit of exchanging banalities find few occasions to exchange more than that, and less and less need, perhaps, to do so. In the temporary community of a classroom, or in an informally organized reading group, we enact the phenomenon that so interested Jane Austen, the play of language generated by the differences and similarities among very different individuals. It is pleasurable, human, even socially useful to weigh one's own perceptions against other people's, to gauge the difference between what can be said and what must remain unspoken, to notice how much good writers can manage to say by focusing on some things and leaving some things unsaid.

PART 3

> [T]he most crucial lesson in composition; namely, that what makes a narrative good is not the story itself but what follows what.
>
> Joseph Brodsky

Jane Austen herself went to school for barely a couple of years. But the schoolgirl habit of ganging up and giggling at the duller kids can be traced through not only the Juvenilia but also her mature works: it fairly sends you back to fifth grade. Consider, for instance, this exchange between his favorite daughter and Mr. Bennet, over Mr. Collins's fatuous and over-written letter:

> "Can he be a sensible man, sir?"
> "No, my dear; I think not. I have great hopes of finding him quite the reverse."
> (*PP*, 64)

Many latter-day readers feel constrained to condemn Jane Austen's linguistic (therefore social) elitism: Geoffrey is one of them. He was a quiet member of the graduate seminar that starred Sarah and Keith, and he has come to my office now to pick up a letter of recommendation. Irrelevantly, I recall the pain that crossed his sensitive face when he observed that Jane Austen made it impossible for people like Lucy Steele—narrow-minded, grasping, and ungrammatical people, that is—to read *Sense and Sensibility*. (Lucy would not be able to pick up the book, he complained; but can anyone who does pick it up see herself in Lucy?) Committed to the belief that anyone can be educated and improved, Geoffrey is a dedicated teacher of composition. Jane Austen is way off his screen, now: in the three institutions that employ him, only regular, full-time faculty members have the privilege of teaching the great literature of the past. No problem, he tells me: he likes teaching comp. The son of a tax lawyer, he has decided to take his chances in an uncertain profession; not only does he love to read and write, but for him (he says it without pomposity) teaching is a vocation. He protests that his taste runs to torn sweaters, rice and beans, and free music on public radio— but he does get huffy when colleagues with tenure condescend.

As he prepares to interview for a full-time job that would give him three sections of composition per semester, Geoffrey cheers himself up by reviewing his best moments in the classroom.

"I always teach only one thing," he tells me. "I try to show them how to make an argument; sometimes it works, sometimes not. I remember a student I had once—I can't believe I forgot her name—who got it straight off. 'You have too many ideas in this paragraph,' I told her, 'you need to choose one of them, and have the confidence to develop it.' I explained that throwing out so many ideas was a sign of lack of confidence, and she got it right away and I knew right away that she got it. In the next paper she did exactly what I told her to do, and she was all right from then on. Other times, you say exactly the same thing and it doesn't work, they don't understand what you're saying, they come in and they say, 'But you told me to do it this way, and I did, and now you're telling me it's wrong.' I can't believe I can't remember her name."

She might not be able to remember his name either, but their connection for a critical moment had been real, close, intimate, personal. Something made it possible for him to move in past her paragraph to her sense of self; something made her feel recognized rather than threatened, and able to build self-confidence on what she might have heard from someone else as damningly faint praise (so many ideas!). Was the exchange charged by an erotic element? I wouldn't know. But I'm not sure that he or she would be able, either, to list the factors that contributed to their momentary perfect understanding: the weather or a recent encounter, successful or not, with someone else; a quality of voice or expression; the hole in his sweater; the paint on the wall; the subject she had so many ideas about; a certain slant of light. My point is that in the process of teaching composition, especially if you teach it well, you often get personal. (An ancillary point: this work is vital, and people like Geoffrey should be paid well for doing it.)

But I am being disingenuous: "personal criticism" as the phrase is used in academic parlance today is something quite specific and particular. Usually, the term refers to books and essays by literature professors who acknowledge or explore their own subjectivity, sometimes as a point of departure but sometimes, especially when the critic is well-known, as the subject itself, more or less shocking, revealing, and/or accessible. The cultural sources of this kind of writing are multiple and various. One, surely, is seventies feminism and its central insight that the personal is the political, which gave women—and then men—permission to make the private life public, to find pleasure and perhaps empowerment in sharing once unspeakable experiences. Literary or literate feminism by the way created new kinds of marketable literary products charged with sexual interest: Everywoman's life, in newly explicit detail, went public and found readers. From another angle, writing about the literary-critical self was encouraged by very different groups of scholars, who analyzed readerly practices and responses, or critical canons and approaches, or the history and politics of English studies. When they emerged, identity politics and queer theory nourished writers who spoke "as" or "for" different groups, and others (sometimes they were the same people) who were moved to confess they hated theory and jargon. The simple human interest that professors, like everyone else, have in their own lives and words was encouraged by their admiring, envious, prurient students, and by the media's embrace of some lucky academic stars, whose colleagues also aspired to cross over. Meanwhile, of course, off and on campuses, everyone was affected by confessional talk shows, the vogue for biographies of literary figures, politically motivated searches for sexual scandal, and the general tendency to let it all, sex especially, hang out. Forty years ago, no one dared talk about the erotics of reading Jane Austen in the manner of Eve Kosofsky Sedgwick or my student Keith or Richard Jenkyns, who wrote wonderfully in *The New Republic*, about her enduring popularity, that "she has possibly given pleasure to more men in bed than any woman in history" (Jenkyns 33).

But bringing personal matters and personal feelings into the literature classroom is not new; neither is questioning the hierarchical relation between dignified professor and respectful student. Gossip has always been a staple of English departments, whose members after all have read Jane Austen. Graduate students have been calling even the professors they aren't sleeping with by their first names since the mid-seventies—those heady years of student-faculty interaction when one man in my department regularly spent his first class walking around the room with his composition students, encouraging them to bump gently into one another and him, before sitting them down in a circle to discuss the experience, and write about it from their different points of view. Freshmen have been encouraged to write "personal experience papers" for decades, at least since the early sixties, when I started teaching—accounts of their summer vacations, descriptions of their relatives and their rooms, or responses to the ingenious essay topic that a colleague of mine devised, "How it Feels to be a Neat Child in a Sloppy Family," or an otherwise X child in a Y one.

What's somewhat new, perhaps, is the creation of a genre of professorial self-revelation, and the emphasis on performing selves rather than the earnest authentic one that was in vogue twenty years ago. Performing in their classrooms, on the page, even on the screen, teachers and critics stage a relation to other people. No matter how distanced or abstracted, whether or not it makes an outright claim to be representative of a group, this politicized self demands more than merely personal attention. Nevertheless it rests its claim to attention on the personal: the assumption of real intimacy, the insistence on a gendered, sexed, racialized self, the in-your-face physical body.

Personal criticism also appeals to writers whose impulse is not only or not exactly confessional—people with a taste for the revealing anecdote told almost, if not quite, for its own sake. Often offered in the first person, such an anecdote is not necessarily, not strictly, derived from a meaningful personal experience. It might be, rather, a story in search of a meaning, an insight, an irony, a perception, a connection that eludes flat-out, flat-footed exposition. Academics of my generation, especially those of us who "work on" fiction, are drawn to such anecdotes. In the late fifties, when I was in college, my friends and I made jokes about the existentialist at the local hang-out who explained he was an actor not a waiter, and for that reason slow in bringing the ketchup. Me, personally, I'm a novelist not a theorist. It's a matter of style and taste, for which as we all know there's no accounting. I write what has been called personal criticism because I'm most moved to say something by an incident that seems to me somehow telling, because I tend to reach for an anecdote when I think I have something to say.

The writing game is partly, crucially, a matter of deciding how much of your hand—of your self?—you want to show. Reading, we imagine ourselves to be intimate with other, real or imagined, people; writing, we aim—not only, perhaps, but always also—to connect. The best student papers—and dissertations—have always been the ones most strongly inflected by the writer's voice, probably the ones that crystallize around a personal conviction or preoccupation, an idiosyncratic perception. The most memorable classes are those in which the people make connections with one another and with new sides of themselves around the book they've read. Discussions of what's said and meant in a story, of other people's motives, morals, and language, generally leads to some measure of self-reflexiveness, therefore of self-revelation. Book groups meet, authors read aloud to audiences, for these reasons; although we are baffled, as a society, by the question of what education is and what it is for, making connections with others on or around words is something that people seem to continue to crave. Contemporary analysts of taste and distinction, and gender and race, have made it hard to keep the awareness of bodies and persons, and unexamined tendencies to secrecy and sharing, out of even the most aestheticizing classroom—where they always have been. Interpreting texts, we cannot but hear ourselves moving in and out of character, performing our more and less representative selves. Isn't telling yet not telling, telling by not telling, what English class has always been about?

11 "THE WORLD NEVER ENDS"
Professional Judgments at Home, Abroad

JOYCELYN K. MOODY

In my Cape Town diary, I wrote:

7:39 a.m. Thursday 5-18-00

Woke up in great anger: last night I finished grading the papers on Derricotte's *The Black Notebooks*. Two students of color—Mimi and José—never even turned in their papers. Mimi said she'd turn her paper in to me on Tues. night, but then she went to the movies w/Dagni! This is the hazard of living with one's students! But I know she decided not to submit it—or shit, to *write* it—after I spat out at her, "Not without a penalty—but *do* turn it in," when she asked—or told me, rather—if she could hand it to me later that evening. I was furious with her for not making the paper a priority last weekend. As for José, he has been ill with his wisdom teeth impacted, but by my observation, not so much that he could not have submitted his paper before leaving for his oral surgery, as he'd called to tell me he would. But my anger is really directed at Jennifer and Andrea: they both wrote lousy, for-shit essays that have left me truly insulted. I don't know if they meant to insult *me* as much as they seem to have wanted to insult Derricotte, to mock her injunction to "tell the truth" by presenting papers that so clearly are falsehoods of their feelings. Andrea told me while doing my hair the other night that she read *The Black Notebooks* as arguing for the kind of "color blindness" that two students had insisted in class is possible between "friends" of different races. I just said, "Oh, no; not at all." I didn't engage her on the issue in part because I was sick of the book after a weekend of absorption with it, in part because it was so late at night (nearly midnite), and in part because I knew Andrea and I would not come to an agreement about the book's worth. I don't regret that decision. But I am certain that my reading of the book is right on this issue. I *am* interested in hearing Andrea talk about how she reaches this conclusion about "color blindness"—but only *if*, IF she's also willing to disclose her feelings about other aspects of the book—less her rational inferences than her genuine feelings. That's why I'm so perturbed: neither she nor Jennifer was willing to make the stretch that Derricotte demands. In this reading, I find that Derricotte is not as honest as I'd first thought, and I am happy to be critical of her book and some of its contentions, but there's no getting around the challenge the book makes for readers to do what Derricotte claims she does.

Oh shit, I am just pissed off! I don't want to be friends with two women who are so damn smart and so damn afraid! I have invested so much time and energy in them in many more ways than with others on the trip because of what I inherently believe about their politics and their past experiences. That's it: I feel betrayed by them. As always, I ask that my friends and students put *themselves* on the line no more or less than I am willing to myself, and I feel failed by Andrea and Jennifer in this instance. Andrea did try to talk with me about her paper—no, she tried to talk to me about her resistance to the text, but I did not give her much latitude to do so: instead I asked her how far she was and inasmuch as she admitted that she had not finished the book, I insinuated that I would talk with her about the book only after she finished it. I suppose she inferred my admiration for Derricotte's "candor" or well, her performance, for the final product, and doesn't share it. I still think it is an important book, one that demands our introspection.

This is another problem with living among students. With Rebekah I came to infer that the students have been unwilling to take certain risks in the classroom, but now I am seeing that they were actually unwilling to take risks in their papers as well. I mean, over and over all term I have heard one student or another allude to conversations about the text to which I have not been privy: they have had these conversations in small groups with each other. Partly I'm glad to know that the texts have provoked and inspired them; that's terrific! But partly I needed to be in on these conversations or to have them represented to me in more formal, less casual, ways if the students are to have earned credit for them. Their papers are by and large so lousy that the benefit they've gained from those conversations without me do not show up in their writing. Maybe they keep journals and their insights are there, but anyway while I trust that they *have* been talking about the books among themselves, I have no way of knowing the extent and utility of those other conversations—only the ones in the classroom, which have been so disappointing.

Partly I'm feeling brought up short, foolish, sheepish, victim of the mask— Andrea's black mask that made me suppose that based on her class participation in the discussion of *The Black Notebooks* her paper was sincere, that at the very least, she would be no more evasive of the critical issues *for her* re Derricotte than she was of the critical issues that Sapphire's book brought up for her. And Jennifer's lesbian mask, perhaps strengthened by her sometime need to closet her queer identity. In other words, partly my anger is with myself and my own assumptions and desires. It's hard not to have the desire that those FOUR students in particular would engage the text more "honestly," more personally. What would I have done if I'd been asked to do what I asked them to do? Well, I think my personality is too much like Derricotte's for me not to have written a paper like Jacquelyn's, doggedly trying to clarify my own racialized subject position. Shit, I know I would have. All day everyday, goddammit: there I am with my heart out.

What's the lesson here? That perhaps I should be more generous in my consideration of the students' reticence. No, I will not. At the very least, I would have wanted the kind of engagement that I got in the Sapphire papers—like Rebekah's: *this book bothers me because* _____. It's hard to feel generous or sympathetic when I simply feel left out of their process or frustrated that they resisted a certain process. It occurs to me that Mimi, Jennifer, and Andrea might actually have done some soul searching with each other in their conversation, but that particular combination of women—all Othered in at least one way—indeed, each (self-) Othered in several diverse ways by class, race, sexual orientation, chosen family, and so on—they would not be honest with each other because in the end they profoundly distrust each other. I guess that's what this boils down to—not voyeurism, or petulance that my friends had a party to which I wasn't invited, but that my friends and my students did not seize an opportunity I tried to provide for them—perhaps because they couldn't, perhaps because they wouldn't, perhaps because they did not perceive it as any "gift" on my part at all. Jennifer told me that she'd written in her journal exactly what I was complaining about re *The Black Notebooks*, that in it Derricotte asks me to meet her challenge of honesty and I just feel revolted and inadequate. I don't want to be as honest as she says she is, as she intimates I need to be; I already feel inadequate to meet the challenge and I don't want her insistent notebook to remind me of my inadequacy around exploring the depth of my internalized racism. I'm the more hurt that Jennifer would concur in my kitchen, but not in her paper. I'm angry with her, and ashamed of her that she wouldn't take this risk. And yet all week I've been wondering and worrying just how—*if*—I can deliver on the proposal to turn this teaching experience into a chapter on the personal in pedagogy. Exactly a year ago, I was agonizing over whether or not to publish an account of my experiences as a pregnant college coed on welfare[1]; now I find myself again having to decide just how much to disclose of my private life, my personal pain, how much to share in the name of effecting social and academic change. I wonder if this isn't megalomania or narcissism or just plain nuts. I must have a monstrous ego. Well, as ever, I can still say no or choose another focus. Everything doesn't have to be so personal, for Pete's sake.

[*End of diary entry*]

It is the first Sunday in June 2000, the last morning I am to spend in Cape Town. I am sitting in Mug and Bean, the Waterfront store of an extensive South African coffee shop chain. I have just finished a brisk walk in dense fog with Rebekah and Aaron, two of the University of Washington students in the Study Abroad program that we have all recently completed. Before departing, I want to take advantage of this opportunity over breakfast to get some insight from them, ideas I can apply to a paper I have agreed to write on the intersection of the personal and the professional in the academy. As it happens, they are two of my brightest students, and I am already feeling nostalgic for our quarter-long course (African American Women's Autobiography), only five days over now, for their enthusiastic participation in it. It is my first mention to them of the professional paper that will come out of the course, and truly curious students, they are immediately captivated—and they have an opinion or two to share. I tell them that I am thinking of starting the paper by revealing that all fifteen of the students in the program, save two or three, have seen me in my underwear, including Aaron, who narrowly escaped a glimpse of my bare brown thighs one morning as he eagerly entered my studio flat to ask about his grade on a class presentation. Aaron interrupts me—Aaron interrupts everyone, he is so garrulous—though he struggles touchingly not to be so. He launches into the memory of his growing awareness in the first few days of the program that there would be few if any boundaries between the program participants, between the program components. He remembers an agonizing moment after class one day when he realized, and warned his roommate about, the encroaching borders—or rather, the lack of them. This June Sunday, the program nearly a week over, he shakes his head in passionate resistance still. "The world never ends," he announces in a mixture of anguish and awe.

Indeed not: how many times was there a knock at the door to my studio flat, followed straight away by its bellowing open to admit a four-year-old imp, demanding to know if her mother, the single most intelligent student I have ever taught (luscious wonder!), can borrow today a bit of butter, yesterday extra batteries for a Walkman, the day before my dictionary.

How did having students casually borrow from me or find me in various stages of undress affect my teaching, especially in a graded, five-credit course? It was sometimes very hard to keep my authoritative teaching persona separate from the more sociable "me" I wanted to cultivate at the Cascades Holiday Apartments where we lived for eleven weeks. While I rarely, I want to say never, found it difficult to perform my teaching self in the classroom, it was challenging, however, to keep my teacherly self at bay when class was not in session. I remember how proud I felt when Savitri unexpectedly announced her admiration for my ability to do so. I too was surprised that some situations blurring the lines of my disparate "selves" did not burden me more. I could see, for example, that Savitri is sharp and used to getting good grades. Yet she worked only minimally to improve the middling grades she consistently earned in my course. Her apathy did not disconcert me: I recognized it as a greater privileging of the adventure of foreign life; in her place as student, I might easily have made the same decision. At "home" in the Cascades, I found it relatively easy to separate the critical, "professional" self who marked Savitri's papers from my black woman self eager to befriend this fascinating British-black, Sri Lanka-born American woman. When she remarked my ability to draw a clean line between my professional self and my personal identity, I realized, as she apparently did not, that constructing such a distinction required fierce concentration.

For her part, at breakfast that last Sunday Rebekah observed that I had had a tendency to mother the students. I vehemently denied it. The characterization of my professional work as "maternal" burdens me still, for though I am certain that Rebekah was unconscious of the connotations it has for me, the label disparages my work among predominantly white students as mammying. But the charge did fit. It was impossible to feel detached from them in a maternal way when I felt so keenly responsible for their safety, especially in as capricious a place as Cape Town is: its current crime rate against women especially daunted me, traveling as I was with twelve women students and a woman co-director. But Rebekah added that she appreciated my balanced sense of when to back off, which, coupled with my maternal "nature," provided her own sense of security. Looking back, I realize I endeavored to ensure my own self-assurance as much as theirs: I dreaded the prospect of having to telephone their parents or loved ones with tragic news. Undoubtedly, this acute fear had much to do with the fact that the students were approximately the same age as my son Patrick.

Initially, I had expected to make here a case against what I deemed the ridiculous notion that it is possible, even desirable, to be objective in academic work. (Writing this now, the concept of "objectivity" seems fluid, even elusive; my comprehension of its meaning shifts with each usage.) Imagining an audience composed primarily of professors of English, I expected my readers also to devalue objectivity as impossible and undesirable. Influenced by post-structuralism, we no longer regard "reality" as hard, fast, and concrete. I believed that English professors of every ilk resist the fallacy of objective reality, and in its place erect something like *perspective* or *performance*. But as I write now, this seems an irrational expectation; after all, I can readily name professors who do not meet it. Furthermore, I had imagined arguing that my experiences in Cape Town taught me that the personal and the professional necessarily commingle and complement each other—not only when one is a Study Abroad coordinator/ professor, but in any academic situation. Indeed, I have published essays arguing that literary analysis and pedagogy are sharpened, strengthened when one takes personally one's scholarship and teaching, no less than the traditions with which one works. Now, to my amazement, I find my perspective has shifted, for I have learned in unexpected ways that my own sense of "professionalism," however tenuous, requires me to honor barriers between my so-called professional identity and my so-called private life, borders that keep the world's multifarious locales from bleeding into each other.

I am thinking of the Saturday morning that I lingered in bed recovering from a severe cold and reading J. M. Coetzee's *Disgrace*. A small group of us were waiting to see if the thick fog over the Atlantic in the harbor at Green Point would lift to permit an afternoon hike up Table Mountain. (As *Disgrace* is a novel about an English professor at the Technical University of Cape Town who fuses his professional and personal identities with devastating consequences, my reading of it among students at the Cascades forms one more episode in this saga.) As I recall, Andrea came in first to share her six law school acceptances; she was followed by Jennifer, followed by Savitri, Mimi and Khathulla, followed by Dagni, followed by Jessica. Before I knew it, still lying in bed in my pajamas, I was surrounded by a roomful of women wanting my "undivided" attention for a variety of purposes—to plan the hike, but also to gossip about a lesbian love triangle, to discuss strategies for revising an essay, to nurse—if not medicate— an unrelenting cough, to mirror a black woman self-image, to dole out program funds for an individual field trip. I remember talking earnestly with Andrea—in my pajamas, still in bed—now as Professor, now as Black Woman Mentor on the Continent, when Jennifer walked in. Immediately, I shifted to a much more casual, relaxed persona—to signify to Andrea, Jennifer's best friend, that our "formal" time was momentarily over. Perhaps because we had both been tending colds, Jennifer (a buddy from the Seattle lesbian community) and I had not had any time for private conversation in several days. The last time I had seen her literally had been the previous Thursday, the same morning I'd awoken in a rage at the poor quality of her essay on Derricotte's *The Black Notebooks*. That morning when I had mentioned to a small group of students that I would be returning their marked papers later that afternoon, she had spoken up: "Oh, I'd like to schedule some time to meet with you about that paper." I remember tucking my chin to hide whatever expression was in my face: fury, hurt, disappointment, amazement at her casual audacity. I remember struggling to assign her and Andrea the same grade on those wretched first versions of the Derricotte paper: my temptation had been to award to Jennifer a higher mark, to find more redeeming qualities in her equally inferior work, though in the end, after several rounds of reviewing them "with detachment," I flatter myself, I had to award them the same unsatisfactory grade. I had been considerably more disappointed in Andrea for what seems to me her greater descent into poor work. I had realized almost immediately in our living arrangement that Andrea procrastinated in preparing her coursework. But that seemed only minorly operative in the Derricotte debacle: she procrastinated in this instance because she did not want to write the paper at all. When she and Jennifer revised their respective papers, each took extensive time, I believe because they were then committed to doing better—not simply in terms of higher grades, but also expanding the quality of their reasoning and their articulation of their revised perceptions. I took each woman's steadfast, exemplary effort made in her revision over the next weeks as a personal triumph—hardly an "objective" perspective.

What is it about the fiction of "objectivity" that renders it so powerful in our profession? Why is it that the academy insists on it? Surely the answer has something to do with so-called empirical knowledge, with the lies we academics tell ourselves about the nature of truth. Even among literary critics, objectivity's siblings—"detachment," "rationality," "disinterestedness," "impartiality," "neutrality"—are thought to yield a fairness deemed vital to knowledge. *As if.*

Back at home for only a week as I begin this essay, at some point in each day I wince at my aloneness, my separation from the group. I miss the students terribly. This is unusual for me: when I teach a course *at* UW, not simply *for* UW, I leave my students after two hours twice a week. Occasionally, one or two of them drop by my office for an additional half-hour of my time. I do not develop an abiding attachment to them as I did to the students I lived with in South Africa. At home, I thrive on solitude; by preference I live alone with my cat. I feel very fortunate in this regard, especially as a black woman. Not many of us have the means to live alone, especially in the affluent conditions as I enjoy in my private space. Conversely, many do not consider it culturally feasible or desirable to live alone, a fact that sometimes activates my black authenticity complex. At any rate, even when I feel particularly close to a group of students, such as I did in Winter 2000 with my mostly Women Studies and English majors to whom I spoke through tears about a student-*cum*-friend who died at age 34 of cancer, I still do not feel particularly disoriented when the course ends. More rarely, a class establishes an attachment to me, as was also the case last winter with my seminar students who manifested tremendous separation anxiety at the end. Those recent examples strike me as extraordinarily different from attachments I have had to earlier courses (though perhaps only because they are recent). However, it may be that cultural and geographical adjustments fall along a single continuum. For two consecutive nights in the week I returned from Cape Town, I dreamed of the students, and I continue to think of them in my waking hours. Although I did not enjoy the same degree of connection to each of the fifteen, I still feel very bound up with our group. Ironically, while in Cape Town, I constantly sought privacy and often locked the door to my apartment even when I was home and receptive to guests, simply because I felt it a measure of privacy and control and distance to have to choose to admit students. Had I locked the door less often, surely they would all without exception have managed to catch me in some state of undress. I quipped to my friend Barbara via email that the students seemed to intuit when I was grading their papers, for a veritable pall fell over our sixth floor flats at those times. Perhaps I should have pretended to grade papers more often so as to carve out some additional private time. For we all needed "space" from each other's intrusions and demands, from the sense that, as Wordsworth grieved, "the world [was] too much with us." Not only did I need it as a private, introspective person used to living alone, but I needed it especially because my duties rendered me so intricately immersed in their lives as teacher, program coordinator, mentor, and neighbor—each an identity wrought with complexity and contradiction.

Students sometimes have ironically different understandings of notions of separateness and objectivity. More than one Study Abroad student mused (naïvely, as it happens) that they were all probably going to work harder for my course than for any other in their college career: it would be too shameful to encounter the prof in the Cascades having done less than their level best in the course. They implied that our proximity would make it impossible for me to remain objective, *not* to develop bias against their indolence or apathy. And yet the standard of objectivity seems rooted in part in defense of students, that is, in place for their protection. Like the U.S. legal system and other social institutions, the academy promises assessment—of ideas, of intelligence, of performance—controlled by theoretical paradigms rather than professors' prejudices. Indeed, this promise constitutes one measure of what we call academic freedom.

Talking with Aaron and me that last Sunday morning Rebekah singled out as one of her best program experiences dancing with me at Café Manhattan one memorable Thursday night. Our dancing together distinguished for her the maternal hovering she experienced from me at other times. She would have pronounced me entirely (too) maternal, she reported, but for occasions like Women's Night when I released both dorm director and prim professor to become her dancing partner. (That night also she ironically exhibited her own maternal concern for me). In my diary a few days later (on May 1) I wrote:

> Rebekah and I both enjoyed ourselves—often dancing w/each other, w/Bernedette, and w/Kellye. We danced on the jam-packed little floor, and I drank red wine first, then switched to shots of tequila, mostly so that I wouldn't have to slosh my drink or get someone to hold it for me while I was dancing. Fortunately, I also drank several tall glasses of water and kept dancing, and Rebekah and I kept going outside to give our lungs a break. She was worried that her severe allergies would act up from the heavy smoke. Plus we were sort of flirting with a lovely woman selling queer souvenirs outside. If we hadn't been careful of the smoke and the booze, I might've ended up in worse shape. As it is, Rebekah insisted on my staying at the Cascades instead of taking a taxi across town back to Kenilworth [a suburb where I house-sat for ten days during our spring break]. Then Friday she and I took the train from town to Claremont with Andrea and Zipporah. The four of us spent a slow, desultory afternoon in Kirstenbosch Gardens, some one of the 9,000 different species of plants bringing on a sinus attack I suffered the rest of the evening.

Last night I babysat Zipporah while Andrea was at the Mary J. Blige concert with a UCT student. After I put her to bed, I spent a couple of hours talking quite intimately with Rebekah in her room next door. So weird how closeness develops after a certain amount of sharing. We began talking about tomorrow's class and about teaching, about the differences between Kareem's course [on changes in education since the end of apartheid] and mine [on black women's autobiography], about Kareem's personality and mine. Where his is relaxed and cozy, my class feels tight, overwrought. Of course, central to the differences between our courses is that he does not live with the students; he is not Rebekah's next-door neighbor, for example. I tell her that, whatever Kareem thinks he is doing with the students, for myself, I want them—my white students especially—to forge significant and specific impressions of life among African American women. I say that what they take from the course not only means something to me, it means something *about* me: their behavior as adults in my society has far-reaching implications. I tell her that I have become a professor in large part precisely to have this kind of access to shaping the opinions of my fellow citizens. The investment Kareem makes in them as an indigenous South African is different from that I make, whatever his pedagogical goals: they will leave South Africa, he knows, whereas I am not willing to chance that any of my students will *not* leave the US. He is a man, too, with a man's "natural" authority, and that matters, even to the Women Studies majors on this trip.... It was a fascinating talk, but I don't think I learned anything that will make our class sessions more relaxed. But *is* being relaxed essential to learning? I dunno.... I do know it's hard living so close together, and I guess I did come to realize that that proximity not only makes it hard for the students to share with me, to trust me, but also to take risks with each other. Rebekah and I were talking about a kind of anonymity we both covet, especially scholastically—how we create diverse personae for different courses. That can't be done here since we live so closely together, so *with* each other.

I read the excerpt from my diary entry of May 18 with which I began this essay, and marvel at the shifts in terminology within my own discourse: the conflation of *student* with *friend* exposes the violation of a personal code of ethics. I have virtually never thought of students as friends while they were still under my tutelage. Instead, I have asked friends who are UW students—like Jennifer—not to take my classes so that I will not have to evaluate friends' work. In Cape Town, however, something changed as a result of having Jennifer in my course, and also perhaps as a result of having Andrea in a *fourth* course. Something changed as a result of living among my students, of interacting socially with them, of having dinner together regularly, shopping together, and moreover, of facing the unknown together, of protecting each other when possibly in harm's way, of bolstering each other against culture shocks. I find in my diary page after page lamenting my lack of privacy in the

Cascades. During the chilly, rainy week that I lived alone with a strange cat in a suburb called Kenilworth, I wrote long passionate paragraphs luxuriating in the respite that solitude wrought at Easter. In the emails I sent back to the States, I relentlessly complained of constant interaction with the group. We could not even *walk* alone. Though many of us exercised alone in Seattle to gain clarity and peace, there doing so seemed fraught with danger: we dare not "lose ourselves" in our thoughts while walking unaccompanied on the Sea Point Promenade for very fear of "losing ourselves" in some dangerous predicament. No wonder, then, that my May 18 journal reveals such awesome paradigm shifts as the discussion of a course text with a current student *in my kitchen* and the avoidance of a similar discussion with a current student who *grooms my hair in my living room at midnight*. By the time that I came to write that entry, contrary to previous restrictions in my personal code of professional ethics, I had developed a closeness with several of the students in the program—had even developed a dependence on them, and I felt protective of all fifteen of them. Although I have always cared deeply whether or not my students learned and though I have often been acutely affected by classroom dynamics—behaviorists tell me that I do not quickly "return to baseline"—I have also not cultivated relationships with students beyond the ten weeks when I am teaching them. Hundreds of undergrads have sat in my courses at UW without my developing the slightest interest in getting to know them personally; what I do care about is whether or not they learn from me. I have sufficient friendships in other areas of my life such that searching for friends among my students is for me neither ethical nor desirable. For all that, however, living among students in Cape Town transformed me into the kind of professor who drinks and dances with her students without experiencing an ounce of anguish about ethicality or propriety.

After dancing with Rebekah, I do not recall a moment of doubt that I would be able to read her paper "objectively." When I am training graduate student assistants to mark my undergrads' papers, I caution them to address the quality of the paper, never of the student. "Refer to the essay when you're writing comments," I tell them. "Don't write '*You* did not . . .' when you mean that *the essay* did not do a particular thing. After all, you are not judging the student; you are judging her work, the paper itself." Thus, dancing with Rebekah at Café Manhattan surely did not render me unable to assess her work "objectively." Despite our exhilarating revelry on Thursday night or our compelling tête-à-tête the following Sunday, I did not worry that I could not mark Rebekah's paper with dispassion, even with severity. We had talked briefly, haltingly of her difficulty in reading Sapphire's *American Dreams*; it was a text she would not discuss with me except to say that she found it "painful to read."

Unfortunately, her essay did not clearly articulate just what distressed her, why she was so repelled and captivated at once by the text's horrific imagery. Indeed, after the extraordinarily close time we spent together during the last days of our interim vacation, I confess that I was the more disappointed that Rebekah had produced so ineffectual a paper—and once I returned it marked and graded, she and I never alluded to it again. To what degree, however, was my assessment of her work influenced by that enjoyable time we shared during the break? Am I right—that is, both precise and fair—to think that the pleasure of her company then did not affect my grading? Is my being in a situation that gives rise to such questions a betrayal of my own professional code as a professor of English?

Undergraduates in English courses, like their peers across the university, rightly trust not only that an "objective" set of criteria will be used to evaluate their work, but also that the discipline is disciplined by a concrete set of rules and norms that form it. My association with Rebekah aside, a paradox often develops in English courses in particular, however. On the one hand, students regard English professors with suspicion because those disciplinary conventions can seem so elusive, so nimble, as to leave the students' work frighteningly prey to professors' opinions. Yet on the other hand, those same students often insist on the legitimacy of their own undisciplined readings on the premise that literature by definition is so "open to personal interpretation" that any reading goes, that individual readings are only "opinions" anyway. And in the case of black professors teaching race(d) literature, are not (white) students in still graver danger of being subject to whim, to political correctness, to assessments not of their comprehension or competence, but rather of their personal attitudes toward blacks?

Disciplinarity is not the only determinant of reliability, though. For even when the professor—whatever her or his ethnicity—is a social scientist teaching about race, respect for experiments and analyses, in other words for objectively collected data, falls away.[2] Anxiety about harmful discrimination and unethical academic practices—within and outside of the academy—has led to vast changes in national law. Certainly, grievously, the effect of this kind of distrust is the aberration of tighter regulations for greater adherence to "objectivity." Witness *Bakke*, *Hopwood*, California's Proposition 209, and Washington's Initiative 200—all cases based on a perceived need to protect citizens. The recklessness of these decisions and the students' misapprehensions undergirding them help me to recognize that whatever disappointment I had in Rebekah's paper on *American Dreams*, that paper did not meet the disciplinary criteria for satisfactory work by which I evaluated *all* of my students' papers on Sapphire's text.

One student's question about theories of objectivity and professionalism still has me reflecting on these issues. Andrea, my most outstanding student, came to me in that oblique way she sometimes deploys, to ask about the staff's decision to get to our UCT classroom earlier that day, despite our arriving an hour late. Every Tuesday afternoon we gathered up our books and papers, and herded ourselves to the Center for African Studies for our three-hour class period. On the first Tuesday after the break, our pre-arranged driver failed to show, so we stood at intersection of Vesperdene Road and the Main Road in Green Point, desperate to hail transportation to school. No matter what time class began, we were rigidly committed to returning to the flats by five, in order to get Zipporah before her day care center shut down for the day. The money collector for the *kombi* (i.e., taxi) that we'd verbally contracted to take to school assured us that the driver would be along within seconds; in the meantime, a second *kombi* drove up to whisk us away. We wanted to honor our word to the first man, but then realized that the driver he accompanied was being given a traffic ticket a block away. We were already half-hour behind schedule at this point, and it seemed that a dispute had evolved between the driver and the cop ticketing him. So we cautiously opted to go ahead with the second driver—painfully aware that *kombi* negotiations often end in fatal and near fatal shoot-outs between these desperate drivers. By the time we got settled in our classroom at the Center, we had only two hours of class time left, one of which was to be used in discussing Jennifer Haaken's complicated theoretical essay "The Recovery of Memory, Fantasy, and Desire in Women's Trauma Stories"[3] (which most of the students had either altogether neglected to read or had only skimmed over the vacation). I planned to use the remaining hour to begin our discussion of Sapphire's complex and unexpurgated collection of autobiographical poems and stories about psychosexual and physical violence in American families. I knew that the students had very definite impressions of *American Dreams*, and wanted to spend some time addressing those concerns about what language ought to be used to do and to express, as well as about how different Sapphire's little book was from the previous autobiographies we had read.

That night Andrea wondered if our decision to spend the time waiting for the taxi, then settling the taxi driver dispute that had ensued had been worth the use of class time. Specifically, she said that we had had "everything we needed"—professor, students, texts—even before we left the sixth floor. Why hadn't we simply opted to stay in one of the apartments for the class period? Not only that day, but also each class day, especially considering that we were doling out a hefty amount of program funds to get to campus. Having had three courses with me already, she was proud of my authority. Andrea says she told the other students at the outset that no matter how casual and open I was with them outside of the classroom, they would know that in the classroom, I was very serious. She herself marveled at the difference in my persona. I knew it was a matter of racial pride for her. If she admires anything about me, it is clearly my tacit command of each class session: "This is my time and we will use it wisely." Her penetrating question goes right to the heart of the arbitrariness of fundamental academic idea(l)s, among them objectivity and propriety. "So you want to have class in someone's bedroom?" I responded. But of course, we held program meetings all the time in "someone's bedroom," in the living space of the student assistant—significantly never my own flat, with the exception of the spontaneous gathering of women that morning I lay reading *Disgrace* while waiting for the fog to lift. In the student assistant's flat we played Spades, decided program field trips, met with somber visitors, made "bring-and-share" (i.e., potluck) dinners for each other, and watched a South African soap opera called "Backstage" that featured a vibrant diva who regaled us with stories of her childhood in a local township. Why not also hold class there as well, Andrea insisted. Why maintain the fallacy of separate spheres even here, in this foreign place? Why maintain the illusion that "the world" never ends?

I remember my initial struggle not to be teacherly at the Cascades. I remember the nearly crushing exigency of clearly demarcated lines between power and neighbor.

Pondering her question, I think, *If we say we can only have class in university classrooms, then we contend that there are borders in our lives. School is only There, not Here as well. If we say we can have class wherever we have professor, texts, and students, then we expose the fallacy of separate borders in our lives.* Paradoxically, however, our group affirms the reality, the fixity, as well as the permeability of separate *national* borders since we were in fact outside of the U.S. borders. Moreover, my (in)valid reasoning troubles the conceptualization of "class" or "school," and provokes the juxtaposition of *class* with *learning*. For surely my students were learning when I was not with them every time they discussed the course texts in significant ways—in a *kombi* to or from the UCT campus, in a Cascades flat, on a walk to the Waterfront, wherever a small group chanced to be—*sans* professor. Perhaps Andrea includes erroneously "professor" among requisite signs of learning. Musing even further, I wonder whether the excision of "professor" from learning contexts is not increasing, as universities move to learning communities comprised solely of individuals and their (im)personal computers. Is *that* a move toward greater objectivity? Will the elimination of professor in the twenty-first century produce more objective "long distance" learning?

Having returned to the UW in Seattle, will I remain a "transformed" professor? I know that I cannot: there is too much at risk here. One reason that the students were so silent during class is that they were unwilling to risk exposing the extent of their own social ills. We had started the course with Jamaica Kincaid's *A Small Place*, in which she names the North American a particularly "ugly tourist." Her little polemic stings with its vivid reminders that here in the West we are trained from birth to be imperialists. My students in Cape Town did not relish this book, even though virtually each of them thanked me for the exposure to it, and so immediately upon our arrival in South Africa. When I taught *A Small Place* in Seattle during the months before departing for Cape Town, many of my students resented Kincaid's "angry" tone and repelled her virulence for Americans; safely at home they could insist that they were exempt from Kincaid's vitriolic charges. But the students abroad had to confront Kincaid's charges in the geopolitical context of RSA (Republic of South Africa), where we formed a small homogenous community transplanted into a different world. Perhaps one interpretation of Aaron's extraordinary pronouncement that "the world never ends" is that wherever westerners go, we inevitably, as Kincaid castigates, take our values and biases with us. Perhaps my students feared that they would reveal too much of themselves in that context.

But again, in considering the impediments to my maintaining the same "professional" attitude in Seattle as I manifested among students in Cape Town, I have to identify students' attitudes towards race, specifically towards blackness, and therefore towards me. Not all of my students abroad were white; more than one-third of them represented American ethnic minority groups: a Filipina, a Chicano, an African American, an American Pacific Islander, a woman of both African American and Korean ancestry, the black Sri Lankan who praised my intact boundaries. And yet even were I to have in Seattle a class composed of only students of color, I could not relax my professional demeanor here in the same way that I could—by compelling circumstance—there. Above I noted that standards of objectivity, however illusory they are, are designed to protect students—students of color from racist professors and practices, women students from sexist policies, and so on. Indeed, these same standards are those to which Katouria Smith appealed when she charged the University of Washington Law School as having admitted an "inferior" student of color but rejected her (whiteness) in the late 1990s. Those same standards are in place to protect me as a woman professor of color—from allegations of unfairness, favoritism, bias.

In Cape Town, I wrote:

> Just as the students live on the same floor of the apartment complex with me, they do so with each other. Just as they cannot leave class after performing this persona today, that persona tomorrow, they also accompany each other home after class where each

remembers the classroom discussions—and at least tacitly expects and depends on a measure of consistency. Performing a self at home in the Cascades that differs from that in our University of Cape Town classroom would violate a taboo and destabilize the group. And because terms like "performativity," "destabilization of the autobiographical self," and "in-law" and "out-law" performances permeate our theoretical course readings[4], we are especially sensitive to their implications for our lives in Cape Town.

Back in Seattle, I recognize the academic code that requires my own complicity: I must not not be professional, no matter where I am.

In the final week before submitting this essay to the co-editors of this volume, I spoke with Jennifer, Andrea, and Rebekah about my representations of our mutual experiences in Cape Town. In the initial voice- or electronic- mail requesting that they contact me for consultation, I provided both my home and office telephone numbers; as it happened in each case, I spoke with the student by phone from my UW office. Our conversations, still richly laced with the intimacy we shared in the Cascades, were yet distinctly different from former ones. I was myself notably different. My own voice no doubt dropped a few notes into a register of something I fancy sounds like "authority," theirs were hesitant, cautious with concern about the need for such a conversation, given the trust they had come to place in me abroad. With each student I try to convey that I am acting from an ethical place, that the call is not to alarm her, but rather to reassure her. It has come to this (again), now that we are "home." Thus in explaining how my essay tries to protect each of them individually, to maintain as much as anonymity as they deem warranted, and yet serve the profession with some insight into the intersection of the personal and the professional, I must needs try to protect myself. I am aware as I speak, as I disclose the contents of my diaries to them, that yet again my heart must open in this professional capacity, and that conversely, in this instance the students are guarded—by their physical absence that the telephone permits, blocking my access to their faces or body language, by no obligation to comment on *how* I have drawn our experience— only to grant or withhold their permission of my reconstruction of that experience. I am also aware that as students they need and merit this very border. Less than a month after our return, professional ethics, the academic dance, and ironically proximity all restrict the nature of our interactions and exchanges. The old barriers fall into place, whatever I choose to reveal; the world has edges again.

CONCLUSION

Thinking now about what it means that my teaching in Cape Town seemed so different from my teaching in Seattle, I realize that in fact my teaching in the two locations has been less divergent than I initially thought. For one thing, it is worth noting that the students traveling with me were voluntarily in class. None of them opted out of my "required" course altogether, though certainly that option was open to them. It is easy to imagine that morale and collectivity might have suffered, had even only one of them chosen to complete Kareem's course and the program's required internship but not the third curriculum component that my course formed. More than one student, I learned when we returned, had elected to take my course for "Credit/ No Credit," yet while abroad I had little reason to believe that they weren't committed to my course, Savitri included.

Similarly, institutional structures followed us to Cape Town. We were governed by UW standards as much abroad as if we had been at home. For all the intimacy we developed, I do not flatter myself that there were not "situations" involving my Gen X students of which I was unaware. The required internship was designed in part specifically to allow students to cultivate an independent identity, an international responsibility apart from our group. My co-director dazzlingly established, then supervised working relationships between our 15 and the local organizations, activists, and institutions to which they promised volunteer service. In one instance, she and I were chagrined that some students ended up volunteering together, as this shared experience nullified a crucial aspect of the program. (In another instance, though, we were relieved that men students accompanied several women to a township medical clinic outside Cape Town.) That some of them did end up working together, however, validates all the more our faith that we directors still remain completely ignorant of some student experiences during our stint. Surely, just as I was desperate for my own separate peace and realized it, so must have my students. They created their own barriers shielding out authority—in some cases through means as simple and transparent as addressing me professionally, formally; in other cases far more egregiously, as by drinking excessively. In Cape Town as in Seattle, young people impeccably cement each other's secrets against folks Over Thirty. In terms of professional objectivity and ethicality then, I must own that as conscientious as I tried to be, as conscious as I truly was of institutional procedures and demands and of being ever "on duty," there as here some situations were simply beyond my control. And I won't pretend to want to know what they all were.

However, the faculty and staff of the UW Study Abroad Program for South Africa did all we could to try to mitigate as many problems as possible. I tried to make my course as "typical" as possible, as predictable as possible. And I believe that most of the students appreciated my complex shifting of parental, personal, and professional attitudes during those three months. Perhaps what our program illustrates is the time and space specificity of virtually every teaching experience; perhaps no learning experience involving professor, students, texts is finally formulaic, merely "academic." Moreover, in the quarter before our program, two professors quite unsuccessfully led a Study Abroad group through southern Africa and barely lived to tell about it, they moaned. They had worked under conditions very similar to those my co-director and I faced with very happy results. One key difference, ironically, had been that they did not live among the students in their group. And when a younger colleague—black, and queer like me but male—approached me last fall for advice as he set out unaccompanied with 15 students, I heard myself blurt without hesitation, "You will want to live among them." But who is to say that were Dagni and I to return with a different group of students—or the very same ones, for that matter—that our experience would be as gratifying? Academic success too often depends on fortuity. Perhaps the best one can do is trust one's own sense of humility, one's own ethicality, wherever one is.

NOTES

I acknowledge the valuable insight and supportive assistance of Dagni Bredesen, D. Merilee Clunis, Kathie Friedman, Angela Ginorio, Susan Glenn, Lorraine Martínez, Caroline Chung Simpson, and Shirley Yee.

1. "To Be Young, Pregnant, and Black: My Life as a Welfare Coed" is part of a collection of essays on women, rights, and welfare, currently under consideration by Temple University Press. The volume's editors are Vivyan Adair and Sandra Dahlberg.
2. See Vanessa Bing and Pamela Trotman Reid, "Unknown Women and Unknowing Research: Consequences of Color and Class in Feminist Pedagogy," in *Knowledge, Difference, and Power: Essays Inspired by Women's Ways of Knowing* (New York: Basic, 1996). They instructively underscore "unknowing research" which they define as scholarship conducted by psychologists who refuse to know multiple dimensions of the lives of their subjects. Bing and Reid condemn a psychology studies methodology that uses "women of color when researchers are seeking to uncover *atypical* phenomena.... The primary consequence of this approach is to pathologize women of color while leaving their other concerns unaddressed. The continued exclusion of culturally and economically diverse women from research on ordinary problems and issues allows the entire discipline to remain ignorant of the experiences of these women" (186–87). Equally instructive, Bing and Reid identify feminist scholars who insist that "Science . . . is not value-free and theories are riddled with biases, inasmuch as ideological biases influence

the kinds of research questions raised and the results obtained" (194). And they remind us that "self-interest need not be construed as having a deleterious influence. In fact, it can be credited with bringing investigators' assumptions into clear view" (194).

3. Haaken's essay is included in *Women, Autobiography, Theory: A Reader*, ed. Sidonie Smith and Julia Watson (Madison: University of Wisconsin P, 1998). pp. 352-361.

4. Chief among these readings were Sidonie Smith's "Performativity, Autobiographical Practice, Resistance," Julia Watson's "Unspeakable Differences: The Politics of Gender in Lesbian and Heterosexual Women's Autobiographies," and Carla Kaplan's "Resisting Autobiography: Out-Law Genres and Transnational Feminist Subjects," all of which appear in Smith and Watson, eds., *Women, Autobiography, Theory: A Reader*.

PART FIVE
The Social Character of Personal Narrative

12 LEARNING TO TAKE IT PERSONALLY

KATE RONALD
HEPHZIBAH ROSKELLY

There's not much about academic life that's personal. At least, no professional academic is supposed to take any of the activities that make up an academic life personally. The trajectories of our careers—getting hired, published, tenured, promoted, reviewed—are documented in terms of qualifications, criteria, standards. These words feel scientific; they carry with them the respectable aura of observation and impartiality, and academics are encouraged to take comfort in the procedures that determine how—and whether—they will live their professional lives.

Yet of course all academics know how personal a professional life in a university is. What could be more personal than your job interview, sitting on a bed in a small room in the Washington Hilton explaining what you have to offer while They—the nodding Search Committee—declare what they want? How does a writer not take personally a letter rejecting a deeply thought-out essay that begins, "Must we have these 'a funny thing happened to me on the way to the cocktail party' openings?" (First line of first rejection letter of first article sent out by HCR to *College English*.) Or the rejection of a manuscript from a group of Anonymous Reviewers, one of whom begins his/her response with a pitying "I always admired Ronald and Roskelly's work *before*. . . ." (Comment from reviewer of book manuscript by HCR and KJR, later published.) How is a tenure-track professor supposed to use this anonymous evaluation of her published work: "I find this popular, chatty, and obvious." (Written comments from KJR's fourth-year tenure review.) How does a member of a departmental community fail to feel personally hurt by a tenure vote that will cause him to leave that community, lose his job, his house, his students? (Both of us have lost good colleagues and friends to such tenure votes.)

The academic life is a personal life. Professional activities and decisions are also deeply personal ones in great measure because writing and teaching are activities of the spirit and imagination. Evaluations, recommendations, reviews and other instruments that document performance *comment* on those spiritual, imaginative enterprises. Why can't we get real about just how personal our professional lives are and stop pretending that what goes on in a classroom, a department and in our profession is "just business?"

And yet the pressure to reject the personal is strong. The bias in a profession still trying to believe its own press remains with the objectifiable and standardizable. (As the comment from the *CE* reviewer above suggests: it denigrates personal narrative as a "proper" form for an article as much as it criticizes the essay itself. And, as the comment from Kate's colleague's shows: it rejects personal narrative and objects to her personalized relationship with her audience. As you can see, neither one of us has ever forgotten these comments.) In the face of that pressure, and an odd, though real need to feel protected from the personal, academics have a hard time asserting it in their writing, teaching, and—maybe most damaging—in the decisions they make with and about one another in tenure votes, curricular decisions, and promotion and merit evaluations.

Maybe this desire for escape from the personal is especially strong in English departments, where writing forms the essence of both subject and method. The inherently and inescapably messy, idiosyncratic, and defiantly subjective nature of writing and reading is a burden to teachers trying to work within a system that forces quantification, data, results, and hierarchy. So teachers assign grades to stories written by eighteen-year olds about parents dying; they evaluate language clearly shaped by poor schooling; they try to justify—in some terms they can live with—a grade for the performance of self that writing is and must be.

Yet, we recognized the depth of the conflict between personal and professional in teaching and in the whole academic life only dimly at first. As graduate students who had returned to school "late"—Hepsie was a public school teacher; Kate a secretary—we knew our decision, and thus our work, was personal, requiring the sacrifice of security, family time, and money. And as beginning professors who rode the first wave of rhetoric and composition (Kate graduating in 1984, Hepsie in 1985), we understood less of the "professional" side of the conflict than the ever-larger groups who followed us. No one talked seriously to us in graduate school about publication. There was scarcely a conversation about the job search and MLA interviews. It took us a while—and we realize that this admission makes us sound foolishly naive—to understand that being academics—going pro—would mean that we'd leave our home and one another.

This essay is a personal history of two academics' struggle to stay together in a deeply competitive environment, to find, keep, and use the personal within their professional lives. It's certainly not a how-to guide for constructing a life in academe. We have no real model to offer, no reasoned position to defend. But we stumbled upon and then deliberately followed a path around the serious, professional/personal dilemma in our field by using our friendship—and our professional collaboration as writers—as a solace and a guide. Our friendship has, with no exaggeration, allowed us to stay in the profession. So if we don't lay out a plan to follow, or announce a universal truth, we do here what good teachers always do: we tell a story that may suggest something useful to a reader about how to rethink an old problem, or how to offer resistance rather than accommodation to a system intent on ignoring, reducing and constraining the personal dimensions of our professional lives.

INTIMATE MOTIVES

Collaboration, especially group work and peer revision, has become a commonplace in many composition classrooms as teachers have realized the benefits of active talk and listening among students: livelier discussions, deeper investment in writing, awareness of alternative ideas. The pedagogical strategy of creating small groups who talk and write together comes as well from a clearer understanding of theories of learning that suggest people learn more effectively when they articulate, respond to and challenge ideas in social and connected ways. Academic writers in the humanities, especially in composition and rhetoric, have begun to realize some of the same benefits in their own collaborative efforts.

We have been collaborators now for twenty years, writing and speaking together in many classrooms and professional venues. We have team-taught classes, administered programs as a team, presented conference talks, papers and workshops together, co-authored articles, co-edited one collection, and most recently written together a book. But our collaboration did not stem from our sense of applying theory to the test of practice in the classroom or in our own writing. Although we have discovered professional rewards for our work together, that's not the reason we write together either. While our collaboration has developed simultaneously along with the field's embrace of social constructionist theory and practice, working together, for us, has always been more personal than professional.

As graduate students at the University of Louisville in the early 1980s, we were assigned the responsibility of helping direct the composition program. But we soon discovered that more than the contingency of our jobs as co-assistants drew us together. We had both grown up in Louisville, although in different parts of the city. Our educations had been different, too—Hepsie a graduate of public schools and a public university; Kate a product of a Catholic girls' high school and a private Catholic university—but our ideas about learning were much the same. We found similarities in our pasts as well: we both had strong fathers with a clear sense of duty and ethics, supportive mothers who believed in our abilities, complicated webs of family expectations and interactions. And, as we shared family stories, we realized we had been brought up with almost identical aphorisms to guide our behavior and our choices, aphorisms that seemed to be (or at least were put to us as) Southern in sensibility: "Be polite," especially to strangers and guests; "Don't toot your own horn"; "Pretty is as Pretty Does"; and "Act like a Lady, no matter what you are."

We found that we were alike in lots of ways. We both used humor to deflect our own fear and others' potential criticism, and we laughed a lot. We were energetic and optimistic. Maybe most important, we shared a beginning understanding of our calling to teach, and a dawning, shaky awareness of the personal changes that calling might require us to make. All these characteristics made us feel like a team even before we made our first presentation together, at an orientation session for teaching assistants and part-timers at the beginning of the fall semester of 1980. We might have begun that first session by dividing up the responsibility for the presentation; that would have been the way we had been trained to think of collaboration. Kate probably wrote out an outline and presented a prepared bit on the role of the Writing Center, Hepsie no doubt winged it as she described the construction of a syllabus. But near the end of our first session as Assistant Directors of Composition, somebody asked a question about drop/add or their schedules or something. We were standing together on the stage and without hesitating we responded in unison: "In the office." We looked at each other apologetically, and then turned back to the group. "Check next week" we said again. Together. The crowd of slightly bored old hands and more than slightly fearful new instructors laughed. That workshop, and the ones that followed it, began to teach us that together we had a more powerful voice than each of us could muster individually. We had been given the position from which to speak, but neither of us yet had the authority that comes with a terminal degree, publication, tenure, or years in service. Our two voices together, though, somehow could speak to audiences that might not have listened to either of us alone. As time passed, people around us started to run our names together, speaking of us almost always as a unit, and we began to talk consciously about ourselves as a team and cultivate our doubled presence. With this story, we write this reflection down publicly for the first time.

When we spoke together, in meetings and presentations and workshops, we delivered ourselves together, making ourselves open and accountable not only to our audiences but also to one another—honoring and using our individual styles, pace, and predilections. As speakers together, at once performer and audience, we learned how to improvise and use nuance. We became more than usually attuned to each other's words, and more that usually open to modifying our own. The oral beginning of our co-authorship is important to this story because, for us, collaboration remains primarily a matter of talk. The two books we've worked on together both began in offhand conversation about our lives and interests. The preface to each one acknowledges the role of our talk in cultivating our ideas and sustaining them through writing and more talk; the first describing a conversation in the car on a backroad in southern Indiana about why we felt pulled in such opposite directions—in Massachusetts and Nebraska, we were being forced to choose between teaching and research, expressivist and social theories of learning, just to name two of the most pervasive dichotomies that still define the academic life—and the second in the attic at Emerson's Old Manse, where we excitedly talked with one another and the guide who had taken us through the house about Emerson's graffiti and the impact of the personal within the historical. But the important point here is that we were traveling together to be together; the ideas, the writing, grew from that impulse.

Our writing together has always in large measure been a way to keep our talk, our friendship going. From the beginning, we made choices that perhaps seemed less than professional but which turned out to be the most professionally astute moves we could have made. After our stint as Assistant Directors was over, Kate was appointed Director of the University Writing Center, a move which would take her to a new office. Kate had started out in the Writing Center as a tutor when she quit her secretary's job and tentatively entered graduate school. Hepsie had never taught in the Writing Center. Yet, faced with separation, we decided that Hepsie would just move into the Director's office with Kate. Thus, we continued our administrative collaboration whether the university made it official or not. We team-taught English 098, the most basic basic writing course, the back door to the University, and there we learned even more about how to move, talk, and think together with students. The Writing Center staff came to view us as co-directors, and when Kate left to take her first job at Nebraska, Hepsie moved officially into the Director's position.

In the fifteen years we've been separated by several states and even the Mississippi River, having an excuse to talk has been central because our collaboration was born mainly from separation, bound up with our memories of the presence we had enjoyed in graduate school versus our present reality working alone. We made all the right professional decisions, accepting the best tenure track jobs we were offered, and those decisions made it seem important at first to carry on the kind of talk that had allowed us to make those professional moves in the first place. One of our most powerful memories is a moment outside the Writing Center, after comps, when we were hit (again, naively) with the realization that all this good work meant that we would have to leave. We burst into tears, held onto each other, and laughed while we cried over how much we would have to give up in order to reap our professional rewards.

We no longer shared work in one place, and we missed it. So we decided to write and present research together at the CCCC meeting in 1984, our first professional meeting as professors. We proposed the paper together, drawing on our team teaching in U of L's Writing Center. We were cautioned by convention organizers that, together, we only had twenty minutes. At the session, it was clear that we were expected to deliver separate performances, and there was some confusion about how to introduce two people with only one paper title. The physical space at the podium was too tight to allow us to stand together. It was awkward: while one spoke, the other had to stand a step behind, making our usual delivery—where we watch one another, interrupt, make fun, refer back—difficult to pull off. But we managed it. Many people came up afterwards, not to comment on the substance of our "paper," but on the fact that we delivered it together. The audience seemed surprised, sort of delighted, as though our talk let them become part of the interaction. People wanted to talk to us not professionally, but personally, about how natural, easy, and intimate our performance had seemed. That presentation became our first co-authored article, and working long-distance to prepare it for publication, talking about working on it, we realized we had a scheme for protecting the personal in our new and separate professional lives.

In the fifteen years since then, we've taken on more and more professional responsibilities—chairing composition programs, directing graduate studies, directing dissertations, leading teacher education and writing across the curriculum programs—and we've sacrificed more and more of our personal lives to those responsibilities. But we've perhaps lost less of those personal lives than many academics because our talk always blurs the line between friendship and work. We're now always writing together, or planning to write together, or talking about writing together. We never compartmentalize, even in stolen weekend sessions supposedly devoted to writing a chapter. In the middle of a discussion of Peirce's pragmatic maxim, we're likely to go off on a fantasy about where and how we'll retire together. Instead of chastising ourselves for inefficiency, we have learned to value the way our talk slips between personal and professional. It's no accident that our latest work together has explored the uses of romantic rhetoric and pragmatic philosophy for the teaching of writing; our collaborative lives have been sustained by a spirit of hope and belief, but at the same time carefully managed by practical moves and decisions that keep us talking and writing together.

Academics will tell you that they write for many reasons; because they have an idea they think is important, because they have to publish to get ahead, because they want to teach others. All writers will tell you that they write to connect; we simply add one more, very important connection to that process: the connection with each other. But there are lots of other advantages of collaboration too. Looking back at the beginnings of our work together, it's easy enough to see us as two women in search of a voice within an academic world where we were not at all sure we belonged. We remain in this world largely because that voice has been created in our collaboration. We were able to find an "other," a responding voice, that was not alien. And we discovered another big advantage as we practiced this way of writing together: collaborating in our talky way allows—even insists on—a speech-like quality in the discourse that gets inside even our most academic prose. And we like that. Our talk easily turns into writing, and our writing becomes a way to *image* our talk. We see ourselves speaking together as we write and rewrite, rather than reading alone. As we write, we imagine not reading the text, but speaking it together. And because we now theorize this double-voiced relationship consciously, we now recognize the process and the style that has come out of it as one strategy of resistance to the formal, impersonal, discourse and modes of the academy.

As the opening to this essay shows, not every audience approves of this oral style or for that matter understands this kind of collaborative relationship. We have had to counter and respond to criticism about the collaborative path we've followed in our professional lives. For, despite new attention and theoretical support for social theories of learning and discourse, myths about collaboration remain: that there's always a first author and a second; that one member of the team is the creative spark, the other the plodding worker. Perhaps this picture of collaboration comes from science, where research teams have a definite "team leader" with the vision and a bunch of other scientists who work the lab experiments and get to put their names on the finished papers. Or maybe it comes from traditional graduate student/professor collaborations, where the student who dug through the library is allowed to "co-author" with the professor who had the brilliant idea. Whatever its source in academia, there's a pervasive sense that in any team effort, there's no real team. Underneath all the myths about co-authorship is the belief that two people can never have (or be credited with) the same idea.

In our experience, sometimes Kate has the idea; sometimes Hepsie, but the idea very quickly becomes "ours" because it moves between us so fast. When we were in graduate school, we used to joke about having *it*—the creativity, the power, the authority a struggling graduate student needed to teach engaging yet rigorous classes, write stunning major papers, read *The Wings of the Dove* and *The Rhetoric of Motives* in one week, comment with wit and eloquence in seminars, go to the grocery, pick up the kids, and visit aging parents. We'd ask each other, "Do you really need *it* today, or do you think I could have it?" We worked the same metaphor in the process of getting tenure and promotion. *It* seems to be something we share, lend out, trade off, just as we wear the same size in shoes and the same prescription in glasses. Now that this particular essay is completed, for example, just like every other piece we've written together, we can't tell who had the idea that generated its final shape. Our knowledge is joined, shared, and communal—in inception, conception, and delivery.

So we have given up the notion that anybody's idea is hers alone, although, as we've discovered, much of the academy proceeds that way. We have talked to other collaborators who admit "holding the best ideas back" for their individual, future projects. We've heard professors say that they don't want to give their graduate students "too many of their ideas" or they'd have nothing left to write themselves. "What section were you responsible for?" a colleague might ask. In fact has asked. Repeatedly. Of both of us. We always reply "All of it. Both of us." We simply don't buy that belief in ideas or language as individual property. Hepsie wouldn't have re-thought Plato without Kate; Kate wouldn't understand Emerson without Hepsie. We resist the academy's standard of the truly "original" idea, for our collaboration has shown us that all good ideas are remade in the words and minds of others. In our work, there is no clear division of inspiration or labor.

PERSONAL METHOD

Another myth about collaboration is that it divides up work and makes it easier. Sometimes we think that the humanities—which often seems to take perverse pleasure in the difficult—is wary of collaborating writers because there's a suspicion that writing together is somehow easier than writing alone; that somehow the writers escape work by halving their work load. In drafting our projects together, we've found that the writing load doesn't split in half; it doubles. We do not, for example, write separate chapters and then submit them to the other for comment and revision; we don't assign separate tasks or sections although we do play to the strengths we discovered in each other (Kate will do bibliographies and manage the computer disks; Hepsie will write inspiring endings; Kate will write the funny line; Hepsie will find the perfect quote). Our way of writing together has become so integrated that even these examples, however, sound false to us as we write them.

Our organic process of writing together, obviously, is always pretty messy. When we get an idea—from what we've been reading (and we often read very different things), teaching, observing around us—and we decide that we'll pursue it together, we start talking: "Let's take your freshmen and my business writing students as an example." "So what's going on with Rorty?" "How about using that Anna Quindlen book as the lead-in?" "OK, but let's not forget to bring the Octavio Paz quote back in some way." "I was out working in the roses this morning when our title came to me." As with all the stages in our collaborative composing process, our jumbly drafting or invention is grounded in this kind of exploratory conversation. The talk quickly becomes a stimulant for as well as a record of our thinking. We not only begin to plan and draft the essay in our talk about it; we begin to shape how we'll talk about it.

If we're in the same location, we usually do this talk at the computer, making notes or outlines, then moving to the machine, taking turns at the keyboard. One talks, one writes, and both revise talk and writing as we proceed. The pace is halting, sometimes the fingers of the one on the computer can't move fast enough on the keys; sometimes there are long pauses while we think. "Why is this so hard?" one will complain. We digress and ramble; one walks to the bookshelf, the other says "I've got it," and starts a new paragraph. Sometimes the ideas and revisions come too fast: we've often rebuked ourselves for not using a tape recorder. (Once or twice we've managed it, and it does help, but it also somehow interferes, makes our talk seem too professionalized, too deliberate.) When we're exhausted or our other lives intrude, we print out, read, then make more notes for ourselves for our next session. We proceed this way for as long as we are together or until we have a complete draft. When we are writing together long distance—a much more common occurrence—we talk, write, email, fax, read over the phone, revise separately, revise together. We've never before consciously described this procedure; it hardly seems like one. And yet, we do follow a consistent if meandering path, always listening, responding, backtracking, building, changing.

We usually have a rough sketch very quickly, and then we read separately, talk about what we've read and talk through the whole piece together. Because we are used to working this way, and because we trust the other's words, something interesting happens in this process. Although it's arduous, taking much longer to get from start to finish than a piece either of us might write individually, we find ourselves anticipating the other. One of us might be writing a paragraph and stop to imagine the voice that responds to the thought. Or to imagine not just the other's reaction but the other's production. "Kate will think that's an awkward pile of words"; "Hepsie will find another metaphor that's more eloquent."

We have found, in our disorganized, inefficient method of drafting and revising, the same rejoinders and responses all writers listen for in their audiences. Here, in the process of getting the ideas on the screen, on paper, in the mail, our reasons for writing together in the first place also come into play. Not only will we tell each other, often through silences, that our ideas are simply boring, no good—we also "rejoin" with the kind of support and encouragement that every writer needs. Hepsie writes in a letter to Kate, with the latest version of an introduction "This is a great story to begin with." Kate faxes revisions to Hepsie and says that her explanation of Peirce's triadicity make sense, which is no small feat. At the lonely moments in front of the computer, it's easy for a "single author" to abandon an idea; solitary writers have to conjure up the belief themselves. Acting simultaneously as writer and audience, we work out belief together; in other words, we give *it* back and forth to each other.

It's a theoretical commonplace now that the solitary writer's voice doesn't really exist, that all language is constructed in communal contexts. And yet, in academic contexts, the continuing belief in the original and separate voice leads to the false assumption that collaboration causes an individual writer's voice to get lost, that writing produced in tandem becomes devoid of personality, responsibility, and creativity. Our process of writing together does indeed change and challenge the writer's unique voice, but in creative, rather than deadly, or deadening, ways.

It is true that the voice all writers struggle to find and maintain gets altered by working with another writer, by listening and responding to another voice. The first time the other voice says "Do you really need to use the word *organic*"? or "I'd like to begin the paragraph with the story of the train instead," the writer's ego bristles a little. When those sorts of comments continue on both sides, writers can only defend "their" choices, "their" voices, rather than listen for a new one, and that's why, we suspect, so many first time collaborators never become second time practitioners. What we've discovered about voice is that successful collaborative tone doesn't emerge as a duet, or a round, one writer's voice followed by another in uneasy compromise or certainly not from a shouting contest where one voice claims victory over another. The tone in a good collaboration comes from a new *third* voice that emerges in the process.

The great advantage of knowing each other well before we began to write together may have helped us to avoid ego-bruising debates about additions and changes to a growing text. But our earliest attempts were sometimes marked by hesitation as we painstakingly listened for that third voice to assert itself. "Why don't we put Eudora Welty here?" one of us would say. "Then we can talk about reader-voice in the students' writing later." The shift to "*we* need to" from "*I* think *you* need to" led us to take responsibility for all the sentences that we were producing. Using that "we" soon became a method for establishing our third, collaborative voice, to hear it and nurture it along. This small stylistic matter clearly illustrates our collaborative voice: we quickly realized that, to avoid confusion, the only "we" that could ever appear in our work together had to refer only to us—Hepsie and Kate—not to teachers in general, the profession, or humanity. Forced, then, to eliminate the royal "we" from all our prose in favor of the particular, intimate "we" of our partnership, we write perhaps more humbly and with more immediacy and accountability than we might have otherwise.

You don't lose your individual voice by writing together. If anything, we've discovered, you find it more easily, hear it more directly as a result of writing as a team. We are as single writers more conscious of style and of effects on an audience now. Here, in single-authored words, so rare for us, are some of the lessons we've learned about our own writing from one another:

Hepsie: From Kate, I've learned the value of attention. I'm a writer who generalizes, who makes sweeping—often sermony—statements. I'm a writer who'll sacrifice too much to a metaphor or to a clever turn of phrase. Kate keeps me honest. I wouldn't have known these things about my writing had it not been for Kate's example of careful reasoning, thoughtful presentation, meticulous stylistic decisions. I've learned to move down in my writing as well as out, and I've learned just how important the merger of support and generalization are. Plus, Kate's funny on paper and in person and her clear sense of humor permeates my own thinking now.

Kate: From Hepsie I've learned to let go and to believe. I'm a writer who hesitates, who edits too quickly, who writes in fits and starts. From her I've learned to follow and trust a metaphor, to mine it and not be afraid to stretch. (From her I've learned to start sentences with "from her"; she claims she's not a stylist, but her parallel constructions give her writing an oral style that is terribly effective.) More than anything, she's taught me that the process itself is what matters. Hepsie resists closure; for her, it's the exploration of the idea that's important. Where I tend not to look down the sideroads, not stop at historical markers along the way, because I want to get there and be finished, Hepsie's continually looking around, wondering about connections, taking the scenic route. And she's also a very funny traveling companion.

As you can see, our approaches to writing alone have been strengthened by hearing the unexpressed query or affirmation of our partner's response. In other words, the "rejoinder" has become an overt part of our individual writing. We automatically hear the other's voice. And now, since we write together so often, looking for that voice leads us to the point at which we no longer remember which one of us wrote which sentence. More importantly, it reminds us to remain tentative in the face of an evolving draft, to remember that the "we" being created is more important than the "I" that we're letting go. Bakhtin talks about how every word is in reality "half mine/half someone else's." Our composing together extends this definition of meaning to something more like "all mine and all hers." And, this realization of community, of communion, is the reason, years ago, we entered academia in the first place.

THE PERSONAL IN THE PROFESSIONAL

The ideology of individualism, firmly in place in American culture, especially in school and most especially in the humanities, often prevents collaboration or makes it less powerful and successful than it might be. The icons of

American literature, at least up until the last part of the twentieth century, have depicted the individual, heroic and embattled, against a group or a society that limited and tried to defeat individual choice or belief. Hester Prynne, Nick Adams, Jay Gatsby, Edna Pontelier, Bigger Thomas, and dozens of others that come to mind, all faced unfeeling or repressive groups that prevented them from becoming or enacting themselves. As well, some of our most cherished cultural ideals in this country—the cowboy, the entrepreneur, the poor boy who becomes president—celebrate individual striving and accomplishment in stories and songs, in movies and comics, and in history books. (It's unsurprising, although worth noting, that these heroic individual models have, for the most part, been decidedly male). No wonder then that school replicates and reinforces the cultural prescription. Achievement in school, in sports or academics, is by and large all about competition, what an individual (or group acting as an individual) can do, above and against group norms or predictions. We love the Cinderella story in life and in basketball.

Because English studies is at heart about the production and reception of writing, premised on cultural and literary models that glorify the individual creator, teachers carry the myth of the individual firmly into classrooms as we teach and into our offices as we write. Despite all the theory of how writing actually happens, how creativity is sparked—socially, communally—and despite acknowledgments pages at the beginning of books and dissertations, the academic model of success too often fails to make theory practicable in writers' own working lives. The recent film *Shakespeare in Love* shows young Will Shakespeare practicing writing his name rather than penning Romeo and Juliet until he talks to his friends in a bar. He uses the words, the ideas, and the experiences of everybody around him to find and illuminate his own creative energy. All writers know from their own experiences as writers that ideas are engendered and transformed in conversation, in collaboration, with those around us, with books we read, with stories we hear. But academics ignore that truth too often.

It may be because academics are so driven to assess achievement that we continue to promote and perpetuate the individual at the expense of the communal. It seems hard to reward two rather than one. The system drives us to ask: Who did what? Who had the idea first? Which part is yours? We want to make sure that the individual gets credit. Our students feel this conflict too when they work together. Most teachers and students have had unhappy experiences with "group presentations" where "one person did all the work" but all the others get similarly rewarded for the final product. When teachers do assign team writing, it's often in the name of efficiency rather than a nod to the social nature of language, a practical attempt to cut down the workload of evaluating individual writers. And one of the mainstays of collaborative writing assignments is the individual's statement of contribution to the project, or the team's assessment of each individual's work. Despite what the academy is learning about team writing in professional and business contexts, collaboration remains suspect.

In spite of the humanities' problems with collaboration, there are some well known and successful practitioners of dual authorship and dual presentation style. Sandra Gilbert and Susan Gubar have written together for years, and from their initial study *The Madwoman in the Attic* (1984) to the *Norton Anthology of Women's Literature* (1999), the profession has tended to think of them as always together, always as Gilbert and Gubar. Lisa Ede and Andrea Lunsford form another writing team that has merged into one unit—almost; moreover, their co-authored articles and their study of collaboration (*Singular Texts/Plural Authors*) have helped the profession take collaborative writing seriously as a practice and as an area of research. In fact, at a Coalition of Women Scholars meeting during the College Composition and Communication meeting in the Spring of 2000, Lunsford argued that the "structures of the academy get in our way" and must be changed to allow and reward collaborative writing, particularly collaborative dissertations.

We think that change would require a real shift in the academy's conception of effort, achievement, and reward. The individual still holds center stage, often even within collaborations themselves. We've noticed that many collaborative pairs of writers steadfastly retain the markers of individual effort, perhaps because collaborators feel the pressure of the individualist model so strongly. For example, in their latest collaboration, *John Dewey and the Challenge of Classroom Practice* (1998), Stephen Fishman and Lucille McCarthy sign individual chapters with individual names, even marking each one's contribution in co-authored chapters with "first" and "second" authorship. This convention is an acknowledgment of a method of collaboration that doesn't risk a loss of individual autonomy or threaten academic, literary, and cultural models of individual achievement and accountability. The work is divided rather than combined. The two writers are in dialogue with one another and with their subject, but they retain their own selves as they write. As we've shown, our writing together doesn't work that way. We're interested in what happens when we create a new voice and blend facets of an idea; we use our talk as a method of creating that third voice or idea, rather than as conversation between our separate selves.

We're not saying that this process is easy, nor are we necessarily recommending our method, or any method, of collaborative writing to any of our readers. We still exist in a profession dominated by an individualistic, competitive model, and, as writers, we had to understand, early, that the academic life we entered expected and tried to require us to be in competition with one another. That model is the source of questions like "What percentage of this article did you write?" Or "Why is she listed as first author?" We have to resist that model, not only to write together, but also to be friends, which has always been the basis of our writing together at all. The process we've described is our way, not necessarily the way, to resist such a model.

But because of our friendship and the values and insights we've gained through writing together, we have continually (and successfully) fought against the destructive effects of professional competition. Just as we were taught at home, we are still polite; we still believe that pretty (or scholarly or teacherly) is as pretty (or scholarly or teacherly) does, as we serve as supporters but also critics and watchdogs for each other's temptations toward professionalized stances and language; we still try not to toot our own horns too much (although we toot the other's, a much more "ladylike" and happy stance). And we have retained, thank god, the silliness of those first years as co-administrators and team teachers, our ability to see the hilarity of so much of the academic life, as well as its high seriousness—the lives at stake, including our own—in our teaching.

Our writing together has remained one way, and a significant one, that we've been able to stay in a profession that routinely suspects its members and to confront the over-specialization in our field, the esoteric, dry voices that too often dominate oral and written performance, the destructive over-competitiveness that stymies real growth and learning and risk-taking. Our writing as a pair has become a way to keep believing in the personal worth of what we're doing, to remember that the professional is always personal. For us, the personal collaborative relationship that we've nurtured in writing and in talk—both privately and publicly and in real attempts to blur that line—remains the ground of all our work and its method.

We're better writers and thinkers, storytellers and teachers in part because we both remember and use each other's memories (sometimes we remember them better than our own.) We count on one another's words to help us teach, and we use our friendship to mentor younger members of our profession as we assert, implicitly and explicitly, its importance in our academic lives. And in our administrative, departmental work, in the painful decision making processes that all academic units engage in, we are braver colleagues than we would be without the example and sympathy of the other. Whether it's a policy matter or a tenure decision, we're less willing to accept objectivity as a defense, secret ballot as a refuge, tradition as law. Simply put, our collaboration has taught us that the personal is never merely that; "taking it personally" is not a condition to be overcome but a platform from which to act.

13 CUENTOS DE MI HISTORIA
An Art of Memory

Víctor Villanueva

A Memory. Seattle, 1979.
> She is a contradiction in stereotypes, not to be pegged. He likes her right off. She wants to go to Belltown, the Denny Regrade, to take photos. He wants to go along. He does, feeling insecure and full of bravado, slipping into the walk of bravado he had perfected as a child in Brooklyn. Stop into a small café at the outskirts of downtown, at the entry to the Regrade. It's a French-style café, the Boulangerie, or some such. To impress her, he speaks French.
>
> "Un tas de café, s'il vous plais. Et croissants pour les deux." Don't correct it. It's how he said it.
>
> He's an English major, a senior, quite proud of having gotten this far in college. But insecure about what this will lead to (since he had only gotten as far as deciding to stay in college till he's finally in over his head), he tells her of a novel he will write some day. His description goes something like:
>
>> I've been thinking about a novel about a white Puerto Rican kid who buys into the assimilation myth, hook, line, and sinker. He does all the right things—learns the language, learns how to pronounce "r's" in words like "mother" and "water" and how not to trill the "r" when he says "three," and he does well in school. He's even a war hero. Does it all, only to realize that assimilation just can't happen. Yet he can't really be Puerto Rican. And he isn't allowed into the Assimilation Club. So maybe he goes to Puerto Rico to find out who he might have been and what he is tied to. I don't have it all worked out.

The plot line might not have been worked out, but this was the impulse nevertheless—to keep alive the memory of assimilation denied, a truism turned to myth, to try to hold on to, maybe even to regain that which had been lost on the road to assimilation.

In some sense, the impulse gets worked out some years later with *Bootstraps*, the assimilation myth explicit in the title; the story told then elaborated upon with research and with theory. It's an attempt to play out a kind of Freireian pedagogy: the political explored through the experiential. And it does more. It's

> an autobiography with political, theoretical, pedagogical considerations. The story includes ethnographic research. The story includes things tried in classrooms. The story includes speculations on the differences between immigrants and minorities, the class system and language, orality and literacy, cultural and critical literacy, Freire, ideology, hegemony, how racism continues or the ways in which racism is allowed to continue despite the profession's best efforts. And in so doing the story suggests how we are—all of us—subject to the systemic. This is the personal made public and the public personalized, not to self-glory nor to point fingers but to suggest how, maybe, to make the exception the rule. (xviii)

Now some part of that first impulse re-asserts itself, fictionalizing, telling the story, reaching back to the heritage that is at risk of passing away quickly.

> Remember to call your grandpa "abuelo." He'll like the sound of that, since none of my sister's kids have called him that. If you let him, he'll just watch baseball day and night and not say much. Push him for the stories of Puerto Rico during his childhood. Ask him about catching shrimp with his hands, and the stories of how the neighborhood boys got a Model A Ford, about the revolutionary who hid out in el Yunque, about his time in the Army. Ask about my grandfather, Basilio, and gardening, and working as a groundskeeper and gardener for the University. And ask about Tío Vicente, the tall farmer, inland, on the coffee hills. "Inland" is important about knowing about being Puerto Rican, about Puerto Rico. I remember when I met him. A tall PR Man, that was very cool. And he gave me sugar cane from his farm, and a coffee bean, and a lemon that he had cut a hole on the top of. And he told me to chew on the been, squeeze lemon juice on the tongue, and chew on the cane. I wish I could give you that memory, mi'jitas. Now, Mom is easier. She loves to talk. But she'd rather forget the past. And I don't want the past forgotten, so press her too.

The fiction, the bootstraps retold and fictionalized would have to begin back then, not quite a generation after the change of hands, when the Spanish colony was handed over to the U.S., the changes seen by three generations—*Boricua* to *Nuyorican* to the middle class of color far removed from the cultural soil of either of the generations, maybe even a wheatfield in Eastern Washington. It's important. The memory.

So many have said this so well, that it's hard for me to reiterate without breaking into the academic discourse of cite-and-quote—Adell, JanMohamed and Lloyd, Omi and Winant, Saldívar, E. San Juan, Singh, Skerrett, and Hogan, Smorkaloff, and the "standards" like Anzaldúa or hooks—all have written about the connections between narratives by people of color and the need to reclaim a memory, memory of an identity in formation, constant reformation, the need to reclaim a memory of an identity as formed through the generations. And, I'd say, the need to reclaim and retain the memory of the imperial lords, those who have forcibly changed the identities of people of color through colonization.

> Nelly, the department's graduate secretary, hands me a flier for a meeting of the Pacific Islander's group, inviting me to join the students, staff, and faculty (which includes two department chairs I work with often). We smile at each other. Her cultural ways—Filipina—and mine are so different really—except that we have two out of three imperial lords in common: Spain and the US. It binds us. Our first were before the world got large, more local: the Japanese and the Caribes. We laugh, while others look and listen on with looks of wondering. It's not their memory.

Memory simply cannot be adequately portrayed in the conventional discourse of the academy.

I am grateful for the acknowledgment of perceptions that academic discourse provides, for the resources the conventions of citation make available, for the ideocentric discourse that displays the inductive or deductive lines of thought, a way to trace a writer's logical connections. But the cognitive alone is insufficient. It can be strong for *logos*. It can be strong for *ethos*. But it is so very weak in *pathos*. Academic discourse tries, after all, to reach the Aristotelian ideal of being completely logocentric, though it cannot be freed of the ethical appeal to authority. Here: A demonstration. Agustín Lao, in "Islands at the Crossroads: Puerto Ricanness Traveling between the Translocal Nation and the Global City," writes that

> Puerto Ricans (as other racialized diasporas) function within multiple and ambiguous registers of race and racism. As colonized subjects, all Puerto Ricans are "colored" by colonial discourses. On the other hand, differential processes of racialization can either nominalize Puerto Ricans as "ethnic" and/or allow some light-skinned Puerto Ricans to "pass" as "white." ... A single Puerto Rican "transmigrant" can be classified as *trigueña* on the island, black in Ohio, and Latina in New York. (178-79)

Now consider the rhetorical effect of Professor Lao's assertion (though with qualification) and a couple of stories from a light-skinned Puerto Rican. Both take place during the Summer of 2000. First story:

> He was picked up at the registration desk of the hotel in Iowa City. The limousine (really a van) driver walks up, a man in his late fifties or early sixties, buzz cut, thick build, surely one more accustomed to hard physical labor, a farmer, one would imagine given the locale. Says at least the guest is on time, kind of to the person behind the registration desk, kind of to himself, maybe even to the guest. He goes on to say that the last guest he'd picked up had been fifteen minutes late then didn't pay the fare.
>
> Once in the van, the story of the deadbeat develops. It was a family of four, including an infant. No car seat.
>
> "I coulda had my license pulled, with no car seat for the baby. Then he tries to pay me with a $100 travelers' check, like I carry that kind of money at five in the morning."
>
> "Were they foreigners?" assuming the passengers would have overestimated the fluidity of travelers' checks.
>
> "Who can know these days. The guy wore a turban. What are you?"
>
> Internal soliloquy: He didn't say "rag head," so maybe this is more the condition of the international seaports flowing into the middle of America, the in-migration of the newest immigrants and those new immigrants from the 1930s, a land no longer completely owned by those of Scandinavian and German ancestry. But 1898 and 1917 really should mean something in a situation like this. [NB: 1898: the US acquisition of Puerto Rico; 1917: US citizenship conferred on all Puerto Ricans].
>
> "Me? I'm American."
>
> "Coulda fooled me!"
>
> "Yeah. I'm from New York."
>
> The conversation ends. The next passenger turns out to be a black man with a crutch coming out of an upper-middle-class home in the suburbs of Iowa City. Kind of felt sorry for the driver and his comfortable assumptions.

Second story:

> It was another one of those receptions produced by the dean of the graduate school. This one was to welcome Doctoral Fellows in Residence. Most were persons of color. I was there as a department chair and as one of the mentors to a couple of the fellows.
>
> The scene: Back porch of the house, clusters of folks with drinks in hand or paper plates with guacamole and chips, talking, smiling, over-

looking cows grazing in the valley below, and green soft rolling hills nearby, maybe 300 yards away, where there will soon be wheat, blowing beautifully in the wind.

A conversation ensues with one of the fellows, a woman who grew up in the black area of Boston, Rockport (CH). Listening in is an associate dean (MT), originally from Central Asia, overtly happy to be away from Russian bureaucracy. The conversation turns to race in the wheatland.

VV: "Around here folks don't know if I'm Spanish, Jewish, Italian, from the Middle East, or from South Asia."

MT: "I would have thought you were Italian"

CH: "I don' know. He looks pretty Portorican to me."

Sure, she knows the hue, she sees the "niggerlips," one of those names I endured as a child, just like Martín, Martín Espada:

> Niggerlips was the high school name
> for me.
> So called by Douglas
> the car mechanic, with green tattoos
> on each forearm,
> and the choir of round pink faces
> that grinned deliciously
> from the back row of classrooms,
> droned over by teachers
> checking attendance too slowly.
>
> Douglas would brag
> about cruising his car
> near sidewalks of black children
> to point an unloaded gun,
> to scare niggers
> like crows off a tree,
> he'd say.
>
> My great-grandfather Luis
> was un negrito too,
> a shoemaker in the coffee hills
> of Puerto Rico, 1900.
> The family called him a secret
> and kept no photograph.

> My father remembers
> the childhood white powder
> that failed to bleach
> his stubborn copper skin,
> and the family says
> he is still a fly in milk.
>
> So Niggerlips has the mouth
> of his great-grandfather,
> the song he must have sung
> as he pointed the leather and nails,
> the stubbornness of a fly in milk,
> and all you have, Douglas,
> is that unloaded gun.

Professor Lao, I would contend, is not quite right. Those of us who are light-skinned don't pass for white; we're just not automatically sorted into the appropriate slot. But more to the point is that Lao's academic discourse (complete with scare quotes and nominalizations) is insufficient, lacks emotional appeal. And though Aristotle thought it not right to sway with emotional appeals, he knew that the greatest impact on listeners is emotional. The personal here does not negate the need for the academic; it complements, provides an essential element in the rhetorical triangle, an essential element in the intellect—cognition *and* affect. The personal done well is sensorial and intellectual, complete, knowledge known throughout mind and body, even if vicariously.

And for the person of color, it does more. The narrative of the person of color validates. It resonates. It awakens, particularly for those of us who are in institutions where our numbers are few. We know that though we really are Gramsci's exceptions—those who "through 'chance' . . . has had opportunities that the thousand others in reality could not or did not have"—our experiences are in no sense unique but are always analogous to other experiences from among those exceptions. So more than narrating the life of one of color so that "one creates this possibility, suggests the process, indicates the opening," in Gramsci's terms (*Cultural Writings* 132), we remember the results of our having realized the possibility, discovered the process, found the opening, while finding that there is in some sense very little change on the other side. This is what Ellis Cose describes as *The Rage of a Privileged Class*.

As I've written before ("On Colonies, Canons, and Cose"), Cose explains, mainly by way of anecdote, the reasons why African Americans in particular continue to be angry even after having crossed over to the other side. He explains the ways in which little slights continue to display the racism inherent in our society. Those "Dozen Demons" are

1. Inability to fit in.
2. Exclusion from the club.
3. Low expectations.
4. Shattered hopes.
5. Faint praise.
6. Presumption of failure.
7. Coping fatigue.
8. Pigeonholing.
9. Identity troubles.
10. Self-censorship and silence.
11. Mendacity.
12. Guilt by association.

I haven't been called a "spic" in many years (except by others of color). Yet little things happen that betray the underlying racism that affects us all, no matter how appalled by racism we might be. I read Anzaldúa or hooks or the poetry of Espada or Cruz or Esteves or any other writing of color, and I know I haven't become clinically paranoid. I know that I've been poked by one of the demons, a little triton to the ribs. Some of the slights signified by Cose are self-imposed, Fanon's internal colonialism. Some are imposed. All can be laid bare through the personal made public.

> There's the story of the academics of color who wrote about the subtle ways in which they find themselves victims of some of Cose's demons—exclusion, expecting less, presuming failure, pigeonholing as "brown-on-brown" research rather than disinterested research (read: white and classical-empirical). Someone far away reads the essay once published and files suit for slander. The authors had never heard of the person. This is a very funny story to people of color who have heard it—the laughter of verification and white-guilt gone awry.
> The converse:
> "Man, I loved your book [or article or essay]. I could relate. The same things have happened to me," told to the author time and again wherever he travels. Identity minus troubles among Cose's demons, association guiltless, a new club formed.

Somehow, the spic does remain, despite all the good fortune and accolades, not only within me, but from without. While a good academic piece would help me to remember, rich narrative does more for the memory.

And the precedent is old. *Memoria* was the mother of the muses, the most important of the rhetorical offices. Now rhetorics of writing seem to go no further than invention, arrangement, and style, when delivery is still there, the matter of "voice," and memory is tied in as well, surely for people of color. It's as if we have accepted Plato's prophecy that literacy would be the downfall of memory, leading only to remembrance, so that memory in the rhetorical canon seems all but forgotten, except as an historical artifact. And the canon of rhetoric only seems to note the contradiction that a prolific writer would write against writing (Kennedy 42,58). But Plato's writing is significant because of its genre, an attempt at representation of dialogue, of story telling, of the play. Plato's literacy took shape not as logocentric discourse but as a representation of discourse in action. Though folks like Volosinov have shown that all discourse, written as well as spoken, is dialogic. Plato is maybe the coolest [yes, coolest] of the philosophers because of the resonance of the dialogue, the possibility for humor, the clear presence of all three points in the rhetorical triangle and the unspecified (at least by Aristotle) dimension which is context. I don't mean to wax Platonic here, really, only to suggest that there's something to Plato's notion of memory as more than recollection and to his leaning on a written discourse that approximates orality as a means toward arriving at that big-m Memory. The narratives of people of color jog our memories as a collective in a scattered world and within an ideology that praises individualism. And this is all the more apparent for the latino and latina, whose language contains the assertion of the interconnectedness among identity, memory, and the personal. There is a common saying among Puerto Ricans and Cubans: *Te doy un cuento de mi historia*, literally rendered as "I'll give you a story about my history": me, history and memory, and a story.

A thousand years before the first Europeans arrived on Puerto Rico, the native peoples of the mainland and the lesser Antilles migrated to Puerto Rico, where they could live in relative peace, able to fish and live off the fresh vegetation—pineapple and varieties of tuber that have no name in English. We don't know the names of the first inhabitants of Puerto Rico. Our history is the history told by the Europeans who, conferring their values on the land, took the language of the local imperial lords. We only know the names given the first Puerto Ricans by their first colonizers, the first to raid them, the first to enslave them, the ones the Europeans honored by naming the region after them. These first colonizers were the peoples of Carib. And they named the people of that island Arawak and the culture of the Arawak was called Taino. And their island was named Boriquén. Then came Columbus (or Columbo or

Colón—I'm glad we've stopped translating people's names, or I'd have to walk around with the name Conqueror Newton). And then Ponce de León. And then the priests. And we don't really know what happened when they spoke, what transpired between the priests of Spain and the Boricua Arakwakas of Taino Ways.

So, to the analogous:

> *The scene is Peru. It's the end of the fifteenth century. Father Valverde, a Franciscan, is speaking to the Incan philosopher-rhetorician about the ways of the world. The Franciscan intends to be instructive, an attempt to raise the indigenous from its ignorance. The Incan doesn't recognize the developmental mindset and enters into dialectical interplay. Having heard of how things work according to Father Valverde, the Incan responds:*
>
> > You listed five preeminent men whom I ought to know. The first is God, three and one, which are four, whom you call the creator of the universe. Is he perhaps our Pachacámac and Viracocha? The second claims to be the father of all men, on whom they piled their sins. The third you call Jesus Christ, the only one not to cast sins on that first man, but he was killed. The fourth you call pope. The fifth, Carlos, according to you, is the most powerful monarch of the universe and supreme over all. However, you affirm this without taking account of other monarchs. But if this Carlos is prince and lord of all the world, why does he need the pope to grant him concessions and donations to make war on us and usurp our kingdoms? And if he needs the pope, then is not the pope the greater lord and most powerful prince of all the world, instead of Carlos? Also you say that I am obliged to pay tribute to Carlos and not to others, but since you give no reason for this tribute, I feel no obligation to pay it. If it is right to give tribute and service at all, it ought to be given to God, the man who was Father of all, then to Jesus Christ who never piled on his sins, and finally to the pope. . . . But if I ought not give tribute to this man, even less ought I give it to Carlos, who was never lord of these regions and whom I have never seen.

The record of this meeting at Atahualpa notes that,

> The Spaniards, unable to endure this prolixity of argumentation, jumped from their seats and attacked the Indians and

grabbed hold of their gold and silver jewels and precious stones. (Dussel, qtd in Villanueva, "On the Rhetoric," 645)

And when the slaves of Puerto Rico rebelled, slaves from Africa were brought in, and the Boricuas ran inland, away from the fortressed walls of El Morro, and the rebels acquiesced to the Spanish while trading with Dutch and English, French and Italian pirates who would find other ways to enter the island. This subversion became jaibería. *And I understand Angel Rama, when he says that it is in the Caribbean that "the plural manifestations of the entire universe insert themselves" (qtd in Smorkaloff vii). My mother's name is Italian (the line is never lost in the Spanish tradition, my mother becoming María Socorro Cotto deVillanueva, and my becoming Víctor Villanueva y Cotto until I was Americanized as Victor Villanueva, Jr.) My mother's name: Italian. The memory of that first Italian? Lost.*

Centuries later, I am Puerto Rican—a product of the first migrations of Puerto Ricans to New York in the late 1940s, though my mother arrived through what was euphemistically called "indentured servitude," what others called "white slavery," as if somehow more barbaric than the slavery of Asians and of Africans. And I assimilate. And I don't. But I know how to seem to be—jaibería—and the memory provided by stories told. Memory does hunger. And it's fed through the stories told.

I'm trying to figure this out, somehow: who I am, from where, playing out the mixes within. It isn't a question for me, whether public or private discourses. I am contradictory consciousness. The discourse should reflect that. I am these uneasy mixes of races that makes for no race at all yet finds itself victim to racism. The discourse should reflect that. I am, an American (from the Americas), an academic, a person of color—and organically grown traditional intellectual, containing both of Gramsci's intellectual formations and not quite his new intellectual. The discourse should reflect that. And I am in a wheatfield, attempting to pass on a memory as I attempt to gather one. Personal discourse, the narrative, the auto/biography, helps in that effort, is a necessary adjunct to the academic. No binary. No contradiction. Just the key to remembrance.

14 PERSONAL LANDMARKS ON PEDAGOGICAL LANDSCAPES

Katya Gibel Azoulay

In order to reflect on my pedagogical orientation and scholarly interests I will begin and conclude with my book, *Black, Jewish and Interracial: Its Not the Color of Your Skin but the Race of Your Kin and Other Myths of Identity* (1997). This work represents the culmination of a forty-three year work in progress which divide into two formative periods: childhood and adolescence in the United States and adulthood in Israel. I write this essay from a third moment – an unfolding set of middles: middle-age in the middle of Iowa in the middle of the U.S. In *Black, Jewish and Interracial*, I worked against voyeuristic expectations of an introspective narrative as well as against adding to the exhausted topic of relations *between* Blacks and Jews in the United States. My specific objective, which I now consider a guiding principle in my pedagogy, was to unveil and theorize the abstract notion of *identity* as a practice and a performance whose multiple meanings are derived in the context of social interactions, themselves shaped by historical and political conditions. While I was interested in considering some of the existential and political meanings of racial identities in general and being *both* Black *and* Jewish in particular, the genesis of the book originated in a dissatisfaction about premises and habits of scholarly thinking about identities which, it seemed to me, overemphasized individual narratives at the expense of historical and political contexts.

Some autobiographical details may serve as a point of departure: two months after graduating from The Brearley School in New York, I made *aliya* [1] to Israel. Twenty one years later, I moved back to the US with my three children and (now ex-) husband to pursue a doctorate at Duke University in Cultural Anthropology. Intended as a temporary sojourn, almost a decade later, a feeling of transience remains—a sentiment familiar to those who cannot give a brief response to the question "where are you from?" I definitely did not anticipate that ten years later I would reside in the heartland of America. It is from within this site that reflections on the vocabulary of place and space offer a semantic refuge in which to comprehend this stage of my life. Iowa is foreign territory among people with whom I have little in common; our points of reference and departure are radically different. As a first generation American who emigrated to Israel at the age of 18, I am neither and yet always both immigrant and native. In Iowa, unlike cosmopolitan New York City or Jerusalem, this has felt particularly anomalous. It is a relief to find this cognitive feel of difference articulated by scholars whose global perspective is defined by their multilingual, multicultural backgrounds rather than merely acquired and cultivated through education. The distinction between these two ways of comprehending multiplicity lies in the roots of consciousness; as Ahiwa Ong usefully describes it, "multiply inscribed subjects" are characterized by an "in-between consciousness of difference"(352). This is the consciousness I bring to the classroom.

I was born and raised in Manhattan to a Jewish refugee from Nazi Austria and a Black Jamaican. My parents and grandparents did not come to America with a desire or interest in assimilating or shedding the past. Perhaps this accounts for the comfortable synthesis of my own multiple identities which incorporate a politicized notion of Blackness, Jewishness as well as motherhood, among others. These identities shape perspectives which invoke memory and history and provide a context for understanding relations of power and politics. Increasingly, I have come to realize that my presence (and not just my persona) is often (however subtly) perceived as an obstinate interruption precisely because it signifies a refusal to comply with or submit to accepted protocol and disciplinary procedures.

The question "where are you from?" is not a neutral one. In my case, it signals, on the one hand, involuntary migrations before my birth (which made my birth possible) and, on the other hand, my children who evidence the contingency of reading bodies as texts: two of my children appear "white" while my middle child is "brown." Practically, this means that although I teach at a predominantly white liberal arts college, on the first day of a semester I never assume that the white-skinned young people in my classroom are necessarily White[2] or privileged. The in-between consciousness of difference conditions the kind of introductory information I seek from students whom I ask, "where are your people from?" (instead of "where are you from"). This is a strategy for immediately making salient the contextual and relational factors which define diverse identities and knowledge students bring into the classroom even where it might appear, visually, as if they were a homogeneous group of people. This strategy also serves to demonstrate a theory: identity originates in and is manifested through social interactions which, in turn, are shaped and influenced by legal, economic, political and religious institutions.

The act of identifying one's people in the public forum of a class requires the ability to cite genealogies and geographies as well as to ponder gaps in family histories. A few students, who rarely have the opportunity to reveal their histories on their own terms, are visibly pleased that they can present their background without being perceived as antagonistic. They are usually students of color who have either resigned themselves to silence in order to avoid being the resident authority on people of color in a predominantly white classroom or invoke their background in order to refute stereotypes about people of color. Once in a while, a student whose physical appearance belies assumptions of classmates, seems to relish the opportunity to forestall misidentification. Most of my students are Euro-American of English, German and Dutch background; they find the exercise curious and more than a few are perplexed. For the first time they are confronted with family histories whose origins have vanished into obscurity and their bewilderment sometimes leads them back to the stories their grandparents had forgotten about. My primary purpose is not to act as an intermediary between the generations: I am interested in motivating students to think beyond themselves and to grasp the connections between the past, the present and the future. In addition, working consciously against the prevalent trend to teach race, class and gender as separate units of study, I organize my syllabi to reflect their constant intersection which, hopefully, broadens and sharpens the way in which they engage with current political events outside the classroom.

Beginning a semester with family histories opens the door to a broad range of topics and cautions against universalizing from personal experience. For example, the process through which "undesirable" European immigrants from the nineteenth century became generic white Americans in the twentieth century is reflected in the different ways in which white students of English and Scot heritage relate to the notion of assimilation than those whose ancestors are of Eastern and Southern European ancestry. Using Mathew Frye Jacobson's book *Whiteness of a Different Color* in a course titled Anthropology of American Culture, students learn, usually for the first time, that from 1840 and until 1924, Europeans were also classified by race which included Saxons, Teutons, Slavs, Semites and Celts (Jacobson 1998). In general, American history classes do not overemphasize the significant "fact" that the presumption of an *inherently* Anglo-Saxon character reflects the successful colonization ambitions of 17th century English settlers. In 1790, fourteen years after they won their independence, the new Americans restricted U.S. citizenship to "free white persons" but never imagined that this would invite a mass influx of European immigrants very different from themselves.

Students are amazed to read about "white-on-white" racism culminating in the 1924 Johnson-Reed Act, which closed the door on immigration, articulated by prominent eugenicist Harry Laughlin, who testified on behalf of the legislation to the US Congress, "Racially, the American people, if they are to remain American, are to purge their existing family stock of degeneracy, and are to encourage a high rate of reproduction by the best endowed portions of their population, can successfully assimilate in the future many thousands of Northwestern European immigrants . . . But we can assimilate only a small fraction of this number of other *white races*; and of the colored races practically none" (qtd. in Jacobson 82; italics added). The majority of my students have not been taught that the term "ethnicity" was introduced as a move away from biologizing differences between Europeans and marks the rapid consolidation of a white identity or that *the melting pot* registered a belief in the *biological* fusion of different European races into one white race – a process Jacobson terms "the alchemy of race." Introducing them to Jacobson's formidable study, directing them to the footnotes and the bibliography is a conscious effort to heighten their awareness of the enormous amount of documented history that has been edited out from their education. Jacobson, like a number of other scholars who have gone into the archives to retrieve highly charged political debates from the past, serves as a model for good scholarship that is politically engaged without being polemical.

Pan-white supremacy reigned in relation to Blacks, American Indians and Chinese.[3] Yet precisely because my students are overwhelming white and have been socialized in predominantly white environments, I believe it is critical to accentuate how the descendants of immigrant groups from Eastern and Southern Europe moved from the margins of whiteness to its center. Monolithic whiteness – in its invisibility and normativity, which is quite different from the self-consciousness of white supremacy which continues to accentuate purity—was facilitated, particularly in the North, by government sanctioned *affirmative action*. With the return of soldiers from World War Two and the baby boom, government subsidies, low-cost mortgages, tax breaks and finally the 1956 Federal Highways Act with its expansion of freeways, enabled the construction industry to embark on a building spree and the phenomenal growth of suburbs from which Blacks were deliberately and carefully excluded (Hannigan 1998). The combination of social engineering and racial exclusion in housing can be mapped out in the labor sector, in education and healthcare to explain persistent patterns of racial inequality despite the abolition of legal discrimination (Barrett and Roedgier 1997).

Matthew Frye Jacobson's text serves as a prelude to Ian Lopez's *White By Law* which provides an analysis of the racial prerequisites to naturalization (rescinded only in 1952) entitling the inclusion of all white-skinned European immigrants but excluding Asians and most Middle Eastern applicants regardless of skin color or anthropological taxonomies (Lopez 1996). The laborious efforts defining race are marvelously accented by the exclusionary effect of the combined 1790 naturalization act and its 1870 amendment which extended citizenship rights—by law, but not in practice—to "aliens of African nativity and to persons of African descent" which excluded those who were neither "white persons" nor "of African descent."[4]

From a pedagogical perspective, Jacobson and Lopez provide students with a deeper understanding of the *process* encapsulated in the cliche "race is a social construction;" i.e. they come to appreciate the intense labor invested in *racing* people. When students discuss the formation of class consciousness among Kentucky miners a few weeks later, particularly after viewing *Matewan* (dir. John Sayles, 1987) and *Grapes of Wrath* (dir. John Ford, 1940), they are better prepared to notice, and then to interrogate, the naturalized linkage of whiteness and civility which presumes the synonymity of white and "middle-class." This leads to the corollary revelation, quite evident in *Grapes of Wrath* (and unusually salient in the representations of ice-skater Tonya Harding, whom they remember), that to be *poor* and white is to be *less* than white—to be disposable or "trash"—and to be a person of color and middle class is to become "just a human being." As we near the end of the semester, most of my students appreciate, without my commentary, that the model of the "human" invoked is white by default. They are more attuned to the vocabulary used in their social circles, on the news, in the movies and they notice the carefully crafted advertising images on television, CD covers, in magazines and newspapers – and for the first time, these predominantly white students are able to discern the routinization of difference: there are human beings and there are Blacks, Asians, Latinos.

I could have my students read essays that more directly tackle questions of "race relations." For instance, Patricia Williams' excellent essays in *Seeing A Color-Blind Future: The Paradox of Race* which opens with an anecdote about three nursery-school teachers insisting that her son was color blind. After a visit to the opthamologist, Williams discovers that, as a result of their well-meaning but misguided intentions, he had "resisted identifying color at all." She writes, "the very notion of blindness about color constitutes an ideological confusion at best, and a denial at its very worst" (4). Instead of Williams, however, I tend to choose texts which analyze the roots and phenomenon of inequality with more subtlety precisely because I am more often than not, the first black professor these students have encountered up to that point in their lives (there are four black professors in different departments at my college and a small number of students deliberately try to take a course with at least one of us). I know they anticipate discussions about race—but I also realize that they come burdened with assumptions and stereotypes: race is about people of color and blacks are rappers, basketball players, poor people. Many are quite comfortable with generalizing phrases like "the white patriarchial system"—but if asked to explain it, they are at a loss. They are even more surprised when I take it out of their vocabulary for the duration of the semester. In order to avoid the tension that arises when white students contemplate their own racialist biases, encouraging them to grapple with the complexity of racism, classism and sexism from a broader, less subjective perspective seems preferable. Selecting texts which make whiteness visible in a narrative style that *seems* disengaged, facilitates a greater appreciation for the arguments that equality cannot occur without strategic intervention and that a color-blind world cannot be willed into being by insisting on the pretense that we are all "just" human beings.

It is obvious that the choice of material and teaching methods are informed by a silent autobiography which integrates interactive and lecture strategies to engage students with ways in which race-based identities and experiences are neither "natural" nor a manifestation of biological differences. Instead they have been conditioned by and constructed through struggles whose battlefields included courtrooms as well as socializing institutions such as school, church and work. This places the issues of power and privilege within a wider time frame and beyond the superficial boundaries conjured up by attention to perceived *cultural* differences, where culture serves as a metonym for race. For most Jewish Americans whose ancestors immigrated from Europe and for whom white skin has provided inconspicuousness, racial identity is delicate as they confront the slippage between whiteness and Jewishness with a Jewish professor who is Black and easily draws on experiences from Israel to illustrate points under discussion. For African-American students, loosening American hegemony on definitions of Blackness invites a recognition that it is a *constructed* category which in turn requires, as Stuart Hall noted in 1989, acknowledgment "of the weakening or fading notion that 'race' or some composite notion of race around the term black will either guarantee the effectivity of any cultural practice or determine in any final sense its aesthetic value" (*New Ethnicities* 443).

For the majority of white Christian students, most of whom are from the Mid-West, critical engagement with race and racial identities interrupts (at least for the semester) the benign security of white normativity as most of them learn for the first time that "white skin"—*looking* white—has historically *not* guaranteed legal recognition of *being* white (Jacobson 1998; Kaplan 1949; Thomas 1997). They learn about the manner in which the analytic construct *ethnicity* was adopted into the social sciences in order to move away from speaking of *racial* differences between Europeans while consolidating a white identity, regardless of class differences, in opposition to Blacks, American Indians, Mexicans and Asians. The significance of vocabulary becomes important in unveiling habits of thought which have been entirely erased from both academic and popular discourse. Retrieving the history of the terms "race" and "ethnicity" serves to underline the multifaceted manner in which opportunities available to immigrants incorporated as "white" Americans was purposely denied to "native" people of color in general and Americans of African descent (of any color) in particular.

A few years ago, I introduced a course titled "Postmodernism and Anthropology" and used the first third of the semester to walk my students through David Harvey's *The Condition of Postmodernity* and Jean Francois Lyotard's *The Postmodern Condition*. These were followed by essays which interrogated the analytical utility of the concept "postmodernism." The challenge was in keeping students focused on the debates and reflections which shaped the emerging discourse in the 1980s, weaning them away from a vague collective assumption that postmodernism was mainly about giving voice to the silenced Others—aka people of color, women of all colors and poor people.

Postmodernism, an elusive concept, is inseparable from late twentieth century capitalism and alludes to the conditions and production of knowledge in highly industrialized and super technological societies. As a conceptual point of reference, it is about language games and rhetorical skills: asking students to restrain their impulse to make judgements about exponents of postmodernism was a pedagogical strategy that represented an intellectual exercise to *discipline* them: "bracket your intuitive reactions until you can map out the arguments of this text." Yet their distaste for postmodernist discourse intensified the more adept they became at deciphering texts and demystifying the author's linguistic prowess. By mid-semester, many noticed a pattern: theorists advocating—and sometimes critiquing—postmodernism were themselves assembling a body of canonical figures and self-referential texts predominantly authored by white men and white women and failed either to mention, or did so only in passing, black thinkers who had raised similar issues more than a hundred years earlier. Women like Phyllis Wheatley, Sojourner Truth, Ida B. Wells, Anna J. Cooper had already interrogated the politics and power of experts in the production of knowledge which percolates into the public sphere as commonsense or circulates within medical circles and among policy makers and informs legislative decisions. We ended the semester with Hanif Kureshi's film, *Sammy and Rosie Get Laid* (UK 1987) in order for the students to experience a cinematic version of the explosion of difference in which whiteness does not serve as a norm (Chatterjee 1996). Kureshi, whose parents are, respectively, Pakistani and English, offered them an opportunity to experience the inadequacy of traditional analytic constructs (race/ethnicity/nationality) and required a discussion which disentangled questions of political power and privilege from vague references to the ambiguous notion of "culture."

One of the decisions I made after teaching Postmodernism and Anthropology, was to eliminate certain key terms from my students' vocabulary for the 14 weeks they are with me. One of these words is "culture." Noting that in all my classes, students use the word as a synonym for society, race, ethnicity—in other words, any time they want to politely refer to what/whom they perceived as different from themselves—I now ask them to specify whatever they are talking or writing about. If the reference is to values, attitudes, behaviors or social practices, then they need to state this; if they are speaking about racial difference, they are asked to specify what these are. By closing the short-cuts which code words facilitate, my objective is to encourage students to think more carefully and therefore more critically about the ways in which they think about the world around them. A careful selection of readings which provide a new conceptual framework to move beyond essentialist notions, helps ease the difficult transition for students to make for they are not accustomed to reading carefully and often they rehash opinions rather than acquiring a more informed perspective from which to engage with past or current events. Ultimately, it is an empowering experience for students who are in the classroom in order *to learn*—in the old- fashioned sense of discovering, revising and refining ideas with new information and analyses. I do want them to be aware of, and to question, the implications behind the false homogeneity of everyday vocabulary such as "African-American," "white," "diaspora" or "middle-class."

I entered the field of cultural anthropology when the politics of representation was being confronted more directly. Who gets represented, what gets selected and given attention, what remains in the shadows and festers while new rhetorical strategies are refined in texts which are read, evaluated and validated by a small circle of privileged capitalists (capital here being both symbolic and cultural as well as economic) (Behad 1993). These are issues anthropologists were forced to confront precisely because, as a discipline, anthropology remains an inquiry rooted in the delineation and objectification of an Other. This objectification is not in itself violent—it is the tendency to universalize the unmarked author which is an act of violence. And yet, despite its popularity, the notion of "textuality" and fashionable emphasis of "texts" conceal the fact that texts do not speak back. An imagined notion of popular culture and textual analysis remains inadequate without a conceptual framework that persistently interrogates the space of theoretical procedures and the conditions of theory's claims (D. Scott 1992).

Viewing the world as a text can be a strategy which actually disempowers and reinforces the marginal positions of people who have been kept out of the center. As Jonathan Friedman, in describing the "agonistic relation of anthropology to the contested realities of formerly silent others," points out, "the ideas that culture can be negotiated and that invention is a question of sign substitution, a kind of cognitive exercise in pure textual creativity, are linked to a structure of self and of culture that is perhaps specific to capitalist modernity. The notion of culture as code, paradigm and semiotics is very much a product of modern identity. Some of the cynical dismissal of other peoples' constructions of their pasts is merely a product of modernist identity in defence of itself" (855).

Embodying diversity entails living comfortably with contradiction and dissonance. This contributes to theory-making and also necessitates political commitments to social justice, which explains my attraction to scholarship that goes against formula and dogma. I actively seek out material that assists me in directing students to question the assumptions behind their knowledge so that they can sharpen their ability to notice and therefore question presuppositions underlying texts they read. My physical presence challenges many of the concepts which dominate and constrain scholarship on "ethnicity", "race" and "culture" as well as the history behind these analytical constructs: what is the history of these words whose meanings are taken for granted until, on closer examination, they are shown to be contested and convoluted? Until students have acquired a broader base of information, I make an effort to guide them away from an over-reliance on the personal precisely, as Joan Scott argues, because of the self-evident assumptions embedded in the notion "experience" (J. Scott 1992). Only when students can contextualize personal experience, are they in a position to perceptively employ their own embodied genealogies and subjective histories as resources.

If the business of exploring the tensions and contradictions of concepts has been seductive, caution mandates an explicit recognition that some insightful analyses employ metaphors which render comprehensible events and phenomena in *particular* ways for *particular* purposes to the benefit of *particular* persons. Take the popular metaphor fluidity—for whom is identity "fluid?" What do the metaphors of absorption and solvency convey and imply for communities with claims to self-determination. And for whom are borders and boundaries "porous?" The concrete material reality is that those who wait for entry visas and exit permits, will find little enlightening about the vocabulary of "porousness" when their request is deferred. When my oldest son, Gabriel, was born, I tried to register him at the U.S. Consulate in East Jerusalem so he would have the advantage of dual citizenship. The clerk smugly informed me that my child was not entitled to American citizenship since I had left the States without the necessary five years after my fourteenth birthday, and his father was a foreigner. Bewildered, I left without argument but halfway down the street, the spirited rage of a 22 year-old pushed me back to demand—loudly—to see the Consul. Standing across from President Gerald Ford's photo, an inch taller in an Angela Davis Afro, I adamantly declared, "I am an American citizen and demand to speak with my Consul!" It was the first time in my life that I had occasion to even *think* these words.

The Consul—a stocky white man with a Marine crew-cut—emerged from his office as the clerk and I engaged in an escalating exchange ("he's busy and you can't see him;" "watch me"). With a conciliatory manner, he invited me into his office. After reviewing the file, he patiently explained the constitutional statute on inheriting citizenship. The law was amended shortly before my daughter, Dorit-Chen, was born—now one needs only two years after the 14th birthday—so she has U.S. citizenship but the changes were not retroactive. When I moved back to the States for graduate school, my father had to file an affidavit for my husband and two sons so they would have the privilege of permanent residence, the coveted green cards (which are, in fact, not green). When my husband and I divorced, his pending application for citizenship was halted and he had to resubmit despite the fact that we had been married for 22 years. Married to an American he could file after three years in the country; single, he had to wait at least five years and is now caught in the backlog of applications.

I have simplified an arduous and frustrating process: borders, boundaries and access to citizenship are concrete constraints on one's autonomy and mobility. When a mean-spirited clerk or an archaic law stands between the applicant and the visa, the barriers are anything but metaphorical constructs. In subtle and invisible ways, experiences like standing on lines in the U.S. consulate, traveling on an Israeli passport to Jamaica and Germany, and living in a working-class neighborhood in Jerusalem inform my perspectives as much as the identities of Blackness and Jewishness.

Given my interest in the manner in which audience can alter the meaning of ideas, the question of porousness and fluidity can also serve as a useful example for the ways in which seemingly similar theoretical insights can communicate radically different ideas. For instance, when *identity* is understood as a process articulated in the context of social interactions and political contexts, the reference to fluidity does not imply fiction or invention but rather addresses the complex subjectivity which includes, but is not overshadowed by, conscientious commitments to group-based identities. However, when the concept of *identity* is analytically disassembled without respect for the significance of the complex ways in which people position and are positioned in relation to other social beings, then the metaphor of porousness can be disabling if not paralyzing. Here I tend to agree with David Scott's critique of the manner in which theory is taken for granted as a "narrative that was authored (and authorized) the hegemonic career of the West." Despite my own dismay with the use of *culture* as a metonym of *race*, Scott correctly questions the motives behind the drive to discredit the *culture concept*: "this recognizably 'anti- essentialist' characterization of 'culture' as mobile, as unbounded, as hybrid and so on, is itself open to question: for *whom* is 'culture' unbounded—the anthropologist or the native?" (375f).

The presence and voice of a professor shapes the intellectual orientation and practical issues of selecting subject matter and organizing syllabi. For instance, in 1995 I was invited to Grinnell College to rejuvenate the Afro-American Studies Concentration. Looking at the available offerings across the general curriculum, I broadened and reorganized the structure of the program under the title Africana Studies introducing two bookend courses, Foundations of Africana Studies and a Senior Seminar. The Foundations course registers the influence of my biography which fostered a pedagogical inclination emphasizing the complicated histories of people in the African diaspora. This introductory course highlights the significance of interrogating the intersection of "blackness" as an experience and as a trope, and the grammar of roots and routes which characterizes—and thus summons—a broad interdisciplinary approach to studies about people of African descent. This translates into a course which, though focused on the experiences of Black people in the United States, constantly questions the ghettoization of Black people in the academy through texts such as Toni Morrison's *Playing in the Dark: Whiteness and the Literary Imagination* and excerpts from Paul Gilroy's *Black Atlantic*.

The effort to use theory—and not be used by theory—requires stepping into the dirt (to borrow from Stuart Hall) of tension and contradiction without being paralyzed by anxiety. This means valuing and validating any source which helps to reconceptualize and reformulate questions *with the specific purpose*—however utopian it may seem in these cynical times—of making the world a more humane place (Hall *Race*). Critical thinking refuses to be imprisoned by discipline and control. In this sense, intellectual creativity needs to be tempered by the contradictions of real lived experiences. My personal background produced and reflects a predisposition to question judgments, evaluations and conceptual frameworks of those who write from perspectives they presume are universal even where they include disclaimers of this position in their introductions. For example, the acquisition of another language (Hebrew) for everyday use, along with immersion in Israeli life, fostered a persistent and conscientious recognition of the suspect nature of all translation—a consciousness about the gaps in communication which result from being positioned differently. From the mid-1980s, my articles critiquing Israeli relations with pre-Mandela South Africa as well as dismissing vacuous, though popular, analogies between the two countries appeared in *The Jerusalem Post* and *New Outlook* (written while I was Coordinator on South Africa on the Foreign Affairs Committee of RATZ, the Civil Rights Party of Israel) but it was the essays on ethnic discrimination and elitism in the Israeli Peace Camp which foreshadowed my growing frustration with the gap between political rhetoric and social activism.

In Israel, after acquiring the credentials necessary to secure a recognized public voice, I witnessed processes of exclusion which became sensible only later in graduate school.[5] French sociologist Pierre Bourdieu remains instructive: "movements of rebellion on the part of the privileged are extraordinarily ambiguous: these people are terribly contradictory and, in their subversion of the institution, seek to preserve the advantages associated with a previous state of the institution" (*In Other Words* 45). One personal example concretely illustrates Bourdieu's insight.

In the Fall of 1982, I approached a social scientist who is also a founding member of Israel's largest peace group, *Peace Now*. At the time, we resided in Neve Yaacov, a working class Jerusalem neighborhood with a large population of Georgians (from the USSR) and Jewish Israelis of North African background. Asked whether it was possible to organize activities in this neighborhood, the professor recoiled in horror, "we don't go to those places." Both she and I were American-born Israeli women. The parents and older siblings of my Israeli-born (ex)husband emigrated from Morocco in 1949 and our social network was primarily composed of Israelis of middle-income and Mizrahi background.[6] The social scientist moved in academic circles which, at the three main universities, are still predominantly Ashkenazi. Most of the people in her social network frequently travel between the States and Israel on academic or politically-oriented visits. Such trips often include speaking engagements focused on the Middle East conflict and Israeli foreign policy. Their proficiency in English and visible positions in the peace movement also make them convenient resources for the foreign press which in turn enhanced their visibility.

Beginning with the election of Menachem Begin, prejudice against Mizrahi Jews by people described as "leftists" because they favored territorial compromise with Palestinians was a sensitive topic in Israel although it received little attention among American Jews who tend to be poorly informed on the country's domestic issues. For instance, the chair of a powerful non-partisan feminist lobby featured regularly in radio and newspaper interviews, often invited American Jewish women to speak out against the oppression of Palestinian women. At the same time, and despite the fact that her reputation as a feminist was built on advocating affirmative action for women, she repeatedly stated her distaste for the "levantization" of Israeli society. In a newspaper interview in *The Jerusalem Post* in July 1986, she described Israel as a lovely country until the Moroccan Jewish immigration: "As far as interpersonal relations are concerned, (things) took a turn for the worst, I remember, in the early 1950s, when the Moroccan immigration began. Until that point, there wasn't any violence.

But the North Africans really pulled knives . . . Of course, *I must confess that at that time I had almost no contact with people from the Edot Hamizrah (Eastern Jews), I never even took a bus, so this wasn't a phenomenon I personally encountered*" (25 July 1986; italics added).

A Moroccan colleague from Hebrew University responded, condemning the stereotype of North Africans as criminal deviants (7 August 1986). Not only did the professor *not* retract her statement, she reiterated her perspective (4 September 1986). Three years later, she responded—in her capacity as chairperson of the Israeli Women's Network—to my op-ed in *The Jerusalem Post* chastising elitism among women in the peace camp with the following comment: "what is most disturbing about Ms. Azoulay's article is the totally unsubstantiated accusations of elitism and ethnic exclusivity. It *is in the nature of leaders to lead and perhaps unfortunately, to be ahead of and different from their fellow men and women*. To interpret this as being elitist or a sign of rejection of those one hopes to lead is reverse snobbery of the very worst kind" (20 July 1989, italics added).

The same summer, following considerable debate over whether *Reshet*, a new umbrella for feminist peace activists, should concern itself with the issue, I organized a symposium, "Identities in Israeli Society and Peace: the Place of Mizrahi Women in Political Activities." The event was held at Tel Aviv University through the sponsorship of the Forum for Women's Studies. As a result, it momentarily generated academic recognition to the topic and, in Bourdieu's currency, symbolic capital. The discussions focused on Mizrahi Jewish women in an attempt to directly confront the obvious absence of Mizrahi women in the peace camp. Six college educated, articulate Mizrahi women, all of whom have been involved in political activities for a number of years, presented papers to a forum of 153 women and 5 men (most of whom were not Mizrahi) on a hot Thursday evening in Tel Aviv.

The size of the audience exceeded expectation and was viewed by *Reshet* as a success. Most of the Ashkenazi women, the main audience, had never engaged with women with a specifically Mizrahi consciousness, convinced that there were no Mizrahi women with the necessary skills who could assume central roles in the organization. Strategically, the symposium demonstrated the possibility of dramatically altering the image of yet another peace group which looked like, and spoke to a predominantly elite Ashkenazi audience. The potential existed for bringing together Mizrahi women and Ashkenazi women with a network of powerful contacts through family connections and with media and political parties, as well as among philanthropists and professional activists abroad. These connections trace a specific social and class position, thus networking was not merely a metaphor, but an efficient and convenient means of empowerment and advancing a particular cohort of women.

These Mizrahi women represent 60% of Israeli Jews, relate to, work with and are sensitive to a working class sector whose marginalization and resentment often led to support for political parties intransigent on the Palestinian-Israeli conflict (Lederer-Gibel 1984). Unlike their Ashkenazi sisters, the Mizrahi women who addressed the symposium linked their politics to both domestic social issues and the Palestinian-Israeli conflict. They viewed these as interconnected, part of a political process through which an image of Israel as a western nation has been constructed.

The possibility of a joint effort between these two groups of women within the coalition of *Reshet* remained hypothetical. The association of academic and professional credentials exclusively with political insight and expertise severely reinforces structural inequities, reproducing overlapping ethnic and class discrimination. But it was lack of symbolic capital, rather than academic credentials, that was the greatest impediment to propelling educated Mizrahi women into pivotal positions even in newly-formed "leftists" women's organizations.[7]

1990 was a turning point and in October, I submitted an application to one doctoral program abroad. Then, a few weeks before I left for Duke University, a group of Mizrahi activists requested a meeting with Tikkun publisher and editor Michael Lerner, then organizing a major peace symposium in Jerusalem. During the meeting, he asked me to participate in the plenary. The plenary papers were later published in Tikkun *with the exception* of the *one* which focused on both peace *and* ethnic chauvinism although (as *The Jerusalem Post* favorably noted) it was greeted by "thunderous applause." I relate this anecdote in order to highlight the lesson I internalized about how events are written and erased even as they are in process. The frustration of being thus canceled has been channeled into an acute awareness of the many situations in which new voices, insights and directions are censored by people vacillating over altering the *structures* of power *unless* they have secured their own position and explains why I am attracted to interrogating the process through which particular narratives are privileged over others, by whom and why. Herein lies the reason why my students are encouraged to historicize events—to return to sources and their contexts in which particular ideas and people were actively promoted while others were conscientiously concealed.[8]

When I returned to the States, I was not prepared for the extent to which 1970s demands for, and resistance against, the inclusion of people of color in courses and on faculty continue. Focusing on race as a central theoretical and pragmatic subject of study continues to challenges many white faculty and administrators who perceive themselves as raceless and their actions as unmarked by the inflection of their racialized positions (Azoulay 1998; Dovidio 1997; Mills 1997).[9] As a social scientist interested in group relations in the U.S.,

I privilege race as a significant social fact which needs to be at the center of analysis. From this perspective, to study the invention of the Negro—the invention of Africa and Africans—obliges an inquiry into the invention of Man and Whiteness; the invention of the West (Trouillot 1991). Here too, the constraints of racial categories and their corollary stereotypes surface as objects of study in my classroom.

Interest in the question of Black and Jewish identities in the context of the United States begins with my own socialization, but it also emerged from a renewed curiosity about Euro-American notions of "interraciality." I left the States when "Black is Beautiful" anticipated a moment of political transition but returned to celebrations of an ahistorical biraciality where *Black* had been displaced by the hyphenated *African-American* and demands for faculty of color and curricular diversity echoed those of my youth.

Dissatisfaction with public conversations on fragmented anxiety-laden multiple identities motivated my initial research focus. I wanted to accentuate the conditions that make it possible for individuals who embody and thus inherit membership in different socially marked groups to identify with both groups and thereby name their identity in the language of coupling rather than contradiction or fractions. I intentionally distanced myself from providing idiosyncratic experiences that satisfy a voyeuristic desire for the exotic or the traditional search for insights into race relations via a purient fascination with the products of interracial sex (Yu 1999).

Consider the language of biracialism which silently obscures and yet saliently evokes the multiracial history of American Blacks. In the seventeenth century, English legislators in the colony pondered the status of children of Englishmen and Negro slave women. Was the child slave or free?—*not* was the child black or white. The question was settled rather quickly by changing English laws of inheritance and introducing status through maternal descent—a child was bond or free according to the status of the mother. With the abolition of indentured servitude and the institutionalization of slavery only for people of African descent, slavery and the stigma of color were formally linked. By the mid-nineteenth century, the stigma of inferiority associated with blackness was given scientific legitimacy which enabled the language of species and hybrids. Nineteenth century racial classifications introduced the discourse of black and white *species* whose sexual encounters produce *hybrids* updated in today's vocabulary of *interracial* couples. Many of the children whose mothers are *not* Black/Afro-American increasingly identify as *biracial* and *mixed race* without grasping that these terms testify to a legacy of scientific racism which is stronger than the disclaimers that race is a social construction. For instance, despite the plethora of newspaper and popular journal articles celebrating multiracialism, racial blending does not forecast a color-blind society although, in a throwback to the melting pot metaphor of fusion, it does expand the boundaries of *probationary* whiteness for children of interracial unions. Increasingly, the *absence* of recognizable signifiers of blackness lends itself to racial ambiguity which facilitates the individual's right to control information about herself. This, in turn, serves to shield the individual from discrimination and to diffuse the *stigma* of blackness by accentuating identities with greater social currency (Goffman 1963). In *this* context, accentuating biraciality, instead of blackness, suggests that "(w)ith the pinning of racial hope upon blood mixtures in such a literal way, there comes a sneaky sort of implied duty to assimilate—the duty to grab on to the DNA ladder and hoist oneself onward and upward" (Williams 1997, 53).

Although I want students to understand that race is a social construction which we reproduce with each invocation, I do not want them to imagine that we can merely wake up one morning and claim to be raceless. (Appiah 1992; Azoulay 1996). The tendency of the media to present biraciality, multiracialism and multiculturalism as a barometer of national moral health presumes a biological component to racial groups in which fusions are the prescription to their dissolution and an antidote to racism. But, as Carol Camper, editor of *Miscegenation Blues: Voices of Mixed Race Women* writes, "We should not be forced into a 'closet' about White or any other parentage, but we must recognize that our location is as women of colour." Her political position is underscored by the selections of essays in her book which do not include "the idea that racial mixing would be the so called 'future' of race relations and the future of humanity . . . I strongly disagree with this position. It is naive. It leaves the race work up to the mixed people. It is essentially a racist solution" (1994, xxiii).

As we move into a new millennium, theorizing and historicizing race should not be deployed against the efficacy of race-based communities of meaning (Outlaw 1996). Therefore, it is of crucial importance that students understand the *processes* which constitute the social construction of race in particular and other socio-political units of analysis. Unfortunately, too often they learn to use code words (such as "social construction") without a clear understanding of what they encapsulate and for this reason are unable to export them into in-depth analyses of topical political issues.

While writing *Black, Jewish and Interracial*, I found it useful to step outside the limitations of normative western Christian bounds which informed almost all the academic and political texts I was reading. I returned to a Jewish source—Genesis, the story of Creation in Hebrew Scripture—in order to rethink "identity" in a way that cohered with my experience. The creation of complementary and complimentary domains resonated with Stuart Hall's notion of the logic of coupling: the conjunction "and" without polarity and opposition (*Minimal Selves* 29). Although attracted to philosophical explications on identity, the solipsism of Descartes' pronouncements—the inadequacy of "I think therefore I am" resolved by "I cannot doubt that I am doubting"—seemed to honor the self in isolation. As Levi-Strauss commented in response to Sartre's claim, "Hell is other people," an identity which presumes the primacy of self is easily sociologized into a collective "we" who assume the right to reshape the world in its own image (*BJI* 38). That year, during the Passover Seder, I realized that while Benedict Anderson's *Imagined Communities* was interesting, the annual recounting of the Exodus already recognized the effort required in maintaining a collective sense of identity among a disparate group of individuals whose self-interests often bring them into conflict with each other. In sum, the in-between consciousness of difference provided a foundation from which to revisit rather than reproduce ideas about racial identities in the United States.

Philosopher Adrian Piper's reflection resonates well: blacks who refuse to accept a subordinate role and expect to be treated with respect as valuable people "reveal their caregivers' generationally transmitted underground resistance to schooling them for victimhood" (25). How exciting, in this context, to be introduced to Michel Foucault's appendix to *The Archaeology of Knowledge*, "The Discourse on Language," when he writes, "It is always possible one could speak the truth in a void; one would only be in the true (*dans le vrai*), however, if one obeyed the rules of some discursive 'policy' which would have to be reactivated every time one spoke" (224). And yet, crossing disciplinary boundaries inheres a sense of empowerment precisely because these boundaries are regulated, governed and controlled by procedures, rules and gatekeepers. My family history is complicated *only* when defined against the norms of homogeneity. Consequently I accentuate the complicated histories of people, the emergence of diasporic communities, and the significance of interrogating political signifiers. This approach lends itself toward uncoupling those hyphenated identities currently channeled into and imprisoned within hyphenated departments: those marked areas of studies—African-American studies, Asian-American studies, Latino Studies which reinforce, rather than challenge, the equation and primacy of Anglo-American studies as *authentically* American.

There are many new voices on the academic scene who do not fit the imposed traditional categories of ethnicity, race, and nationality. Although they—like me—may assert a particularistic identity in the public sphere, their in-between experiences and genealogies motivate and direct their scholarship toward an interrogation of traditional lines of inquiry and processes through which disciplinary canons have been instituted and institutionalized. Their repertoire of courses and syllabi selections as well as research projects reflect intellectual inquiries that have been shaped and crafted from the advantage of multiple perspectives.

In conclusion, an insight from South African writer Andre Brink has significant relevance for how I perceive my vocation, teacher and scholar, as a practice. Reflecting on the distinction between *an act* that is a commitment—it obligates—and *a gesture*—which is merely a performance for an audience—Brink notes that the political distinction is profound: "An act, implies involvement in the whole chain of cause and effect; it leads to something; it has direct moral or practical bearing on the situation in which it is performed; and thereby it commits the (wo)man who performs it. The heroic rebel, in other words, is committed to rebellion not *against* but *toward* something." (61) Rather than dismissing canonical legacies, interventions to reveal their archaeology witness efforts toward highlighting the personal fusions and cross-cultural diffusions that underlie any and all academic pursuits. My education and life experiences have led to the conclusion that one goal of any teacher should be to guide students toward valuing knowledge learned in the classroom and finding a way to put it to practical use in their daily lives. It is a deceptively modest objective.

NOTES

1. Jewish immigration to Israel is referred to as *aliya* and quite literally means to go/rise up. One goes up to Israel and Jerusalem – every other geographical movement is just to go or to go down.
2. I am here using a capital W to indicate white as a racial identity and not merely an adjective.
3. At different moments, discrimination against Mexicans, Japanese and Hindu Indians reinforced a generic sense of whiteness. However, it should be noted that despite negative attitudes towards Asians in general, the Chinese Exclusion Act of 1882 was the only legislative ruling to explicitly name a nationality for the purpose of their specific exclusion.
4. Chap. CCLIV, sect. 7, An Act to amend the Naturalization Laws, Forty-First Congress, July 14, 1870.
5. In 1988, two feature articles on my activities, (see Tom Segev, "The Raymond Suttner Affair," *Haaretz*, 23 September and the Jerusalem weekly *Kol Hair*, 30 September) importantly helped highlight the case of detained South African lawyer, Raymond Suttner. At the time I believed that extensive attention to South African Jews who were anti-apartheid activists was needed in order to buttress criticism of Israeli foreign relations with the apartheid government.

Over time, cynicism has displaced naivete as I realized that *all* government policies are dictated by pragmatism and not principle. The military contracts between Israel and Pretoria continue—only the signatories changed.

6. Mizrahi—which explicitly refers to the East—is used more frequently than *Sepharadim* for Jews from Afro-Asian countries. While the term was initiated by political concerns, historical accuracy encouraged it's incorporation into daily use.

7. See Ayala Emmett's informative chapter, "East Confronts West: What the Left Eye of Israel Does Not See" (1996, 133-170).

8. As in my book, I refer to Bourdieu's statement from *Homo Academicus* about the temptation "to adopt the title *A Book for Burning*, which Li Zhi, a renegade mandarin, gave to one of those self-consuming works of his which revealed the rules of the mandarins' game. We do so, not in order to challenge those who, despite their readiness to denounce all in inquisitions, will condemn to the stake any work perceived as a sacrilegious outrage against their own beliefs, but simply to state the contradiction which is inherent in divulging tribal secrets and which is only so painful because even the partial publication of our most intimate details is also a kind of public confession (Bourdieu 1988,5).

9. In 1997, George Yancy interviewed William Jones, founder of the first formal Committee on Blacks in Philosophy, whose reflections on institutional rigidity in the American Philosophical Association of the 1970s saliently resonate as accurate for the academy of the 1990s: "We have found that oppressors go through three denials. They would describe the present situation such that the labeling of oppression is inaccurate or inappropriate. You can use internal criticism to have them relinquish the first denial. But then they're going to move to the second denial, Well I'm not the cause. But then again, through internal criticism, we get them to relinquish that claim. So, they admit that there is oppression, that they are culpable, and that there is something that must be done to correct this oppression. But this is where the third denial emerges. The oppressor will select a method of correction that will *not* correct. The APA did not see the oppression in their structures or in their policies because they were not looking at it from the angle of analysis that would reveal such things as oppression." (Yancy 1998).

15 THE ANXIETY AND NOSTALGIA OF LITERACY
A Narrative about Race, Language, and a Teaching Life

Morris Young

February 1, 1973
   Speech evaluated—Missing central incisors.
   No apparent speech defect; however omits initial /s/ in blends (st, sw).
   Difficulty could be due to missing teeth.
   Good stimulability—Recheck. Waiting list.
                                                        J. Takano, Speech therapist

I look up from my chair at the stranger who has come to take me to an unfamiliar classroom. My legs dangle over the chair seat, feet not reaching the floor as I prepare to hop off. The building this classroom is in is different from my school—more sterile and hospital-like with the long corridors and chairs placed outside doors along the hall. In the yard there are no swings or jungle gyms to play on, a strange absence if this was indeed another school. As we enter the classroom, I notice the walls are not covered with kiddy cartoon figures or alphabet letters or big funny pictures like my kindergarten classroom. And it's dark. Not pitch black but more gray and gloomy as if a storm were approaching this room alone.

The walls are hospital green—not quite the blue-green of the ocean but not grass green either; more the pale mint of tooth paste. The furniture is familiar with kid-size tables and chairs. Easels stand on either side of the table—one with a paper pad and markers propped up on it, the other holds a felt-covered board with felt letters, numbers, and shapes that stick to it.

Mom and Dad wait on the other side of the closed door as I sit across from a young woman. She looks like a teacher but is friendlier than the teachers I knew back at my kindergarten. She asks me questions, has me pronounce words and letter-sounds, and read a little. I do as I am told, unsure why I am being drilled this way, especially when everything is so easy. I know my alphabet—A, B, C, D, E, F, G, H, and the rest. I read a little—"See Spot run" or some other simple sentence. And I answer all of her questions—"How old are you?" "I am six. My birthday was last month. I go to Kapalama School." Why was I pulled away from Saturday morning cartoons (though I remember vaguely being bribed with the promise of a chocolate covered wafer bar)? Why was I in another classroom far away from my regular school that was just next door to my home?

> January 1, 1974
> Speech eval.: Spacing bet./teeth—Slightly distorted /s/. Often omits /s/ in blends. Difficulty with /l/. Enroll for therapy.
>
> J. Takano, Speech therapist

I walk up to the main office building, leaving behind the rest of my classmates in Room 34. This has become a weekly routine as I miss story hour every Tuesday to meet with Mrs. S. But Mrs. S is nice and I don't mind talking with her. It's those worksheets that annoy me. Why do I need to fill the sheet with L's and S's? Why do I have to practice the "ST" and "SW" sounds when I can do them already? But I go to speech therapy and I bring home the worksheets to show Mom. "Look Mom. Listen Mom. S S S S S. ST ST ST ST ST. L L L L L." I continue to practice even when my missing tooth makes the air whistle through the gaps. Then I stop going to speech therapy. I don't remember why. It just seemed to stop. I stayed in Room 34 and sat for story hour with my classmates on Tuesdays now. And sometimes I would stop by the main office building on my way home and say "hi" to Mrs. S.

I look back at this time and wonder how much this early experience with language has shaped my life? Is it just coincidence that the study of language has become part of my professional life? Why did I become engaged with language rather than alienated like so many other students who may have had similarly "negative" experiences? Or was it a negative experience? Despite the "scariness" of being evaluated and the potential for resentment as I was sent off by myself on those afternoons, I was comfortable with language and perhaps even amused at the treatment I was receiving. Why was there so much interest in me? What about those other kids who seemed to have the same "problems" but did not receive the same attention I did?

> April 18, 1974
> Speech re-eval. No further therapy recommended.
>
> J. Takano

Here is the first clue that my life would be shaped by language:

> Born today, you are an intellectual by nature. Your head rules your heart almost exclusively and you make all decisions without emotional involvement. Such an approach to life is good when it comes to furthering your career, but it could prove a drawback in your personal relationships. No one likes to feel that he is friends with a machine. You have a great gift for the written word and often do better in your relationships with others if you can communicate by letter rather than face-to-face.
>
> "Your Birthday—By Stella" (21 January 1967).

As I read this horoscope thirty-two years later, clipped and saved by my mother, I am amused by the "accuracy" regarding my interpersonal skills, and am amazed by the final line's attention to "a great gift for the written word." I had never seen this horoscope until I began rummaging through the File, the personal record my mother kept on each one of her children. The File is selective and includes many of the expected things: report cards, notices of achievement, important school and personal records. But then there is also a hodge podge of items that illustrate a life filled with literacy. Among my favorites are the programs from the pre-kindergarten story-hour at the neighborhood library and my first library card.

Now with the kind of predestination indicated by the horoscope, it is no wonder that I have become a writing teacher (though I still find it difficult to call myself a writer) who researches literacy practices, and finds himself writing about writing in these pages. And as I reflect back on my life it is not surprising that some of my most vivid memories from my childhood are about language. Before I started kindergarten I attended story hour at the neighborhood public library where I would receive the aforementioned handmade program that listed the stories for the day and an animal shaped nametag. My opening memory about that Saturday morning speech evaluation is often replayed in my head as I look out at my classes everyday and speak publicly with them. On a family vacation when I was twelve, I found myself in New Orleans at an open market looking at some used comic books (my passion at the time) when the burly man who ran the stand looked at me accusingly and said in a gruff voice, "Don't you understand English?" as he pointed aggressively to a "no reading" sign. I only stared back at him, *speechless*, knowing that somehow my Asian features and dark skin had marked me as illiterate in his eyes. I am not sure why these memories stay with me. Perhaps because these were encounters with language I have internalized them and have become aware of the everyday uses of language and their contexts. Or I recall these experiences now because at the time they occurred I didn't understand their implications. Wasn't story hour just fun? What was a speech pathologist? Did I look as if I didn't know English? Did I look foreign? Or, as my horoscope suggests, perhaps language was simply part of my destiny.

In these memories, I see Sylvia Scribner's three metaphors for literacy—Adaptation, Power, and State of Grace—often the common tropes that drive our narratives about literacy. I see Adaptation in my experience with the speech pathologist where I needed (or was expected) to modify and develop my language skills to participate fully in school. Literacy as Power is clear when my English language skills were conflated with my race by that man who ran the comic book stand and acted to disempower me by questioning my literacy. And perhaps I am experiencing literacy as a State of Grace now since I am able to make language my career and experience the promise of literacy—a good education and a good job. There are variations in these stories about literacy, but usually recognizable characters, themes, and actions emerge to create a familiar cultural script. This script naturalizes experiences and creates master narratives of transformation and success that seem like easily achievable and desirable goals. These stories can evoke nostalgia, recuperating meaning for those who want to remember their literacy experiences in uncomplicated ways and who seek confirmation of their place in society. However, these stories can also create anxiety because they can further marginalize those who have already been marked as Other by privileging one story over another. In the stories I tell here I explore the anxiety and nostalgia of literacy in my own life, not to prove myself or to share myself. Rather, I consider my own struggles with literacy and identity in order to acknowledge the struggles of others who have often found themselves unsure, confused, and immersed in the contradictions of their lives and literacy.

In his book, *The Call of Stories*, Robert Coles explains that "one keeps learning by teaching fiction or poetry because every reader's response to a writer's call can have its own startling, suggestive power" (xix). As a teacher, I value the emphasis that Coles places on pedagogy and how a teacher's own learning can inform his or her practice. As a reader and student of literature I also believe that Coles is right when he suggests that the "call of stories" plays a very important role in a reader's life. When stories are read there is an attempt, whether conscious or unconscious, to make a connection between stories and personal lives. Those narratives about education, about literacy and language, hold even more sway because memories about these types of experiences (whether negative or positive) resonate with a bit of "truth," offering readers at least a glimmer of familiarity if not outright identification with these stories.

However, there is also a danger in the way stories can be used. The attraction to stories is due partly to attempts by readers to see aspects of their lives in them; to read the narrative of another's life is to sometimes read (or attempt to read) the narrative of one's own life. But it is this very desire of the reader that can be exploited; stories can be employed in ideological projects that act to advance particular views rather than engage the readers in their own self-examination. Harold Rosen suggests that readers keep these "basics of narrative" in mind:

1. that it matters *which* stories we work with and that remembering and comprehending are especially related to the power of a story to engage with the world of feeling and thought in the listener;
2. that receiving a story is an exploration by the receiver(s), not a set of responses to someone else's questions in right/wrong format;
3. that we should ask *why* we should remember a story and not simply *what* we remember;

4. that the most constructive way of examining the hold a story has is for it to be presented in a propitious context and to be retold in an equally propitious one. (229)

Rosen's "basics" provide not only a way to approach stories, but also a way to approach the use of story in our culture. In these guidelines he recognizes the interestedness in the telling and use of story. Rosen proposes a set of critical methods that *readers* of story must utilize in order to understand how a story is working beyond the narrative structures of plot, character, and setting, and in our own larger structures of culture and society. These guidelines seem like common sense since they build upon a reader's own interest in reading story. And yet the need to articulate this critical approach to reading suggests that for some reason readers are more often *uncritical* in their reading and that the potential of stories in their lives becomes a danger if it acts to fill a void through diversion rather than to help them create their own meaningful narratives.

Stories can provide a sense of belonging, can appeal to a desire to belong, or even to confirm a belief that individuals do not quite fit in. While the power of story is that it can bridge differences and appeal to many, this is also its danger. As Rosen notes:

> The very universality of narrative contains its own surreptitious menace. Stories are used to manipulate, advertise, control, above all to soothe, to massage us into forgetfulness and passivity. They are, in the original sense of the word, diversions. (236)

The universality of narrative acts to create a community, and I would also suggest, to create an audience. But while community can provide a sense of purpose through the production of common practices and goals, it can also result in a sense of reality with a very limited view: whatever or whomever falls outside the parameters of the community simply is not part of the story. Raymond Williams's definition of community is similar to Rosen's description of story as soothing, "massag[ing] us into forgetfulness and passivity":

> Community can be the warmly persuasive word to describe an existing set of relationships, or the warmly persuasive word to describe an alternative set of relationships. What is most important, perhaps, is that unlike all other terms of social organization (state, nation, society, etc.) it seems never to be used unfavourably, and never to be given any positive opposing or distinguishing term. (66)

The persuasiveness of story and community can act in the erasure of subjects who do not fit easily into either. In the attempt to create a universal and unifying narrative, stories can erase those minor narratives that tug and pull at the margins and bring into question the universality of a story. Minor narratives are either dismissed as unimportant or too radical, or are "rewritten" to appeal to the larger culture, making sure that the unfamiliar becomes familiar even if it means relying upon stereotype or other overdetermined representations. As Jerome Bruner argues, "The function of the story is to find an intentional state that mitigates or at least makes comprehensible a deviation from a canonical cultural pattern" (49-50). Thus in our culture, stories about education and literacy are often read as stories about becoming American, about the transformation from cultural Other into legitimate American subjects. And as Janet Carey Eldred points out, despite the controversy over cultural literacy in curricular matters and readings of conflicts between literacies, "the myths of self-reliance and of the self-made man who transcends his environment, who succeeds despite his origins, *still bolster critical readings*" ("Narratives" 696, emphasis added). No matter what ideological or political project is at hand, the trope of literacy as transformation or conversion—or to return to Sylvia Scribner, literacy as a State of Grace—occupies an important place in the American consciousness because it brings us back to those nationalist fantasies of self-reliance and success through hard work that have been part of our country's imagined narrative history and character. This is the National Symbolic suggested by Lauren Berlant, where the production of fantasy and the use of traditional icons, metaphors, rituals, and narratives "provide an alphabet for a collective consciousness or subjectivity" (20).

A familiar literacy ritual found in the American classroom in one form or another is the worksheet. Whether these worksheets are the mimeographed dittos of a past era, mass-produced workbooks that accompany basal readers, or new interactive computer programs, they often operate under the illusion of scientific validity. As Patrick Shannon argues, this type of work "maintains the myths among poor and minority students that they are solely responsible for their difficulty in learning to be literate and among middle and upper class students that they are literate simply because they can pass basal tests and other standardized tests" (631). This literacy ritual thus performs a socializing function as students are either made responsible for their own (lack of) social position or are rewarded because of their social position. Students learn what it means to be a good citizen by performing the appropriate labor and completing their own individual (though culturally scripted) narrative of progress.

As we know, the project of schooling for citizenship begins early. Here is another artifact from the File (Figure 1) that is an example of my own schooled literacy being reinforced by institutional practices. The two-page worksheet is dated Oct. 30. There is no year but I suspect it is something I worked on in kindergarten or first grade. Some of the clues: my written answers are in block print and not cursive; and a classmate I knew only in kindergarten and first grade is named.

Figure 1

1. Today I feel *like reading.*
2. When I have to read, *I want to play,*
3. I get angry when *somone takes someing.* ^something
4. To be grown up *you half to be a man.* ^chase
5. My idea of a good time *is playing chace.*
6. I wish my parents knew *I want to have a football.*
7. School is *fun and good.*
8. I can't understand why *I cant play with chalk*
9. I feel bad when *I am mad*
10. I wish teachers *gave me good work*
11. I wish mother *gave me a new book*
12. Going to college *meanslots of work*
13. To me, books *are good to read*
14. People think I *am a good boy*
15. I like to read about *fire truck*
16. On weekends, I *like Miles to come and play.*
17. I don't know how *to take picher s* ^pictures
18. To me, homework *is good*
19. I wish people wouldn't *hit me*
20. I hope I'll never *be a police man.*
21. When I finish high school *I am going to college.*
22. I'm afraid *of dogs*
23. Comic books *are funny to read.*
24. When I take my report card home *I see if I have a good grade*
25. I am at my best when *I study.*
26. My brothers and sisters *are good*
27. I'd rather read than *wirte* ^write
28. When I read math *I think*
29. The future looks *good*
30. I feel proud when *I am good* ^house
31. I wish my father *makes a playhoues.*
32. I like to read when *it is day*
33. I would like to be *a fire man*
34. For me, studying *good*
35. I often worry about *my fish.*
36. I wish I could *have a boat.*
37. Reading science *is fun* ^house
38. I look forward to *going to Miles houes.* ^flies
39. I wish someone would help me *catch butterflys.*
40. I'd read more if *I had a new book.*
41. Special help in reading *means tooters.* ^tutors
42. Every single word is *not a combond word.* ^compound
43. My eyes *see good*
44. The last book I read *was in school.*
45. My mother helps *in my homework.*
46. Reading in junior high school *is hardwork.*
47. My father thinks reading *is good*
48. I read better than *Scott.*
49. My father helps *me with my reading*
50. I would like to read better than *my brother.*

On the worksheet there are fifty prompts that are to be completed by the students. There are the standard, "Today I feel ..." and "I get angry when ...." But as part of the ideological project of schooling there are also prompts like "School is ...," "I wish teachers ...," "Going to college ...," "To me, books ...," and "I'd rather read than ...." There are a number of these prompts that act to reinforce schooling in a positive way. And the completion of these prompts are often glowing portrayals (for a 5-6 year old) of school. Now I admit I was probably well-prepared for school. I had much older siblings who did well in school, my Mom had worked as a teacher's aide before I was born, and there were tons of books and magazines around the house. So when I read over these worksheets I am not surprised at my answers—I was socialized to be a "good boy" (see #14) and to reproduce the positive attributes of school, literacy, and family. The worksheet acts to write the standard literacy narrative, prompting students to rehearse the "school is good" mantra and perhaps transforming students to believe this.

Patrick Courts argues that the basalization of literacy teaching and learning has diminished literacy by its attention to decontextualized language learning and creation of an artificial performance by the students. As Courts points out, worksheets become an instance of literacy that exists for itself:

> Either you must fill in the blank (or does the blank fill you in?—they have lots of blanks) or you must identify the correct or incorrect answer by circling it, or drawing an X through it. In addition to all of this, students will find that learning to spell involves copying the definition; and learning to write involves writing a sentence or two using the word they copied five times and looked up in a dictionary.... In surprisingly few cases does one find kids reading in order to have fun or to learn something because they are too busy reading in order to read. And to the extent that they write at all, they are writing-to-write; they are practicing correct punctuation and usage and business letters—getting ready for the day shift, so to speak (Courts 47-48)

While Courts's description of the classroom critiques our culture's capitalist impulses to prepare workers for an existing labor market, I find that his own belief in education is perhaps overly romantic. Certainly it would be nice to have "fun" or to learn something simply because of curiosity or joy or pleasure. However, the idea that education and learning are unquestioned positive and enlightening experiences has its own ideological underpinnings. As my own experience has shown, I can take such enlightenment ideals for granted because of my middle-class upbringing and my parents' belief in the cultural value of education.

I find my own worksheet actually very clever because of what I see as its ideological project of promoting good schooling. And I hope that students at an early age can have these positive, perhaps less heavy-handed, literacy experiences. But when I read over these questions and prompts I also wonder about the students who could not comprehend prompts #12 or #21 because going to college seemed like a very remote possibility. Or about those students who could not expect to get a new book as I did in prompts #11 and #40. Or who did not have parents who were available to help with homework (see #45 and #49).

How do students feel when faced with a worksheet like this that asks them to draw upon literacy and educational tropes that while seemingly familiar in our expectations of American Culture—that is, white middle-class culture—may not be familiar in their daily lives? Hawai'i writer Lois-Anne Yamanaka captures this anxiety about not being a part of white middle-class culture in her novel about growing up in the islands, *Wild Meat and the Bully Burgers:*

> I don't tell anyone, not even Jerry, how ashamed I am of pidgin English. Ashamed of my mother and father, the food we eat, chicken luau with can spinach and tripe stew. The place we live, down the house lots in the Hicks Homes that all look alike except for the angle of the house from the street. The car we drive, my father's brown Land Rover without the back window. The clothes we wear, sometimes we have to wear the same pants in the same week and the same shoes until it breaks. Don't have no choice. (9)

In this expression of anxiety, the character Lovey Nariyoshi, a working class/poor Japanese American girl, recognizes how language and class are often conflated in our culture. To counter this anxiety Lovey creates a nostalgic scene of what she understands American culture to be:

> Sometimes I secretly wish to be haole [white]. That my name could be Betty Smith or Annie Anderson or Debbie Cole, wife of Dennis Cole who lives at 2222 Maple Street with a white station wagon with wood panel on the side, a dog named Spot, a cat named Kitty, and I wear white gloves. Dennis wears a hat to work. There's a coatrack as soon as you open the front door and we all wear our shoes inside the house. (10)

For me, this scene captures the tension between the anxiety of being a marginalized subject and the nostalgia for an unfamiliar life that has informed an understanding of what it means to be American, to be average or normal, to be literate.

> *The moist air sits on my skin as I walk slowly through the New Orleans streets. Gray colors the sky and the ground as tiny puddles mirror back the dark clouds.*
>
> *"Mom," I whine, "Can't we go back to the hotel? It's sooooo hot."*
>
> *Mom looks down, "We should look around—we're only in New Orleans for a couple of days."*
>
> *A bead of sweat moves down her forehead as she tries to be positive. I drop my head and follow her, Dad, and my sister Genny, as we wind through the open air*

French Market. God why is it so hot? The humidity is worse than Hawai'i. The streets are dirty, and there's a fishy smell from the docks a few blocks away.

"This French Market is soooo boring," I complain to Genny. "It's only fruits and vegetables—we can see this stuff anywhere."

Genny pats my head. She looks tired too but she trudges on through the crowds trying to look interested. This family vacation has lasted too long I think to myself. We started two weeks ago in Seattle and made our way across Canada, down the East Coast, and now New Orleans. Why can't we just go home, to my comic books and friends? This is grown-up stuff. I'm twelve and I'm stuck on the mainland without anything to do and no one to hang out with. My own family is holding me hostage.

"Hey, look over here," Genny calls to me."

I drag myself over to a table she's standing next to. I'm expecting to see some New Orleans thing—voodoo dolls, pralines, or some such junk. I look down at the table and there are stacks and stacks of comic books. Not just newer comics, but lots of old ones too. Maybe I can find some X-Men or Legion of Superheroes, those really old ones that cost $2.00 at the collector's store. I'm excited as I start to rifle through the stacks. No I have that one. What's with all of these old Superman's? Isn't there anything good here?

"Hey boy!"

I don't look up.

"Hey boy! What'cha doing there?"

I slowly raise my head and look over to where the voice is coming from.

"Hey! Can't cha read English? Don't cha know English?"

A finger wags in my face as I follow where it points to: "No Reading Comic Books" warns the sign.

I look back at the man behind the finger. He's staring at me with contempt. His plaid shirt is pulled over a big belly and he leans toward me as he squints. I pull back, not sure how to respond. "Of course I know English," I think to myself, "Why do you think I'm looking at the comic books?" But I remain silent, unable to speak, unable to prove that I know English. I turn my back and walk away, feeling a little frightened and a little indignant. Who is he to ask if I know English?

I meet up with Mom, Dad, and Genny who are a few stalls down looking at some souvenirs.

"Didn't you buy something?" Dad asks.

"No, there wasn't anything good," I reply meekly. I turn back to look at the old grouch at the comic book table. What was wrong with me? Why did he think I didn't know English? Did I look—foreign? I continue to shuffle after Mom, Dad, and my sister wondering if we all looked foreign, wondering if others on the mainland didn't think we were American.

Up to now I have only provided glimpses of my life through my literacy experiences. Let me set some of the conditions of my own narrative-in-progress, creating a clearer but also more complicated portrait through history, story, and theory. I was born and raised in Hawai'i, on the edge of downtown Honolulu in the working-class neighborhood of Kalihi. Perhaps another sign of predestination was my home on School Street just next door to the elementary school I attended. This school had been an English Standard School much before my time but it was a distinction that was often remembered by teachers as well as my family. The English Standard Schools were part of a two-tier public education system that existed from 1924-1948 that separated students based on the quality of their speech, leading to de facto racial and class segregation. This system emerged during the height of the Americanization campaigns of the teens and twenties and was aimed at separating the children of immigrant laborers from Asia and the Native Hawaiian population from the children of Hawaii's growing white middle class who could not afford the elite private academies. Even today, the legacy of the English Standard School has an impact as debates about the use of Standard English, complaints about pidgin-speaking students, and concerns about the poor quality of public schools continue in Hawai'i.

I rehearse this short history because the creation of racialized subject positions is a primary condition in the production/emergence of my literacy narrative and in the cultural discourse about literacy and education. I do recognize that writers who have been marginalized in other ways (i.e., gendered, classed, queered, Othered, etc.) also produce narratives in response to the ways they have been constructed by and/or excluded from dominant culture. However, I focus on racialized writers in particular, partly because this is my own position but also because these writers find themselves so ideologically infused by dominant culture and carrying so much cultural baggage that they are more susceptible to being read as non-citizens, often as "foreigners" in their own land. Though the expected impulse is to prove proficiency (even expertise) in Standard English (note my Ph.D. in English and my specialization in literacy practices), there is also an impulse to resist Standard English, or at least to resist the *imposition* of Standard English by dominant culture. My own racialization becomes a way for me to reconfigure the literacy narrative as a strategy for resisting appropriation by a dominant American culture. Instead of undergoing a metaphorical naturalization to American citizenship by proving my literacy in Standard English beyond a doubt, I choose to *denaturalize* Standard English in order to unpack the ideology that accompanies our belief in the promise of literacy. In the story written by dominant American culture racialized subjects are included only marginally, reduced to cultural Other, or presented as "good Americans" who have successfully assimilated—think of the ways Frederick Douglass and Richard Rodriguez have been represented in mainstream culture. George Lipsitz's concept of "counter-memory" inverts this story, and cultural Others begin to use local moments in order to critique larger master narratives of history and culture (213). The inversion of Standard English, not the dismissal of it, begins the process of analyzing literacy tropes and how they operate in literacy narratives.

My New Orleans story is not uncommon. In his introduction to *A Different Mirror: A History of Multicultural America,* Ronald Takaki recounts his own experience with being "foreign":

> I had flown from San Francisco to Norfolk and was riding in a taxi to my hotel to attend a conference on multiculturalism. Hundreds of educators from across the country were meeting to discuss the need for greater cultural diversity in the curriculum. My driver and I chatted about the weather and the tourists. The sky was cloudy, and Virginia Beach was twenty minutes away. The rearview mirror reflected a white man in his forties. "How long have you been in this country?" he asked. "All my life," I replied, wincing. "I was born in the United States." With a strong southern drawl, he remarked: "I was wondering because your English is excellent!" Then, as I had explained many times before, I explained: "My grandfather came here from Japan in the 1880s. My family has been here, in America, for over a hundred years." He glanced at me in the mirror. Somehow I did not look "American" to him; my eyes and complexion looked foreign." (1)

Why is there an expectation of foreignness? If we were to continue the story, the cab driver, now defensive, might insist that he does detect an accent since traces of Takaki's Hawai'i accent may slip through. However this would open up another set of expectations and constructions as the trope of Hawai'i relocates Takaki. Every day in our culture we see examples of how language, literacy, identity, and race are often connected, constructed, and talked about in often problematic ways. The Asian markings of Takaki's body defines him as foreign despite any other signifier that would mark him as American. His use of Standard English, his credentials as an academic at an elite university (The University of California, Berkeley), his expertise in American history, seemingly will not supersede his racialized body.

Here is another example. When United States Senator Alphonse D'Amato mocked Judge Lance Ito on a radio talk show by using an exaggerated Asian accent reminiscent of Japanese villains in old World War II movies, he displayed an attitude that often constructs Asian Americans as less than literate and as less than full citizens in America. *The New York Times* reported:

> In a rapid-fire conversation with the radio talk show host Don Imus on Tuesday, Mr. D'Amato sharply criticized and belittled Judge Lance Ito over his handling of the

Simpson case and used an exaggerated Asian accent, like that of villainous Japanese characters in old World War II movies, in talking about the Judge . . . "Forever and ever, because Judge Ito will never let it end," Mr. D'Amato said in his version of a Japanese accent. "Judge Ito loves the limelight. He is making a disgrace of the judicial system. Little Judge Ito. For God's sake, get them in there for 12 hours; get this thing over. I mean this is a disgrace. Judge Ito will be well known. And then he's going to have hung jury. Judge Ito will keep us from getting television for the next year." (6 April 1995)

While we might give the cab driver in Ronald Takaki's story the benefit of the doubt since his interaction with Takaki was probably limited and overdetermined to start, it is harder to dismiss Senator D'Amato's willingness to construct Judge Ito as a Japanese caricature with a pronounced "foreign" accent. Ito had been seen and heard on television often. His position as a judge seemingly provided an authority and legitimacy that located him securely as an American citizen. And yet D'Amato felt he had license to portray someone with an Asian body as a foreigner with a recognizable marker of foreignness, an accent, as well as the use of "Yellow English."

I look at these different scenes because they illustrate the complicated representations of literacy and race that exist in our culture. The ability to participate in public discourse, to be perceived as fully literate (and without an accent) often becomes a marker of citizenship and legitimacy. Our culture's discourse of literacy (the ways in which we talk about and deploy literacy), its inherent construction of race, and the implications for the teaching of writing are problematic not just because literacy is often constructed in uncomplicated terms, as an unquestioned public good; rather, the discourse about literacy is also problematic because it is often coded as a way to talk about race, citizenship, and culture in America by raising the specter of crisis.

According to John Trimbur, the idea of a national literacy crisis entered into the nation's popular consciousness with the *Newsweek* story "Why Johnny Can't Write" (December 8, 1975). The tone of the story by Merrill Sheils certainly invokes crisis. Education at all levels is questioned, the threat to the labor pool is emphasized, and the cultural life of the nation is at risk:

> If your children are attending college, the chances are that when they graduate they will be unable to write ordinary, expository English with any real degree of structure and lucidity. If they are in high school and planning to attend college, the chances are less than even that they will be able to write English at the minimal college level when they get there. If they are not planning to attend college, their skills in writing English may not even qualify them for secretarial or clerical work. And if they are attending elementary school, they are almost certainly not being given the kind of required reading material, much less writing instruction, that might make it possible for them

eventually to write comprehensible English. Willy-nilly, the U. S. educational system is spawning a generation of semiliterates. (58)

This opening paragraph to the story does not only describe a perceived crisis, it participates in the making of a crisis by playing on the anxieties of parents who not only had to worry about the economic and political difficulties of the 1970s, but now had to consider the "poor" education their children were receiving. If their children were not being taught the very basics of reading and writing, what could parents expect for their children's future when the outlook at the time was already bleak?

The conflation of very different issues into a single literacy crisis is also problematic. Sheils draws together issues about writing instruction, language politics, literary culture, and discourse communities without ever discussing fully the complexities of any of these single issues much less the construction of them as all about "good writing," or in this case, "poor writing." As Trimbur points out, the construction of a crisis is meant to provide an explanation for events and conditions that have shaken the confidence of a culture, "resolv[ing] in imaginary ways actual tensions, anxieties, and contradictions" (281).

Just as Benedict Anderson suggests the "imagined community" as a way of organizing relations among diverse subjects, this imagining of crises is also a way to organize relations and to draw together a community. Citizenship and its attendant practices (such as literacy) becomes a way to both create and resolve these imagined crises, to enforce dominant practices as well allow the more subtle powers of hegemony to operate. In the case of both citizenship and literacy, subjects are made to desire these conditions and yet are also made to suffer the exclusionary consequences when citizenship or literacy is unavailable to them. Henry Giroux describes this process and appropriately emphasizes its pedagogical aspects: "The concept of citizenship must also be understood partly in pedagogical terms as a political process of meaning-making, as a process of moral regulation and cultural production, in which particular subjectivities are constructed around what it means to be a member of a nation state" (7). Renato Rosaldo suggests a term, the "polyglot citizen," which is extended by Mary Louise Pratt to describe the "changing realities in the U. S., notably the arrival of large, new immigrant populations," but to also account for the realities of a polyglot history of the United States ("Daring" 6). The polyglot citizen, in Pratt's construction, is "a point of intersection of multiple threads that weave in and out to make the dense fabric of society" ("Daring" 8).

The use of an autoethnographic moment, to build upon Mary Louise Pratt's definition of autoethnography, allows these Othered subjects to theorize their subjectivities through their literacy practices as well as the literacy practices and expectations of the metropolis. That is, these subjects can interrogate literacy by investigating how they are situated and how they participate in constructing representations of literacy. This autoethnographic moment within the literacy narrative is a way for the tension between nostalgia and anxiety to be reconfigured as a productive and no longer debilitating act. Talking about literacy is a complicated and often quite frustrating experience because the term "literacy" is just as ambiguous as it is powerful. When it is invoked, it is used to describe a standard in our larger society (perhaps most often manifested in our educational institutions), a standard that is never clearly defined and often relies heavily on "Western" assumptions and contexts and the modernity of nations. Literacy becomes a marker of membership, and those who can demonstrate this membership gain both access to and privilege in the dominant structures of power. Those without membership often face economic and political disadvantage, limiting their participation in the community in various ways. The implications of literacy, then, are greater than just acquiring reading and writing abilities that meet the community's "standards": literacy often becomes the marker of citizenship and this assignment of legitimacy is often "required" to enjoy the full benefits of citizenship or even of basic human rights. The incentive for individuals to be identified as literate is great; for individuals to question literacy is a great risk.

First Day, First Semester, First Year, First Job

I enter the classroom nervously, surveying the room and trying to maintain some semblance of authority. I am beginning my first full-time teaching position and my first class is first-year college composition. Twenty-three fresh faces stare back and I worry about learning all of their names. As I scan down the roll sheet I notice there are two Kristins, a Kristine, a Kirsten, and two Jeffs. Everyone looks alike to me except for one young African American woman. I take attendance, trying to burn faces and names into my brain. I ask students to introduce themselves: where are they from, what are their interests, why are they here? I try to assure the class that I'm experienced, have my Ph.D. from a prestigious university, and can identify with them since I've lived in the Midwest for six years. Then I go into my routine about being from Hawai'i, that faraway place that evokes dreams of Paradise—I exploit my "exoticness" to gain some cultural capital in this class. After reading through the syllabus and asking for questions, I dismiss class. Only fifteen more weeks in the term. Only forty-three more class meetings. I hope they like me. No, I hope they respect me. Please, I hope they learn something.

Third Week, Second Semester, First Year, First Job

I enter the classroom to the strained humming of the Hawaii Five-0 theme song—dada da da daaaaaaaa da. . . . John, a student from my first semester course welcomes me with this tune everyday. Its become my theme song, a way to prepare me mentally, and to signal the start of class. It's the second term and I'm teaching a Composition and Literature course, the second part of a year sequence writing requirement. I survived the first semester—I enjoyed the first semester.

This week the class is preparing for its first essay assignment. Last semester students generated essays around various topics and responded to a wide range of texts: essays, magazines, television, music, lived experience. This term they focus on reading and responding to written texts. As a form of practice and demonstration I bring in a sample essay for them to work on. I want them to read and respond in productive ways and I provide something that is similar to the writing assignment I just gave them. The only directions: they should give this essay the same attention they would to a classmate's essay—treat this like a workshop paper. Afterwards, I plan to go over the essay with the class, partly to model a way of responding but also to illustrate how I evaluate writing.

This time the practice essay is something I had written as a sophomore in college. I must admit that when I looked over the essay with the instructor's comments and the final grade of "B," I was a little embarrassed to use it in class. Terms weren't defined, the thesis was a little shaky, and I didn't provide page number citations for the quotes I used from The Adventures of Huckleberry Finn. *But as I reread the essay, I saw some originality in an underdeveloped idea that actually seemed to have something interesting to say. I saw some rhetorical flourishes, a nicely turned phrase, and even some sophisticated sentence structure. There was something to the essay. I did get a "B" (revised up from a "C+" I think) but the instructor was tough and intelligent, and extremely generous as a teacher and person—the kind of teacher I hoped to be. I felt pretty good about that "B" and what I felt was a wake-up call from the empty "pretty" writing I had been doing. There were problems with the essay but also some good points as well. A good essay for the class to critique—a piece that needed work but also a piece that had something there.*

"The introduction is boring."

"There's no thesis—maybe if the first couple of paragraphs were combined."

"The author seems to have some good ideas but it also seems like he's just trying to sound smart."

"This is at best a C paper."

I stared back at the class, grinning because I was embarrassed about the essay, but perhaps also because I saw myself in these students. The confidence, the assured evaluation of the essay's quality, the real belief that they knew what "good" writing looked like. That was all me as a college freshman and sophomore. Until I did get a "C" on that essay and everything in my world seemed to fall apart. The skill I had the most confidence in, the ability that I felt was most natural had let me down. What now? Could I even get a "B" for the course? I was literate, even intelligent. Why (in my mind) was I failing?

Rereading my sophomore writing and hearing other students respond to it forced me into their place once more. I was not always the "professional" writing teacher. I did not always have the "authority" that I suppose I do now. I was a student trying to write essays I thought were smart and interesting. And perhaps they were smart and interesting—to me—but they were also in need of revision and lots of work. When I respond to writing now I cannot help but think of that teacher who dared to give me a "C." He was generous, understanding, and tough, and taught me to approach writing in a different way. I begin to take risks.

First Class, First Week, First Semester, Second Year

A new year and a new class. This time I am another writer in a roomful of writers, cramming the night or morning before class in order to bring a draft to our writing groups. Teacher and student, the lines are blurred as everyone writes, shares, revises, and learns. Another risk.

As a writing teacher, I often ask students to think about the experiences that have brought them to this point in their lives—college—and how these experiences have shaped who they are, how they think, why they believe, and what they write. I also ask them to think about their literacy: what is literacy? What does it mean to them? How do they know they are literate? I do not ask them to write about their personal lives though some choose to do so. And I do not ask them to reveal intimate or private moments though some do because a particular experience is necessary in their making of meaning. What has become apparent to me the more I teach is that our lives are so intertwined in our learning that whatever we do in the classroom both as teachers and students has some reference, no matter how small, to an individual's lived experience.

In my case, I cannot help but address my lived experience in my teaching everyday. As an Asian American who was born and raised in Hawai'i, the difference in/of my life is in front of me as I look at my classes and usually see students who do not look like me. I understand this. Hawai'i is a state where 63.1% of its population is Asian/Pacific American and whites are the minority at 33.4%. Contrast this to Ohio, where I presently live and teach: 87% of the population is white; 1.1% is Asian American. At the university where I teach, 93% of the student population is white and 7% non-white. I cite these statistics not to lament about the lack of diversity, especially since no place in the US can match Hawai'i for its varied population. However, I do raise these figures because of what it has meant for my classroom. In 10 courses I have taught so far, I have had 18 students of color out of 242, slightly better than the 7% minority population at the university. But when you break down these courses, I have had classes with minority enrollments of 1, 4, 0, 1, 0, 2, 0, 0, 1, 4, 0, 1, 1, 0, and 1. What does it mean for these students to be in a situation where they are often the lone student of color? What does it mean to me when I am the only person of color in the classroom? And what does it mean to both my students and myself when I am perhaps the only teacher of color many of these students may ever have?

It means I am tired. Tired not because of the teaching but because of the extracurricular work I feel I must do. While I have never been directly challenged in my classroom about my "agenda" (read Race) or my qualifications (read Affirmative Action hire), I still work very hard to not let others assume anything about me. When people ask what I do, I tell them I teach writing and literature, not English, because they may assume that means English as a second language (or is this my own fear?). On the first day of class when we all introduce ourselves, I often say I have lived in the Midwest for a number of years before revealing I was born and raised in Hawai'i. I make it clear I earned my doctorate in English from an elite university. And I assure the students that I have taught many writing classes. Just as I see in front of me a sea of mostly white faces, I am sure they are looking back at me and my dark features, their Asian American (if not only Asian) teacher.

But when I look out at those mostly white faces, I also see "diversity" (a problematic though perhaps necessary term) and work hard not to categorize these students who have been labeled members of J. Crew U (or now, Abercrombie & Fitch U). When these students write, they bring their lives into their work, analyzing, arguing, or narrating about their culture and their place in it. My work as teacher is to work with these students as they make and shape meaning in their lives. I can only hope my presence as a person of color is part of this meaning making and shaping even if just a tiny bit.

In my memories about language, I have tried to uncover the pervasiveness of the ideology that has formed my anxieties and fueled my nostalgia for my literacy, whether achievements or shortcomings. I want to offer one last scene that perhaps illustrates the ideological force of Standard English and Asian American anxiety to a point of absurd indulgence. One evening I was in the video store with a friend looking over the rental possibilities when one box cover caught my eye. It was a Hong Kong action movie that starred two actresses whom I recognized from another action film I had recently seen. That was partly why I took a closer look, but under the movie credits at the bottom of the box was what really caught my attention. It read: "With Yellow English Subtitles." I was amazed. I called my friend over and declared to her that this video was racist. I could not believe how blatant the video producers were in advertising that Yellow English was a feature, if not highlight, of the movie. Of course I refused to rent the tape; my friend did rent it. The next day after watching the video, she promptly called me and explained that "Yellow English Subtitles" meant the subtitles were yellow so they would show up on the screen better. "Oh" was my only utterance.

I describe this scene because it illustrates the power of ideology and the discourse of literacy. The problem, however, was that it was my own ideological project which was driving this reading of literacy and race on the video box cover. Because of my own immersion into the discourses of literacy and race I had become hyper-sensitive to those possible eruptions of racialized representations of literacy. It seemed if it wasn't Alphonse D'Amato and Lance Ito in the middle of an uproar over racial stereotypes and accents, then it was a much publicized debate about Ebonics and the Oakland School Board's policy on literacy. If it wasn't someone approaching me and inexplicably beginning to speak in Japanese then it was another complaint about the use of Pidgin in Hawai'i and the lack of standards in the schools. As Thomas O. Beebee says, "The ideology of genre is all around us" (3). I take this to mean that generic conventions are always already set up waiting to be activated. Ideology drives genre when there are investments in reading cultural texts and culture in specific ways.

However, this raises an important question for me. While I can see my own expressions of anxiety about literacy and race in my willingness to read beyond generic conventions in order to fulfill my own needs, what is it that allows other genres to exist which are blatantly racialized if not racist? What allows the *National Review* (24 March 1997) to portray President Clinton, Vice-President Gore, and Hillary Rodham Clinton as racialized Asian subjects with the stereotypical features of buck teeth and Fu Manchu facial hair? Why does golf sensation Tiger Woods become the center of so much attention because his racial identification is a contradiction for so many people: he is coded as African American; he is "actually" more Asian American (one-quarter Thai, one-quarter Chinese, one-quarter Caucasian, one-eighth African American, and one-eighth Native American) (Leland and Beals 59, 60).

These questions about racial identity and the discourses our culture uses to talk about race create much anxiety not only for dominant culture but for all subjects who often only have their identities to hold on to. While we must work to make the ideologies which drive (the seemingly neutral/natural) discourses about literacy and education visible, to see how literacy and citizenship are intertwined with race and class, we can also assert agency, to act upon these discourses as James Berlin describes:

> Of equal importance, the subject in turn acts upon these discourses. The individual is the location of a variety of significations, but is also an agent of change, not simply an unwitting product of external discursive and material forces. The subject negotiates and resists codes rather than simply accommodating them. (78-79)

While there are ideological projects that allow for racist formations both as part of hegemonic cultural practice or as a more radical expression, marginalized subjects can and must respond. As I have begun to argue in this essay, the writing of narratives becomes an important strategy for marginalized subjects in their negotiation of and resistance to the discourses of dominant culture. The use of story (and not simply to resist or invert dominant culture) creates the possibility of expressing a fuller experience.

In Neil A Lewis's *New York Times* article (5 May 1997) about critical race theory, he focuses on storytelling as a primary feature that allows individual experiences or parables to provide different contexts for the interpretation and understanding of minority lives. Professor Kimberle Crenshaw, a proponent of critical race theory who was interviewed for the article, says that storytelling aims at "challenging versions of reality put forward by the dominant white culture" (Lewis A11). However, critics of critical race theory find the use of storytelling to be weak scholarship because it reduces complex issues to personal experience:

> But for Professor Sherry, "storytelling doesn't bear the slightest pressure once you start to examine it." Such storytelling, she said, starts with conclusions, "and when you start with conclusions, it's all too easy to make arguments that won't withstand any scrutiny."
>
> Her co-author and colleague at the University of Minnesota, Daniel A. Farber, who, like Professor Sherry, is white, said another problem with storytelling, especially personal narratives like the one by Professor Banks, is that when someone challenges a story, "you're not just criticizing someone's scholarship, but you're attacking their life, something that goes to the heart of their identity." Dr. Farber added, "That can make a dialogue very difficult." (Lewis A11)

While I certainly agree with Dr. Farber that dialogue can be very difficult, dialogue has often been difficult for marginalized subjects forced to enter a public discourse that has constructed them and yet rarely allowed them to participate in meaningful ways. That is, while marginalized subjects are often portrayed in the American Story, their own stories are either naturalized, reduced, or even erased in order to maintain the ideological and genre requirements of America.

The point that opponents of critical race theory miss is that storytelling creates a fuller picture of the American experience. I share some of my own stories here not to authorize this project or to use my personal life as a shield from attack. Rather, I use my stories to provide a context for this discussion about literacy and for the ways I do research and teach.

A former student once offered a definition of literacy that I have always found compelling: "[Literacy] meant the ability to stay healthy, thus survive and succeed, by being honest and open about the way I feel" (Nye and Young 69). In the scenes of literacy I have provided here this definition is at work. While writers/characters often contend with definitions and representations of literacy and race constructed by dominant culture, they also come up with alternative definitions of literacy which allow them to survive and succeed. In my work when I have read the literacy narratives of others I have gained an increased awareness of the complexities in representing and constructing culture and identity, the complexities of reading lives, and the complexities of life.

When I examine the literacy artifacts from my own life, reread my stories, and begin to write my own literacy narrative, I see both the virtue and the danger in my performance as an elementary student some twenty-odd years ago, as a college sophomore a dozen years back, and as a teacher today. How can I not be nostalgic, as I'm sure my mother was whenever she placed something in the File, as I look back at what I achieved at five or six years old and consider the cumulative effect of these collected literacy moments. No wonder I am a professor of English and teach writing or courses on the teaching of writing. But I also feel an anxiety because of the contradictory experiences in my life that have told me that despite my literacy I am open to being questioned and challenged or to being held up as a model of assimilation. Perhaps it is my destiny as my horoscope told me to live a life with words. In writing my own literacy narrative here, I have begun to understand the many layers of experiences and the many layers of culture which make up my life. It is this understanding and these experiences which become the foundation for my life as a teacher and a scholar as I continue to read the literacy narratives in my classroom and in our culture and to write my own life's story.

NOTE

This essay was written and workshopped in my Advanced Composition course in the Fall 1998. I thank the following students for their feedback and honesty: Jennifer Dobbins, Nick Hiltunen, Mike Leesman, Jon Masica, Carrie Ostermeyer, Melissa Quigley, Jami Riley, Megan Saulnier, Shelly Siemering, and Drew Stricker.

16 WHERE I'M COMING FROM
Memory, Location, And The (Un)making of National Subjectivity

CHRISTOPHER CASTIGLIA

In memory of my father, Joseph Anthony Castiglia.

My father didn't finish high school and my grandfather, a first-generation Sicilian immigrant, left school even sooner. Very little prepared me for my life as not only a college graduate but a college professor, except my sense that my passage through higher education somehow finished a journey started almost a century earlier by my grandfather. In my family, the worst insult was "caffon" ("greenhorn"), a label that summed up a state of ignorance, at once academic (awkward grammar, bad spelling) and national (an inability to adapt to pot-melted "American" culture, a habitual repetition of "Old World" practices and beliefs). By attending college (much less graduate school), I set out to eliminate the last traces of "greenhorn" in my family tree, learning the lessons that would make me not only more learned, but a better American, fluent in the national lexicon.

That lexicon, as I quickly discovered, consisted in a series of abstractions: not only the notoriously ill-defined generalities of America political discourse (truth, justice, liberty), but abstractions *away* from other, previous forms of identification and belonging. I was learning, among other things, to forget: to distance myself from my family and its awkward adjustments to the New World, away from my body and the traces it bore of that history, away from the collective sense of self. The process of "abstraction" began long before I entered the Ivory Tower, with my grandfather's passage through Ellis Island, with my father's decision to move from his parents' home and settle in a more "mainstream" suburb, in our increasing participation in the national economy. The essay that follows begins to tell that story.

While those "historical" thresholds have been well analyzed within literary and cultural studies, however, the role academia itself—its disciplines and its disciplined desires—plays in mediating between the ethnic and the national, the collective and the individual, the emotional and the rational, the particular and the abstract, has remained far less scrutinized (the ground on which critics stand always being the last explored). Yet the process of learning to forget involves learning a way of thinking, of valuing, and of composing, and those ways are structurally connected to the nationalizing discipline of "good" citizens. By learning to think and write in a certain way I was learning to operate in the national lexicon, the outcome my family and I hoped for. Yet at the same time, less legibly, I was learning to forget the source of that desire, the beginnings of that process, and in so doing I denied other, potentially productive models of belonging, other means of making sense of the world, of composing my "self."

In the essay that follows, I want to argue for the importance of making those (only ever half-forgotten) alternatives more visible, more critically central, within academia, using not only the stories of our movements through national pedagogy in order to understand *as content* the ways citizens must embody the interests of the nation-state, but also to analyze how the *styles* of academic writing—abstract, analytical, dispassionate—serve those interests as well. The reintroduction of the "personal" into scholarly essays potentially serves both ends, creating a hybrid of styles—emotional *and* analytical, particularized *and* generalized, distancing *and* collectivizing—that saturate the lived experiences of so many Americans and that are separate only in the disciplinary how-to's of the national/academic pedagogy.

Nationalism both requires and presents itself appositionally to the "particular." It requires competing cultural specificity, for only when emotion, collectivism, or particularity become the involuntary effects of certain (raced, gendered, sexed, classed) bodies can abstract knowledge be a privilege of others. At the same time, nationalism requires that members of those groups always believe themselves somehow inferior, marginalized, or incapable citizens. Locked in "identities" they must (but cannot, fully) disavow to enter full citizenship, members of particularized (hyphenated, gendered) communities exist in a liminal position that can potentially take the self-shaming form of national longing. But that liminality can also give rise to challenging forms of hybridity, and I am arguing for personal criticism as a potent form of strategic combination and culture-crossing. Not surprisingly, personal criticism has been taken up primarily by those with the most to gain from challenging and altering the forms of national belonging.[1] While national citizens are said to occupy a publicity characterized by abstract and disinterested principle, the "personal" is supposedly private, particular, and embodied. Those furthest from full citizenship are, not coincidentally, most closely associated with "balkanizing" cultural identities, with private domestic spheres, and with the markings and excesses of their bodies: women, gay men and lesbians, people of color, immigrants, the poor, the disabled. Members of those identity categories have taken up personal criticism in compelling and challenging ways to refuse the false divisions of body and mind, deriving and inventing, memory and theory. At the same time, its best practitioners use personal criticism to stress the mediated nature of the "personal," questioning the transparency of self-knowledge. In so doing, personal criticism, like much poststructural theory, potentially deconstructs—and, *unlike* much poststructural theory, powerfully *re*constructs—the national subject. Our "personal" lives (which is to say, our lives) are the place where national subjectivity is made and unmade, giving rise to an anxious tension that might be said to be the normative state of national affect. In our prose, academics have tended to bifurcate that process, crediting either the making or unmaking, normativizing or subverting, of citizenship, and in a parallel (but usually unrecognized) way, our *style* of analysis has effected similar splits between the personal and the analystic. By bringing those styles together I hope to suggest the complex dangers and pleasures of a family's movements into and away from national subjectivity, and thereby to suggest an academic *approach* for those forced to live within the "personal."

ROCKY NATIONALISM

I grew up in Emerson, New Jersey, a suburb of New York City and a typical "bedroom community." In contrast to the public production of capital, the bedroom community is supposedly private, a secluded place of rest and repose. But what kind of bedroom contains not the solitary slumberer or even the tranquil family, but an entire community? If my hometown was a bedroom, it contained multitudes, and not all eyes were sleeping: as the term "bedroom community" suggests, the privacy of the suburb is collective and, therefore, highly scrutinized. Moreover, the generic term "bedroom community," by rendering distinct townships interchangeable, suggests a linkage between suburbs and sameness that, however fictional, is the pride of the bedroom community, the source of its citizens' mutual knowledge and shared interest. Sameness requires the surrender of particularized distinction to generalized abstraction, and suburbs encourage such surrender in their inhabitants. In these bedrooms, the community maintains a watchful eye over the private lives of citizens, turning the peaceful resident of the bedroom community into a disembodied cipher, a representative of abstract values—fair play and hard work, duty and liberty—rather than a dreaming, drooling, snoring subject.

The suburb might be said to form a nation threshold, on one side of which is affective loyalty and on the other a disembodied abstraction ("citizenship") that allows bodies to circulate interchangeably within the national rhetoric.

Attaching affections experienced as private and particular to abstractions that promise a "sameness" that becomes the precondition of public belonging, suburbs are a nationalist training ground. Not surprisingly, the two things most ex-suburbanites can say of their hometowns is that they were indistinguishable from all others, and yet they inspired fierce civic pride. A particular pride in an interchangeable abstraction: this affective state is, finally, the birth of national emotion. That identification with abstractions ultimately puts the nation-state at the service of rhetoric ("the public") and not of individual citizens (who become "private interests") matters little compared to the entitlements (legal coverage, institutional power, geographic prestige) that citizenship confers.

In saying that national abstractions remove the state's obligation to particular citizens, I don't mean to imply that national "ideals" don't serve the interest of particular citizens. Access to national abstractions and the citizenship they generate is, like virtually every form of access in the United Stated, economically determined. Despite its claims to generic—and hence, presumably, democratic—sameness, Emerson's marked neighborhoods reveal the economic basis of national status. The town's high- income neighborhood was called Soldier Hill, ostensibly in reference to a Revolutionary War battle fought in the vicinity. In contrast, the town's lower income neighborhood, Frog Town, put residents so far from universal citizenship that they were hardly human at all. While lower income residents were naturalized, then, its wealthier residents were nationalized (the heart of the neighborhood was a field with a flagpole that flew the Stars and Stripes). "Universals," as Emerson's internal divisions demonstrate, are defined in relation to localized particulars, and if some citizens become "public" through identification with universalizing abstraction, other (quasi)citizens bear the "private" burden of hyper-embodiment.[2]

As will often happen in bedrooms, economic privilege and regulated conformity to interchangeable abstraction arose as self-generated desire at the level of our most cherished pleasures. A highlight of my youth was the March 1974 opening of the Paramus Park Mall one town over. Through the familiarity of its stores' names and the regularity of its architecture, its musak and controlled climate, Paramus Park endorses on the level of its physical structure the interchangeable sameness that is reportedly the defining characteristic of bedroom communities. Like its shoppers, however, Paramus Park represents sameness as distinction, packaging mass-produced fashions as indicators of individual style and character. Even Paramus Park's standardized architecture promises a different kind of sameness. As the area's first enclosed mall, Paramus Park offered new attractions, especially the central food court overlooking a two-story tiered waterfall, unsoiled by the flock of paper birds hanging perpetually suspended above. The waterfall, by virtue of its status as impromptu wishing well, rendered consumption not only natural but metaphysical: by "throwing away" money, the mall promises us, we purchase something as intangible and satisfying as a wish, a desire. My family's favorite dinner spot was the mall's franchised creperie, The Magic Pan, where we could, while enjoying a family dinner, watch hundreds of others, carrying the same bags and doing the same things we did. This remembered vista suggests the connections between mass-production and the "nature" in/of the mall, the "Park" betraying the suburb's claim to organic sameness as an innocent emanation of affinity.[3] At the time, however, I experienced it as a natural enjoyment, for the mall, with its cascading waters, tree-lined corridors, and origami birds, soothingly naturalized uniformity and consumption.

As a scrutinized location for merging, through an economic nexus, "private" desire and "public" conformity into the sameness of knowledge and the oneness of interest, bedroom communities, like their malls, are national productions.[4] That my hometown is named Emerson adds a particular layer of national irony to this sleepy suburb. The community in which being "different" was tantamount to being a communist or, worse, a bad consumer, took its name from America's philosopher of independence, self-reliance, and individual transcendence.[5] On our way to becoming true Emersonians, our most deeply-held belief was that, as we came to identify with the scripts of nation, we would lose the excesses of our particular bodies so as better to merge into the "oneness" that is the precondition of belonging. The dream of most of the boys in my high school class was to be on the football team, the Cavaliers, working out every day until their bodies became trim instruments of town pride, their distinction ironically marked by donning uniforms. These were the sons of second and third generation Italian Americans and Eastern European Jews who understood well the incentives to trim off what one was born with in order to achieve the American Dream, even when that dream amounted to little more than not getting picked on in the locker room. On fall afternoons, crowds of Emersonians poured out to worship these living products of routine discipline, personifications indeed of their hometown.

Even though I didn't play football, the dream of translating my marked, excessive body into abstract citizenship nevertheless suffused what was, for me, the most "private" space in that bedroom community: my particular bedroom. On the wall over my bed was a poster of Sylvester Stallone as Rocky Balboa, the media idol of the bicentennial year. An out-of-shape Italian-American boxer who gets a shot at the heavyweight title when he's selected to fight the champ, Rocky was for me a hero who transcended the squalor of his ethnically marked friends and family to participate in the national culture that promises economic success and fame if one can erase one's past and eliminate competing loyalties. Little wonder that Rocky appealed to the Castiglias' oldest son. My mother worked as a self-taught bookkeeper for a large machinery manufacturer, while my father slowly made his way from butcher and truck driver to a salesman for and eventual president of a wholesale hardware firm. While my parents worked, I lived with my grandparents in their house decorated with framed jigsaw puzzles of *The Last Supper* and occupied by aunts and uncles with names like Chappie and Pippi who sat at a large table in the basement and screamed at each other in broken English over meals that seemed to melt into one another. By the time I entered high school, my parents had acquired a suburban home is Emerson, and my father, expelled in eighth grade for throwing a classmate out the schoolroom window, became the town's mayor. Like Rocky, he had worked from his ethnic roots to the American Dream: the leader of all Emersonians, he had become a Representative Man.

Continuing in my parents' footsteps, I enacted my ethnic disloyalty by applying to college, writing out my applications on my bed, under the eyes of my hero. My plan to go to college was the great secret of my adolescence, but I had internalized communal scrutiny and mine was the open secret the whole town shared. In attempting to differentiate myself, I continued the same paradoxical logic that drove my parents' lives; I imagined, as they did, that Americanness waited always around the next corner, in that mysteriously elusive public sphere of entitlement that I would enter if I could only learn the national idiom.[6]

At the end of the movie, Rocky realizes that he has been used by promoters who have no real intention of letting him win the title, at which point he is unable to return to his old friends who, in any case, have acknowledged their own ethnic shame by cheering his rise into a national symbol. We ignored this ending, however, to our own detriment. Having momentarily reached his dream, my father lost his bid for a second term in the year of Reagan's reelection, his business during the Bush presidency, and his Emersonian house in the first year of Clinton's term. I too achieved and lost my dream: having been accepted to Tufts University, I declined the offer, unable to tell my parents I was going to an elite private school. Eventually, after attending a state university for a few years, I transferred to the kind of privileged institution I dreamed of attending and did gain a greater proximity to national knowledge. As a result of the road that began in that bedroom (community), linking national belonging and "private" affect, today I enjoy the benefits of education, but the satisfaction I imagined would come remains elusive, as one can see from the fact that in writing this essay I continue to "trade in" (in both senses) my family to earn academic credentials. The search continues. For me as for my parents, the desire for full citizenship keeps us all working for something that exists solely as a promise, an incentive, that took its being only in our moments of desire, as what we lacked.

SLY SEXUALITY

If my bedroom registered and reinforced my national desire, it was the site of other, less predictable if equally emblematic desires as well. Besides my Rocky poster, my walls were decorated with scores of Playbills. To the right of my bed was a record player and along one wall ran my record collection, comprised of the soundtracks of Broadway musicals. Holding a candle in place of a microphone, I would croon broken-hearted laments or belt out-show-stoppers, but only when the house was empty: staying home from football was one thing, staying home to rehearse "Some Enchanted Evening" was quite another. At fifteen I was a major homo—or at least a homo major—learning the lessons that would allow me to imagine other belongings that would take me (I believed) out of the suburbs and the life (marriage, children, lucrative career) it seemed to require. Lying in bed at night so I could stare at his overdeveloped pectorals, I made Stallone the object of my desiring gaze, turning Rocky into my own private knock-out.[7]

What's a boy to do? On the one hand, my hero promised the privileges of ethnic transcendence and disembodied citizenship. On the other hand, the same hero occasioned a knowledge of my body that marked me as "different," as deviant, and as dangerous. Once, on *Room 222*, a boy was being picked on by his classmates because he had VD. "What's VD?" I asked my parents, but all my mother said was, "Watch the show." Her response told me that VD had something to do with sex, and from the show I gathered that sex led to ostracism and, in the viewing scenario, family silence. If that's what VD led to, what would come of masturbating with Stallone? That boy on TV became the focus of everyone's gaze, his diseased, abnormal body—which is to say, his *body*—constantly on display while his tormentors became increasingly invisible, taking the final form of anonymous graffiti on his locker. Karen Valentine may have saved him eventually, giving her English class an essay assignment instructing them that sex was really love and that love was natural or that tolerance was groovy. I don't remember. What stood out for me was the shame of his embodiment, a lesson I had already begun to learn in my own school during, say, "war ball," the game we played weekly in gym class, in which the loser is the person standing alone, his body bombarded by rubber balls fired from across the gym by anonymous enemies. My classmates *became* anonymous by targeting a (more often than not, my) body, for only when deviants are embodied can the citizenry achieve effective abstraction, become normal to the point of oneness. Far from the disembodied cipher of national belonging, then, I, like the boy in *Room 222*, was undeniably embodied.

Growing up in Emerson, I learned through my body that the ontological stability of the suburb's most fabulous and destructive ideal—"community"—and its constituent abstraction relied on the marking and (at least fantasized) banishment of bodies, an exile that took literal form in the Hudson River, which separated us from the decadent city, home to the suburb's nightmare "others."[8] Despite its fantasies of group-coherence-through-banishment, however, "queers" were always at the heart of the suburb, not just because, as the liberation slogan runs, "we are your sons and daughters," but because, as my story suggests, the popular culture that mediated suburban life was also the "stuff" of urban queerness. I've come to realize that precisely such mediations—records, radio, television, theater, movies, malls—not only created suburban repression, but also brought me suburban relief.[9] Instead, my national memories are filtered through movies, television, and records, proving Berlant's point about the mediated nature of modern citizenship. If the disembodied citizens of the bedroom community had their transparent eyeballs on my body, my embodiment became the source of mediated pleasures that revised the disciplined regularity I experienced in my everyday life.

My favorite teacher in high school was Ed Peretti, the chorus director, who taught us the scores of *Pippin* and *Man of La Mancha* and cast me as Pappy Yokum in my first musical, *Li'l Abner*. Mr. Peretti gave me a way to think about and to resist the relationship between my body and the "fictive ethnicity" inscribed upon it. If chorus is itself a fitting symbol of the "community," creating harmony out of potential discord, Mr. Peretti, by introducing me to musicals, was offering distinctly dischoral materials. Musicals are notoriously conventional affairs: if you can't tell the entire plot from the first ten minutes, you're not really watching a musical. At the most predictable moments, however, an actress (men never have big numbers on Broadway; women, not men, are the embodied subjects *par excellence*) steps out of the plot and delivers a showstopper, a term that indicates the disruptive quality of the performance. These numbers present the body as a register of unconventional longings: No longer a set piece in a routine script, the actress becomes, for a moment, a spectacular exception, whose presence as longing body—where else is that breath-grabbing music coming from?—will force us to clap, to cry, to stand and shout—in short, to remember that we, too, have bodies.[10] Not surprisingly, my favorites continue to be concert reenactments of musicals that include the audience reactions: the surprised gasps, the ecstatic cheers when, say, Angela Lansbury comes on stage, making my listening part of the performance, linking performance and sensation into an "imagined community" that would reassure but not reincorporate me.[11] By relying on the kindness of strangers, I used the pleasures of my body to turn aside, for a moment, the admonishing glower of the community in my bedroom.

Such mediated encounters quickly became the core of my imaginative life in Emerson, enabling me to find in the midst of regulated disembodiment the creative possibilities of my own and others' bodies. I began to meet men who desired other men, not in the urban Sodom but in the Paramus Park Mall, the suburb's emblematic core. These encounters were remarkably comforting, opening up realms of imaginative adventure that made my adrenaline pump and kept my mind busy for days afterward. What mattered to me in these encounters, which rarely involved any talk, was not "knowing" others like me in the model provided by the suburb (establishing a conformed "sameness" that allows mutual knowledge), but exactly their difference, which became an opportunity to invent, to pose, to perform. My identity, therefore, was not "discovered" within my "self" or across the river in the city, but in the mediated cultural forms that brought people together without making them one: the mall's actual, rather than its virtual, function.

If I learned the lessons of embodiment in Emerson, I also learned this: if the promise of "freedom"—of transcendence that would free me into the disembodied abstraction that was my natural self—was a constant source of disappointment, the pleasures that came from what Lauren Berlant calls performing *unfreedom*—acting within and against, but not outside, the forms of cultural determination at hand—became the most satisfying and reliable source of agency I've found.[12] Such revisions acknowledge our perpetual confinement within national rhetorics ("unfreedom") while also demonstrating that those rhetorics may be re-articulated ("performed") to draw attention to their failed promises and ulterior motives and to assert a public agency for those who re-articulate them. In advocating "unfreedom" as a powerful form of agency I do not want to underestimate the physical locations and deployments of power that sometimes make movement a necessity of survival. But Americans have too often believed that movement *in itself* constitutes agency, misrecognizing dislocation as transformation or freedom. My story is, however, not of a move from oppression to liberation, from suburb to city, from family to college, or from body to nation (or back again to subculture), but of mediation between symbolic orders (suburban, urban, national, sexual), that allows me to use one order to read and, to a certain degree, to resist the other. The suburbs are an historic articulation of the nation; they do not precede or "reflect" America. It is in places like Emerson that "fictive ethnicity" is formulated, taught, enforced, and perhaps most importantly, contested. I had to go home to begin this exploration of liberal community and its discontents, of resistance and alternative social formations, of ontological fictions and the preconditions of national belonging. My efforts to "transcend" Emerson seem to me to have demonstrated the strongest hold of its values upon me; maybe only when I stayed put, when I felt most stuck in my bedroom in my ethnic family's split-level in an all-American suburb, that I was able to become most "other" to myself, to imagine different narratives of what life could be, of where and how I could belong.

HOME SCHOOLING

The gesture of "staying put"—of performing unfreedom rather than engaging in the fiction of transcendence—turns out to be easier said than done. As I'm writing this, my mother telephones. "Are you cooking?" she asks, sensing the distraction in my voice. "No," I reply curtly, "I'm writing." She begins to apologize, says she'll call back. I hesitate and then click on "save." "No, it's okay. I can come back to it." She tells me about the antics of her grandchildren, sales at the local supermarket, the terminal illness of a cousin I've never met, the sauce she's making for dinner. Not much response is called for: I giggle, cluck my tongue, express mild surprise. Eventually she runs out of news and it's my turn, but the censor clicks on: I've had a tough day writing. I attended a lecture. I proposed a panel for a professional conference. None of this, I think, would mean a thing to her; I worry that she would think that my life sounds pretty boring, if not to say easy, not equal to the frustration I express. Not that my mother would give me any basis for these fears; she would respond the way she would to eating play-doh, missing a sale on boneless chicken, making marinara sauce: she would find a way to translate. It's I who wonders how important my work is, why I'm doing it. So I say, "Nothing new here," and leave it at that. What I'm really saying is: my life is so different from yours that you couldn't possibly understand; I have no way to express myself to you. I assert her failure to transcend along with me (thereby claiming my own successful transcendence), my failure to find a way back.

So I still want to leave them behind, to use academic forms to turn my family and the other people of my childhood into two-dimensional figures of discipline and deconstruction. Even while disavowing the push towards national abstraction, I repeatedly position the details of my parents' everyday lives (*Play Doh*, marinara sauce) against the "explanatory" abstractions of academic theory ("interpellation," "discourse"). For better or worse, my sense that academia could teach me the national idiom—would transform a private body into a privileged abstraction—was for the most part right.

Once I chose academia, the road led to an increasing belief in the national myths of originality and heroic individualism, discovered in my chosen "field" rather than in the prairies of a manifest destiny. Yet those myths too often lead, as the American Adams and Eves of yore discovered, to crippling sensations of competition and isolation. At a recent MLA panel, someone read a story from local paper in which a hotel clerk remarks that he doesn't understand academics: we don't spend a lot of time eating or sleeping with one another, he claimed; we just go back to our hotel rooms alone and cry. This remark elicited laughter from the audience, but also groans of recognition and defensive explanations: the horrors of the job market, betrayal played out on panels and in coffee shops throughout the conference. Such glosses fail, however, to recognize these phenomena as systemic components of the larger, isolating effects of academic culture and a good deal of criticism.

I saw this very clearly when I asked a colleague to read an early draft of this essay. "Why are your footnotes so nice?" he asked. "I know you. You're pretty skeptical. But I'd never know that from your footnotes. Get rid of them. They're too nice." In many ways it was the feedback I hoped for, suggesting that my intellectual debts are not as overwhelming as I had claimed. Entertaining the possibility of changing my text, however, I realized that I had not experienced the footnotes as admissions of debt at all; indeed, they were a comfort, a source of pleasure. The footnotes formed a countertext to my argument itself, for even while leaving my family behind, even while using the essay to criticize the values of community, I was reconstructing those values in the footnotes.

The impulse to eliminate uncritical footnotes is one of the many conventions that tie academia to Americanization. Footnotes that acknowledge academic connection—rather than stressing critical distance—smack of collectivism, while "derivativeness" (the worse quality academic prose can possess) carries the whiff of Ellis Island. Deriving (coming from somewhere else) retards one's emergence as the individualistic self that is the true American citizen. Since one is self-made, not defined by one's relatives or competing ethnic loyalties, being in conversation with others, agreeing and witnessing rather than contesting and debating, is suspect, a hindrance towards Americanization no less than a sign of academic laziness. Despite my academic training, however, I *did* derive from some place—or rather, from some *places,* for the Americanizing suburb I called home was only one of many locations of my childhood: my ethnic family and my queer love of show tunes were also homes to me, and their influence—as well as their competitive jostlings—shape who I am, how I can belong in the world.

My great-grandmother, Barbara Ciardella, lived along the railroad tracks in a rowhouse with faded green awnings and a steep front stoop, much like those of her predominantly Italian-American neighbors. In the morning she would put on a pot of coffee that simmered all day, serving a steady procession of friends and family who came to sit at her table, talk to her occasionally in Italian (she spoke no English) and watch the soap operas or, in season, the Yankees. But most of all they gossiped. All visitors, male and female, young and old, passed around stories seemingly without point, punctuated with emotional highlights, that everyone already knew. Over coffee and cookies, for hours at a time, among constantly changing players, they established lines of affiliation and familiarity.

This was the backdrop to a distinct early memory: I was having enormous difficulty learning math, and these guests of my great-grandmother's paused in their gossip long enough to write out problems for me, wrestling with long division themselves so as to help me along. When I solved these problems successfully, they clapped and cheered, our glory collective and expressive. When I failed, my great-grandmother's woeful moans, when the situation was translated to her in hushed tones, made me resolve to try harder next time, for their sake as well as my own. This was another kind of education, a competing model of belonging, although a harder one to recall.

In evoking memory's capacity to articulate an instability within the presumed coherence of national identity and its abstractions, its models of belonging, and its academic rationalizations, I don't want to naturalize memory or its subsequent expression in personal criticism as transparent "experience." Rather, personal criticism can demonstrate the fictive nature of identity, memory, and collective belonging, without mitigating their power either to destabilize national fictions or to pose enabling alternatives. To return again to my great-grandmother's kitchen: the Ciardellas were well aware of the fictive quality of the memories that served as the basis of their connections, at least as indicated by one piece of family lore. My great-grandmother had two sons who died, one soon after the other. My great-grandmother's grief upon the death of the first son was so extreme that when her second son died, the family took up the task of writing her letters "from" the second son. I became haunted by this story of my aunts and uncles keeping their sibling alive through the years, textually. When my great-grandmother died, her children and grandchildren stopped coming together, and I lost this communal connection. I mourn that loss, and if this text can revive them a while, so be it.

In the end, my extended family proved more adaptable to my "difference" than I could have anticipated. When I finally did graduate from that elite New England college, my whole family made the trek to graduation. My father, crying, told me it was the proudest day of his life. When I was worried about coming out to my family, my brother invited over a gay member of his fraternity who told me how my brother had made a speech to the whole house saying that making the frat safe for gay men made it safer for all their differences; my grandmother, who upon the birth of each of her grandchildren crocheted an elaborate tablecloth to give as a wedding present, gave my partner and me my tablecloth when we bought our house. To be sure, these efforts inscribe me in the heteronormative discourses (marriage, home-ownership, homosocial bonding) that structure their lives; yet my family's efforts to transform those discourses—their own performances of unfreedom—have, in many ways, allowed me my life. Even in the course of their suburbanization, what my family retains, as memory, from competing models of social organization and belonging—a willingness to incorporate newcomers into the family; a raucous and at times indecorous sense of humor; a trust that our bonds can withstand a heated discussion; that open displays of affection, by men as well as by women, are healthy—has in many ways made me a poor academic (too hungry for community, too quick with tactless speech), but has also brought other forms, other styles, to this essay. My family stays in touch, mediates our lives, induces me to use the "save" function. If Americanness was only half achieved, other forms of belonging were only half deserted.

There's the hope.

PUBLIC INTELLECTUALS, PERSONAL CRITICISM

The power of personal criticism to upset the nationalizing functions of academic discipline became strikingly clear to me when I began delivering early versions of this essay, provoking a mixture of anger and despair best summed up by one scholar: "If you're right," he exclaimed, "then everything I've always believed is wrong, and you might as well put me on a shelf like a can of Campbell's soup." This odd metaphor for "out-datedness" drew less on the shelf-life of minestrone than on the art of Andy Warhol, whose famous Campbell's Soup silkscreens suggest not only the mass production of contemporary desire ("um-um good"), but, when Warhol used the same style in his multiple-panel portraits, of "personal" identity. With his images of riot police and electric chairs, Warhol extended his exploration of identity under Fordist capitalism to include the disciplines of the state as well.

Thinking about this scholar's unlikely metaphor, I've come to believe that my essay troubled him not because it revealed anything startling, but because it was uncannily familiar, suggesting how the life narratives of academics, like Warhol's silkscreens, are composed through the repetitious overlay of the national, the economic, and the personal. The dismayed scholar was resisting the recognition that he is, like me, invested in those very structures—capitalism, the state, other people's identities—upon which academia supposedly grants a transcendent perspective. He *is*, in short, a can of Campbell's Soup.

The academic desire to segregate "the personal" from "the professional"—to keep identity "private"—is part and parcel of broader cultural currents: If the public is taken in American civil discourse as a synonym for the national, then the private or personal become the nation's other. From right-wing outcries against governmental regulation of "private" enterprise to liberal protests against state intervention in "personal" choices (sexuality, abortion, physician-assisted suicide), a wide and often contradictory range of "private" experiences is presented as an enclave against the nationalized public. These distinctions especially occur in discourses of the body and its markings: race, gender, class, and sexuality. Insofar as the "personal" may be said to be over-located within the discourses of the body, that privatized body is dis-located from the national public. The Warhol allusion suggests that my interlocutor was especially troubled, however unconsciously, by the specter of that most private of marked citizens, the American queer (why Warhol and not, say, Lichtenstein?), claiming a structural relation to the national public and its academic institutions.

Academia would never be so vulgar as to adopt the terms of the popular press or of explicitly nationalist literature. Yet the obsession with drawing absolute and value-laden distinctions between public and private—and with marking those distinctions by setting limits on the body—has found an academic inflection in debates over personal criticism. The association of much (particularly Leftist) scholarship with the private (its "jargon") and with the bodily discourses of race, sex, and gender (the "p.c.") has occasioned a vigorous effort to create a public—and yes, even national—scholarly position, evidenced by the renewed call for "public intellectuals" (where have we been all along, if not in public?). In this effort to claim a public academic status, personal criticism has often been a scapegoat, irrationally distinguished from rigorous (read: abstract, disinterested) scholarship. The call for public intellectuals corresponds with the rise—and disavowal—of personal criticism, just as the creation of a national public correlates with the abjection of marked "private" bodies.

In defending personal criticism against these charges, however, I also urge its practitioners to avoid making "personal" synonymous, not only with "private," but also with "individual." Our stories are never private or only our own. As Michael Berube argues, "one's understanding of one's observations has been formed by the various historical forces that have formed the landscape that makes those observations possible" (1065). If personal criticism does not shed light on what Berube calls "intersubjective relationships," but pauses on self-absorbed fascination with the particular, it misses the opportunity to challenge the self-determined autonomy of one's "personal" story and to analyze the academy's role in the workings of state interpellation. The theoretical promise of personal criticism lies in its potential demonstration of how the subject circulates between public and private spheres, abjection and entitlement, the state and the subject, subject positions and global economies. Such circulations undermine clear distinctions between the national public and the experiential private, and it is precisely that deconstructive circulation—articulated not from a transcendent and abstract position but from an experiential and implicated one—that comprises personal criticism's potential to challenge, not only what Nancy K. Miller calls "the nationalism of the 'I'" (xix), but nationalism itself.

NOTES

A fellowship from the National Endowment for the Humanities made this essay possible, as did the generous support of the staff of the Newberry Library. This essay was truly a community project, for many friends encouraged me, read drafts, and offered invaluable commentary. For those loving services, I want to thank Lisa Brawley, Robert Caserio, Anne Dalke, Allen Frantzen Leigh Gilmore, Kim Hall, Sasha Hemon, Jean Howard, Joe Janangelo, Paul Jay, Kate Jensen, Rachel Kranz, Tessie Liu, Dana Nelson, Jean Pedersen, Gerry Reed, Mary Kay Reed, Mary Beth Rose, Carl Smith, Julia Stern, Priscilla Wald, and Peggy Waller. David Bleich and Deb Holdstein improved the essay with their enthusiastic and insightful editing. Above all, I thank Chris Reed for making the "personal" a splendid place to live.

1. I am thinking of such works as *Getting Personal* (Nancy K. Miller), *French Lessons* (Alice Kaplan), *Crossing Ocean Parkway* (Marianna Torgovnick), *Alchemy of Race and Rights* (Patricia Williams), *Leaving Pipe Shop* (Deborah McDowell), *Alias Olympia* (Eunice Lipton), *Colored People* (Henry Louis Gates, Jr.), *A Life in School* (Jane Tompkins), *BorderLands* (Gloria Anzaldua), *My American History* (Sarah Schulman), and *Cures* (Martin Duberman).

2. My thinking here owes much to Lauren Berlant's argument that the nation's "norms of privilege require a universalizing logic of disembodiment, while its local, corporeal practices are simultaneously informed by the legal privileges and—when considered personal, if not private—are protected by the law's general proximity" ("Queen," 470).

3. Several commentators note the mall's blurring of public and private spaces, especially as the mall replaces the traditional downtown shopping area. Lizabeth Cohen argues that the mall's appropriation and commercialization of public space means that a "free commercial market attached to a relatively free public sphere (for whites) underwent a transformation to a more regulated commercial marketplace . . . and a more circumscribed public sphere of limited rights" (1099). In contrast to Cohen, who uses the regulated "private" space of the mall to naturalize the "freedoms" of public space *outside* the mall, I am arguing that the public sphere and the private sphere are coterminous and mutually structuring, not distinguishable "opposites."

4. It seems nearly impossible for critics writing about suburbs not to nationalize them, as is evident in the subtitle to Kenneth Jackson's classic study, *Crabtree Frontier: the Suburbanization of America*. Neil Harris similarly nationalizes malls when he claims, "In joining modern pleasure in large, unadorned surfaces to an older, baroque theatricality, the best of these buying machines remind us, once again, that the commercial spirit has nourished much of our most interesting American design" (288). Without

denying the commercial spirit behind the design of malls, I want to suggest that the architectural designs of the malls *generate*, not simply reflect, the national character and the "commercial spirit" that Harris sees as motivational—and hence prior—entities.

5. Emerson, incorporated in 1903, was originally named Etna, but its mail was being delivered to a town of the same name in New York; a name change was necessary, but firehats had already been ordered with an emblazoned "E," and so the town changed its name in 1909 to Emerson. I am grateful to town historian Bill Wassman for the details of this story. The name change is perhaps fitting: Christopher Newfield argues that Emerson endorses "corporate liberalism," a belief that the principle social pleasure is submission to an amorphous and unappealable power before which both personal action and collective democracy lose all effective agency. Given Newfield's analysis, perhaps the naming of my hometown was not ironic at all.

6. I am building here on Etienne Balibar's theory of "the nation-form." Subjects, Balibar argues, are formed as part of a "fictive ethnicity," a national collective, purportedly possessed of a common ancestral "nature," that dissolves all competing localities and identifications. That idealized projection is productive, however, of a haunting dissatisfaction—a misrecognition—characterizable as "desire." Such a desire—for a belonging never quite achieved, a recognition never quite completed—is necessary to the state, insofar as it produces both voluntary labor and patriotic striving. My desire was not only overdeternmined, then, it was doomed from the start, ironically in similar ways to how my parents' had been. Although my access to disembodied logic as an academic seemed to resolve my embodied status as a queer, both "identities" functioned to foreclose my options for national belonging, and paralleled how my parents' lack of education and desire for upward mobility disqualified them. As Lauren Berlant argues, "excesses to the norms of body and language" mark "American failures, citizens unfit to profit from their talents in a national symbolic and capitalist system" ("Infantile" 502). My parents' newly bourgeois bodies, like my queer body, their undereducated language, like my overeducated language, placed us outside the national norm that fueled all our desires in the first place.

7. Rocky may not have been, as I imagined, my private fantasy after all, either sexually or socially. I was startled, watching *Saturday Night Fever* recently, to see the same *Rocky* poster on the bedroom wall of John Travolta's character, himself a notable Italian American hero who leaves his ethnic Brooklyn family for his new life with a name-dropping social climber in Manhattan. The use of the poster in that film indicates that others have seen its symbolic value for Italian-American boys with social ambitions. The same scene, in which John Travolta parades around in a pair of tight black briefs, extends

the homoerotic potential of the poster through Travolta—whose sexuality, the subject of endless speculation, has formed its own open secret—to the male viewer, indicating that the sensational effects caused by Stallone's body enjoyed a wider circulation than I imagined.

8. I have focused on queerness as the suburban "other," but the most suppressed suburban category of difference is race. One of the central misconceptions of the suburbs is that by moving farther from the city, citizens become more white, and hence more American. At the heart of white flight is white fright: a fear that one's privileges, stolen from others and enjoyed compulsively (activities projected onto the urban black or Hispanic criminal and drug addict), will continue to be haunted by the suburb's projected "others." Kenneth Jackson reports that African Americans comprised only 8.7% of the 54.1% of the suburban population of New York's metropolitan area in 1980. Lizabeth Cohen notes that between 1950 and 1960, the population of the ten largest U.S. cities shrank, with three whites moving out for every two non-whites who moved in. Arguing that the suburbs subtly reversed the gains of the Civil Rights movement, Cohen concludes that "suburbanization must be seen as a new form of racial segregation in the face of a huge wave of African American migration from the South to the North during the 1950s (1059). When I called the borough clerk of Emerson to find out how many African Americans live in Emerson now, she informed me that the township does not keep numbers on "such things," a statement that testifies to the white hegemony of my hometown.

The irony of suburban racism is that it reproduces the snobbish exclusion that first forced the Protestant elite out of the cities to escape exactly the immigrant populations who now project the same stereotypes upon African American and Hispanic city dwellers that were initially projected onto them. This irony was brought home to me on a recent visit to my parents. Driving home from the airport, my father noted that the roads were dangerous because of black ice. My mother, mishearing, assured him that there wouldn't be many black guys on the roads of those suburbs. My mother's mishearing arose from my father's strong Italian-American accent (the rendering of "c" as "g," the extension of sibilant "s" into "z"). The very linguistic traits that marked them as "racial" to me translated, for my mother, into an assertion of their white privilege in relation to the "black guys" who could never, as they had, escape the city for the suburb.

9. Lauren Berlant notes a shift in national education from monumental to technological culture; "global media formations," she argues, "are the real citizen-heroes" ("Infantile," 504), not the founding fathers enshrined in Washington D.C. Although I along with my ninth grade class made the national pilgrimage to the Capitol Berlant writes of, I can't remember a thing about it.

10. Michael Moon discusses his identification, as a fat "protogay" boy in rural Oklahoma, with the excessively embodied opera divas, "radiating authority and pleasure," he saw pictured in *Look* magazine ("Divinity," 215). Both weight and sexuality, as types of "excessive" embodiment, incite ridicule, and hence are violations of the abstract body at the core of American citizenship.
11. Building on Benedict Anderson, I am claiming a form of memory here that acknowledges the national pressures to forget (one's family past, one's bodily sensations) requisite to the forming of imagined national communities, but also works against that pressure by forming national media into subcultural countermemory.
12. Berlant writes that Harriet Jacobs, Frances Harper, and Anita Hill "represent their deployment of publicity as an act made under duress, an act thus representing and performing unfreedom in America." Such performances "represent their previous rhetorical failures to secure sexual jurisdiction over their bodies, challenging America to take up politically what the strongest individualities could not achieve" ("Queen," 458).

17 THE PERSONAL AS HISTORY

RICHARD OHMANN

When I summon up remembrance of my early teaching years, lively courses and fine students swim to the surface, but chiefly a feeling of inadequacy bordering on desperation. A 23-year-old standing in coat and tie before privileged 18-year-olds, I took attendance with gravity, carefully announced that papers would be due or would be returned at the end of the hour, passed around a list of conference times, said OK, please turn to Orwell's essay, and withal sought to prolong the safe time during which there could be no question who was in charge. I knew the script. They knew the script.

"Mr. So-and-so" (no first names; students were "Mr.," I was "Mr.," our famous professors were "Mr.," this was Harvard) "Mr. So-and-so, what is the assumption behind that first sentence?" My lesson plan spoke through me, but would it speak through Mr. So-and-so? If yes, back to the script, but suppose he got it wrong: should I put the same question to Mr. Such-and-such and keep going until someone hit the answer that matched my plan? Kindergarten stuff. Come back to Mr. So-and- so? Try to figure out the nature of his mistake? Tease the right answer out of him? Suppose he didn't know what an assumption was? Suppose he hadn't read that part of the assignment? A bad breakdown in the script. Do I reprimand him? By what authority? Suppose he wasn't listening? Doesn't care what an assumption is? Can't see why he should be studying logic and rhetoric instead of writing like Thomas Wolfe or playing squash? A worse breakdown, especially if he should through an intonation or a gesture or glance at his friend in the next seat open up such vistas of indifference. Suppose, worse still, that he is unhappy, homesick, afraid, needs me to be something other than a nervous teaching fellow, trying to make it through this difficult hour, on script?

The hour might—usually did, I guess—include moments when learning happened. Certainly there were times I thought I had something to teach: how to explicate "The Unknown Citizen," or which introductory paragraphs on a dittoed sheet from students' essays were stilted or superfluous, and which purposefully taut. I remember one or two times (doubtless there were more) when students talked with animation to one another and to me, and the class felt more like a conversation among smart people about matters of serious interest than like a test of my skill at impersonating a professor. But the high point of the hour was that of its cresting toward a close—of astonished realization that I could once again surf onto the beach with my hoax intact. Then the low-stakes busyness of giving out the next assignment, returning or collecting papers, perhaps sympathetically granting an extension, assuring a dutiful student that his missing next Wednesday's class would not leave him in too deep a hole. Human exchanges. Then out the door and the rest of the way back to a life I could recognize as my own. Buoyantly if the class had gone "well," with shame or relief if not. Two days or five days or a week before I had to stare down humiliation again.

How I spent those intervals: reading for orals, working on my dissertation, drinking with friends, being domestic. Work or play—at first with ease of mind, with teaching anxiety at a distance. It came nearer each day. Procrastination, then panic. Grading papers helped. A practical step, a manageable duty. But it, too, could let the spectre into my study if I relaxed my guard. Sure, I was way ahead of most freshmen (but not of a precocious few) in my command of grammar, usage, diction—the comp teacher's trade secrets. On the other hand, why did I seem to be spattering as many "dics" and "grs" and "trs" and "awks" on each batch of themes as on the batch before? "Work harder on organization," I would write, but hadn't I said that last time? And when I peeked at my grade book before settling on a judicious C+, depressing to see that I had given him C+ last week, too, and every week except for the beginning-of-semester D-, which had terrorized him into paying attention. What was I teaching, really?

Back to panic, and a quick end to "the sad account of fore-bemoaned moan" allusively promised in the opening sentence of this essay. When panic got the better of avoidance, I began what I thought of as preparation for class—an activity so excessive and so poorly attuned to the challenge of helping students improve their reading and thinking and writing that there should be another term for it: depreparation? pedagogical disablement? I read tomorrow's text as if it were Talmud, amassing enough commentary to fill a semester's class hours and put the most rabbinical of students to sleep. A few years later, in my first regular job, the problem shifted: now I often taught about daunting Great Books (Homer, the New Testament, Dostoevsky), already encrusted with commentary I had no time to learn while trying to keep one chapter or book ahead of my students. Either way, nights-before developed along the same pattern. A gathering awareness that I could never build my teacherly fortress high enough; 1:00 am, 2:00 am, I'll finish in the morning, can't sleep, guzzle a quart (truly? so memory tells me) of cheap sherry, destroy consciousness; set the alarm for 5:30, shatter my coma with its ringing; waken consciousness again with a Molotov cocktail of coffee, shower, and fear; cobble together a disorderly sheaf of teaching notes; proceed grimly to class, do the opening rituals, and launch my professor act one more time.

To be sure, another part of my memory says it can't have been that dismal. Some students told me how much they thought they had learned from my classes. A few hung out in my office, seemed to value my conversation and even advice, became friends. The director of the freshman writing course, Harold C. Martin, visited my class, read my comments on papers,[1] said I was doing fine. Later he made me "head section man," then invited me to collaborate in the making of two text books.[2] I came to Wesleyan (my first and only regular job) trailing clouds of pedagogical glory. Tenure was quick and easy, though I wonder still if I would have made the grade had my judges paid even the most perfunctory attention to students' views of my teaching. There was no scheme of assessment in the early 1960s. Hearsay ruled. Wesleyan promoted those making a mark in scholarship, and assumed their teaching to be commensurate. We were "scholar-teachers," with the teacher part in rhetorical boldface, but the scholar part dominant in tenure case law. No surprise, that, to anyone familiar with academic folkways and the economy of institutional prestige.

"Scholarship." The word resounds with dignity, implies solidity and permanence. ("Scholarship sublime," mocked Gilbert and Sullivan.) By contrast, "teaching" suggests interminable activity, pushing a boulder up the mountain, never reaching the top. The end of a course: respite, free time for scholarship. The end of a career: a fading hologram of Mr. Chips, while one's scholarship endures, in print, on one's curriculum vitae (a telling phrase), and in the edifice of knowledge—monuments of unageing intellect. These hyperboles seem to me to capture something powerful in the ethos I learned without being exactly taught. Scholarly writing was to be my real career. I was to pursue truth and get it into print when I found it. Fantasy whispered that I might become a hero of the intellect. Short of that, my fresh and yet solid contributions to knowledge would, along with the learning that grounded them, earn me repute and fund my authority.[3]

It is a common criticism of the academic institution that the privileging of research devalues teaching. I am after a related but different point: that one's authority as a teacher is supposed to *derive* from one's effort and achievement in research. That relation may hold pretty well in a research seminar for graduate students and post docs in biochemistry. And indeed it worked for me in similar settings: giving an MLA paper was a breeze compared to teaching an English 101 class. But universities house many renowned chemists who fail in introductory courses, and they at least "know" the whole field of chemistry, while for my generation (and to an extent still), advanced study and research in English added scarcely a tittle to one's authority as a composition teacher. In a liberal arts college like Wesleyan, there were in fact very few settings where advanced training and research translated into classroom authority. I was, in the early 1960s, amassing scholarly credentials at a good pace, while floundering in my courses in spite and because of the extravagant labors I have described.

Now clearly, something was askew in the expectations we bright boys had for unity of academic being. The ideology of research as guarantor of good teaching collapses for the reason just stated, and for a still more obvious one: scholarship and teaching are very different social relations. Among many dimensions of difference I will stress two. Getting ahead in research and publication is a matter of pleasing, impressing, and often contending with one's peers and elders; teaching is chiefly a relation with less entitled juniors. And: scholarly intercourse takes place over spatial and temporal distances, through measured exchanges and with the personal mediated and defended by professional conventions and crafted styles; teaching, except in the mass-production format, happens live and on the wing, with the instructor's plan and persona open to a thousand unpredictable responses (including dreaded indifference) and needing constant adjustment. The teaching moment can yield ease and even exhilaration, but neither those pleasures nor the enlightenment of students can be had by transposing relations of scholarship into the classroom.

To do so literally is impossible. Students are not journal referees or fellow specialists. Students are right there with you; they talk back in the middle of the exposition rather than framing a decorous response after it's over (and of course you need them to talk back). So no teacher tries to be an expert with students in the modes of authority and discourse he or she has painstakingly learned through apprentice scholarship. But since those are the modes that have *made* you an authority—earned you the right to *be* teaching—the impulse to rely on them is powerful. How else do you signify and enact that right?

On this account, it's not that teaching is personal and scholarship impersonal. No social practice can be entirely one or the other. But we screen and project ourselves differently in these two practices. Scholarly conventions—and I resume the past tense here—scholarly conventions demanded the etiolation or bracketing or erasure of much that pertained uniquely to the individual presenting research. Out of bounds were, for example, the writer's gender (though we have learned since that it was unmarked and so male), his age and physical characteristics, his life history, the labor and conflict and perhaps uncertainty that went into production of the written or spoken text, how the writer was feeling at the moment (I'm cold and a bit edgy right now, but it's unseemly for you to know that), how the reception of his writing mattered to him beyond acceptance of its contribution to certified knowledge, and so forth. He might imply such information through style; probably he couldn't *help* conveying some of it to the canny reader. But the conventions largely forbade its explicit communication, restricting the scholarly persona to a disembodied fund of old and new knowledge, mobilized in accepted forms of argumentation and circulated among other such disembodied personae.

In class it was a struggle to wall out so much of the personal, but it also seemed both proper and safe. Physical appearance was ineradicable, but we did our best by wearing the professorial uniform. I, like most, flattened the social field by being Mr. and calling students Mr. or Miss. Although during my early teaching years the legal barriers against sexy literature were beginning to crumble (*Lolita, Tropic of Cancer, The Group, Naked Lunch,* etc.), and although a style of reading all texts as sexual (via phallic symbols and the like) was wildly and naughtily popular, silence was to shroud our own sexualities—and, needless to say, the erotics of teaching. Political conviction, autobiography, family? I thought it permissible to voice anti-fascist or anti-communist sentiments, speak of having met a poet whose work we were studying, or accept congratulations on a newborn child, but beyond such admissions of a life outside the classroom lay risky terrain.

A remembered incident: I was teaching about seventeenth century poetry, which necessitated a good deal of annotation on everyday Christian theology. A student asked if *I* believed these things. With no pause to think through the implications of one or another reply, I said I couldn't talk about that, but would be glad to discuss it with him outside of class.

In fact I disbelieved Christianity across a cool distance. Neither ambivalence nor sensitivity on the subject had anything to do with my reticence, which proceeded automatically, in response to a novel question, from the rules of impersonality as I had learned them.[4] Only my professional self, stripped down for intellectual work, was to be present in class. And of course I was tacitly asking students to abstain, reciprocally, from the personal. No sloppy revelations here, please; we're practicing objectivity together. Did I want their approval? Their affection? Certainly; but I could not be a person who wanted affection at the same time I was being a teacher.

It is embarrassing yet also therapeutic to write these things, to write personally.[5] Retrieving experience and posing its authenticity against the dissembling and the public half-truths we let pass in accommodating our individual lives to myths of professional solidity: these are by now common manoeuvres. And when put forth in writing, such disclosures usually enable and are enabled by another common manoeuvre: my experience is *not* after all just personal. Maybe its idiosyncrasies, explored with a psychiatrist, would have come together in a healing story of neurosis. But read another way—almost always privileged—they tell a more social narrative, showing how the teller is like other people so situated, not distinct from them.

As I recalled my experience of teaching earlier in this essay, I found myself easing into the second mode, giving weight to the "so situated," providing social coordinates for my discomfort, intimating ways in which it might be understood as exemplary.[6] I referred it to the way academic authority was constructed, to the valuation of scholarship over teaching, and in general to professional ideology, which (especially then) muted the personal and charged experience with certain kinds of tension. Other elements of my social location surely helped constitute that experience. I will not explicate, just mention a few topoi for analysis. Maleness: the drive to be emotionally invulnerable. Middle class upbringing: the importance of scripted self-presentation, the undesirability of surprises, the imperative never to make a scene. The 1950s: boom time, rapid expansion of the university system, professional aggrandizement, Cold War ideology in the disciplinary form of literature freed from historical circumstance.

I could go on,[7] but my aim is not to spin out such an analysis, only to remind readers how it conventionally goes. We evoke the personal, in venues like this one, to show how thoroughly social it was and is. The social may not exhaust the personal; there may be a residue of pure, individual difference; but we tell these stories to look *through* personal history at the ghosts of other, similarly situated people.

❦

But where did this convention come from? How did it establish itself in academic practice? I will approach these questions, too, through personal history: my own is perhaps both odd enough and commonplace enough to launch a discussion of more general interest.

Like most of my academic cohort, I maintained an easy skepticism toward the building of US hegemony through the postwar years and the triumph of "business society." We took Cold War pieties with a grain of salt, deplored McCarthyism, rooted for Stevenson, sniffed at commercialism and advertising— all from the platform of our allegiance to the best that had been thought and known. Needless to say, we also accepted the status and advantage afforded us by postwar economic arrangements. Some habitually but vaguely sided with workers and negroes and poor people—in my case, upbringing in a New Deal family had taught this affinity, which was then transmuted into parlor socialism by my immersion in G. B. Shaw's work, on the way to a dissertation. But until Michael Harrington rediscovered poverty, it could seem that the rising tide of the economy was lifting these groups, too, along with us happy humanistic few. We championed Culture in our daily work. Politics, beyond voting liberal, seemed irrelevant. My one activist sally in the fifties, marching against the bomb, was in behalf of life on earth.

Oppositional politics moved closer in the early sixties. Two colleagues of mine at Wesleyan had been freedom riders; others flew down to march at Selma. I stayed on the sidelines, though with rising sympathy and anger. Vietnam pushed me by degrees into politics. Why was my government entering a civil war, backing the wrong (undemocratic, corrupt) side, using my taxes to slaughter peasants? I wrote in private rage to Congressmen, signed a public letter to Lyndon Johnson ("Mr. President, please stop the bombing"), withheld the portion of my income tax that went for war, turned in my draft card. The latter two actions made me a criminal with an FBI file.[8]

The law and its institutions of enforcement, made and adjusted over centuries by white men of substance, constitute people like me as good citizens. They draw around us an invisible circle of respectability and allow us to conduct secure lives—except when exceeding the speed limit—in no conscious relation to police and the courts. When such a person steps outside the circle, everything taken-for-granted becomes problematic. I felt myself to be in a new and unstable relation not just to the State and the FBI but to other ordinary people (most of whom, in 1966, would have thought me unpatriotic or worse, had they known) and to the institutions of daily life. Its elements came unstuck.[9]

Mine were individual crimes, though of course not of my own invention. In 1965 I had heard that Chomsky (whom I greatly admired) and others were refusing to pay taxes, and by 1966 many young men had burned or otherwise unburdened themselves of draft cards. But I did not act with them or belong to their groups, and when I did band with others in organized opposition, that was a sharper breach from apolitical habit. I phoned antiwar colleagues and asked them to sign a public statement of support for Wesleyan students who refused induction; this felt very different from politicking with them about, say, a change in graduation requirements. Prompted by a phone call from Mitch Goodman (see the beginning of Mailer's *Armies of the Night* for an amusing account of the call *he* received from Mitch), I joined an action at the Justice Department before the 1967 march on the Pentagon. At the end of the rally, a few dozen of us (beyond draft age) filed across the steps of Justice, announced our names, and dropped our draft cards (in my case, a classification card, since I no longer had the other) in a sack of a thousand or so cards collected from draft age men around the country, and watched as the sack was carried inside and given in peaceful defiance to an official. My participation in this ritual brought me a predictable office visit the next Monday from two FBI agents, and some less predictable visibility. Walter Cronkite's evening news ran a five-minute clip of our civil disobedience, including my pass by the sack and declaration that I was "Richard Ohmann, Wesleyan University." This cameo appearance led to puzzled inquiries from two of our trustees that weekend at the inauguration of a new president (I was by then Associate Provost), and a call from my mother asking if I was all right—meaning was I under arrest yet and also, I surmise, how could I have so departed from her tutelage as to make a rude display of our family on national television?

Soon after, I helped found RESIST, an organization supporting various kinds of resistance to the war, legal and illegal. I signed its "Call to Resist Illegitimate Authority," and went to work on its board. We were all on the FBI's radar now (my mid-1970s file included many RESIST bulletins with every name on the masthead but mine blacked out), and some (the "Boston Five") were brought to trial for conspiracy. We encouraged civil disobedience and committed it. I found myself part of an informal network helping draft refusers and deserters leave the US, among other felonies that the FBI apparently did *not* detect. But self-criminalization was by then as habitual as lawfulness had been just a few years earlier. The change I felt most keenly in my social activity and location was membership in a big, loose affiliation called the anti-war movement, and soon the larger and looser one called simply The Movement. In this heady, naive moment we saw it as embracing civil rights and black power, women's liberation, student power, youth liberation, then gay rights, environmentalism, and so on, with a penumbra of sex rebels, drop-out communards, drug advocates, left sectarians—everyone saying no to the tyrannies and complacencies of the old order. In spite of deep and ultimately insuperable rifts, around 1970 it was possible to see ourselves as millions of people not only joined in opposition to "illegitimate authority" but working together for a free and egalitarian society. The word "revolution" was in play.

New organizations came together, new forms of collectivity. In addition to RESIST, I belonged for a while to SDS, worked in the New University Conference (left and feminist academics), helped form professional radical caucuses, checked out a couple of vanguard parties but couldn't accept democratic centralist discipline or adherence to "the line." We tried to live democracy, in New Left groups: the end would be our means. At the same time, many of us sought to subvert or reshape existing institutions such as the National Council of Teachers of English and the Modern Language Association—that they were malleable or even (in the case of NCTE) friendly shouldn't have been a surprise, since many of their members had passed through the same revulsions and illuminations as had activists from my quarter. Likewise the universities where we worked: clearly they were part of "the system" (a common term whose vagueness suggests the primitive nature of shared analysis at the time). They were complicit in war-making, white supremacy, capitalist rule. Maybe we could remake them to serve peace, justice, and ordinary people.

Here's the part of my experience that was odd. While positioning myself with the disempowered and against "the system," I had landed in its middle echelons, propelled by the momentum of my early career. In 1966, just when anger was spilling into protest, I took a job as Associate Provost in my college's administration, and became editor of *College English* as well as a member of the governing committee for NCTE's College Section, sponsor of the journal. I thought to facilitate reform at Wesleyan (reduced requirements, more interdepartmental studies, less autocratic tenure procedures, etc.) and a critique of the field of English (its aping of more scientific disciplines, amassing of endless New Critical explications, weakness in theory, inattention to its professional folkways). By 1970, when chaotic local events had elevated me to the post of interim Chancellor,[10] I had passed through the estrangements described above. Not reform, but radical change was my agenda. Yet at work I was charged with holding things together *against* radicals like me, and as editor of *CE*, with sustaining the dignity of a profession whose structure and practices I now thought carceral.

At *CE* the contradiction was tolerable and often productive. Colleagues around the country were furiously rethinking literature, writing, culture, pedagogy, and professional ideals in a fluid mix with power, injustice and democracy, war and peace, soon gender and sexuality. Manuscripts tumbled in. I accepted many that more conservative editors would have found unmannerly or outlandish. I also contracted with guest editors for clusters of articles or whole issues on themes heretofore incompatible with a professional or scholarly context: feminism, marxist criticism, the rebellion in MLA, emancipatory curricula in community colleges, gay liberation. These projects made *CE* controversial and of course offensive to some; though I published conservative articles, too, the journal was hardly a model of "balance" through this period. But neither was it completely out of step with thought and action in the field, or with the interests and concerns of NCTE's generally populist leadership, which at least tolerated and usually encouraged these editorial adventures.[11] I and my associate editor Bill Coley made a habit of transgression, but in the supportive company of very many readers and contributors, also caught up in "The Movement" or sympathetic to it.

At Wesleyan the contradiction was intense. Not that the trustees or my administrative superiors condemned my activism or made my tenure precarious: to the contrary, they seemed ready to boost me up a notch in the administrative hierarchy whenever campus tensions heightened. A few of them hated the war as much as I did; some demurred but sincerely endorsed the value of academic dissent and debate; perhaps some thought my presence a palliative to student and faculty radicals. (The word "coopt" came unpleasantly to mind.)

The problem was one of structure, not antagonism. An academic administrator like me can put out a few ideas and rally support for them, but most of his time and energy go to negotiation and compromise. Collect the desires and demands of faculty members and students, try to reconcile them with one another, see what the budget will stand, patch together a proposal, see how it fares in committees, hope that the result will be at least an incremental improvement. Not much leverage in the process for one's own passions against the weight of custom, institutional constraint, and other people's entrenched interests. In daily work, I was a sort of conduit.

Worse, in those frenzied years I often did crisis management. Our administration would drop all routine when protest or disruption threatened, and huddle in endless strategic sessions. How would we respond to the black students' occupation of a building? To the blockade of a military recruiter in the administration building? To a sit-in at the admissions office by Puerto Rican students demanding that more of their number be recruited? To a midnight assault by two black students on a white student who had written an insulting letter to the newspaper? To women faculty members and staff demanding that Wesleyan depart from its old, boys' club practices? I might be put on assignment to negotiate or control damage or write a bit of judicious administration-speak to faculty and students. Given my job, this made some sense, but always my sympathies were with the protesters, if not with a particular expression of their politics.

Sometimes the ambivalence of my position worked out all right, as when I sat with the black students' organization (after their takeover of a classroom building) to plan what eventually became our African American studies program; or negotiated with the women's group—among other things, for the hiring of a woman associate provost, who turned out to be the admirable Sheila Tobias.[12]

More often the dissonance was somewhere between comical and shattering. Toward the comical end: insisting that a Grateful Dead concert not be cancelled for fear of riot; declining to host a national SDS conference (I knew that SDS was about to implode in revolutionary adventurism); missing a meeting of the Student Affairs Committee, which I chaired, while in jail after doing civil disobedience outside a Sikorsky helicopter plant; representing Wesleyan at the inauguration of a new president at Mt. Holyoke, and standing—red-gowned, back turned to him and the other platform dignitaries, in protest against a ceremonial address by the war criminal McGeorge Bundy; giving a talk in a rally at Southeastern Massachusetts University against its autocratic president, and seeing our own president, deluged with angry letters from alums, respond to the effect that I was not representing Wesleyan, just exercising my right of free speech. Not a bad place to work.

Far from comical: having to decide in the middle of the night whether to accept or reverse the Dean's decision (he reported to me) to expel, without due process, the black students who had beaten up the white student;[13] in the conflict that followed, being thrown out of Malcolm X house along with the President as we were trying to make peace; being sent to observe the blockade of the military recruiter and being mistaken by my antiwar friends there for a fellow blockader, with quite understandable recriminations to follow; going to negotiate with the Puerto Rican students in the admissions office and being held hostage there myself. I lived uncomfortably in two polarized milieux: the educational bureaucracy and the movement challenging its legitimacy, along with the legitimacy of almost everything else.

A prickly contradiction it seems, even today. But I think my two-world experience, though perhaps unusually intense, was deeply congruent with that of many other thousands caught in the same historical turbulence. Teaching assistants and instructors, only somewhat less than full professors and the occasional provost, had labored to win academic authority, to master professional decorum, to build the kind of invulnerability I have described. Teaching, we performed routines of talk, dress, gesture, and classroom order legitimated by the bodies of knowledge that grounded our disciplines. Researching, we enacted loyalty to those knowledges even when we sought distinction by contesting their received truths. Going to meetings, which is to say administering, we paid tribute to the dignity of the institution even when trying to modify it—however we might ironize its rigidities and chafe at its demands.

But by 1968 or so, those who had followed a trajectory from anger at racial injustice or protest against the war to a conviction that our society was laced together with bad power had come to question the solidities that underlay those routines of daily, working life. The knowledges we professed were honeycombed with pockets of inexcusable ignorance (e.g., of women and black people), or shaped to the needs of Cold War ideology. They served technocratic domination or (worse) surveillance, terrorism, and war. The beloved institution—the university—appeared now to be complicit as well. "Who ruled Columbia?" and "Who ruled America?" turned out to be two forms of the same question. Our enclave of free inquiry and emancipatory culture looked instead like a conveyer of ideas that made Vietnam possible, and of students into predictable slots in the social hierarchy. I report these discoveries laconically, but don't mean to patronize them. They proceeded from feverish investigation and analysis, driven by both political and intellectual need—a "ruthless critique of all things existing," in one of my favorite phrases from Marx—and they decisively altered scholarship and curriculum in all traditional fields except the sciences. That's what the culture wars of the 80s and 90s have been about.

Through the time of these revaluations, the unbearable tension I have described between academic rituals and the injustice in which they were embedded began to look systematic. At first it read something like this: how can I be seriously deliberating whether to put a B or a B+ on this student's paper while the government is napalming peasants in my name? As ruthless critique proceeded, however, the disjunction reconfigured itself into a perceived unity: my painstaking enactment of the rituals *enables* warmaking (or helps this student escape the draft and sends that one to Vietnam; or reinforces the whiteness of the university system; or perpetuates the habits of male supremacy; or greases the skids of class reproduction and makes it look fair—and so on). The caucuses and study groups and activist organizations and coalitions and professional insurgencies and consciousness-raising groups that were piecing together a dissident, wholistic understanding of U.S. society and its imperial outreach turned the analysis, inevitably, back in on the institutions in which we worked, and on our own unexamined practices.

Of those, teaching came under the most careful scrutiny. For the first time in my experience groups of like-minded college teachers gathered outside the context of staff meetings to talk about pedagogy, because we saw it as political, in the broad sense of the term newly salient.[14] Every customary procedure that our professional training had naturalized now seemed laden with political relations, chiefly undemocratic: the lecture format, the inflexible syllabus, the canons it transmitted, the insularity of the disciplines, the exam, the unchallengeable paper topic, the gap between assignment and finished product wherein "process" later took up residence, the independence of each student's work, the grade meted out according to immutable standards. Classroom etiquette, too: last names, formal dress, discussion dominated by the more assertive, the absolute distinction between instructor and student. Architecture itself spoke hegemony. The form of the amphitheater, the lectern in front, ranks of desks bolted to the floor, all enforced the "banking concept" of education.

As we knocked down the walls that had set apart profession, pedagogy, and politics, a fourth "p" came forward: the personal. Famously, the women's movement legitimized public talk of the personal, in fact insisted upon it. That talk was in part a refuge from and assault on domination of antiwar venues by, well, us: by male "heavies" with "correct" political lines. But it also joined with and fortified a critique of professional detachment and scholarly objectivity already underway. To tell one's own story and hear the stories of others, we were learning, was to restore differences hidden behind *the* instructor and *the* student and *the* reader. Provided with genders, class locations, and so on, these characters now garbled the professional script in which they had been asked to perform as universals. A pedagogy of the lyric poem, meant to open vistas of timeless unity, might instead work for a first-generation student at a state college as a class put-down—the "laying on of culture," in a phrase we took from John MacDermott. An actual female reader of *Lady Chatterley's Lover* might not willingly take up the part assigned to her by Lawrence or by the male instructor. *The* profession meant something different for an adjunct writing teacher in a community college than for an ivied professor. Such banalities were fresh in 1968 or so, and narratives of personal experience were as crucial to the interrogation of professional ideology as to the making visible of male supremacy in interstices of daily conduct.

I think it important that the personal turn of the late sixties happened in groups of people joined by common purposes and shared anger—for me, the MLA Radical Caucus, the New University Conference, various faculty and student groups at Wesleyan (including, later, the Women's Studies collective), like-minded colleagues in NCTE and around my work for *College English*. In David Bleich's term (*Know and Tell*, see especially pp. 13-19), ours were *disclosures* of previously silenced experience that showed one person's discomfort or inadequacy or embarrassment or pleasure to be not after all unique, not inherently private. They expanded our affiliations and drove our activism as they deepened our understandings, and so helped "bring the subjective and the collective categories of experience together" (16). Sure, I recall explosions of runaway bitterness, indulgent confession, unusable ego—including my own. But the personal mode settled into movement process because it raised consciousness, and because it knit people together by clarifying the social relations in which we found ourselves and by hinting at how they might be changed.

Not that disclosure and political resolve automatically charted the way to worthwhile change. To speak only of teaching—my point of departure in this essay—the furious experimentation of the years around 1970 threw up a number of strategies that were largely stylistic. Wearing blue jeans to class instead of dresses or suits, using first names, meeting in informal spaces, sitting in circles or on the floor: these signalled eagerness to renegotiate authority in the classroom but did not forge new contracts, and by themselves led to "grooving in the grass"—structureless, feel-good pedagogy. Other strategies collided with invisible walls outside the classroom and the university itself. Take grading. Everyone saw that grades were invidious, poor incentives for learning, incompatible with serious collaboration, and (especially when linked to the military draft) consequential beyond anything intended by the award of a C rather than an A. So instructors tried no grades, pass-fail grades, giving all As, grading by lottery, self-grading, peer grading, and doubtless many other arrangements. All failed because students needed grades because in turn employers and graduate programs and draft boards required them. Our assignment was not just to teach and to generate certificates of learning, but to rank students for purposes of social sorting—the "reproduction," as we later would say, of class and race and gender systems. No socialism in one classroom, then, and we had to find other fields of battle.

This aside, in my view the ferment around teaching yielded healthy and lasting results. A democratic revolution in the U.S. was not one of them, but more democratic relations of instruction and *better* pedagogies did ensue. Collaborative learning, small group work, peer tutoring, flexible syllabi, responsiveness to the capabilities and needs and social positions that actual students bring with them to class, critical reflection on the learning process as it goes along, a humanizing of the instructor and demystifying of his or her authority (not abandonment of it), and many strategies to help students take responsibility for their own learning. The shift will seem old hat to likely readers of this volume because it has been most decisively achieved in women's studies, in writing instruction, and to a lesser extent in literature.

These pedagogical discoveries certainly transformed my own relation to teaching. Even the grooving-in-the grass phase was therapeutic in loosening rigidities of authority that had earlier caused me such confusion and discomfort. Teaching became a field of innovation, not an inflexible heritage of conventions. I could try new formats, decenter my precious authority, let down defenses, rethink the ways learning might happen. This was possible because I now felt teaching must respond to political as well as professional urgencies—Vietnam cried out in every classroom—and paradoxically, those urgencies made it far more personal than before. Still more important, I believe, was the conviction that even in my own classes I was working daily with many student and faculty allies (and of course against powerful antagonists), not striving to meet some heroic standard of individual performance.

Teaching never became easy for me, but challenge, imagination, achievement, and sometimes joy flowed into it. Stress came now from feverish but cheerful overwork, not helpless repetition of my defensive professional routines. There were small collaborative victories, institutions built,[15] pedagogies developed over time (see "Teaching as Theoretical Practice," chapter 8 in my *Politics of Letters*), the irreversible movement by thousands of colleagues in English and American studies to demystify and remake the literary canon. All this amounted to a cumulative and cooperative project, very different from the desperate scramble to escape each semester and turn with relief to the "real" work of scholarship.

About which a word, now, because the upheavals of c.1970 and the assumption of historical agency they provoked made for an entirely different relation between teaching and scholarship from the one I described earlier in this essay.

Those on the left came to see research and writing as charged with political urgency. In caucuses and collectives we intensively reexamined scholarly practices, their theoretical underpinnings, their historical construction, and their institutional housing. (See Kampf and Lauter [1972] for such an effort, in which I had a small part.) Many of us now took up research that aimed to question disciplinary givens and set new directions. Black studies, women's studies, working class studies, and gay and lesbian studies were the most visible expressions of that project, which not only created new subjects and won reputability for them, but changed what could reputably be thought and written about the traditional subjects, The engaged scholarship that ensued has of course been a scandal to the right, and a main battlefield of 1990s culture wars. It was an intellectual liberation for us, and in my view for the disciplines.

Be that as it may, the transformation brought my own teaching and research together in a refreshing and unanticipated way. From about 1972 on, almost everything I wrote answered directly or indirectly to a felt political imperative. In my teaching (I was lucky to be at a flexible college), I transited from English literature to American culture, and from a formalist to an historical outlook, furiously learning about economic and social theory along the way. Politics informed my teaching, and my teaching now became the basis of new research and writing.[16] I left behind my specialized training in linguistics and literature, taught what I studied, and studied what I needed to know to teach.

What I knew always trailed my need to know. And what I knew was always provisional, always in formation. This meant that my authority in class—earlier so precariously and often irrelevantly derived from scholarly credentials—now rested more on the openness of an inquiry whose difficulties I could happily admit, and to which students could contribute questions and insights that taught me things, as well as secure knowledge of their own, especially when the subject was mass culture, about which they inevitably knew more than I, at least experientially. So the social relations of scholarship and teaching overlapped and grew closer. The authority generated as the class moved along was as much as I wanted, and was the more satisfying because collaboratively built.[17]

Did these changes bring on a personal turn in my scholarship as well? Certainly not of the sort that academic feminist writing took, in the early seventies. I did not "speak bitterness," as the phrase went, about indignities and slights and oppressions that invaded my daily life from systemic inequality: how could I, or anyone situated as I was on the privileged side of most social boundaries? But I did let anger flow into my writing from the place it now occupied in my political life: this was a departure from the scholarly conventions I had previously learned, which permitted no tone more personal than huffy indignation at the stupidity of an intellectual antagonist. *English in*

America barely contained the rage that drove its composition—rage at war and oppression, of course, but also at what I took to be the complicity of my own discipline and its institutions. In criticizing these ("exposing" might better characterize what I thought I was doing), I did also give some authority to my own experience, and admitted more personal anecdote than I would have thought permissible before. After that (1976), I adopted a rather conversational academic style that felt personal to me at least in leaving behind the fortifications of tonal distance and disciplinary authority we had all used to guard our collective, professional capital. And more recently, taking advantage of the indulgence granted elderly folk, I have laced several articles with reminiscence. (Does experience somehow gather credibility and a claim on polite attention as it grows hoary?) This is by far my most personal essay,[18] and, since it unsettles me, I doubt I'll prowl farther along this path. In any case, the most important way in which I imagine my scholarship of the last 25 years to have been personal is by following imperatives of the movements in which I claimed membership. The personal is the political, yes, and I want to emphasize how *social* it has been for me, how saturated with affinities and alliances and conflicts both real and (no doubt) fanciful.

At the beginning of the last section I hoped that its first person story would ground "a discussion of more general interest." That, I now attempt, with abundant reservations about what may be justly concluded from any such account—reservations, that is, about whether I've written anything of use to other people, these last many pages. What I've *meant* to do is historicize the personal turn that many academics have taken since 1970. But by means of my own history as I choose to tell it, or maybe can't help telling it? What presumption lies in that strategy: that my experience has been paradigmatic, that I can in this way represent the many people assembled from time to time, without their consent, inside my "we." I'm suspicious of the personal even as I practice it, about which more later.

But first, to draw out the inferences I want from this story: the rules of college teaching and academic writing began changing, around 1970, under pressure from activists in feminism and other movements, to admit a good deal more of personal experience and feeling than had been respectable or even tolerable before. The thinking behind this pressure was simple. Movement people identified rhetorics of impersonal authority with the lies our leaders told us about Vietnam, with the crackpot rationale for war, with the complicity of the corporate university, with cost-benefit analysis that left human suffering and harm to nature outside its equations, with social engineering that treated the lives of poor and non-white people as problems to be solved from above, with male assumptions of privilege, with the bromide that in America we had no social classes, with curricula and pedagogies driven by professional imperatives and thus abstractly "irrelevant" to students' needs, with scholarship that justified or took as natural the world as it was—in effect, with all that seemed ignorantly hierarchical and undemocratic in our supposedly egalitarian society. To recognize experience and speak from it was a step toward truth and decency. Furthermore, in the practice of dissident groups, especially feminist ones, the personal turn at its best delivered radical insight, strenghened sisterhood and solidarity, and helped build new institutions and ways of working together.

The specific conditions of historical possibility that enabled a liberatory personal turn three decades ago are attenuated or gone. The ferment of rage and opposition and experiment and discovery within which we learned to speak truth (personal and otherwise) to power has simmered down. "The movement" that never quite was, but whose idea stirred millions to transformative action, looks naive in retrospect about how much and what kinds of power laced "the system" together, and about what would be required to replace it with something better. Not that the movement disappeared: rather, it dispersed into more specialized campaigns, whose partial victories are everywhere embedded (sometimes precariously) in U.S. society now. Women become physicians, executives, Secretaries of State. Abortion is an embattled right. Migrant farmworkers are powerfully organized. African Americans attend previously white colleges and law schools in large numbers, travel where and how they will, buy homes in suburbs, are heard from in national media (and constructed as avid consumers in TV commercials, right alongside white yuppies). Gay and lesbian people have meager but previously unimaginable rights. Corporations cannot destroy the natural world with complete impunity. Vietnam is free of U.S. occupation, and what was known for a while as the "Vietnam syndrome" now apparently prevents us from invading countries (but allows us to bomb up to four per year) Anyone can add to this list, and although to do so is simultaneously to realize how incomplete and disconnected the advances have been, they are not nothing, either.

And my list omits the site where movement gains have taken root most deeply: the university—or rather, that part of it where we study the humanities and social sciences, and where we pursue and debate "personal effects." Here, the change is tectonic. Look around at the various "studies" programs that were unimaginable in 1965, each the academic sedimentation of a social movement. Look at how we have changed the subject within traditional fields—the texts that appear on syllabi, the questions that can be asked about them, the vast enlargement (in the humanities) of what we take culture to be, the intellectual seriousness and partial autonomy of rhetoric and composition studies, and the infusion of politics (broad sense) into all these studies. Look at the changes in teaching and scholarship that have been my topic in this essay. The liberal arts curriculum, understood most deeply as the texts and problematics and ways of thinking that we put on students' and our own agendas—the curriculum has become quite another thing in three decades, gradually transformed by the urgencies of c. 1970.

It's almost enough to cheer up a decaying leftie. But as I was saying before this optimistic swerve, history has left behind the conditions that brought personal experience into fruitful play back then. First, the academic movement that changed our work has grown apart from the activism that initially inspired it. (With many commendable exceptions, but still.) We now enact and dispute the personal in a conversation chiefly among ourselves, on terms that have more to do with academic politics or even fashion than with changing the world. Second, "the" movement that didn't quite happen has fragmented into largely separate social movements, so that when the academic "I" does reach out beyond the academy it tends to make contact with identity politics, where who "I" am is most saliently female, or disabled, or Asian American, or gay, or. . . . In this situation the personal tends to imply that identities are given and fixed, to reify difference, to veer away from disclosures that might strengthen a universalist solidarity or even point toward coalitions.

Third, the gains of sixties movements provoked a reaction from the New Right. By 1964, it had already come in from the fringe (the John Birch Society, and such) around Goldwater's candidacy, and it took new strength from its opposition to what the sixties came to mean for much of "middle America ." Through the 1970s, it established right wing foundations, organized among Christian fundamentalists, contested for power within the Republican Party, and gradually reconfigured American politics. It vigorously challenged the liberal hegemony of the postwar decades, and in the process demonized the social movements that had built momentum within that hegemony. The culture wars of the 1990s were one manifestation of that conservative reaction, and in them the Right took aim as much at positions won by radicals *in the university* as at those won in Congress and the courts. Whatever weight the personal may still carry in our internal conversations, it seems to me ill-adapted to a defense of the university against charges of political correctness or of multiculturalism grounded in identities.

And finally: since 1970 our economic system and social formation have been passing through a fairly deep transformation. This is not a subject to be wrapped up in a paragraph. Let me simply gesture toward globalization: the rapid movement of capital (in a hundred new forms) around the world, the proliferation of new products and services, the repackaging and incessant commodification of knowledge, the breakup of the old Fordist work force, the casualization of labor, the application of market logic to institutions of all kinds, and so on. These forces have been at work in and on the university, needless to say, producing there a crisis whose dimensions—from the erosion of tenure and collapse of the old job market to the marketization of academic services and research—are familiar enough to likely readers of this essay. Our profession (along with medicine, law and most of the others) is in decline. The personal turn was in part a challenge to its claims of authority, and those of the fat and complacent postwar university. Does it still have that meaning? Do we want it to, in our present circumstances?

Those circumstances are much on my mind: I imagine the tasks of and threats to a democratic left at millenium's end to be starkly different from what they were in 1970. If I'm right, is that cause for those who share egalitarian and democratic goals to abandon the personal, to declare it mined out and anachronistic? It's hard to separate that question from my own uneasiness with disclosure—doubtless evident enough to the reader of this mixed essay, so determined to become an argument or a master narrative, so uncomfortable in its personal moments, so burdened with its author's male, middle class, childhood instruction in the shame of making scenes or showing vulnerability. No wonder such a person, even after decades of contrary instruction, tends to hear accounts of personal experience in academic or other public discourse as outbreaks of self-indulgence among the privileged, or competitive displays of victimization, or unsporting claims on sympathy, and in any case distractions from the urgent work at hand.

No, I do not think the personal vein is bled dry or politically irrelevant. But let me add two thoughts to the caveat embedded in my attempt to historicize it. The personal itself is not a stable category, any more than the "real" in literary representation. Conventions of privacy change. Richard E. Miller tells a nice anecdote of his Rutgers seminar for beginning teachers of composition. By request, he included a session on coming out as gay or lesbian in class, a topic not just taboo but inimaginable, thirty years ago. Excited discussion, revelation, story upon story, until one TA came out to the seminar as a *Christian*, and revealed her fear of doing that in her comp section. Consternation and silence. Miller comments that "what gets seen as merely merely personal and better left unsaid in the academy has shifted over time and across locations. . ." (280). Globalization and the crisis of the university have brought coming-out stories by graduate TAs, adjuncts and other casualties of the new order, linked to organizing struggles on university campuses and in organizations like MLA. Are there other realms of what used to be "better left unsaid" to be explored now, by way of building new memberships and collectivities?

Second, it is easy to understand how the word "objective" sprouted cynical quotation marks, how "abstract" and "impersonal" became pejoratives, how "formal," "linear," and "adversarial" came under censure.[19] No plea, here, for a return to the blindly self-assured, contestatory, male academic conventions of 1965. But the inheritors of sixties movements have real enemies who can't be conjured away by forswearing the adversarial style. We need (maybe more than ever) new knowledge of this difficult world in order to try changing it; that knowledge will have to be in part abstract because real relations are not evident on the surface of things; and we can't get there without working through the impossible ideal of objectivity. (Would "fairness" and "open-mindedness" be more acceptable terms?) The knowledge we need must be personal, too, but will not accord epistemological privilege to personal experience. Joan Scott: "When experience is taken as the origin of knowledge, the vision of the individual subject . . . becomes the bedrock of evidence on which explanation is built," and "the constructed nature of experience" becomes invisible, along with the "given ideological systems" in which experience offers itself as pristine and natural (Scott 777-78). For all that, the personal turn has I think been more beneficial than not. It is in any case irreversible. I hope we can keep alive in it the social and the political, from which it has historically been inseparable, and without which it is at best incomplete and isolating.

NOTES

1. Here's a symptomatic story: one paper was a third-person account, modeled on Henry Adams, of "the boy's" first walk into Harvard yard. Hal Martin thought it was wonderful, and wanted to submit it to the alumni magazine (which did in fact print it). I had given it a B+, and asked Hal if he thought that a little ungenerous. Yes, he said. I changed the grade to A. Did the student benefit from my exquisitely high standards? A grad student colleague of mine, when asked why a grade was so low, would say: "For a B, you have to write as well as I do; for an A, as well as Hemingway." Western civilization was safe in our hands.
2. Mentor and friend, Hal saw better than I what I could do, and launched my career.
3. No one spoke these lessons to me and my graduate student cohort; they were in the air we breathed. Yet in time I did actually take vows of scholarship, administered with great seriousness to inductees into Harvard's Society of Fellows, by such as W. V. Quine, Wassily Leontiev, and my dissertation director Harry Levin. For example:

You will practice the virtues, and avoid the snares, of the scholar. You will be courteous to your elders who have explored to the point from which you may advance; and helpful to your juniors who will progress farther by reason of your labors. Your aim will be knowledge and wisdom, not the reflected glamour of fame. You will not accept credit that is due to another, or harbor jealousy of an explorer who is more fortunate. You will seek not a near but a distant objective, and you will not be satisfied with what you may have done. All that you may achieve or discover you will regard as a fragment of a larger pattern of the truth which from the separate approaches every true scholar is striving to descry.

A high vocation, a heady moment.

4. What a missed opportunity for discussion of literature and belief, of my and the students' relations to the texts we were reading and the culture we were studying.
5. To have done so at the time would have been all but unthinkable, in a context such as the present one. I remember a few personal essays about teaching, for instance Theodore Roethke's marvelous "Last Class" (*College English*, 18:8 [May, 1957], 383-86). But see: reminiscence was a prerogative of poets and novelists.
6. In the process I became more explicitly the interpreter, as well as teller, of my tale. It's hard for the "personal turn" to displace lifelong habits of academic authority.
7. And have done: see my "English and the Cold War."
8. When I obtained it in the mid-1970s, under the Freedom of Information Act, I was surprised to find how many tax dollars the FBI had squandered clipping my letters to the *Middletown Press* and to Wesleyan's student newspaper, and also miffed that its agents had sized me up as a sincere but harmless protester, not a dangerous enemy of the State.
9. A friend stopped me on the street: his first grade kid came home from school with the news that I was likely to go to jail. I had tried to explain what I was doing to *my* first grade kid, and she disclosed her version of the story in "show and tell."
10. Translation: academic vice president. Since our president more or less vacated the premises that year, I and the other vice president found ourselves in charge, though hardly in control.
11. Objections from readers of *CE* were plentiful, and I dutifully printed those that came in as letters. A few members of NCTE called for my ouster. But in the twelve years of my editorship, those in the Council to whom I was directly responsible grumbled aloud to me only once: not about unpatriotic or marxist or feminist sallies in the journal, but about a 1974 special issue on "The Homosexual Imagination." Interesting.

12. And for a parental leave policy, the one idea too much before its time to be enacted.
13. I supported the Dean. He went on to become president of a big state university. I returned to teaching as fast as I was able.
14. The discussion spilled out into journals, as well, particularly in English. My own commitments are perhaps enough to explain the proliferation of articles in CE that reexamined pedagogy under the sign of the political, but the same interest invaded the pages of *College Composition and Communication*, whose editor (William Irmscher) espoused politics very different from mine.
15. For instance, the student-led course, "Towards a Socialist America," which reproduced itself at Wesleyan through shifts in political climate, official opposition, a softening of purpose and of title, over twenty years. (See Arneson et al.) The course was accorded a surprising honor when Lynne Cheney attacked its catalog derscription (ignorantly) on the editorial page of the *Wall St. Journal*, March 14, 1996.
16. *Selling Culture*, my most learned work, germinated in a course I taught on American mass culture (with invaluable help from undergraduate TAs) in the late seventies, and gained momentum from several other courses that I devised along the way—courses very far from my early training and interests.
17. Yes, I doled out the grades; no escape from that. Two strategies eased the contradictions. First, I made grading a subject of explicit discussion, often in the context of power and social reproduction as these topics came up in the course. Second, in comments on papers I excused myself from the task of explaining the grades I had given. I credited students with having taken seriously an intellectual challenge and written something they stood behind, not just having tried to please me in an academic exercise. (This working premise was of course not always correct.) I framed my comments as responses to their ideas, often critical but not according to some paradigm of A-ness or C+-ness to which I had privileged access. If they wanted to know why I had assigned the grade I had, and how to get a better one, they could come and talk with me about that. Few did. And I came to take intellectual as well as teacherly pleasure in reading sets of papers.
18. Even so, I can hear the muse chiding: look at what you've left out—family, friends, health, sex, disaster, guilt, pleasure, everything *really* personal. True. By comparison with, say, Jane Gallop (whom I admire), I'm a timid hand at this.
19. For a lexicon inflected this way, see, e.g. Freedman et al., especially the introduction and the essays by Frey and Jane Tompkins. I agree with them but want to save some of what they object to, in both intellectual and political work.

REFERENCES

Abel, E. 1993. Black Writing, White Reading: Race and the Politics of Feminist Interpretation. *Critical Inquiry* 19.3.

Abraham, N. and M. Torok. 1994. *The Shell and the Kernel.* Volume I. Ed. and trans., Nicholas T. Rand. Chicago: University of Chicago Press.

Ackroyd, P. 1999. Biography: The Short Form. Review of *Marcel Proust* by Edmund White and *Crazy Horse* by Larry McMurtry. *NY Times Book Review* 10 Jan.

Adan, J. 1991. *The Children in Our Lives: Knowing and Teaching Them.* Albany: State University of NY Press.

Adell, S. 1994. *Double-Consciousness/Double Bind: Theoretical Issues in Twentieth-Century Black Literature.* Urbana: University of Illinois Press.

Anderson, B. 1994. Exodus. *Critical Inquiry* 20.2.

———. 1991. *Imagined Communities: Reflections on the Origin and Spread of Nationalism,* Revised Edition. London: Verso.

Anzaldua, G. 1987. *Borderlands/La Frontera: The New Mestiza.* San Francisco: Spinsters/Aunt Lute.

Appiah, K. A. 1992. *In My Father's House: Africa in the Philosophy of Culture.* NY: Oxford University Press.

Arneson, E. et al. 1978. A Student Initiated Course in Socialism. *Radical Teacher* 9.

Ashton-Warner, S. 1963. *Teacher.* NY: Bantam Books.

Atwell-Vasey, W. 1998. *Nurturing Words: Bridging Private Readings and Public Teaching.* Albany: State University of NY Press.

Atkins, G. D. 1992. *Estranging the Familiar: Towards a Revitalized Critical Writing.* Athens: University of Georgia Press.

Austen, J. 1933. *The Novels of Jane Austen,* ed. R.W. Chapman. London and NY: PRESS?

Awkward, M. 1995. *Negotiating Difference: Race, Gender, and the Politics of Positionality.* Chicago: University of Chicago Press.

Axtell, J. 1997. Twenty-Five Reasons to Publish. *Journal of Scholarly Publishing* 29.1.

Azoulay, K. G. 1998. (White) Women and (Racial Diversity) in the Academy: Reflections on Intentions and Interventions. *The Review of Education/Pedagogy/Cultural Studies* 20.3.

———. 1996. Outside Our Parent's House: Race, Culture and Identity. *Review of African Literature* 27.1

———. 1997. *Black, Jewish and Interracial: It's Not the Color of Your Skin but the Race of Your Kin and Other Myths of Identity*. London & Durham: Duke University Press.

———. 1989. Familiar Themes. *The Jerusalem Post* (18 November)

Bachman, L. 1995. Unpublished essay.

Bachya, A. 1993. *Biur al ha-Torah*. Ed. Chaim Shavel, Vol 2,. Jerusalem: Mossad Ha-Rav Kook.

Bain, A. 1867. *English Composition and Rhetoric: A Manual*. NY: Appleton,

Bakhtin, M. M. 1981. Discourse in the Novel. *The Dialogic Imagination*. Ed. Michael Holquist. Austin: University of Texas Press.

Baldwin, J. 1957. *Notes of a Native Son*. Boston: Beacon.

Balibar, E. and I. Wallerstein. 1991. *Race, Nation, Class: Ambiguous Identities*. NY: Verso.

Bartholomae, D. 1985. Inventing the University. *When a Writer Can't Write*. Ed. Mike Rose. NY: Guilford.

Bartholomae, D. and A. Petrosky. 1986. *Facts, Artifacts and Counterfacts: Theory and Method for a Reading and Writing Course*. Portsmouth: Heinemann.

———. 1999. *Ways of Reading*. 5th ed. Boston: St. Martin's/Bedford.

Bauer, D. 1995. Personal Criticism and the Academic Personality. *Who Can Speak? Authority and Critical Identity*, ed. Roof and Wiegman. Urbana: University of Illinois Press.

Becker, S. 1995. Ugly Letters. *The Virginia Quarterly Review* 71.1.

Beebee, T. 1994. *The Ideology of Genre: A Comparative Study of Generic Instability*. University Park, PA: Pennsylvania State University Press.

Begam, R. 1992. An Interview with J.M. Coetzee. *Contemporary Literature* 33.3.

Behad, A. 1993. Traveling to Teach: Postcolonial Critics in the American Academy. *Race, Identity and Representation in Education*, ed. McCarthy and Crichlow, 40-49. NY: Routledge.

Behar, R. 1996. *The Vulnerable Observer: Anthropology That Breaks Your Heart*. Boston: Beacon.

———. 1995. Writing in My Father's Name: A Diary of *Translated Woman's* First Year. Behar and Gordon.

——— and D. A. Gordon. 1995. *Women Writing Culture*. Berkeley: University of California Press.

Belenky, M. F., et al. 1986. *Women's Ways of Knowing: The Development of Self, Voice, and Mind*. NY: Basic Books.

Benhabib, S. 1992. *Situating the Self*. Routledge, NY.

Benjamin, J. 1988. *The Bonds of Love: Psychoanalysis, Feminism, and the Problem of Domination*. NY: Pantheon.

Benjamin, W. A 1986. Berlin Chronicle. *Reflections*, trans. Jephcott. NY: Schocken Books.

Berlant, L. 1991. *The Anatomy of National Fantasy: Hawthorne, Utopia, and Everyday Life*. Chicago: University of Chicago Press.

———. The Theory of Infantile Citizenship. In *The Queen of America Goes to Washington City: Essays on Sex and Citizenship*. Durham, NC: Duke University Press.

———. 1995. The Queen of America Goes to Washington City. In C. N. Davidson and M. Moon, eds. *Subjects and Citizens: Nation, Race, and Gender from "Oroonoko" to Anita Hill*. Durham: Duke University Press, 455-480.

Berlin, J. 1996. *Rhetorics, Poetics, and Cultures: Refiguring College English Studies*. Urbana: NCTE.

———. 1987. *Rhetoric and Reality: Writing Instruction in American Colleges, 1900-1985*. Carbondale: Southern Illinois University Press.

———. 1988. Rhetoric and Ideology in the Writing Class. *College English* 50.5.

———. 1982. Contemporary Composition: The Major Pedagogical Theories. *College English* 44.8.

Bérubé, M. 1994. *Public Access: Literary Theory and American Cultural Politics*. London: Verso.

———. 1996. Against Subjectivity. *PMLA* 111.5.

———. 1994. Beneath the Return to the Valley of the Culture Wars. *Contemporary Literature* 35.1.

———. 1993. Discipline and Theory. *Wild Orchids and Trotsky*. NY: Penguin.

Bhabha, H. 1994. Respondent in panel Homi Bhabha: The Location of Culture. MLA Convention, San Diego.

Bing, V. and P. T. Reid. 1996. Unknown Women and Unknowing Research: Consequences of Color and Class in Feminist Pedagogy. *Knowledge, Difference, and Power: Essays Inspired by Women's Ways of Knowing*. NY: Basic Books.

Bleich, D. 1978. *Subjective Criticism*. Baltimore, MD: Johns Hopkins University Press.

———. 1995. Academic Ideology and the New Attention to Teaching. *New Literary History* 26.

———. 1988. *The Double Perspective: Language, Literacy & Social Relations*. NY: Oxford. Rpt 1993, Urbana: NCTE.

———. 1998. *Know and Tell: A Writing Pedagogy of Disclosure, Genre, and Membership*. Portsmouth NH: Boynton/Cook.

Bloom, H. 1994. *The Western Canon*. NY: Harcourt, Brace.

Bloom, L. 1995. Review: Voices from the Ark. *College English* 57.

Booth, W. 1966. *The Rhetoric of Fiction* Chicago: University of Chicago Press.

Bourdieu, P. 1984. *Distinction, A Social Critique of the Judgment of Taste*. Trans. R. Nice. Cambridge, MA: Harvard University Press.

———. 1988. *Homo Academicus*. Cambridge: Polity Press.

———. 1990. *In Other Words: Essays Towards a Reflexive Sociology*. Stanford: Stanford University Press.

———, and J. D. W. Loic. 1992. *An Invitation to Reflexive Sociology.* Chicago: University of Chicago Press.

Boynton, V. 1996. Desire's Revision: Feminist Appropriation of Native American Traditional Stories. *Modern Language Studies* 26.2-3.

Brecht, B. 1964. *Brecht on Theatre.* trans. John WIllet, London: Methuen.

Brink, A. 1983. *Mapmakers: Writing in a State of Siege.* London: Faber and Faber.

Britzman, D. 1998. *Lost Subjects, Contested Objects: Toward a Psychoanalytic Inquiry of Learning.* State University of NY Press.

Brodkey, L. 1996. *Writing Permitted in Designated Areas Only.* Minneapolis: University of Minnesota Press.

———. 1994. Writing on the Bias. *College English* 56.5.

Boone, J. 1996. The Inevitability of the Personal. Forum. *PMLA* 3.5.

Brodbribb, S. 1992. *Nothing Mat(t)ers: A Feminist Critique of Postmodernism.* North Melbourne, Victoria: Spinifex.

Bruner, J. 1990. *Acts of Meaning.* Cambridge, MA: Harvard University Press.

———. 1996. *The Culture of Education.* Harvard University Press. Cambridge.

Buber, M. 1955. The Education of Character. *Between Man and Man.* Boston: Beacon.

Burnham, C. 1993. Expressive Rhetoric: A Source Study. *Defining the New Rhetorics,* ed. Enos and Brown. Newbury Park: Sage.

Butler, J. 1997. *The Psychic Life of Power: Theories of Subjection.* Stanford: Stanford University Press.

Caesar, T. 1996. Letter. Forum: Problems with Personal Criticism. *PMLA* 111.5.

Campbell, G. 1969. *The Philosophy of Rhetoric,* ed. Bitzer. Carbondale: Southern Illinois University Press.

Camper, C., ed. 1994. *Miscegenation Blues: Voices of Mixed Race Women.* Toronto: SisterVision.

Capra, F. 1975. *The Tao of Physics: An Exploration of the Parallels between Modern Physics and Eastern Mysticism.* Boulder, Colorado: Shambhala.

Cassity, K. 1998. E-mail to author. 27 January.

———. 1997. Embracing Student Voices: A Journey into Peter Elbow's Composition Classroom. Master's Thesis, University of Hawaii.

Chambers, I. 1990. *Border Dialogues: Journeys in Postmodernity.* NY: Routledge.

Chamoiseau, P., R. Confiant, and J. Bernabé. 1990. *Éloge de la Créolité.* Baltimore: Johns Hopkins University Press.

Chatterjee, R. 1996. An Explosion of Difference: The Margins of Perception in 'Sammy and Rosie Get Laid.' *Between the Lines: South Asians and Postcoloniality,* ed Bahri and Vasudeva. Philadelphia: Temple University Press.

Chiseri-Strater, E. and B. Sunstein. 1997. *FieldWorking: Reading and Writing Research.* Upper Saddle River, New Jersey: Prentice Hall.

Chodorow, N. 1978. *The Reproduction of Mothering: Psychoanalysis and the Sociology of Gender.* Berkeley: University of California Press.

Cixous, H. and C. Clément. 1991. *The Newly Born Woman*. Trans. Wing. Minneapolis: University of Minnesota Press.

Cohen, L. 1996. From Town Center to Shopping Center: The Reconfiguration of Community Marketplaces in Postwar America. *American Historical Review* 101, 4: 1050–1081.

Cohen, R. 1987. Reviewing Criticism: Literary Theory. *Literary Reviewing*, ed. Hoge. Charlottesville: University of Virginia Press.

Coles, R. 1989. *The Call of Stories: Teaching and the Moral Imagination*. Boston: Houghton Mifflin.

———. 1999. *Black Writers Abroad: A Study of Black American Writers in Europe and Africa*. NY: Garland.

Coles, W. E., Jr. and J. Vopat, eds. 1985. *What Makes Writing Good: A Multiperspective*. Lexington: D. C. Heath.

Connolly, M. F., and D. J. Clandinin. 1988. *Teachers as Curriculum Planners*, Toronto: OISE.

Cooper, A. 1988 [1892]. *A Voice from the South*. NY: Oxford University Press.

Costello, B. 1991. *Questions of Mastery*. Cambridge: Harvard University Press.

Courts, P. L. 1991. *Literacy and Empowerment: The Meaning Makers*. NY: Bergin & Garvey.

Crapanzano, V. 1990. On Dialogue. *The Interpretation of Dialogue*, ed. Maranhao. Chicago: University of Chicago Press.

Crawford, M. and R. Chaffin. 1986. The Reader's Construction of Meaning: Cognitive Research on Gender and Comprehension. Flynn and Schweickart.

Crews, F. 1970. Anaesthetic Criticism. *Psychoanalysis and Literary Process*, ed. Crews. Cambridge, MA: Winthrop Publishers.

Daly, B. 1998. *Authoring a Life: A Woman's Survival in and through Literary Studies*. Albany: State University of NY Press.

———. 2000. Weeping for the Mother: A Feminist Daughter Calls for Continuing Change in the Public Schooling of Girls. *Women's Issues in Literature and Life Assembly*. Vol IX.

Danticat, E. 1991. *Krik? Krak!* NY: Soho Press.

Davidson, C. 1996. Critical Fictions. *PMLA* 111.5.

Davies, C. 1996. Letter. Forum: The Inevitability of the Personal. *PMLA* 111.5.

de Certeau, M. 1984. *The Practice of Everyday Life*. Berkeley: University of California Press.

Delia, M. 1991. *Killer English: Postmodern Theory and the High School Classroom*. PhD. Diss. University of Maryland, College Park.

Delpit, L. 1988. The Silenced Dialogue: Power and Pedagogy in Educating Other People's Children. *Harvard Educational Review* 58.3.

Dewey, J. 1984. The Quest for Certainty. *The Collected Works of John Dewey: The Later Works, 1925-1953*, ed. Boydston. Carbondale: Southern Illinois University Press.

DeSalvo, L. 1996. *Vertigo: A Memoir*. NY: Penguin/Dutton.

Dickstein, M. 1998. A Man Nobody Knew. *NY Times Book Review*. Sept. 20. 43.

Dinnerstein, D. 1976. *The Mermaid and the Minotaur: Sexual Arrangements and Human Malaise*. NY: Harper and Row.

DiPardo, A. 1989. Narrative Knowers, Expository Knowledge: Discourse as Dialectic. ED304688. Berkeley: Center for the Study of Writing.

Dovidio, J. 1997. 'Aversive' Racism and the Need for Affirmative Action. *The Chronicle of Higher Education* (25 July), A60.

Dowling, W. C. 1997. Saving Scholarly Publishing in the Age of Oprah: The Glastonbury Project. *Journal of Scholarly Publishing* 28.3.

Duberman, M. 1991. *Cures: A Gay Man's Odyssey*. New York: Dutton.

Duster, A. M., ed. 1970. *Crusade for Justice: The Autobiography of Ida B. Wells*. Chicago: University of Chicago Press.

Eakin, P. 1985. *Fictions in Autobiography: Studies in the Art of Self-Invention*. Princeton: Princeton University Press.

Ede, L. and A. Lunsford. 1990. *Singular Texts/Plural Authors: Perspectives on Collaborative Writing*. Carbondale: Southern Illinois University Press.

———. 2001. Collaboration and Concepts of Authorship. *PMLA* 116.6.

Edmondson, M. ed. 1993. *Wild Orchids and Trotsky*. NY: Penguin.

Elbow, P. 1995. Being a Writer vs. Being an Academic: A Conflict in Goals. *CCC* 46.

Elder, D. 1994. Different Climbs. *College English* 56.5.

Eldred, J. 1991. Narratives of Socialization: Literacy in the Short Story. *College English* 53.6.

Elshtain, J. 1981. *Public Man, Private Woman*. Oxford: M. Robertson.

Ellsworth, E. 1997. *Teaching Positions: Difference, Pedagogy and the Power of Address*. NY: Teachers College Press.

Emigh, J. 1996. *Masked Performances: The Play of Self and Other in Ritual and Theatre*. Philadelphia: University of Pennsylvania Press.

Emmett, A. 1996. *Our Sisters' Promised Land: Women, Politics and Israeli-Palestinian Coexistence*. Ann Arbor: University of Michigan Press.

Espada, M. 1994. Niggerlips. *Cool Salsa: Bilingual Poems on Growing Up Latino in the United States*. Ed. Lori M. Carlson, NY: Fawcett Juniper.

Faigley, L. 1992. *Fragments of Rationality: Postmodernity and the Subject of Composition*. Pittsburgh: University of Pittsburgh Press.

Fanon, F. 1967. *Black Skin, White Masks*. Trans. Markmann. NY: Grove.

———. 1965. *The Wretched of the Earth*. NY: Grove.

Farrell, T. J. 1979. The Male and Female Modes of Rhetoric. *College English* 40.

Felman, S. 1993. *What Does a Woman Want: Reading and Sexual Difference*. Baltimore: The Johns Hopkins University Press.

Fenton, J. 1996. A Short History of Anti-Hamitism. *NY Review of Books*. 43.3.

Fields, B. 1990. Slavery, Race and Ideology in the United States of America. *New Left Review*. No. 18.

Fischer, K. 1997. The Soul of America: An Increasingly Fractured Society Sends the Nation on a Quest for Faith. *Smith Alumnae Quarterly* (Spring).

Fish, S. 1985. Anti-professionalism. *New Literary History* 17.

———. 1988. No bias, no merit: The case against blind submission. *PMLA* 103.

Fishman, S. and L. McCarthy. 1998. *John Dewey and the Challenge of Classroom Practice*. Urbana, IL: NCTE.

Flynn, E. 1988. Composing as a Woman. *CCC* 39.

——— and Schweickart, P. 1986. *Gender and Reading: Essays on Readers, Texts, and Contexts*. Baltimore: The Johns Hopkins University Press.

Foucault, M. 1972. *The Archaeology of Knowledge*. NY: Tavistock.

Freud, S. 1989. Mourning and Melancholia. *The Freud Reader*, ed. Gay. NY: Norton.

Frank, A. 1995. Lecturing and Transference: The Undercover Work of Pedagogy. *Pedagogy and the Question of Impersonation*, ed. Gallop Bloomington: Indiana University Press.

Franklin, B. 1889. *The Autobiography of Benjamin Franklin*. NY: Alden,

Fraser, N. 1989. *Unruly Practices: Power, Discourse, and Gender in Contemporary Social Theory*. Minneapolis: University of Minnesota Press.

Frazier, C. 1997. *Cold Mountain*. NY: Atlantic Monthly Press.

Freedman, D. P. 1992. *An Alchemy of Genres: Cross-Genre Writing by American Feminist Poet-Critics*. Charlottesville: University Press of Virginia.

———. 1996. Autobiographical Literary Criticism as the New Belletrism. *Confessions of the Critics*, ed. Veeser. NY: Routledge.

———. 1992. The Creatively Critical Voice. *The Bucknell Review*. (Sep).

———, O. Frey, and F. M. Zauhar, eds., 1993. *The Intimate Critique: Autobiographical Literary Criticism*. Durham: Duke University Press.

Friedman, J. 1992. The Past in the Future: History and the Politics of Identity. *American Anthropologist* 94.4.

Froula, C. 1989. The Daughter's Seduction: Sexual Violence and Literary History. *Daughters and Fathers*, eds. Boose and Flowers. Baltimore: Johns Hopkins University Press.

Gallop, J. 1985. *Reading Lacan*. Ithaca: Cornell University Press.

———. 1988. *Thinking Through the Body*. NY: Columbia University Press.

———. 1996. The Inevitability of the Personal. Forum. *PMLA* 111.5

———. 1997. *Feminist Accused of Sexual Harassment*. Durham: Duke.

———, M. Hirsch, and N. K. Miller. 1990. Criticizing Feminist Criticism. *Conflicts in Feminism*, ed. Hirsch and Keller. NY: Routledge.

Gannett, C. 1992. *Gender and the Journal: Diaries and Academic Discourse*. Albany, NY: State University of NY Press.

Gates, H. L, Jr. 1994. *Colored People*. New York: Knopf.

———. Goodbye, Columbus? Notes on the Culture of Criticism. *American Literary History* 3.4

———. 1992. *Loose Canons: Notes on the Culture Wars*. NY: Oxford University Press.

———, et al, eds. 1997. *Norton Anthology of African-American Literature*. NY: Norton.

Gee, J. 1990. *Social Linguistics and Literacies: Ideology in Discourses*. London: Felmer.

Geertz, C. 1983. *Local Knowledge: Further Essays in Interpretive Anthropology*. NY: Basic.

———. 1980. Blurred Genres. *American Scholar* 49.

Gilmore, L. Policing Truth: Confession, Gender, and Autobiographical Authority. *Autobiography and Postmodernism*, ed. Ashley, Gilmore, and Peters. Amherst: U Massachusetts Press. 1994.

Giroux, H. 1988. *Schooling and the Struggle for Public Life: Critical Pedagogy in the Modern Age*. Minneapolis: University of Minnesota Press.

———. 1995. Who Writes in a Cultural Studies Class? Or, Where is Pedagogy? *Left Margins: Cultural Studies and Composition Pedagogy*, ed. Fitts and France. Albany: State University of NY Press.

Glass, J. M. 1993. *Shattered Selves: Multiple Personality in a Postmodern World*. Ithaca, NY: Cornell University Press.

Glatzer, N. 1953. *Franz Rosenzweig: His Life and Thought*. NY: Schocken.

Goell, Y. 1989. We Are Not and Never were Like the PLO. *The Jerusalem Post* (19 Nov).

Goffman, E. 1963. *Stigma: Notes on the Management of Spoiled Identity*. Englewood Cliffs, N.J.: Prentice-Hall, Inc.

Gradin, S. L. 1995. *Romancing Rhetorics: Social Expressivist Perspectives on the Teaching of Writing*. Portsmouth: Heinemann.

Gramsci, A. 1971. *Selections from the Prison Notebooks*, ed. and trans. Hoare and Smith. NY: International.

———. 1985. *Selections from Cultural Writings*. Trans. William Boelhower. Ed. David Forgacs and Geoffrey Nowell-Smith. Cambridge: Harvard University Press.

Gray, J. 1994. Essentialism and the Mulatto Traveler: Europe as Embodiment in Nella Larsen's *Quicksand*. *Novel* 27.

Green, M. 1998. *Accompanying Young People on Their Spiritual Quest*. London: National Society of Church House Publishing.

Grosfoguel, R., F. Negrón-Muntaner, and C. S. Georas. 1997. Beyond Nationalist and Colonialist Discourses: The *Jaiba* Politics of the Puerto-Rican Ethno-Nation. *Puerto Rican Jam: Rethinking Colonialism and Nationalism*. Minneapolis: University of Minnesota Press.

Grumet, M. 1990. On Daffodils That Come Before the Swallow Dares. *Qualitative Inquiry: The Continuing Debate*, ed. Eisner and Peshkin. NY: Teachers College Press.

———. 1995. Scholae Personae: Masks For Meaning. In Jane GalloPress. ed., *Pedagogy: The Question of Impersonation*. Bloomington: Indiana University Press.

———. 1988. *Bitter Milk: Women and Teaching*. Amherst: The U of Massachusetts Press.

Gubar, S. 1999. Notations in *Medias Res. Critical Inquiry* 25.2.

Guest Column. 1996. Four Views on the Place of the Personal in Scholarship. *PMLA* 111.5.

Haaken, J. 1998. The Recovery of Memory, Fantasy, and Desire in Women's Trauma Stories. *Women, Autobiography, Theory: A Reader*, ed. Smith and Watson. Madison: University of Wisconsin Press.

Halbertal, Moshe, and Tova Halbertal (1998). The Yeshiva. In Amelie Oksenberg Rorty, *Philosophers on Education Historical Perspectives*. London: Routledge. 458–469.

Hall, J. C. 1995. Toward the 'Success' of a 'New Canon': Radical Introspection as Critical Practice. *Teaching a New Canon? Students, Teachers, and Texts in the College Literature Classroom*, ed. Goebel and Hall. Urbana, IL: NCTE.

Hall, S. 1996. New Ethnicities. *Stuart Hall: Critical Dialogues in Cultural Studies*, ed. Morley and Chen. NY: Routledge.

———. 1996b. Race: The Floating Signifier. Northampton, MA: Media Education Foundation.

———. 1987. Minimal Selves. *ICA Documents*, 6.

Hallet, M. 1999. Personal Effects: Grief, Loss, and the Pedagogies of Writing. *Journal of Curriculum Theory* 15.2.

Handelman, S. 1982. *The Slayers of Moses: the Emergence of Rabbinic Interpretation in Modern Literary Theory*. Albany: State Univ. of NY Press.

———. 1991. *Fragments of Redemption: Jewish Thought and Literary Theory in Scholem, Benjamin, and Levinas*. Bloomington: Indiana University Press.

Hannigan, J. 1998. *Fantasy City: Pleasure and Profit in the Postmodern Metropolis*. NY: Routledge.

Harding, S. and M. B. Hintikka, eds. 1983. *Discovering Reality: Feminist Perspectives on Epistemology, Metaphysics, Methodology, and Philosophy of Science*. Boston: Reidel.

Harris, J. 1990. *Expressive Discourse*. Dallas: Southern Methodist University Press.

Harris, M. 1987. *Teaching and the Religious Imagination: An Essay in the Theology of Teaching*. San Francisco: HarperSan Francisco.

Harris, N. 1990. *Cultural Excursions: Marketing Appetites and Cultural Tastes in Modern America*. Chicago: University of Chicago Press.

Hassoun, J. 1997. *The Cruelty of Depression: On Melancholy*. Reading: Addison-Wesley.

Heilbrun, C. G. 1988. *Writing a Woman's Life*. NY: Ballantine Books.

———. 1997. *The Last Gift of Time: Life Beyond Sixty*. NY: Ballantine.

Herman, J. L. 1992. *Trauma and Recovery*. NY: Basic Books.

Herron, J. 1992. Writing for My Father. *College English* 54.8

Higgins, G. V. 1996. A Letter to the Copy Editor. *Sewanee Review* 104.3

Holland, N. 1996. The Inevitability of the Personal. Forum. *PMLA* 111.5.
Holquist, M. 1990. *Dialogism: Bakhtin and his World*. London: Routledge.
Hooks, B. 1994. *Outlaw Culture: Resisting Representations*. NY: Routledge.
———. 1992. *Black Looks: Race and Representation*. Boston: South End.
———. 1994. *Teaching to Transgress: Education as the Practice of Freedom*. NY: Routledge.
———. 1990. *Yearning: Race, Gender, and Cultural Politics*. Boston: South End.
Hunter, P. 1992. 'Waiting for an Aristotle': A Moment in the History of the Basic Writing Movement. *College English* 54.8.
Jackson, A. M. 1996. Letter. Forum: The Inevitability of the Personal. *PMLA* 111.5.
Jackson, K. T. 1985. *Crabgrass Frontier: The Suburbanization of the United States*. NY: Oxford University Press, 1985.
Jamison, K. R. 1995. *An Unquiet Mind*. NY: Knopf.
Jan Mohamed, A. R. and D. Lloyd, eds. 1990. *The Nature and Context of Minority Discourse*. NY: Oxford University Press.
Jenkyns, R. 1998. Janeism. *The New Republic*, May 4.
Johnson, B. 1985. Thresholds of Difference: Structures of Address in Zora Neale Hurston. *Critical Inquiry* 12.1.
Jouve, N. W. 1991. *White Woman Speaks with Forked Tongue: Criticism as Autobiography*. NY: Routledge.
Kallen, H. M. 1960. Quoted by Sidney Hook in The Centrality of Method. *The American Pragmatists*, ed. Konvitz and Kennedy. NY: Meridian.
Kampf, L. and P. Lauter, eds. 1972. *The Politics of Literature*. NY: Pantheon.
Kaplan, A. 1993. *French Lessons: A Memoir*. Chicago: University of Chicago Press.
Kaplan, C. 1998. Resisting Autobiography: Out-Law Genres and Transnational Feminist Subjects. Smith and Watson.
Kaplan, L. D. 1998. *Family Pictures: A Philosopher Explores the Familiar*. Chicago: Open Court/Carus.
Kaplan, S. 1949. The Miscegenation Issue in the Election of 1864. *The Journal of Negro History* 34.3.
Kazin, A. 1942. Criticism at the Poles. *On Native Grounds*. NY: Reynal and Hitchcock.
Keller, C. 1986. *From a Broken Web: Separation, Sexism, and Self*. Boston: Beacon.
Kennedy, G. A. 1980. *Classical Rhetoric and Its Christian and Secular Tradition from Ancient to Modern Times*. Chapel Hill: U North Carolina Press.
Kerdeman, Deborah 1998. Between Interlochen and Idaho: Hermeneutics and Education for Understanding. In Steven Tozer, ed. *Philosophy of Education 1998*. Urbana Illinois. Philosophy of Education Society. 10.5.
Kincaid, J. 1997. *My Brother*. NY: Farrar, Straus, and Giroux.
Kolodny, A. 1998. *Failing the Future: A Dean Looks at Higher Education in the Twenty-first Century*. Durham: Duke University Press.
Kirsch, G. 1993. *Women Writing the Academy: Audience, Authority and Transformation*. Carbondale: Southern Illinois University Press.

——— and J. S. Ritchie. 1995. Beyond the Personal: Theorizing a Politics of Location in Composition Research. *CCC* 46.

Kittay, J. and W. Godzich. 1987. *The Emergence of Prose: An Essay in Prosaics.* Minneapolis: University of Minnesota Press.

Koppelman, S. 1993. Excerpts from Letters to Friends. Freedman, et al.

Krieger, S. 1991. *Social Science and the Self: Personal Essays on an Art Form.* New Brunswick: Rutgers University Press.

Kumin, M. 1978. Friendship Remembered. *Anne Sexton: The Artist and Her Critics,* ed. McClatchy. Bloomington: Indiana University Press.

Kutz, E. 1990. Authority and Voice in Student Ethnographic Writing. *Anthropology and Education Quarterly* (Dec).

La Capra, D. 1987. History and Psychoanalysis. *Critical Inquiry* 13.2.

Langer, S. K. 1957. *Problems of Art.* NY: Scribner's.

Lao, A. 1997. Islands at the Crossroads: Puerto Ricanness Traveling between the Translocal Nation and the Global City. *Puerto Rican Jam: Rethinking Colonialism and Nationalism.* Minneapolis: U Minnesota Press.

Larson, A. 1995. *Marya, a Life, by Joyce Carol Oates: Masochistic behavior as a recovery strategy of the abuse survivor.* Thesis, Iowa State University.

Larson, R., T. McCracken, and J. Entes, eds. 1998. *Teaching in College English and English Education.* Urbana: NCTE.

Lather, P. 1991. *Getting Smart: Feminist Research and Pedagogy with/in the Postmodern.* Routledge, NY.

———. 1996. Troubling Clarity: The Politics of Accessible Language. *Harvard Educational Review* 66.

———, and C. Smithies. 1995. *Troubling Angels: Women Living With HIV/AIDS.* Columbus: Greyden.

Lederer-Gibel, I. 1984. Israel's Radical Chic Helps the Radical Right: Writing Off the Sepharadim. *Christianity & Crisis* 44 (15 Oct).

Leibowitz, N. 1976. *Studies in Exodus.* Trans. Aryeh Newman. Jerusalem: World Zionist Organization.

Leland, J. and G. Beals. 1997. In Living Colors. *Newsweek.* 5 May.

Lentricchia, F. 1993. My Kinsman T.S.Eliot. *Wild Orchids and Trotsky: Messages from American Universities.* Ed. Mark Edmundson. NY: Penguin.

Lenzo K. 1995. Validity and Self-Reflexivity Meet Poststructuralism: Scientific Ethos and the Transgressive self. *Educational Researcher* 24.4.

Levi-Strauss, C. 1966. History and Dialectic. In *The Savage Mind.* Chicago: University of Chicago Press.

———. 1973. *Triste Tropiques.* Translated by John and Doreen Weightman. NY: Atheneum.

———. 1978. *The Origin of Table Manners.* NY: Harper & Row.

Levinas, E. 1981. *Otherwise Than Being, or Beyond Essence.* Trans. Alphonso Lingis. The Hague: Martinus Nijhoff.

Lewis, C. S. 1961. *A Grief Observed*. London: Faber Pub.

Lewis, N. A. 1997. Black Scholars View Society With Prism of Race. *The NY Times*. 5 May.

Lipsitz, G. 1990. *Time Passages: Collective Memory and American Popular Culture*. Minneapolis: University of Minnesota Press.

———. 1994. *Dangerous Crossroads*. London: Verso.

Lipton, E. 1994. *Alias Olympia: A Woman's Search for Manet's Notorious Model & Her Own Desire*. NY: Meridian.

Lopate, P. 1995. *The Art of the Personal Essay: An Anthology from the Classical Era to the Present*. NY: Doubleday.

Lu, M. 1992. Conflict and Struggle: The Enemies or Preconditions of Basic Writing? *College English* 54.8.

Luke, C., ed. 1996. *Feminisms and Pedagogies of Everyday Life*. Albany: State University of NY Press.

Lunsford, A. and Lisa Ede. 1996. Representing Audience: 'Successful' Discourse and Disciplinary Critique. *CCC* 47.

Lutz, C. 1995. The Gender of Theory. Behar and Gordon.

Luttrell, W. 1997. *Schoolsmart and Motherwise: Working-Class and Women's Identity and Schooling*. NY: Routledge.

Lyotard, F. 1988. *The Postmodern Condition: A Report on Knowledge*. Trans. Geoff Bennington and Brian Massumi. Minneapolis: University of Minneapolis Press.

Mackey, N. 1995. *Strick: Song of the Andoumboulou*. Spoken Engine compact disc 7 90807 16252 9.

Maher, F. A., and M. K. T. Tetreault. 1994. *The Feminist Classroom*. NY: Basic Books.

Malin, I. and I. Stark, eds. 1964. *Breakthrough: A Treasury of Contemporary American-Jewish Literature*. NY: McGraw-Hill.

Marcus, G. E. and M. Fisher. 1986. *Anthropology as Cultural Critique: An Experimental Moment in the Human Sciences*. Chicago: U Chicago Press.

Max, D. T. 1998. The Carver Chronicles. *NY Times Magazine* (Aug 9).

McClaren, P. 1997. The Ethnographer as Postmodern Flaneur: Critical Reflexivity and Post-Hybridity as Narrative Engagement. *Representation and the Text: Reframing the Narrative Voice*, ed. Tierney and Lincoln. Albany: State University of NY Press.

McDowell, D. 1996. *Leaving Pipe Shop: Memories of Kin*. N Y Scribner.

McKay, N. 1996. The Inevitability of the Personal. Forum. *PMLA* 111.5.

———. 1998. Naming the Problem that Led to the Question 'Who Shall Teach African American Literature?': or, Are We Ready to Disband the Wheatley Court? *PMLA* 113.3.

McKeon, R., ed. 1941. *The Basic Works of Aristotle*. NY: Random House.

Mehta, V. 1998. The *NYer*'s Mr. Shawn. *The Atlantic Monthly* (Apr).

Michaels, A. 1996. *Fugitive Pieces*. Toronto: McClelland and Stewart.

Middlebrook, D. W. 1991. *Anne Sexton: A Biography*. Boston: Houghton-Mifflin.

——— and D. H. George, eds. 1988. *Selected Poems of Anne Sexton.* NY: Houghton Mifflin.

Mill, J. S. 1875. *Autobiography.* NY: Henry Holt.

Miller, J. L. 1991. *Creating Spaces and Finding Voices: Teachers Collaborating for Empowerment.* Albany: State University of NY Press.

Miller, N. K. 1991. *Getting Personal. Feminist Occasions and Other Autobiographical Acts.* NY: Routledge.

———. 1996. *Bequest and Betrayal: Memoirs of a Parent's Death.* NY: Oxford.

———. 1991. *Getting Personal: Feminist Occasions and Other Autobiographical Acts.* NY: Routledge.

Miller, R. E. 1996. The Nervous System. *College English* 58:3.

———. 1998. *As if Learning Mattered: Reforming Higher Education.* Ithaca: Cornell University Press.

Miller, S. 1991. *Textual Carnivals: The Politics of Composition.* Carbondale: Southern Illinois University Press.

Mills, C. W. 1997. *The Racial Contract.* Ithaca: Cornell University Press.

Mohanty, S. 1995. Colonial Legacies, Multicultural Futures: Relativism, Objectivity, and the Challenge of Otherness. *PMLA* 110.1.

Moon, M. and E. K. Sedgwick, 1993. Divinity: A Dossier, A Performance Piece, A Little-Understood Emotion. In *Tendencies.* Durham: Duke University Press, 215-251.

Morgan, D. 1998. Opinion: Ethical Issues Raised by Students' Personal Writing. *College English* 60.3.

Morson, G. S. and C. Emerson. 1990. *Mikhail Bakhtin: The Creation of a Prosaics.* Stanford: Stanford University Press.

Munger, K. 1997. Reading and Writing Outside the Lines: Radical introspection and Teaching *Beloved.* Final Paper, English 521, Iowa State University.

Nachman of Breslov. 1959. *Likkutei Moharan.* Jerusalem: Agudat Meshek Ha- Nahal.

Neumann, A. and P. L. Peterson., eds. 1997. *Learning from Our Lives.* NY: Teachers College Press.

Newfield, C. 1996. *The Emerson Effect: Individualism and Submission in America.* Chicago: University of Chicago Press.

Newkirk, T. 1997. *The Performance of Self in Student Writing.* Portsmouth: Heinemann.

Nissen, A. 1996. The Inevitability of the Personal. Forum. *PMLA* 111.5.

Nye, E. and M. Young. 1999. Service-Learning and the Literacy Connection. *The Literacy Connection*, ed. Horning and Sudol. Cresskill: Hampton Press.

O'Brien, M. 1981. *The Politics of Reproduction.* Boston: Routledge and Kegan Paul.

O'Donnell, T. 1996. Politics and Ordinary Language: A Defense of Expressivist Rhetorics. *College English* 58.4.

Ohmann, R. 1976. *English in America: A Radical View of the Profession.* NY: Oxford University Press. Rpt. 1996, Middletown: Wesleyan University Press.

———. 1987. *Politics of Letters.* Middletown CT: Wesleyan University Press.

———. 1996. *Selling Culture; Magazines, Markets, and Class at the Turn of the Century.* NY: Verso.

———. 1997. English and the Cold War. In *The Cold War and the University*, ed. Chomsky et al. NY: The New Press.

Olds, S. 1997. Prose comment. *Approaching Poetry: Perspectives and Responses*, ed. Schakel and Ridl. NY: St. Martin's.

Oliver, E. 1994. *Crossing the Mainstream: Multicultural Perspectives in Teaching Literature.* Urbana: NCTE.

Olson, D. R. 1994. *The World on Paper.* Cambridge: Cambridge University Press.

Omi, M. and H. Winant. 1994. *Racial Formation in the United States: From the 1960s to the 1990s.* NY: Routledge.

Ong, A. 1995. Women Out of China: Traveling Tales and Traveling Theories in Postcolonial Feminism. Behar and Gordon.

O'Reilly, M. R. 1990. Silence and Slow Time: Pedagogies from Inner Space. *Pre-Text* 11:1-2.

———. 1993. *The Peaceable Classroom.* Portsmouth: Boynton/Cook.

Orner, M. B. 1992. *Teaching Otherwise: Feminism, Pedagogy, and the Politics of Difference.* Dissertation, University of Wisconsin, Madison.

Ostriker, A. 1982. That Story: Anne Sexton and Her Transformations. *The American Poetry Review.* (Jul/Aug).

Outlaw, L. T. 1996. *On Race and Philosophy.* NY: Routledge.

Pagano, J. A. 1990. *Exiles and Communities: Teaching in the Patriarchal Wilderness.* Albany: State University of NY Press.

Palumbo-Liu, D. 1996. Historical Permutations of the Place of Race. *PMLA* 111.5.

Paley, K. 1998. The Social Construction of Expressivism, Expressivist Pedagogy: The Politics of Teaching the Personal Narrative. Diss. Northeastern University.

———. 2001. *I-Writing: The Politics and Practice of Teaching First-Person Writing.* Carbondale: Southern Illinois University Press.

Parker, P. 1983. *Movement in Black.* Trumansburg NY: Crossing.

Patai, D. 1994. Sick and Tired of Nouveau Solipsism. *Chronicle of Higher Education* (23 Feb).

Patten, R. L. 1987. Reviewing Reviewing: From the Editor's Desk. *Literary Reviewing*, ed. Hoge. Charlottesville: University of Virginia Press.

Pettit. A 1995. Few Last Words, First. *Studies in the Novel* 27.3.

Phelan, P. 1993. *Unmarked: The Politics of Performance.* London: Routledge.

Pinar, W. 1988. Autobiography and the Architecture of the Self. *Journal of Curriculum Theorizing* 8.1.

——— and M. Grumet. 1976. *Toward a Poor Curriculum.* Dubuque, Iowa: Kendall/Hunt.

Piper, A. 1992. Passing for White/Passing for Black. *Transition*, 58.

Pollard, D. 1997. I Hear You, I Hear Myself: The Struggle to Find Voice. Conference on Research on Women and Education. Ames, IA.

———. 1997. Mother-Hunger: A Struggle to Find My Voice. Unpublished paper.

Poovey, M. 1984. *The Proper Lady and the Woman Writer.* Chicago: University of Chicago Press.

Pratt, M. L. 1991. Arts of the Contact Zone. *Profession 91.*

———. 1996. Daring to Dream: Re-Visioning Culture and Citizenship. *Critical Theory and the Teaching of Literature: Politics, Curriculum, Pedagogy,* ed. Slevin and Young. Urbana: NCTE.

Rashkin, E. 1992. Family Secrets and the Psychoanalysis of Narrative. Princeton, NJ. Princeton University Press.

Rich, A. 1979. *On Lies, Secrets, and Silence. Selected Prose 1966-1978.* NY: Norton.

———. 1995. Split at the Root. *The Art of the Personal Essay: An Anthology from the Classical Era to the Present.* Ed. Phillip Lopate. NY: Doubleday.

———. 1976. *Of Woman Born: Motherhood as Experience and Institution.* NY: W. W. Norton.

Richardson, L. 1997. *Fields of Play: Constructing an Academic Life.* New Brunswick: Rutgers University Press.

Rodriguez, R. 1982. *Hunger of Memory.* NY: Bantam.

———. 1989. An American Writer. *The Invention of Ethnicity,* ed. Sollors. NY: Oxford University Press.

Roethke, T. 1957. Last Class. *College English* 18:8.

Rosen, H. 1986. The Importance of Story. *Language Arts* 63.3.

Rosenblatt, L. 1938. *Literature as Exploration.* NY: Appleton-Century. Rpt 1986. NY: MLA.

Rosenzweig, F. 1930. *The Star of Redemption.* 2nd ed. Trans. Hallo. Rpt 1985. South Bend: Notre Dame University Press.

———. 1965. *On Jewish Learning.* Ed. Nahum Glatzer NY: Schocken.

Ruddick, S. 1989. *Maternal Thinking: Toward a Politics of Peace.* Boston: Beacon.

Rukeyser, M. 1996. *The Life of Poetry.* Ashfield: Paris.

Rylant, C. 1992. *Missing May.* NY: Bantam Doubleday Dell.

Said, E. W. 1978. *Orientalism.* NY: Random.

———. 1994. *Culture and Imperialism.* NY: Vintage.

———. 1991. On Palestinian Identity: A Conversation with Edward Said. *Imaginary Homelands,* Rushdie. London: Granta.

———. 1989. Representing the Colonized: Anthropology's Interlocutors. *Critical Inquiry* 15.2.

Saldívar, R. 1990. *Chicano Narrative: The Dialectics of Difference.* Madison: University of Wisconsin Press.

Salvatori, M. 1997. The Personal as Recitation. (Review) *CCC* 48.

Salvio, P. 1990. Student Autobiography and the Project of Self-Creation. *Cambridge Journal of Education* 20.3.

———. 1999. Reading in the Age of Testimony. *Building Moral Communities Through Educational Drama,* ed. Wagner. London: Ablex.

———. 1999. Teacher of Weird Abundance: Portraits of the Pedagogical Tactics of Anne Sexton in *Cultural Studies*, 13.4.

San Juan, E. 1992. *Racial Formations/Critical Transformations: Articulations of Power in Ethnic and Racial Studies in the United States*. Atlantic Highlands, NJ: Humanities.

Sartre, J. P. 1949. *No Exit and Three Other Plays*. NY: Vintage Books.

Scarry, E. 1985. *The Body in Pain: The Making and Unmaking of the World*. Oxford: Oxford University Press.

Schneerson, Y.Y. 1993. *Seefr Ha-Ma'amorim: Bati L'Gani*. 3rd.ed. Brooklyn: Kehot Pub. Society.

Schneider, A. 1999. Persistence Paid Off for 'Lost Generation' of English Ph.D.'s, Study Finds. *Chronicle of Higher Education Online* 3 Sep. www.chronicle.com.

Schön, D. 1987. *Educating the Reflective Practitioner*. San Francisco: Josey-Bass.

———. 1995. *The Reflective Practitioner: How Professionals think in Action*. Aldershot (England): Arena.

Schreiter, R. J. 1997. *The New Catholicity: Theology between the Global and the Local*. Maryknoll, NY: Orbis Books.

Schulman, S. 1994. *My American History: Lesbian and Gay Life During the Reagan/Bush Years*. NY: Routledge.

Schwab, J. 1978. Eros and Education. *Science, Curriculum, and Liberal Education: Selected Essays*, ed. Westbury and Wilkof. Chicago: University of Chicago Press.

Schweickart, P. 1986. Reading Ourselves: Toward a Feminist Theory of Reading. Flynn and Schweickart.

Scott, D. 1992. Criticism and Culture: Theory and Post-Colonial Claims on Anthropological Disciplinarity. *Critique of Anthropology* 12.4.

Scott, J. 1991. The Evidence of Experience. *Critical Inquiry* 17.4.

———. 1992. Experience. *Feminists Theorize the Political*, ed. Butler and Scott. NY: Routledge.

Scribner, S. 1988. Literacy in Three Metaphors. *Perspectives on Literacy*. Ed.Kintgen, Kroll, and Rose. Carbondale: Southern Illinois University Press.

Sedgwick, E. K. 1991. Jane Austen and the Masturbating Girl, *Critical Inquiry* 17.

Sexton, A. 1960. *To Bedlam and Part Way Back*, NY: Houghton Mifflin.

———. 1962. *All My Pretty Ones*, NY: Houghton Mifflin.

———. 1966. *Live or Die*, NY: Houghton Mifflin.

———. 1969. *Love Poems*, NY: Houghton Mifflin.

———. 1971. *Transformation.*, NY: Houghton Mifflin.

Sexton, L. G. and L. Ames, eds. 1977. *Anne Sexton: A Portrait in Letters*, Boston, MA: Houghton Mifflin.

Shannon, P. .1989. The Struggle for Control of Literacy Lessons. *Language Arts* 66.6

Shaughnessy, M. 1977. *Errors and Expectations: A Guide for the Teacher of Basic Writing*. NY: Oxford University Press.

Shea, C. 1999. Makeover. *Lingua Franca* (Feb)

Sheils, M. 1975. Why Johnny Can't Write. *Newsweek*. (8 Dec).

Simpson, D. 1995. *The Academic Postmodern and the Rule of Literature: A Report on Half-Knowledge*. Chicago: University of Chicago Press.

Singh, A., J. Skerrett, and R. E. Hogan, eds. 1994. *Memory, Narrative, and Identity: New Essays in Ethnic American Literature*. Boston: Northeastern University Press.

Smith, L. Z. 1998. Anonymous Review and the Boundaries of Intrinsic Merit. *Journal of Information Ethics* 7.2.

———. 2000. Make Me a Letter: Personal Criticism and the Epistolary Symposium. *The Personal Narrative: Writing Ourselves as Teachers and Scholars*. Ed. Haroian-Guerin. Portland ME: Calendar Islands.

———. 1998. Prosaic Rhetoric in Still Life and Personal Essays. *Mosaic: A Journal for the Interdisciplinary Study of Literature* 31.1.

Smith, S. 1998. Performativity, Autobiographical Practice, Resistance. Smith and Watson.

———, and J. Watson, eds. 1998. *Women, Autobiography, Theory: A Reader*. Madison: University of Wisconsin Press.

Smorkaloff, P. M. 1999. *Cuban Writers on and off the Island: Contemporary Narrative Fiction*. NY: Twayne.

Snyder, D. 1997. *The Cliff Walk: A Memoir of a Job Lost and a Life Found*. Boston: Little, Brown.

Soloveitchik. J. B. 1993. Ha -Yehudi Mashul L'Sefer Torah [Hebrew]. *Beit Yosef Shaul: Kovetz Hiddushei Torah*, ed. Elchanan Asher Adler. NY: Yeshiva University.

———. 1979. Teaching with Clarity and Empathy in Avraham Besdin, ed. *Reflections of the Rav: Lessons in Jewish Thought*, Vol 1. Hoboken, N.J: Ktav

Southam, B.C., ed. 1995. *Jane Austen: The Critical Heritage 1870-1940*, vol. 2. NY: Routledge.

Spingarn, J. E. 1964. The New Criticism. *Columbia University Lectures on Literature*. 1911. Rpt. in *Creative Criticism*. Port Washington, NY: Kennikat/Harcourt.

Spivak, G. 1990. Postmarked: Calcutta, India. *The Postcolonial Critic*. Ed. Saraj Harasym. NY: Routledge.

———. 1990. Questions of Multi-culturalism. *The Postcolonial Critic*. Ed. Saraj Harasym. NY: Routledge.

Stanislavski, C. 1949. *Building A Character*. NY: Theatre Arts Books.

Staten, H. 1998. Ethnic Authenticity, Class, and Autobiography: The Case of *Hunger for Memory*. *PMLA* 113.1.

Steedman, Carolyn. 1986. *Landscape for a Good Woman: A Story of Two Lives*. New Brunswick: Rutgers University Press.

Stewart, S. 1993. The State of Cultural Theory and the Future of Literary Form. *Profession 93*. NY: MLA.

Stone, L., ed. 1998. *Close to the Bone: Memoirs of Hurt, Rage, and Desire*. NY: Grove.

Suleiman, S. R. 1994. *Risking Who One Is: Encounters with Contemporary Art and Literature.* Cambridge: Harvard University Press.

Sullivan, P. 1995. Social Constructionism and Literary Studies. *College English* 57.8.

Takaki, R. 1993. *A Different Mirror: A History of Multicultural America.* Boston: Back Bay Books.

Tall, D. 1993. *From Where We Stand: Recovering a Sense of Place.* NY: A. A. Knopf.

Tanselle, G. T. 1990. *Textual Criticism and Scholarly Editing.* Charlottesville and London: University of Virginia Press.

———. 1996. Reflections on Scholarly Editing. *Raritan: A Quarterly Review* 16.2.

Tate, C. 1996. The Inevitability of the Personal. Forum. *PMLA* 111.5.

Taubman, P. M. 1990. Achieving the Right Distance. *Educational Theory* 40.1.

Thomas, B., ed. 1997. *Plessy v. Ferguson: A Brief History with Documents.* Boston: Bedford.

Thompson, A. 1998. How Scholarly Writing Makes Readers Work. *Journal of Scholarly Publishing* 29.2.

Thomson, G. 1998. Men (Editors) Are from Mars, Women (Editors) Are from Venus. *The Writer* 111.4.

Tobin, L. 1998. Personal communication. (29 Jan).

Todorov, T. 1993. *On Human Diversity.* Trans. Catherine Porter. Cambridge: Harvard University Press.

Tompkins, J. 1987. Me and My Shadow. *New Literary History* (Autumn). Rpt. in Diane P. Freedman et al.1993.

———. 1990. Pedagogy of the Distressed. *College English* 52.

———. 1996. *A Life in School: What the Teacher Learned.* Reading, MA: Addison-Wesley.

Torgovnick, M. 1990. Experimental Critical Writing. *ADE Bulletin* 96.

———. 1994. *Crossing Ocean Parkway: Readings by and Italian-American Daughter.* Chicago: University of Chicago Press.

———. 1996. Letter. *PMLA* 111.5.

Treichler, P. 1991. AIDS, Homophobia, and Biomedical Discourse: An Epidemic of Signification, in *AIDS: Cultural Analyis, Cultural Activism.* Ed. Douglas Crimp Cambridge: MIT Press.

Trimbur, J. 1991. Literacy and the Discourse of Crisis. In *The Politics of Writing Instruction: Postsecondary.* eds. Bullock and Trimbur. Portsmouth, NH: Boynton/Cook Publishers.

Trouillot, M. 1991. From Planters' Journal to Academia: The Haitian Revolution as Unthinkable History. *Journal of Caribbean History* 25.1 & 2.

Turner, F. 1993. An Exchange. *Contemporary Literature* 34.4.

Twenty-six letters on the personal in scholarship. 1996. *PMLA* 111.5.

Uchmanowicz, P. 1995. The $5,000–$25,000 Exchange. *College English* 57.4.

Vaihinger, H. 1925. *The Philosophy of As If: A System of the Theoretical, Practical, and Religious Fictions of Mankind.* Trans. C.K. Ogden. NY: Harcourt Brace.

van Gelder, L. 1995. D'Amato Mocks Ito And Sets Off Furor. *The NY Times*. (6 Apr).
Villanueva, V. 1993. *Bootstraps: From an American Academic of Color*. Urbana: NCTE.
———. 1996. On Colonies, Canons, and Ellis Cose's *Rage of a Privileged Class. JAC* 16.
———. 1999. On the Rhetoric and Precedents of Racism, *CCC* 50.
Walcott, D. 1998. *What The Twilight Says*. NY: Farrar Straus & Giroux.
Walker, A. 1983. Saving the Life That Is Your Own. *In Search of My Mother's Garden*. San Diego: Harcourt.
Wall, S. 1994.'Where Your Treasure Is': Accounting for Differences in Our Talk about Teaching. *Taking Stock: The Writing Process Movement in the '90s*, eds. Tobin and Newkirk. Portsmouth: Heinemann.
Watney, S. 1987. *Policing Desire: Pornography, AIDS, and the Media* (Minneapolis: University of Minnesota Press.
Watson, J. 1998. Unspeakable Differences: The Politics of Gender in Lesbian and Heterosexual Women's Autobiographies. Smith and Watson.
Webb, C. 1968. *Richard Wright: A Biography*. NY: G.P. Putnam's Sons.
Williams, P. J. 1996. And We Are Not Married. *The Alchemy of Race and Rights: The Diary of a Law Professor*. Cambridge: Harvard University Press. 1991. Rpt. in Bartholomae and Petrosky, eds. *Ways of Reading*. 4th ed. Boston: Bedford Books.
———. 1997. *Seeing A Color-Blind Future: The Paradox of Race*. NY: The Noonday Press.
Williams, R. 1976. *Keywords: A Vocabulary of Culture and Society*. London: Fontana/Croom Helm.
Willinsky, J. 1989. *The Fearful Passage: Romeo and Juliet Do High School: A Feminist Perspective*. Ottawa: CCTE.
Wilson, E. *Axel's Castle: A Study in the Imaginative Literature of 1870-1930*. NY: Scribner's. 1931.
Wilson, M. 1995. Research, Expressivism, and Silence. *JAC* 15.2.
Winterowd, W. R. with J. Blum. 1994. *A Teacher's Introduction to Composition in the Rhetorical Tradition*. Urbana: NCTE.
Wiskind-Elper, O. 1998. *Tradition and Fantasy in the Tales of Reb Nachman of Breslov* Albany, NY: State Univ of NY Press.
Wolf, M. 1992. *A Thrice Told Tale: Feminism, Postmodernism, and Ethnographic Responsibility*. Stanford: Stanford University Press.
Woods, S. 1994. *The Solace of Separation: Feminist theory, autobiography, Edith Wharton and me*. Thesis, Iowa State University.
———. 1997. Wagering It All in Double Jeopardy: Autobiography in a Graduate Paper. *Creating Safe Space: Violence and Women's Writing*. Ed. Tharp and Kuribayashi. Albany: State University of NY Press.
Woolf, V. 1939. *Three Guineas*. NY: Harcourt, Brace, and World. 1966.
———. 1976. A Sketch from the Past. *Moments of Being*. NY: Harcourt Brace and Company.

Yamamoto, T. 1993. Different Silences. Freedman et al.

Yamanaka, L. 1999. *Wild Meat and the Bully Burgers.* NY: Farrar, Strauss, Giroux.

Yancy, G. ed. 1998. *African-American Philosophers: 17 Conversations.* NY: Routledge.

Young, R. J. C. 1995. *Colonial Desire: Hybridity in Theory, Culture and Race.* London: Routledge.

Yu, H. 1999. Mixing Bodies and Cultures: The Meaning of America's Fascination with Sex between 'Orientals' and 'Whites'. *Sex, Love, Race: Crossing Boundaries in North American History* ed. Hodes. NY: NY University Press.

Zawacki, T. M. 1992. Recomposing as a Woman: An Essay in Different Voices. *CCC* 43.

Zeiger, M. F. 1997. *Beyond Consolation: Death, Sexuality, and the Changing Shapes of Elegy.* Ithaca and London: Cornell University Press.

CONTRIBUTORS

KATYA GIBEL AZOULAY is Associate Professor of Anthropology and Africana Studies at Grinnell College. She is author of *Black, Jewish and Interracial: It's Not the Color of Your Skin but the Race of Your Kin and Other Myths of Identity* (Durham University Press, 1997). Her articles have appeared in *American Anthropologist, Cultural Studies, Identities, Research in African Literatures, Review of Education/Pedagogy/Cultural Studies* as well as Israeli publications *The Jerusalem Post, New Outlook* and *Noga: Feminist Journal*. She is currently writing a book on academic and media representations of Ethiopian Jews in Israel.

DAVID BLEICH's recent book is *Know and Tell: A Writing Pedagogy of Disclosure, Genre, and Membership* (1998). He is also the author of *Readings and Feelings* (1975), *Subjective Criticism* (1978), *Utopia: The Psychology of a Cultural Fantasy* (1984), *The Double Perspective: Language, Literature, and Social Relations* (1988). He had edited special issues of *Poetics Today* and *Journal of Advanced Composition*. He is working on a special issue of *College English*, "Materiality, Genre, and Language Use," due out in 2002. At the University of Rochester, he teaches English in Women's Studies, Jewish Studies, Science Studies, and, if appropriate, in the English Department.

RACHEL M. BROWNSTEIN is the author of *Becoming a Heroine: Reading about Women in Novels* and *Tragic Muse: Rachel of the Comedie-Francaise*. She is a professor of English at Brooklyn College and The Graduate School, CUNY, where she runs the Liberal Studies Program.

CHRIS CASTIGLIA, Associate Professor of English at Loyola University Chicago, is author of *Bound and Determined: Captivity, Culture Crossing, and White Womanhood from Mary Rowlandson to Patty Hearst* (Chicago, 1996) and *Interior States: the Romance of Reform and the Inner Life of the Nation* (Duke, forthcoming).

BRENDA DALY, Professor of English and Women's Studies at Iowa State University, has published two books: *Lavish Self-Divisions: The Novels of Joyce Carol Oates* (Mississippi, 1996), *and Authoring a Life: A Woman's Survival in and through Literary Studies* (SUNY Press 1998), an autobiographical scholarly work arguing for a revision of the language arts curriculum in order to meet the needs of women students, an alarming number of whom are survivors of childhood sexual abuse. Daly has also co-authored the collection, *Narrating Mothers:*

Theorizing Maternal Subjectivities (Tennessee 1991) and has published many essays, some of them personal, on contemporary narratives by women.

DIANE P. FREEDMAN, Associate Professor of English and Women's Studies at the University of New Hampshire, is the author of *An Alchemy of Genres: Cross-Genre Writing by American Feminist Poet-Critics* (Virginia, 1992) and numerous articles on personal scholarship; co-editor of *The Intimate Critique: Autobiographical Literary Criticism* (Duke, 1993); and editor of *Millay at 100: A Critical Reappraisal* (SIUP, 1995). Recent projects include two co-edited volumes, one on the Teacher's Body and the other on autobiographical scholarship across the disciplines. Contact her about her evolving website (personalscholar.com) for now via e-mail: dpf@christa.unh.edu.

JEFFREY GRAY is an associate professor at Seton Hall University, where he directs the reading series "Poetry-in-the-Round." His articles on contemporary poetry and African-American literature have appeared in *Contemporary Literature, Callaloo,* and *Novel,* among others; his poetry has appeared in the *Atlantic, The American Poetry Review,* and *The Literary Review.* He is now completing a critical book, *Mastery's End: Travel and the Poetry of Vulnerability,* and editing the *Greenwood Encyclopedia of American Poetry.* A Seattle native, he has lived and taught in Latin America, the South Pacific, Asia, and Europe. In 2000, he was a Fulbright Scholar in Guatemala.

MADELEINE GRUMET is Dean of the School of Education at the University of North Carolina at Chapel Hill. Prior to this position, she served as Dean of the School of Education at Brooklyn College, City University of New York. She is the author of *Bitter Milk: Women and Teaching,* a feminist study of education. She holds the doctoral degree in curriculum theory with an emphasis on humanities and arts education and has published widely in these areas, addressing curriculum theory, teacher education and the uses of autobiographical narrative in educational research and teaching.

SUSAN HANDELMAN is Professor of English at Bar-Ilan University in Israel. She also taught at the University of Maryland, College Park for twenty years before recently moving to Israel. Among her publications are *The Slayers of Moses: The Emergence of Rabbinic Interpretation in Modern Literary Theory; Fragments of Redemption: Jewish Thought and Literary Theory in Scholem, Benjamin, and Levinas.* She has also co-edited *Psychoanalysis and Religion* and *Torah of the Mothers: Contemporary Jewish Women Read Classical Jewish Texts.* Her research interests are the relation of Jewish thought to contemporary literary and cultural theory, hermeneutics, and pedagogy.

DEBORAH H. HOLDSTEIN is Professor of English and Rhetoric at Governors State University. Her essays have appeared in *College Composition and Communication, College English,* the inaugural issue of *Pedagogy,* and other journals and books. Her books include *On Composition and Computers* (1987, MLA, under revision,

2001), *Computers and Writing* (1991, MLA, co- edited with Cynthia Selfe), and *The Prentice-Hall Anthology of Women's Literature* (2000). She is now preparing an essay collection on Judaism and composition. She has been a member of the MLA Publications committee; she is now a member of the Executive Committee of the Conference on College Composition and Communication, Co-Director of the Consultant-Evaluator Service of the Council of Writing Program Administrators.

JOYCELYN MOODY is an Associate Professor of English at the University of Washington, and the author of *Sentimental Confessions: Spiritual Narratives of Nineteenth-Century African American Women*. She teaches courses in African American literature, autobiography, and women's writings, and occasionally directs Study Abroad programs in Cape Town and London.

RICHARD OHMANN taught English and American Studies at Wesleyan University from 1961 to 1996. He edited *College English* from 1966 to 1978, and has been on the board of *Radical Teacher* since its founding in 1975. His most recent books include *English in America* with a new introduction (1996) and *Selling Culture: Magazines, Markets, and Class at the Turn of the Century*.

KAREN SURMAN PALEY is a Visiting Assistant Professor of English at California State University at San Bernardino. Southern Illinois University Press published her book *I-Writing: The Politics and Practice of First-Person Writing* in 2001. Her essays have also been published in the *Journal of Advanced Composition*, *Assessing Writing*, *Reader*, *Diversity*, and the *Ladies Home Journal*. She is currently writing a second book, *Caring for the Whole Person: A Look at Writing Taught in the Disciplines*. For relaxation she lifts weights in Gold's Gym and camps and hikes in the mountains of Southern California.

KATE RONALD teaches composition and rhetoric at Miami University in Oxford, Ohio, where she also works with the School of Business on writing-across-the-curriculum. HEPHZIBAH ROSKELLY teaches composition, rhetoric, and literature at the University of North Carolina-Greensboro, where she also serves as Associate Director of Women's Studies. Their most recent collaborations include *Reason to Believe: Romanticism, Pragmatism, and the Teaching of Writing* (SUNY, 1998); "Untested Feasibility: Imagining the Pragmatic Possibility of Paulo Freire" (*College English*, May 2001); and "Embodied Voice: Peter Elbow's Physical Rhetoric" (forthcoming in *Writing with Peter Elbow: A Collection of Essays to Honor Peter Elbow*, eds. Pat Belanoff, Marcia Dickson, Sheryl Fontaine, and Charles Moran.)

PAULA M. SALVIO is an Associate Professor of Education at the University of New Hampshire where she directs the Doctoral Program in Literacy and Schooling. Her essays on curriculum theory, autobiography and feminist pedagogy have appeared in the *Cambridge Journal of Education*, *Cultural Studies*, the *Journal of Teacher Education*, and *English Quarterly*. Salvio served as section editor for the

Journal of Curriculum Theorizing from 1995-2000. "Loss, Memory and the Work of Learning. . . ." is part of a book-length project on the teaching life of poet, Anne Sexton.

Since 1974, LOUISE Z. SMITH has taught composition theory and pedagogy, 19th-century British literature, and literary nonfiction at the University of Massachusetts—Boston, where she is Professor of English and Chair of her department. She co-authored The Practical Tutor (Oxford, 1987), edited *Audits of Meaning: A Festschrift in Honor of Ann E. Berthoff* (Heinemann, 1988), and contributed chapters to *Teaching Keats* (MLA 1991), *Conversations: Rethinking American Literature* (NCTE, 1996), *Reconceptualizing American Literary and Cultural Studies* (1996), and other books. From 1992 to 1999, she edited *College English*. She was a Fulbright Senior Lecturer at Universität Trier (Germany) in 1997.

VÍCTOR VILLANUEVA is Professor and Chair of the English Department as Washington State University, where he teaches rhetoric and composition studies. His concern is always with racism and with the political moregenerally as embodied in rhetoric, literacy, and college composition.

MARGARET WILLARD-TRAUB is Assistant Professor of Rhetoric at Oakland University in Rochester, MI, where she teaches undergraduate and graduate courses in writing and composition studies. She has published in *Assessing Writing* and *Rhetoric Review,* and is a contributor to the forthcoming volume *(Re)Presenting Our Practice: Documenting Teaching and Learning in Composition Studies* (Heinemann/Boynton Cook, Cross Current series, 2001). She is currently at work on a book project that brings together her interests in writing assessment and scholarly memoir, examining the practice and consequences of reflective writing by students and scholars across the disciplines.

MORRIS YOUNG is currently an Assistant Professor of English at Miami University where he teaches undergraduate courses in writing, graduate courses in composition and rhetoric and literacy studies, and courses in Asian Pacific American literature. His research focuses on the literacy and rhetorical practices of communities of colors, the teaching of writing, and the continuing development of Asian Pacific American literature. Other interests include the use of personal narrative in scholarly writing, alternative discourses and literacies, and the use of portfolios in assessment.

INDEX

Abel, Elizabeth, 56, 57, 60
Abraham, Nicholas, 99, 114, 115, 130
Adan, Jane, 177
Adell, Sandra, 268
ancestry, 66, 245, 270, 279
Anderson, Benedict, 61, 66, 293, 309, 334
Anzaldua, Gloria, 63, 331
Appiah, Kwame, 292
Arneson, Eric, 356
Ashton-Warner, Sylvia, 169
Atkins, G. Douglas, 200
Atwell-Vasey, Wendy, 177
Austen, Jane, 220–230
authorship, 52, 150, 152
autobiography, 37, 46, 49, 51, 71, 74, 86–89, 102, 108, 114, 115, 165, 168, 173, 176, 177, 201, 202, 204, 211, 214, 219, 234, 240, 249, 268, 282, 339
Awkward, Michael, 57, 58
Axtell, James, 160
Azoulay, Katya, 277, 289, 290, 292

Bachman, Linda, 48, 49
Bain, Alexander, 183, 203
Bakhtin, M. M., 30, 31, 37, 88, 149, 150, 263
Baldwin, James, 64, 68, 169
Balibar E., 332
Bartholomae, David, 44, 156, 179, 196
Bauer, Dale, 80
Becker, Stephen, 145
Beebee, Thomas, 314
Begam, Richard, 70
Behad, Ali, 284
Behar, Ruth, 31, 33–37, 40–42, 46, 48, 50, 210, 216
Belenky, Mary, 82
Benhabib, Seyla, 175
Benjamin, Jessica, 82
Benjamin, Walter, 177
Berlant, Lauren, 301, 324, 325, 331–334
Berlin, James, 180, 188–193, 196–198, 204, 314

Bérubé, Michael, 27, 30, 52, 53, 56, 67, 72, 76
Bhabha, Homi, 72, 73
Billings, G. L., 172
Bing, Vanessa, 248
Bleich, David, 74, 80, 87, 114, 200, 205, 207, 209, 218, 331, 347
Bloom, Harold, 60, 67
Bloom, Lynn, 32
Boone, J., 201
Booth, Wayne, 144, 220
Bourdieu, Pierre, 34, 36, 37, 39–41, 45, 49, 221–223, 288, 289, 295
Boynton, Victoria, 58, 60, 92
Brink, Andre, 294
Brodbribb, S., 174
Brodkey, Linda, 27, 40, 46, 152, 156
Bruner, Jerome, 174, 176, 301
Buber, Martin, 135, 136
Burnham, Christopher, 198
Butler, Judith, 96, 106, 111, 112, 174

Caesar, Terry, 74
Campbell, George, 183, 203
Camper, Carol, 292
Capra, Franz, 209
Cassity, Kathleen, 180, 191, 193–196, 198
Chambers, Iain, 59, 61
Chamoiseau, Patrick, 62
Chatterjee, Ranita, 283
childhood, 29, 43, 49, 60, 91, 94, 166, 179, 182, 206, 213, 217, 244, 268, 272, 277
Chiseri-Strater, Elizabeth, 178, 217
Chodorow, Nancy, 81, 170
Cixous, Hélène, 183
classrooms, 58, 81, 83, 97, 99, 126, 182, 189, 192, 193, 197, 201, 207, 230, 244, 255, 264, 268, 271
Cohen, L., 331, 333
Cohen, Ralph, 148, 331
Coles, Robert, 67, 299

Coles, William, 180, 182, 185–188, 190, 299
collaboration, 27, 93, 156, 159, 175, 254–260, 262–266
composition, 27, 32, 44, 46, 56, 107, 146, 156, 161, 178, 180–182, 184, 185, 188–190, 196–198, 200–202, 204, 205, 208, 224, 227–230, 254–256, 258, 265, 310, 316, 337, 350, 352, 353, 356
Conway, K., 82
Cooper, Anna, 283
Costello, Bonnie, 69
Courts, Patrick, 303
Crapanzano, Vincent, 111
Crawford, Mary, 85, 226
Crews, Frederick, 167, 176
criticism, 37, 46, 51–54, 57, 64, 70, 71, 74, 79, 82, 86, 88, 89, 91, 123, 146–151, 173, 175, 176, 178, 180, 181, 197, 201–203, 210, 217–219, 229, 230, 259, 294, 295, 318, 319, 327, 328
curriculum, 89, 90, 96, 105, 114, 166–168, 173, 176, 177, 209, 247, 258

Daly, Brenda, 79, 117, 202, 206, 209, 218, 219
Danticat, Edwidge, 106
Davidson, Cathy, 53
Davies, Carole, 55
Delia, Mary, 140, 141
Delpit, Lisa, 195
DeSalvo, Louise, 209, 210, 219
Dewey, John, 104, 265
Dickstein, Morris, 127
Dinnerstein, Dorothy, 170
disciplinarity, 28, 30, 31, 33, 41, 44, 46, 49, 50, 52, 56, 76, 89, 91, 172, 174, 197, 199, 200, 202, 205, 208, 209, 242, 278, 283, 284, 287, 293, 317, 318, 326, 342, 343, 345, 346, 349, 350
Dovidio, John, 290
Duberman, M., 331

Ede, Lisa, 44–46, 50, 265
Elbow, Peter, 44, 180, 189–191, 193–196, 198, 209, 219
Elder, Dana, 151
Eldred, Janet, 301
Ellsworth, Elizabeth, 115
Elshtain, Jean, 170
Emmett, Ayala, 295
English studies, 43, 55, 65, 68, 79, 89, 90, 93, 96, 106, 108, 128, 129, 140, 143, 146, 153, 158–161, 184, 185, 193–195, 201, 207, 208, 212, 213, 222, 225, 227, 229–231, 236–238, 242, 253, 254, 257, 264, 267, 274, 288, 291, 298, 304–309, 313, 316, 322, 323, 327, 337, 342, 343, 347–349, 356
Espada, Martìn, 271, 273
ethnicity, 56, 61, 63, 65, 66, 70, 72, 73, 75, 125, 126, 171, 175, 194–196, 242, 280, 282–285, 293, 324, 325, 332
expressivism, 150, 180, 181, 192, 197, 198

Faigley, Lester, 32, 40, 180–188, 193, 197
family, 29, 30, 33–37, 40, 42, 48, 49, 69, 90, 91, 94, 97, 98, 105–107, 112, 114, 115, 147, 151, 167, 169, 171, 174, 178, 179, 182, 183, 185, 186, 188, 204, 210, 217, 225, 230, 234, 254, 255, 270–272, 278, 279, 289, 293, 298, 303, 305–307, 317–319, 321, 322, 325–329, 332, 339, 340, 342
Fanon, Franz, 110, 111, 273
Farrell, Thomas, 76, 206, 215
Felman, Shoshana, 86, 87, 102
feminism (and feminist theory), 32, 33, 38, 39, 44–47, 51, 54, 55, 57, 58, 60, 67, 71, 72, 75, 79–83, 86–91, 94, 95, 137, 147, 159, 168–172, 174, 175, 191, 202, 204, 205, 209, 213, 217, 218, 221, 222, 226, 229, 248, 249, 288, 289, 342, 343, 349–351
Fenton, James, 66
Fish, Stanley, 54, 151, 153, 154
Fishman, Stephen, 265
Flynn, Elizabeth, 32
Foucault, Michel, 182, 293
Frank, Arthur, 133, 134
Franklin, Benjamin, 169
Fraser, Nancy, 47, 50
Freedman, Diane, 114, 149, 199, 206, 218, 219, 356
Friedman, Jonathon, 284
Froula, Christine, 90

Gallop, Jane, 38–40, 47, 52, 53, 56, 57, 60, 171, 206, 356
Gannett, Cinthia, 199
Gates, Henry L., 67, 75, 331
Gee, James, 28, 35
Geertz, Clifford, 52, 202, 204, 218
gender, 29, 31, 38, 48, 56, 60, 62, 69–72, 94, 129, 140, 151, 159, 169, 171, 172, 175, 178, 179, 183, 195, 196, 205,

206, 218, 221–223, 230, 231, 249, 279, 306, 318, 330, 338, 343, 346, 348
genre, 47, 128, 165, 167–169, 171, 176, 178, 179, 181–183, 201, 202, 205, 208, 214, 215, 230, 274, 314
Gilmore, Leigh, 106, 114, 331
Giroux, Henry, 194, 309
Glass, James, 88
Glatzer, Nahum, 129
Gradin, Sherrie, 192, 198
Gramsci, Antonio, 80, 188, 272
Gray, D., 146
Gray, Jeffrey, 51
Green, Maxine, 173
Grumet, Madeleine, 81, 82, 114, 115, 165, 168
Gubar, Susan, 265

Haaken, Jennifer, 243
Hall, Stuart, 282, 287, 292
Handelman, Susan, 121
Hannigan, John, 280
Harris, Jeanette, 183
Harris, Maria, 138
Harris, N., 331, 332
Hassoun, Jacques, 110, 116
Heilbrun, Carolyn, 44, 147, 149
Herman, Judith, 89
Herron, Jerry, 151, 152
Higgins, George., 145
history, 28, 29, 37, 46, 48, 55, 58, 62, 71, 72, 95, 99, 100, 102, 104–106, 112, 115, 123, 128, 148, 150, 152, 166, 170, 172, 174, 181, 186, 188, 202, 224, 229, 254, 264, 274, 278–280, 282, 285, 291, 293, 301, 306, 307, 309, 317, 331, 338, 340, 350, 352
Holland, Norman, 200, 217, 218
Holquist, Michael, 30, 38
hooks, bell, 55
humanities, 28, 94, 96, 113, 114, 160, 168, 255, 260, 263, 265, 331, 351
Hunter, Paul, 150

individualism, 31, 46, 61, 70, 87, 135, 192, 193, 263, 274, 326

Jackson, Agnes, 71
Jackson, Kay, 331, 333
Jamison, Kay, 48, 115, 209
JanMohamed, A., 268
Jenkyns, Richard, 229

Johnson, Barbara, 56, 57, 60
Jouve, Nicole, 58, 60
Judaism, 122, 128, 131

Kallen, Horace, 104
Kampf, Louis, 349
Kaplan, Alice, 36–38, 41–44, 50, 331
Kaplan, Carla, 55, 56, 59, 249
Kaplan, Laura, 218
Kaplan, Sidney, 282
Kazin, Alfred, 147
Keller, Catherine, 59
Kennedy, George, 274
Kincaid, Jamaica, 80, 106, 245
Kirsch, Gesa, 31, 47
Kittay, Jeffrey, 148, 149
Koppelman, Susan, 148
Krieger, Susan, 199
Kumin, Maxine, 93, 96, 101
Kutz, Eleanor, 185

Langer, Susanne, 150
Lao, Agustìn, 269, 272
Larson, Angela, 88, 89
Larson, Richard, 89, 146
Lather, Patti, 41, 50
Lederer-Gibel, Inge, 290
Leland, John, 314
Lentricchia, Frank, 60, 181
Levinas, Emmanuel, 123, 124, 128–132
Lewis, C. S., 103
Lewis, Neil., 314, 315
Lipsitz, George, 74, 307
Lipton, E., 331
literature, 51, 54, 56, 58, 62, 65, 67, 68, 70, 75, 83, 87–89, 94, 95, 102, 107, 115, 122–124, 127, 128, 131, 132, 140, 161, 167, 170, 172–174, 183, 187, 200–204, 207, 209, 211–213, 216–219, 221, 227–230, 242, 264, 265, 299, 310, 313, 330, 339, 340, 343, 348, 349, 355
Lopate, Phillip, 178
loss, 43–45, 47–50, 68, 83–86, 93, 95–98, 100–102, 104–106, 109–113, 115–117, 166, 187, 191, 192, 202, 223, 265, 281, 328
Lu, Min-Zhan, 150
Luke, Carmen, 81
Lunsford, Andrea, 44–46, 50, 265
Luttrell, Wendy, 81, 82
Lutz, Catherine, 31, 39
Lyotard, Francois, 51, 283

Mackey, Nathaniel, 69
Maher, Frances, 91
Malin, Irving, 203
Marcus, George, 28, 29, 202, 204
Max, D. T., 145
McClaren, Peter, 175
McDowell, D., 331
McKay, Nellie, 67, 75, 203
Mehta, Ved, 145
Michaels, Anne, 106
Middlebrook, Diane, 96, 101, 116
Mill, John, 169
Miller, Janet, 173
Miller, Nancy., 31, 32, 36, 46–48, 56, 57, 75, 147, 330, 331
Miller, Richard, 27, 45, 49, 353
Miller, Susan, 50, 60, 178, 218
Mills, Charles, 290
Mohanty, Satya, 73
Moon, M., 334
Morgan, Dan, 151, 207, 208
Morson, Gary, 149
motherhood, 79, 88, 278
Munger, Kel, 89, 90

Nachman of Breslov, 132, 134, 135, 138, 144
narcissism, 41, 234
Neumann, Anna, 172, 174
Newfield, C., 332
Newkirk, Thomas, 180, 184, 192, 198, 208, 209, 211
Nissen, Axel, 200, 206
Nye, Emily, 315

Ohmann, Richard, 335, 341
Olds, Sharon, 212
Oliver, Eileen, 195
Olson, David, 28
Omi, Michael, 269
Ong, Ahiwa, 278
Ostriker, Alicia, 94
otherness, 69, 110
Outlaw, Lucius, 292
O'Brien, Mary, 170
O'Donnell, Thomas, 180, 197, 198
O'Reilly, Mary, 126

Paley, Karen, 142, 178, 203–205, 214, 217–219
Palumbo-Liu, D., 65
Parker, Pat, 63–65
Patai, Daphne, 41
Patten, Robert, 155

the personal, 29, 31–36, 38, 42, 44–53, 55, 56, 58, 65, 68, 69, 71–74, 79, 80, 83–92, 95, 96, 98, 100, 106, 108, 109, 111, 113, 114, 121–123, 125, 127–131, 133–136, 138, 144–157, 159, 169, 170, 178–185, 188, 191–193, 197, 199–211, 214–219, 224–226, 228–230, 233–237, 240, 242, 244, 246, 247, 253–258, 260, 262, 263, 266, 268, 272, 273, 276, 277, 279, 285, 287–289, 294, 297–299, 312, 315, 318, 319, 328–331, 338–340, 346–354
Pettit, A., 145
Phelan, Peggy, 49, 109, 113, 117
Pinar, Willaim, 168
Piper, Adrian, 293
Pollard, DeRionne, 83, 86
Poovey, Mary, 222
postmodernism, 174, 202, 283
Pratt, Mary Louise, 47, 59, 74, 309
the private, 19, 43, 44, 61, 79, 89, 99, 121, 147, 150, 151, 169, 170, 172, 177, 180, 189, 190, 193, 194, 196, 199, 200, 212, 214–216, 229, 234, 236–238, 266, 276, 312, 318–322, 329–331, 347
professionalism, 27–29, 31, 32, 34, 38, 44–50, 55, 69, 72, 79, 91, 122, 129, 139, 142, 143, 146, 151, 154, 156–158, 160, 170–172, 183, 203, 205, 209, 210, 215, 216, 221, 232, 234–237, 241–243, 245–247, 253–255, 257–259, 261, 263, 265, 266, 289, 290, 297, 311, 326, 329, 338–340, 342, 343, 345–348, 350, 351
the public, 61, 147, 150, 169, 170, 172, 177, 199, 200, 212, 214–216, 229, 319, 320, 322, 325, 329–331, 346, 353

race, 35, 47, 55, 57–61, 63, 65, 69, 70, 72, 91, 151, 156, 171, 172, 194, 196, 231, 232, 234, 242, 245, 269, 271, 276, 277, 279–286, 290–293, 296, 298, 307, 308, 312–315, 318, 330, 331, 333, 348
Randolph, Laura, 90
Rashkin, Esther, 115
Rich, Adrienne, 47, 147, 151, 179, 209
Richardson, Laurel, 202
Rodriguez, Richard, 35, 36, 68, 75, 179, 307
Roethke, Theodore, 355
Rosen, Harold, 299, 300
Rosenblatt, Louise, 200, 204, 218
Rosenzweig, Franz, 123, 124, 128–130, 132, 139
Ruddick, Sara, 83
Rukeyser, Muriel, 209
Rylant, Cynthia, 106

Said, Edward, 61–63, 73, 74, 98, 188, 224
Saldívar, Ramón., 269
Salvatori, Mariolina, 47, 180, 181
Salvio, Paula, 93, 209, 218, 219
San Juan, E., 269
Sartre, Jean Paul, 41, 124, 168, 169, 293
Scarry, Elaine, 107, 116
Schneerson, Yosef, 137, 138
Schneider, Alison, 27
Schön, Donald, 173
Schreiter, Robert, 197
Schulman, S., 331
Schwab, Joseph, 121, 136
Schweickart, Patrocinio, 187, 200, 218, 360
science, 28, 67, 80, 104, 126, 146, 172, 202, 203, 248, 282, 345, 351
Scott, David, 284, 286
Scott, Joan, 285, 354
Scribner, Sylvia, 298, 301
self-inclusion, 77, 80, 201
Sexton, Anne, 111–117, 217
sexuality, 38, 86, 100, 126, 171, 196, 220, 221, 233, 237, 319, 323, 328–330, 333, 334, 342, 343, 349, 351–353
Shannon, Patrick, 301
Shaughnessy, Mina, 150, 151
Shea, Christopher, 145
Sheils, Merrill, 308, 309
Simpson, David, 51, 71, 72, 74, 308
Singh, Armritjit, 269
Smith, K., 245
Smith, Louise, 149, 154
Smith, Sidonie, 249
Smorkaloff, Pamela, 269, 276
Snyder, Don, 47
Southam, B. C., 221
Spingarn, J. E., 203
Spivak, Gayatri, 66, 67, 71–73, 75
Stanislavski, Constantin, 109
Staten, Henry, 75
Steedman, Carolyn, 48
Stewart, Susan, 75
Stone, Laurie, 211, 216
subject matter, 58, 107, 134, 139, 208, 212, 287
subjectivity, 38–40, 43, 48, 51, 52, 56, 69, 71–73, 112, 126, 139, 168, 173, 175, 176, 182, 190, 191, 202, 219, 229, 286, 301, 317, 319
Suleiman, Susan, 46
Sullivan, Patricia, 180, 202, 337

Takaki, Ronald, 307, 308
Tall, Deborah, 166
Tanselle, G. Thomas, 145
Tate, Claudia, 201
Taubman, Peter, 114
teaching and scholarship, 49, 94, 96, 105, 106, 119, 128, 133, 134, 168, 173, 199, 208, 224, 228, 254, 257, 258, 266, 337, 340, 345, 348–350, 352
Thomas, Brook, 264, 282, 314
Thompson, Audrey, 153
Thomson, Gary, 159
Tobin, Lad, 114, 181, 209, 219
Todorov, Tzvetan, 76
Tompkins, Jane, 32, 47, 80, 139, 143, 150, 151, 200, 209, 218, 219, 331, 356
Torgovnick, Marianna, 29–31, 33, 47, 48, 199, 331
Treichler, Paula, 100
Trimbur, John, 308, 309
Trouillot, Michel-Rolph, 291
Turner, Frederick, 60, 61

Uchmanowicz, Pauline, 151

Vaihinger, Hans, 73
Villanueva, Victor, 267, 276

Walcott, Derek, 68, 70
Walker, Alice, 190, 217
Wall, Susan, 198
Watney, Simon, 100
Watson, Julia, 249
Webb, Constance, 64
Williams, Patricia, 31, 47, 48, 50, 151, 281, 292, 331
Wright, Richard, 64
writing (incl. scholarly), 28, 30, 32, 33, 37, 46, 49, 52–54, 83, 85–89, 145, 160, 184, 199, 204, 210, 217, 318, 337, 339, 343, 348, 349, 350

Yamamoto, Traise, 64, 65
Yamanaka, Lois-Ann, 304
Yancy, George, 295
Young, Robert, 315
Yu, Henry, 291

Zawacki, Terry, 32
Zeiger, Melissa, 95, 100

Dad — the play
Mum — the crowd?
    The closeness to the play
Cancer — No play
    Something you can
        beat, some thing
        you can't
    Some things we can
        Choose To Do.
    Some things have
        to be fulfilled
    — Ours is not to ask to
        guess why